STEPPING FORWARD

STEPPING FORWARD

Children and young people's participation in the development process

Editors and co-authors:

VICTORIA JOHNSON
*Development FOCUS, Consultant to
Institute of Development Studies*

EDDA IVAN-SMITH
Save the Children Fund UK

GILL GORDON
Institute of Education

PAT PRIDMORE
Institute of Education

PATTA SCOTT
Institute of Development Studies

INTERMEDIATE TECHNOLOGY PUBLICATIONS 1998

Intermediate Technology Publications Ltd
103-105 Southampton Row, London WC1B 4HH, UK

© the individual authors; this collection IT Publications 1998

A CIP record for this publication is available from the British Library

ISBN 1 85339 448 3

Illustrations by Patta Scott
The cover picture was drawn by Chini Maya Majhi
of Majhigaon, Nepal

Typeset by J&L Composition Ltd, Filey, North Yorkshire
Printed in the UK by Biddles Ltd

Contents

Abbreviations   xi
Glossary   xiii
Acknowledgements   xv
Foreword ROBERT CHAMBERS   xvi
Preface JUDITH ENNEW   xviii

PART 1: CHILDREN AND YOUNG PEOPLE'S PARTICIPATION: THE STARTING-POINT

1.0 Background to the issues   3
     VICTORIA JOHNSON and EDDA IVAN-SMITH

1.1 Origins and structure of the book   8
     VICTORIA JOHNSON and EDDA IVAN-SMITH

PART 2: BUILDING BLOCKS AND ETHICAL DILEMMAS

Summary   21

2.0 Introduction   22
     VICTORIA JOHNSON

2.1 Degrees of participation: a spherical model – the possibilities
     for girls in Kabul, Afghanistan   25
     EMMANUELLE ABRIOUX

2.2 The developing capacities of children to participate   27
     ROGER HART

2.3 Child participation: ethical values and the impact of mass media 31
     SARAH McNEILL

2.4 Collecting information from child domestic workers: some
     ethical issues   34
     JONATHAN BLAGBROUGH

2.5 Children and decision-making: ethical considerations   36
     CLAIRE O'KANE

2.6 The challenge of keeping participatory processes on track
     towards the achievement of practical goals   42
     MELINDA SWIFT

2.7 Dealing with change: issues arising from young people's
     involvement in educational research and curriculum development   46
     EILEEN ADAMS

2.8 Ethics and approaches   52
     WORKING GROUP REPORT

2.9   Conclusions   59
VICTORIA JOHNSON

PART 3: HOW TO: THE PROCESS

Summary   65

3.0   Introduction   66
GILL GORDON

3.1   Situational analysis with children living in difficult
circumstances in Zimbabwe using participatory rural appraisal   69
CHARITY MANYAU

3.2   Understanding with children: coping with floods in Bangladesh   76
MAHFUZA HAQUE

3.3   Key issues in children's participation – experiences of the Ilitha
Lomso Children and Youth Organization   79
THABANG NGCOZELA

3.4   Participatory research on child labour in Vietnam   81
JOACHIM THEIS

3.5   Children creating awareness about their rights in Ghana   86
ALICE LAMPTEY

3.6   Participatory video-making in Brazil   88
JULIAN FAULKNER

3.7   Towards louder voices: ActionAid Nepal's experience of
working with children   92
JOANNA HILL

3.8   Using matrices for health research with children   96
RACHEL HINTON and RACHEL BAKER

3.9   Involving children as equal participants with adults in
community-wide participatory planning and research   102
ANDY INGLIS

3.10 The Children's Theatre Collective of the Philippine Educational
Theatre Association   105
ERNESTO CLOMA

3.11 Workshop to share experience on children's participation   109
ANDY INGLIS

3.12 Conclusions   112
GILL GORDON

PART 4: CULTURE: ATTITUDES AND PERSPECTIVES

Summary   119

4.0   Introduction   120
PAT PRIDMORE

4.1   Culture, education and development   122
DAVID STEPHENS

4.2 Child work and child development in cultural context: a study
     of children's perspectives in selected countries in Asia, Africa
     and Central America   124
     MARTIN WOODHEAD

4.3 Using participatory approaches in schools: the experience of
     child-to-child in Uganda   129
     KATE HARRISON

4.4 Cultural relativity in Ghana: perspectives and attitudes   132
     CHRISTIANA OBENG

4.5 Children's participation for research and programming in
     education, health and community development: selected
     experiences in Africa   135
     BARNABAS OTAALA

4.6 Participation with Jordanian children to understand and improve
     their role in local neighbourhoods   143
     SAFA HALASAH

4.7 Workshop on culture and children's participation   147
     RACHEL CARNEGIE

4.8 Conclusions   151
     PAT PRIDMORE

**PART 5: CHILDREN'S PARTICIPATION IN SITUATIONS OF
         CRISIS**

Summary   157
5.0 Introduction   158
     PAT PRIDMORE

5.1 Exploring child participation: the Sri Lankan experience   161
     PRIYA COOMARASWAMY

5.2 Children's participation – past experience and future strategy 166
     VESNA DEJANOVIC

5.3 Conclusions   171
     PAT PRIDMORE

PART 6: INSTITUTIONS AND POWER

Summary   175
6.0 Introduction   176
     VICTORIA JOHNSON and PATTA SCOTT

1: Young people and institutions   180
6.1 Patterns for the future: knitting reflection into the practice
     of children's participation   180
     AMY KASPAR

6.2 Children's participation in research: the Paradise Project in
     Grenada   184
     DENISE ALLEN

vii

6.3   The Peace Child rescue mission experience   188
      DAVID WOOLLCOMBE and AMANDA OLIVIER

6.4   Young people and institutions   191
      WORKING GROUP REPORT

6.5   The family in context   194
      WORKING GROUP REPORT

2: Schools

6.6   Participation within the school   199
      AMANDA SAURIN

6.7   Project Grow at the City-as-School High School in New York   203
      MARY ELLEN LEWIS

6.8   The Brighton Centre for active learning and amazing
      achievements   205
      LUCY HARRIS

3: Non-Governmental Organizations

6.9   Child participation in programme planning and implementation
      in the marginalized youth projects, Jamaica   208
      DENISE ALLEN

6.10 Mambo Leo, Sauti ya Watoto: child participation in Tanzania   211
      ESTHER OBDAM

6.11 Involving children in the project cycle: experience from SCF
      Jijiga   214
      ABEBAW ZELLEKE

6.12 Non-governmental organizations – barriers and solutions   217
      WORKING GROUP REPORT

4: Government and International Agencies

6.13 Introducing participation by children and young people into local
      public services: first steps, early mistakes and lessons learned 220
      MARK FEENEY

6.14 Children's participation in local decision-making: the challenge
      of local governance   225
      BARRY PERCY-SMITH

6.15 Child-sensitive local government structures in synergy with
      children's representative bodies   232
      JOHN PARRY-WILLIAMS

6.16 Children as partners with adults: a view from the North   233
      BERRY MAYALL

6.17 Children's conferences and councils   236
      DAVID WOOLLCOMBE

6.18 Promoting children's participation in an international conference: what can we learn from the Save the Children Alliance experience in Oslo?   241
RACHEL MARCUS

6.19 International agencies, government and NGOs working together in Yemen   243
SHEENA CRAWFORD

6.20 Government and international agencies   246
WORKING GROUP REPORT

6.21 Conclusions   253
VICTORIA JOHNSON and PATTA SCOTT

PART 7: CHILDREN AS ACTIVE PARTICIPANTS

Summary   259
7.0 Introduction   259
EDDA IVAN-SMITH

7.1 Shadow of death: growing up in a Jamaican garrison community   263
IMANI TAFARI-AMA

7.2 Voyce: environmental care and young people's participation   266
ADAM HAINES

7.3 Different questions, different ideas: child-led research and other participation   271
ANDREW WEST

7.4 Giving children a voice   278
GRACE MUKASA and VERA VAN DER GRIFT-WANYOTO

7.5 Children, power and participatory research in Uganda   281
ROB BOWDEN

7.6 Approaches to peer education and youth advisory councils – experiences in Honduras   283
DONALD KAMINSKY

7.7 Conclusions   285
EDDA IVAN-SMITH

PART 8: THE WAY FORWARD

EDDA IVAN-SMITH AND VICTORIA JOHNSON

Lines of communication and power   291
Ethics   293
How to: the process   294
Culture   295
Crisis   296
Institutions and power   296
Where do we go from here?   297

ix

Appendix 1: The Workshop Process   300
             PATTA SCOTT
Appendix 2: Ladders of Participation   308
             PAT PRIDMORE
Appendix 3: The United Nations Convention on the Rights of
             the Child – history and background   310
             EDDA IVAN-SMITH
Appendix 4: The Lead Organizations in the Preparation of this
             Book   313
Appendix 5: Children's Participation in Research and Programming
             Workshop: Participants' Contact List   314
Bibliography and References   317
Index   327

Abbreviations

AAN	ActionAid Nepal
ALC	Adult Literacy Class
CAS	City-as-School
CBO	Community-based Organization
CBR	Community-based Rehabilitation
CCPR	Child-centred Participatory Research
CCVD	Children's Committees for Village Development
CDW	Community Development Worker
CEC	Community Education Council
CLC	Child Literacy Class
CRC	Convention on the Rights of the Child (UN)
CTC	Children's Theatre Collective
DA	Development Area
DCWC	District Child Welfare Committee
ECPAT	End Child Prostitution, Pornography, Trafficking
FFW	Food For Work
FGD	Focus-group Discussion
FUNDAR	Foundation for Development, Friendship and Answers
GNCC	Ghana National Commission on Children
GUIC	Growing up in Cities
IDS	Institute of Development Studies
IoE	Institute of Education
ILO	International Labour Office
JLP	Jamaica Labour Party
LGMB	Local Government Management Board
MBE	Ministry of Basic Education (Zimbabwe)
M&E	Monitoring and Evaluation
MTR	Mid-term Review
NCC	National Children's Commission
NGO	Non-governmental Organization
NYC	New York City
OAU	Organization of African Unity
PETA	Philippine Educational Theatre Association
PLA	Participatory Learning and Action
PNP	People's National Party (Jamaica)
PRA	Participatory Rural Appraisal
PV	Participatory Video
RPE	Measure of quality in participation in research, planning and evaluation
SCF	Save the Children Fund
SFI	Salinlahi Foundations Incorporated
SMC	School Management Committees
SWRC	Social Work Research Centre

UN	United Nations
UNCRC	United Nations Convention on the Rights of the Child
UNESCO	United Nations Educational, Scientific and Cultural Organization
UNICEF	United Nations Children's Fund

Glossary

Agenda 21: An action plan for sustainable development for the world in the 21st century. It was drawn up at the United Nations Conference on Environment and Development (UNCED), commonly known as the Earth Summit, in Rio de Janeiro in 1992 (a gathering of 179 heads of state and government).

Bal Sansad: Children's Parliament (India).

Capoera: Brazilian form of martial arts/dance originating in Africa.

Child-specific indicators: Indicators that relate specifically to the well-being of children and their circumstances; these may be indicators identified by children and young people or by adults, or a mixture of both; they may be qualitative or quantitative.

Charland: Mid-channel and bank-line areas in river channels in Bangladesh.

Don: Gang leader/involved in drugs and crime.

Draught power: The use of animals such as oxen and horses to pull ploughs or carts.

Durbar: A large celebration or fair during which people gather to enjoy traditional games and sports and to eat special foods.

Gate-keepers: People who control the access of others to resources, people, venues or information.

Habitat: United Nations Centre for Human Settlements.

Informed consent: Gaining the consent of participants (adults or young people/children) who are fully aware of the process and consequences of a piece of research or an action project. Informed consent for children should be sought also from their parents or guardians.

Logframes: The Logframe or Logical Project Framework is a project design tool that summarizes the main features of a project and provides a means by which progress can be judged. The framework is a 16-box matrix that helps to make transparent the validity of a project design by showing how activities lead to outputs and achieve purposes and goals if certain assumptions are met.

Margolis wheel: This is a participatory method for generating the maximum number of solutions to problems. Seated in concentric circles facing each other in pairs, people on the inner circle suggest solutions to those on the outer circle. By moving around the circle one person at a time, each person with a problem gets ideas from all the advisers. Participants take it in turns to act as advisers and those with a problem.

Namebrand Man: Man who wears designer clothes.

Piece-work: Work that is paid according to the amount of work done rather than by the hour.

Porte Parole: Giving a voice – an open door to words.

PRA/PLA: PRA (also referred to as PLA) describes a number of approaches intended to enable people to share, represent and analyse their life experiences and to facilitate their identification of potential solutions and action. In theory, it represents a move away from extractive-information collection. Examples of techniques include: mapping, transects, seasonal calendars, preference ranking and Venn diagrams.

Rädda Barnen: Save the Children, Sweden.

Redd Barna: Save the Children, Norway.

Role play: In a role play, people act out a given situation. They may act as themselves or play another role. Role plays are made up spontaneously by the actors; there is no script.

Stake-holders: Persons, groups or institutions with interests in a programme or activity because it will affect them in some way, either positively or negatively, or because they have some influence on the outcome.

Triangulation: Uses a mix of methods, sources of information and/or researchers to acquire different perspectives on a situation. This increases the trustworthiness of information generated in research and develops an holistic picture of reality.

Dedication

The editors and co-authors would like to dedicate this book to our children and partners, who have supported us in this work, rarely complaining when we have little time to listen to them: Henry-Wolfe, Gregg and Robert; Claudius; Jon, Vanessa and Njoroge; Oliver, Tom, Tim, Rebecca and John; and Alastair. And also to the children we have worked with in different parts of the world who have inspired us and have been so generous with their ideas and spirit: from Nepal, Vietnam, Kenya, South Africa, Sudan, Ghana, Zambia, Iraq, and The Gambia; Brighton and Hull in the UK.

Acknowledgements

We wish to acknowledge the funders without whom this work would never have been possible, not least in bringing over the overseas participants. The Swiss Development Co-operation (SDC) through the Institute of Development Studies at the University of Sussex (IDS), Save the Children (UK), the Department for International Development of the British Government (DIFD) and the Institute of Education (IoE). Thanks also to those participants from Northern countries who funded themselves to attend and participate so fully.

We are grateful to all who made this workshop and book possible: Robert Chambers at IDS for his continued support in planning and following through this whole enterprise; Judith Ennew for her unwavering assistance on issues of children in development; Jo Boyden and Roger Hart for their advice at the beginning of the process; Andy Norton in DFID for his support on the subject and the project; Charlie Austin for his time and valuable comments on the draft; Juliet Merrifield for her input to the introductory issues; Barry Percy-Smith for his idea of 'Stepping Forward'; Rita Dutta and Felicity Rawlings at IoE, and Julia Brown, Garry and Jenny Edwards and Betty Grimes at IDS for keeping us afloat by organizing logistics and administration; Ann Watson for advice on the workshop and Vanessa Bainbridge at IDS for dealing with awkward requests; to Robert Nurick at Development FOCUS for continued help with technology; and to Meg Howarth, our copy-editor at IT Publications, for giving coherence and shape to this, at times, unwieldy volume.

Last, but not least, we would like to thank those who participated in the workshop and helped to put this book together who are named as co-authors of the chapters and made the whole process so rich with examples, ideas and fun.

Foreword

Participation has entered the mainstream vocabulary of development; inclusion is following hard on its heels. Though practice has lagged behind rhetoric, more and more social groups have been identified as marginal or excluded, and their participation and inclusion seen as priorities. So it has been with women, poor people, ethnic and religious minorities, refugees, the disabled, and the very old. While this has been happening, many have seen children as a different sort of category. Children's health, nutrition and education have long been on the agenda but not their active participation as partners in development.

In part this has reflected the views adults and teachers commonly hold of children and of the young. They are seen as ignorant – to be taught; irresponsible – to be disciplined; immature – to be 'brought up'; incapable – to be protected; a nuisance – 'to be seen and not heard'; or a resource – to be made use of. The pervasive powerlessness of children sustains and reinforces these views; female children or those from low social groups are especially disadvantaged and looked down upon.

With the authority of experience, this book turns these views on their heads. Many old beliefs and attitudes about children cannot survive the evidence presented here: again and again, in different cultures and in whatever context – school, communities or the family, whether as pupils, street children, child labourers or refugees – children are shown to be social actors, with evidence that their capabilities have been underestimated and their realities undervalued.

Appreciating the potentials of children's participation has taken time. An example is the evolution of PRA (participatory rural appraisal) over the past decade. At first, children and younger people were little noticed, even a nuisance. Sometimes they were neutralized by being given something to do – fetching leaves of different trees, or different grasses, or drawing with chalks or pens – to make them useful, keep them quiet or simply for fun. But soon they demonstrated that they could do more than adults supposed. Like older people, they too could make maps, matrices and diagrams. Moreover these showed that their knowledge, realities, preferences and priorities were valid, and differed from those of women and men. Like other 'lowers' they, too, could be empowered to express and analyse their realities and present them to 'uppers'.

Stepping Forward brings together many other illustrations. The experiences described open up a new and wonderful world in which adults facilitate more than teach, and children show that they can do much more than adults thought they could. So we have here children's participation not just in their own social groups but in conferences, councils and community meetings; children's planning and analysis using techniques of mapping, diagramming and matrix scoring; children as researchers; children taking photographs and videos to document their lives; and children designing and performing their own drama, radio broadcasts and television programmes.

For many of us adults, this is more than an ordinary book. It is an invitation to see and relate to children in new ways. The change of view can be compared with becoming aware of gendered roles and attitudes. It demonstrates how much our mindsets about children, like those about gender roles, are socially constructed and reproduced through power relations.

There is, though, a difference. With gender-awareness there have been many adults, mostly women, able and willing to speak out for themselves and others. For children, in contrast, this is rarely possible. In cultures of adult power it is difficult for them to assert themselves, being as they are at once smaller, weaker, more dependent, less articulate, and less able to meet and organize.

For their reality to be recognized and to count they have then to rely on sensitive insight and enabling by adults. These qualities in adults, though still not common, are shown in full measure by the contributors to this book. Working separately in 30 countries spread through five continents, they have explored similar terrain and made similar discoveries. They have faced similar ethical issues in facilitating children's participation. Coming together in the workshop which gave rise to this book, their experiences generated synergy and an infectious excitement. These are now shared in a measured and balanced manner with a wider audience. Richly diverse in culture and context, the findings converge on striking conclusions: that children across the world can do more, and be more creative, than most adults believe; that children's knowledge, perceptions and priorities often differ from what adults suppose them to be; and that giving children space and encouragment to act and express themselves is doubly fulfilling, with rewards for children and adults alike. So this is a book not just about the participation of children and young people. It is also about new forms of fulfilment for adults, the rewards of sharing power and of enabling those who are younger to discover and express more of their potential.

Let me hope that when our children look back from later in the 21st century, they will see this book as part of a watershed in adult understanding and behaviour towards the young. There is perhaps no more powerful way of transforming human society than changing how the adults of today relate to children, the adults of tomorrow. By sharing their explorations and experiences with children and young people, the contributors and editors of *Stepping Forward* have done good service. Their new understandings of children will make many other adults want to change. Their contributions invite us to join them on a steep learning curve. For this, their insights give us a flying start, for they show us how we can enable children to participate and be included more as partners in development; how we can see, relate to and empower them in new ways; and how we can help them discover for themselves more of their remarkable potentials. The message I take from this book is that if we adults can only change our views and behaviour, children will astonish us with what they can do, be and become, and how in time they can make our world a better place.

Robert Chambers
18 July 1998

Preface

There is a widespread tendency to view children's participation with fear, dismay, or at least caution. At one extreme is the argument that children must at all costs be protected from taking any part in what is called 'the adult world'. This is associated with a supposed natural hostility between adults and children, expressed throughout this century in ideas as diverse as the Oedipus complex and the generation gap. At the less extreme end of the non-participation spectrum there are those who argue that children's right to participate should be tempered by the responsibility of adults to protect them from bearing burdens of activity and decision-making that properly belong to adults.

The arguments for child participation perhaps begin with the romance of children's voices, 'smaller voices' to which we are now instructed to listen, but which have tended to be crowded out by the clamour of adult voices, just as female voices have been until recently given no historial hearing. As several contributors to *Stepping Forward* point out, this is an issue of power. Muted groups, such as women, children, prisoners and ethnic minorities are unable to express their reality in ways that are acceptable to the dominant groups that control both means and modes of expression.[1] Nevertheless, the voices of the youngest of our species are now being recorded, listened to and respected as never before, albeit against a background of hostility. Children are being un-muted. Which raises a fascinating question: why should it be that children's voices and children's participation are being advocated at this stage in history?

The editors consistently and correctly ground the debates in *Stepping Forward* in the 1989 United Nations Convention on the Rights of the Child. The idea of participation is one of the many novel features of this human rights instrument, even though the term itself does not occur in any of the Articles that are regarded as 'participation articles' (12–15). Indeed, the word 'participation' occurs only twice in the text of the Convention, once to ensure that children with disabilities can take a full part in society (Article 23) and once with respect to the child's rights to ensure that witnesses take part in court proceedings (Article 40). The so-called participation articles refer to children's rights to influence decisions made on their behalf, express their views, have freedom of thought, conscience and religion and also the right to form associations. Just about all these rights are tempered in the text by the need to take into consideration 'the age and maturity of the child'. This is precisely caught in the definition of participation in *Stepping Forward*:

> Participation in this book does not mean the token involvement of children, but how to incorporate their specific needs and views into decision-making processes within the context of what is possible institutionally and culturally.

Nevertheless, the absence of the term does not mean that participation is not implied in the Convention. Indeed I am tempted to argue that, just as dignity is the undefined basis and touchstone of human rights, participation is the basis and touchstone of ensuring that children are subjects of those same human rights.

Stepping Forward provides many examples of how children can be facilitated to express their opinions and describe their reality using a variety of modes of expression, in the words of Article 13 of the Convention, 'orally, in writing or in print, in the form of art, or through any other media of the child's choice'. This correctly attempts to remove the techniques of domination whereby children's voices have been muted. However, the *structures* of domination, which trivialize or misinterpret children's voices, remain rooted (and virtually untouched) in patriarchy. One of the keys to confronting this is in Article 15, which provides the right to freedom of association and peaceful assembly – a fundamental human right that adults have long been accorded. Nevertheless the right for children to meet and organize on their own behalf and in their own interests is still given by adults, who claim to protect children either from other adults or from themselves.

As contributors point out in *Stepping Forward*, there are now numerous examples of national and international meetings of children with the objective of making children's voices heard on important issues. Yet the role played by adults in facilitating children's meetings and organizations is ambiguous and can be both manipulative and controlling. There are no established methods for ensuring that children are enabled to participate fully and freely, nor definitions of what participation means in this context. Children tend to participate through adult selection rather than as child representatives and it sometimes seems that any child's voice will be regarded as having special authenticity as long as it is heard on a public platform and applauded by adults. In many cases, participation is reduced to tokenism or decoration, to use Hart's terminology, and children's voices are only heard in songs written for them by adults to give support to adult opinions and policies. My own experience of these activities leads me to agree with David Woollcombe's comment, in his contribution to *Stepping Forward*, about child participation in United Nations and other international arenas: 'It is important to understand that visibility does not equal participation or empowerment'.

One obstacle to resolving these and other questions raised in this thought-provoking book is that there is no integrated discourse on child participation, which often appears to have taken over as a fashionable attitude in policy, programming and advocacy from earlier terms such as self-reliance and sustainability. Until now, the debates around participation have tended to be based more on opinion, recall of childhoods past and anecdote than on concrete evidence. Although there are an increasing number of experiences of child participation of all kinds, records are few and there are even fewer evaluations available. Success is generally claimed on the basis of unsubstantiated stories from agencies, rather than being grounded in monitoring processes that use agreed definitions, criteria and indicators. Instances in which children are truly involved in programme planning and evaluation are rare, and examples of child-generated indicators even less frequent. Child participation projects have existed since at least the 1970s, predating the Convention on the Rights of the Child. some of these projects set the precedents for more recent programmes. Most of the older projects work with street or working children, in developing countries. Documentation of these projects is either scanty or nonexistent. Much of the information about the history and progress of both pioneering and more recent projects exists in the form of fundraising publicity, as 'grey material' in project files or in the memories of long-term project workers. Thus a book that presents an inventory and evaluation of methods of child participation is timely, and should help to establish the basis for generally-accepted objectives and methods. The sheer range of papers in *Stepping Forward* makes it an invaluable resource for future debates on children's participation and a stout shield for children's rights advocates against the backlash of patriarchy.

Judith Ennew

Notes

1. Ardener, E. 1975, The problem revisited, in Ardener, S., (ed.), *Perceiving women*, London, Dent, pp. 19–27; Moore, H.L., 1988, *Feminism and anthropology*, Cambridge, Polity Press, p. 3.

PART 1

Children and Young People's Participation: the starting-point

VICTORIA JOHNSON and EDDA IVAN-SMITH

1.0   Background to the issues

VICTORIA JOHNSON and EDDA IVAN-SMITH

Why children?

Several practical examples of research which have taken children's roles and views seriously give a clear answer to this question. Through using more participatory processes and approaches we can start to see how valuable it is to work with girls and boys to understand their differing perspectives and we can also begin to recognize the risks of ignoring their viewpoints. Risks to their own quality of life, but also the failure to achieve the full potential for development ideas springing from more inclusive processes that appreciate and respond to a diversity of views from different members of civic society. 'Participation' in this book does not mean the token involvement of children but how to incorporate their specific needs and views into decision-making processes within the context of what is possible institutionally and culturally.

In an innovative study of child labour in rural Vietnam carried out by SCF UK, gender and age differences in children's work were explored. The study included exploration of the likes and dislikes of girls and boys, the split between time spent on work and education activities and the critical contribution of children to the household economy. The report raises the issue that, although the research project tried to involve children actively, it overlooked 'children's own abilities, capacities, strategies and ingenuity', namely 'what children do to protect themselves, to fight or to evade exploitation and abuse?' (Theis and Thi Huyen, 1997: 38). The report points out that it is important not to assume that children are vulnerable and passive victims, and thereby to reinforce existing power relations. We must recognize children's own coping strategies in the face of difficulties and build on their resourcefulness, at the same time as acknowledging the need for proper protection and provision of services. The research from Vietnam is covered further in this book in Chapter 3.4 by Joachim Theis.

Research primarily carried out with ActionAid Nepal and complemented by case-study examples from around Asia, Africa and Latin America also concluded that children have to be treated as active participants in the development process (Johnson, Hill and Ivan-Smith, 1995). In the resulting publication, 'Listening to smaller voices: children in an environment of change', the authors assert that, 'If the specific needs of girls and boys are not fully understood or addressed, then action to alleviate poverty could affect their quality of life adversely. Instead, only those members of the society with louder voices and more prominent positions within society are likely to benefit; thereby increasing the poverty gap' (Johnson, Hill and Ivan-Smith, 1995, executive summary). Children's participation is, therefore, an issue that should not be ignored by people working on broader issues of participation, social exclusion and poverty alleviation. This work has been followed through

3

and is reported by Joanna Hill in Chapter 3.7 of the book. It is not just an issue for those working on projects that specifically target children. Girls and boys will be affected by action and intervention intended for other targets and roles in civic society and the impact of different strategies on them have to be carefully monitored and understood by developing more child-sensitive indicators for broader development programmes.

We risk more than adversely affecting the quality of children's lives by not listening to their voices and views. We risk missing out on the richness and innovative perspectives that can be offered by children and young people with varying experiences and from varying situations. A pertinent example which demonstrates so clearly, 'why children?' is taken from the experience of Redd Barna and IIED in Masaka District of Uganda (Guijt, Fuglesang and Kisadha (eds) 1994). In the case of Kyakatebe in Masaka District, the children's unique concerns could not be identified by adults, while they could identify other issues affecting both the children and themselves. Denying the children the chance to participate in analysing their situation risks missing out key issues that affect children. Grace Mukasa came to the workshop to discuss Redd Barna's most recent work with children and her paper is included in Chapter 7.4 of the book.

In research carried out on young people's experiences of leaving care (West, 1995), the benefits of using participatory approaches are listed. Amongst these benefits were that young people brought 'fresh categories and perceptions to the research' and that youth enjoyed research carried out by their peers. Involving young people in the analysis of results gave a more legitimate and meaningful structure to the key issues and experiences emphasized. The project was not merely about the research but about the broader engagement of those with and without power, which is bound to be a process of continuous negotiation. Andy West updates his analysis of work with SCF in the UK and addresses some of the fundamental power relationships that need to be addressed, in his paper in Chapter 7.3 of the book.

These examples give us a taste of why children and young people have so much to offer in our analysis of the development process and our planning of interventions intended to improve the quality of life for children and for poor people in different cultural contexts around the world.

In drawing from many experiences of projects world-wide to formulate the SCF Development Manual on Street and Working Children, Judith Ennew comes to the fundamental conclusion that: 'children are capable, resourceful people whose individual histories, feelings and opinions must be respected. It follows that projects must be considered always as working with children rather than for them, encouraging and facilitating the fullest possible participation'. (Ennew, 1994: 6). It is with this spirit that we enter into the issues of children's participation. In this book we try to delve into how and why children have participated in different projects. We also examine approaches that have both worked and also those that have met with difficulties so that we can work towards solutions that respect the contribution that girls and boys of different ages and varying social, cultural and economic contexts can make to civil society.

4

Children, civic society and social exclusion
It is important to try to identify how the inclusion or exclusion in different groups, structures and processes will shape young people's views on their social roles, rights and responsibilities and their feelings about citizenship. 'Social exclusion' is a term used by the European Union to identify a number of economic and social attributes that decrease civic, political and economic participation (Merrifield, 1997). Recent literature on issues relating to youth and citizenship make it clear that the experience of transition into adulthood and full citizenship is shaped in part by factors of socio-economic status, ethnicity and gender, as well as age. Recent research has looked at youth and citizenship (e.g. Jones and Wallace, 1992; Bhavnani, 1991; Willis *et al.*, 1988) from a variety of perspectives: sociological, psychological and political.

It is useful to understand the concepts about social capital and the civil society (an American focus) and about social exclusion (a European focus). In this context, social capital would include democracy, human rights, respect within communities and general social organization of groups of people and the benefits that this accrues. Each of these dimensions adds to our understanding of the ways in which participation is shaped and constrained by the social fabric. It is clear that at the same time that the current youth cohort is making its transition to adulthood and citizenship, the status itself is changing and being changed. What citizenship meant to their parents is not what citizenship will mean to today's youth, and youth itself is not a homogeneous group in their experience of citizenship and participation. People conceive of civic participation very broadly, and include neighbourly acts as well as voting, involvement in community organizations and political parties. Being a citizen is not a passive status, a matter of rights, but an active involvement in the community, however constituted. In some societies the entire civil

Table 1.1: **Key issues identified by children and other members of the community at Kyakatebe, Masaka District, Uganda**

Issues of concern	Team identifying the issues	
	Children	Adults
Child labour	✓	–
Transport to school	✓	–
Inadequate food	✓	–
Supply of teachers	✓	–
Drunken teachers	✓	–
HIV/AIDS	–	✓
Lack of fuelwood	–	✓
Inadequate health facilities	–	✓
Lack of school fees	✓	✓
High level of school opt-out	✓	✓
Orphans	✓	✓

Source: Adapted from: Guijt, Fuglesang and Kisadha (1994): 157/8.

structure has broken down and the concept of citizen or member of the community has to be re-evaluated and approached in a different way. Although there are different ideas and meanings of citizenship globally, there are few areas where all human beings strive to or desire to communicate or organize themselves in such a way that makes them feel less vulnerable and able to make a recognizable contribution. Citizenship, wherever it is, could be said to satisfy these criteria. (Merrifield, pers. com. 1997).

Boyte (1995: 17) in his work on citizenship as public work recognizes that public values are 'created through the ongoing, multi-dimensional work of people with different interests and needs who address common problems'. By recognizing the diversity of views amongst youth, we can start to understand how social capital affects their lives and concepts about the world around them. Wilkinson (1996) argues that individuals who possess optimum social capital enjoy relatively better health than others of the same socio-economic status with less social capital. Putnam (1993: 37) refers to how 'stocks of social capital, such as trust, norms and networks tend to be self-reinforcing'. This highlights the importance of viewing social capital as a dynamic and continually changing concept as we analyse how it affects youth.

Practitioners and researchers are now seeking to understand the processes by which different groups of children and youth become excluded and the way in which social capital can be built and destroyed. Varying concepts of childhood and adulthood will depend on socio-economic status, ethnicity, sexuality, age and gender and these must be explored in order to understand the changing roles and responsibilities of young people in households or families and society. James, Jenks and Prout (1998: 124) raise the debate about one or many childhoods: 'is it ever possible (or desirable) to speak meaningfully about 'childhood as a unitary concept?' Childhood diversity raises the issue that childhood may have a variety of meanings depending on the different circumstances of a child or group of children. It is true that this erects barriers to cross-cultural comparisons and generalizations within cultures. Some, such as Jens Qvortrup, would argue that there is value in understanding the 'childhood of society' and focusing on the aspects and relationships that all children have with the rest of society (Qvortrup, described in James, Jenks and Prout, 1998). What seems to be important is to carry out analysis at different levels of aggregation deemed appropriate in order to gain a better understanding of children's realities, also to portray this to policy decision-makers in a language and style upon which they can act. This means inevitably a detailed level of research and analysis of diverse childhoods so that the varying impacts of change on different children can be linked with a broader analysis of the structural influences that may affect all children in a given society.

It is important, too, to understand that visibility does not equal participation or empowerment. It is tempting to assume that the only hindrance for children's participation is invisibility and that a higher profile will allow them to be heard and for their needs to be met. In many industrialized countries children and teenagers are clearly visible as consumers and are targeted quite aggressively by advertising agencies and producers of a variety of goods. In many areas child labour, such as agricultural work, prostitution or street vending, may be very visible but this visibility does not enable these children to participate in their local communities or, more importantly, to have their contribution recognized and acted upon.

The participatory process can help us to understand social exclusion, social capital and different roles within society from the perspective of young people.

Making participatory processes more child-sensitive
There is a wealth of experience working with excluded people in developing countries using participatory approaches, sometimes referred to as participatory rural appraisal (PRA) or participatory learning and action (PLA). Lessons learnt have not only helped us to understand appropriate solutions to poverty but the processes have been shown to include people in analysis and action which can lead to their better sense of well-being (Chambers, 1997). It is important to link concepts of participation and exclusion in different communities and countries, and in the North and South to learn from each another. Lack of participation may also be recognized as a form of social exclusion. Thus, participation or inclusion can be thought of as a goal in itself, as a response to exclusion. Participation can also help the excluded to act effectively to address the problems they face (Gaventa, 1998). There is growing evidence that participatory approaches can be successful in understanding many issues from the perspectives of a range of people of varying socio-economic and ethnic status in different countries around the globe.

Participatory processes have not, however, always been sensitive to all 'issues of difference', such as ethnicity, wealth/poverty, gender, age and disability (Welbourn, 1992). Although there are tried and tested techniques of wealth ranking and a growing body of examples which have started to analyse differences in people's lives due to ethnicity and gender, there has been less participatory work carried out with young people. In some participatory training manuals people have noted the importance of separating young and old men and young and old women. 'Young', however, does not specifically focus on youth and rarely includes children. Despite this, there is a growing emphasis on working to understand children's and young people's roles in households and in society as reflected in the examples included in the introductory section to this chapter and indeed in the examples throughout this book.

Different levels of participation can be achieved by varying interventions in different contexts and the ladder of participation is referred to in a number of papers. Appendix 2 describes in more detail Arnstein's ladder of citizen participation and Hart's ladder that adapts these concepts to children's participation. This shows levels that start with 'manipulation', 'decoration', and 'tokenism' and move up to 'child-initiated, shared decisions with adults' (Hart, 1997: 41). Participation of young people as addressed in this book cannot stop at their involvement in activities, but explores their increased participation in processes and decision-making that affect their own lives. Thus, the ways in which one works in a participatory way with adults and with different institutions which affect the lives of young people can be vital to a successful outcome from the point of view of the children or young people themselves.

7

The Convention on the Rights of the Child

The UN Convention on the Rights of the Child (CRC) is a theme that runs through the book (see Appendix 3). The rights of a child to participate are central to the convention and should be seen as equally as important and running alongside rights to protection and provision. This is sometimes referred to as the 3Ps – provision, protection and participation. The CRC articles relevant to participation are elucidated in the appendix and set the context for achieving different degrees of participation.

In the book it is seen as important to start from the perspectives of children, but also to look at the contexts that influence their lives and roles. This includes understanding the framework of the rights of the child expressed in the international convention and how this is relevant at different levels of decision-making within different institutional and cultural contexts.

1.1 Origins and structure of the book

VICTORIA JOHNSON and EDDA IVAN-SMITH

Anyone who works on children's participation issues will be familiar with being accused of merely following a development fashion, taking children too seriously, or being asked, why focus on children? Paying serious attention to a group of people deemed powerless, helpless and disruptive can often be met with hostility or incredulity. Very often however, many organizations feel that if they are working on children's issues they have no choice but to involve children more in their work. One of the stimuli behind the growing children's participation movement has been the previous lack of information or knowledge about the reality of youngsters' lives. This has led to programmes and projects targeted at children being less effective, and more broadly targeted development projects having unforeseen circumstances for girls and boys.

Working with children and young people and truly participating with them not only has benefits for them but sharpens the analysis and understanding of the world around us which, without that information, is somewhat one-dimensional. We should be asking why it has taken so long to arrive at the obvious, but the concept of children's participation is not yet well-enough established to elicit that type of enquiry. There remains the sense of the pioneer spirit about the people and organizations that become involved in these issues, and pioneering can at times be lonely, unrewarding and difficult. Conversely, initiatives such as the workshop which spawned this book re-ignite the enthusiasm and excitement of viewing the world through the lens of children and young people.

When working in an institution or on a research project that has the aim of understanding children's and young people's roles and increasing their participation in the development process one has sometimes a strange sense of isolation. Why are you doing this? Why children? Why participation? You realize then that other people do prioritize the same issues, maybe somewhere within your own organization or in a different type of institution altogether, and you realize that there is great value in trying to understand the rich, innovative perspectives that come from the children themselves. It often helps in your own thought and planning processes to look at what others have learnt and to share ideas on the way forward. It was these thoughts that initiated the process that has resulted in this book of case-studies and themes on the participation of children and young people.

The starting-point
In September 1995, a small workshop was held at the Institute of Development Studies (IDS) in collaboration with the International Institute for Environment and Development (IIED), ACTIONAID and Save the Children Fund UK (SCF UK). The aim of the workshop was to share ideas between some 15–20 UK-based practitioners and academics who had begun working on issues of children's participation. Key ethical themes arose as some of the most demanding of discussion and understanding, together with the institutional barriers facing people in their own contexts. A special edition of PLA Notes (No. 25, Johnson, 1996) was published by IIED. This series is produced to share ideas internationally on participatory learning and action (PLA), also referred to as participatory rural appraisal (PRA) approaches. It was suggested at the workshop that it would be a good idea to have a larger international meeting to discuss some of these issues more broadly and to involve more international input. The Education and International Development Group at the Institute of Education, University of London, was at the same time also thinking of an event on children's participation to build on their previous experiences and contact with those involved in the child-to-child movement and with write-and-draw techniques.

In September 1997, an international workshop was held by the Institute of Development Studies, the Institute of Education and Save the Children UK. The objectives of the workshop were to share experiences of children's participation, both positive and negative, and to take the debate forward in terms of process and approach to overcoming institutional barriers and ethical dilemmas. Around 50 participants attended, from the UK, eastern Europe, south-east and west Asia, different countries in west, east and southern Africa, the Caribbean, central America and north America. The agenda for the five-day event that has formed the basis for this book was formulated by clustering into six themes the topics identified by the participants in their abstracts as being important for discussion and further consideration. The organizers of the workshop (for more detail see Appendix 1) tried to make use of the experience and facilitation skills of the participants who had identified similar issues by forming them into teams with responsibility for running their session. It is the participatory nature of the workshop process that has, we think, led to the enthusiasm to share the ideas presented there with a wider constituency of people working with children and young people within the context of the broader development of civic society.

The audience
The book is aimed at two principal categories of practitioners and researchers: those who work with children and young people and are seeking ways of becoming more participatory in their activities; and those who work more broadly on participatory processes and techniques who should value the views and contributions of children and young people as an integral and important part of the broader picture. The contributions made by practitioners from government and non-governmental organizations, youth groups and academics offer a range of perspectives and ways of portraying the issues. We hope this makes the book accessible to both parties.

The themes of the book

The book is divided into eight parts. Parts 1 and 8, by the editors, provide a general introduction and conclusion respectively. Parts 2–7 each cover one of the six workshop themes, mainly in the form of papers presented to the workshop but with the addition of a few specially commissioned pieces designed to cover missed issues or provide a greater geographical spread. The themes are as follows:

Part 2   This looks at the building blocks of communication techniques and ethical approaches that need to be considered fully and planned for within the context of working with children and young people. Not all the answers are given. Instead, key questions and areas are raised that need to be assessed before embarking on a project or piece of research.

Part 3   Different participatory processes are explored, focusing on some of the new and innovative ways of using video, photo evaluation, TV programming and theatre to work with young people. The importance of visualization and of making research processes fun, accessible and inclusive is highlighted.

Part 4   The significance of the cultural context in which you are working is discussed using case-studies from a variety of regions. The ways in which perceptions and attitudes are shaped and moulded in different cultures are appreciated, whilst exploring the concepts of sub-cultures and children's own cultures.

Part 5   This illustrates the sensitivities faced in times of crisis and emphasizes the crucial role that children's participation can play in conflict settings.

Part 6   A variety of institutional settings is explored from the perspective of how children see themselves fitting into different formal and informal structures. The approaches and changes of attitude needed to engender greater children's participation in schools, NGOs, government and international agencies are discussed. The pitfalls of participation and situations where children's participation may be no more than tokenistic are acknowledged.

Part 7   Young people need to be seen as active participants in the development process, not as passive victims. A range of case-studies demonstrates some of the lessons learned in other parts of the book and gives examples of processes in the field, from beginning to end.

The parts of the book

Each of Parts 2–7 has an introduction by the editors, with reference to literature in the field that it is hoped will enable the reader to follow up in greater detail the issues raised. There now follows a brief summary of each of the papers included in Parts 2–7:

Part 2
Emmanuelle Abrioux's hard-hitting and practical chapter (2.1) asserts that the particular socio-economic, political and cultural context within which we work determines the degree of children's participation possible, as well as the methods used to achieve this. The difficulties faced in participatory approaches with girls in Kabul, Afghanistan, are such that she proposes a spherical model which shows degrees of involvement at an individual activity level, considering the context in which one is working and the starting-point of the participants. Roger Hart (2.2) summarizes the recent thinking of contemporary development psychologists conducting research and developing theory that emphasizes the context of development and the processes by which children learn and collaborate. The mistakes of the past in generalizing about children's intellectual development across cultures must be avoided. Hart notes the importance of play in the development of children's social relations, empathy, sense of belonging and skills of self-control and co-operation. He also highlights that for maximum involvement of children of all ages, a wide range of media should be used. Children's participation requires adults willing to change their own attitudes towards children, learn how to listen, and who will allow children to develop a wide range of capacities and skills.

Sarah McNeill's chapter (2.3) raises ethical issues in the context of the mass media. In the media, adult preconceptions of the child as a passive non-contributing member of a community, reinforced by images of the young as mute and victimized, devalue the status of children. This issue can only be addressed through participation, the focus of work now being done by the CRC working group on the child and the media. In actively seeking out examples of good practice the group aims to influence codes of practice in media professions to enhance and enable children's participation.

Jonathan Blagbrough's contribution (2.4) presents research that has been carried out with child domestic workers in a range of countries in Asia, Africa and the Caribbean. Key ethical issues raised in this research relate to the experience needed when working with children and the length of time often required in order to build trust and confidence between them and the researchers. The physical setting and the style of interaction are important in understanding the children's true situation. Stress and depression can affect the children after an interaction and children have been known to run away after an interview. This is a sobering message and Blagbrough highlights the point that a researcher must therefore be willing to follow through with help if it is needed as a consequence of investigation.

11

Claire O'Kane (2.5) raises a range of ethical considerations and practical approaches arising from her work in Swansea, UK. The biggest ethical challenge lies in the disparities in power and status between adults and children. Melinda Swift (2.6) discusses her experience in the use of participatory research methods with children in the Growing Up in Cities (GUIC) project in Johannesburg, South Africa. The research raises the issues of consent and permission. In the final chapter of Part 2 Eileen Adams (2.7) discusses some of the ethical problems of dealing with change from her experiences in educational research and curriculum development: raising expectations within a framework of action research, gaining permission or consent through schools, the risks of participation, and the tensions experienced by adults working with children who are not trained in communication skills. Fundamental issues of power and control are discussed, as well as those relating to the ownership, end-use, interpretation and dissemination of information.

Farhana Faruqui's contribution acknowledges the realities of different childhoods and the conflicting interests and divisions between different groups of children and lists the principal ethical issues arising from her experience.

Part 3
Charity Manyau (3.7) describes a needs assessment in Zimbabwe involving 'bush boarders' who live far from the school and are obliged to squat nearby in shacks. The use of visual techniques, role-play and the role of energizers are discussed. Mahfuza Haques's experience of running a workshop (3.2) in Bangladesh highlights the factors that helped generate interest and participation: time to build rapport; a clear understanding of the purpose of the workshop; time for games and recreation; flexible methods and processes designed for children; and opportunities for children to participate with adults in discussions.

Thabang Ngcozela (3.3) identifies seven key issues in children's participation: needs assessment; expectations; setting, environment and subsistence; methodology; qualities of the facilitator; supporting resource materials; and evaluation. Joachim Theis (3.4) suggests that researchers on child labour in rural Vietnam were caught between two concepts of childhood, that of children as social actors and as helpless victims. Although children were involved in designing, selecting, adapting and testing tools, they did not participate in designing the research agenda, identifying their survival strategies, analysing data or presenting results. The paper points out the difficulties of accessing urban working children and suggests photo appraisal as a useful tool.

Alice Lamptey (3.5) describes how children in Ghana produced their own film for national television to raise awareness of their rights and problems. The challenge now is to reach poorer, rural children, perhaps through radio broadcasts in local languages. Continuing the theme of film production by children and drawing on his experience of working with children in Brazil, Julian Faulkner (3.6) argues that participatory video is potentially transforming. Key questions concern who has control over the camera, microphone and finished product and how this affects whose reality is represented. The author suggests three pillars to participatory video: children's interest and perception of benefits; adults' willingness to allow participation and perception of whose reality counts; and enabling factors of time, money and skills. Joanna Hill

(3.7) describes a network of children's groups working with ActionAid in Nepal. The groups are involved in awareness-raising activities, evaluation and advocacy. The author argues for a need to work for adult rights alongside those of children and to involve children in mainstream development planning. ActionAid Nepal is disaggregating monitoring and evaluation indicators by age and gender to monitor their impact on children's lives. Rachel Baker and Rachel Hinton (3.8) write about the use of two types of matrices with refugee and street children in Nepal and Bhutan to explore illness patterns over the seasons and to show the impact of sickness and sources of treatment. The authors argue that the process of data collection and the comments made are at least as important as the data themselves. Participants in a PRA activity can have very diverse experiences and researchers should avoid making assumptions about values and biases. Presentation and cross-checking with the community is essential for validity.

Andy Inglis (3.9) argues that there are many advantages to using processes and tools that enable children to be equal participants with adults at all stages of the planning process. Facilitators should aim to have 100 per cent visualization of analysis and outcome by participants, with no note-taking by facilitators, because this leads to distortion and bias. An effective outreach strategy, which reaches all sections of the community, will enable people to work in small groups or as individuals in places where they can be secure, comfortable and relaxed. Ernesto Cloma (3.10), in the final chapter of Part 3, describes the work of the Children's Theatre Collective (CTC) of the Philippine Educational Theatre Association (PETA). The CTC specializes in children's theatre aimed at the development of children, working closely with other agencies in a range of educational, training, therapy and advocacy activities. The author describes an exciting and positive cyclical process of work with children using theatre pedagogy.

Part 4

David Stephens (4.1) argues in support of his assertion that the concept of culture should be centre stage in the discourse on education and development. Martin Woodhead (4.2) provides background to the research relating to a Rädda Barnen study of children's perspectives on their working lives. The study, which was conducted in Bangladesh, Ethiopia, the Philippines and Central America addresses central issues about the conditions of work, the work-school relationship, parental attitudes and children's self-concept. Woodhead outlines eloquently the main threads in the debate on child labour, highlighting the pervasive influence of Western conceptions of childhood and child raising throughout the world. He then asserts the rights of children to participate in the debate and describes the methodology in the study to enable participation.

Kate Harrison (4.3) outlines the findings of a small-scale study conducted in Uganda in 1997, which examined the implementation of the child-to-child approach by teachers and children in primary schools. The findings suggest that the approach is conceptualized differently by different actors. Christiana Obeng (4.4) focuses on the impact of culture on children's participation in Ghana. The subservient position occupied by children within society can destroy their initiative and creativity and hinder their participation in community development. Cultural values are, however, changing rapidly, and in this environment the child-to-child approach can enhance children's participation provided children can use their mother-tongue language and that culturally appropriate methods such as drama are used to address sensitive issues such as sexual health.

Barnabas Otaala's chapter (4.5) opens with a discussion about the child-to-child approach in Namibia which he links to those provisions of the UN Convention on the Rights of the Child which underscore children's rights of participation. Broader questions about the influence of child-rearing practices on child development are raised, and he then contends that the conceptualization of children's rights is relative to the context in question. The present need is for a research shift from that which investigates 'the needs and deficiencies of people' to that which explores successful programmes and initiatives.

The changing situation of children in Jordan is the focus of the chapter by Safa Halasah (4.6). Rapid urbanization has destabilized families and social institutions as they wrestle with the multifarious challenges it poses. Halasah outlines the results of a project of participatory research conducted by Questscope, a non-governmental organization. Participatory rural appraisal (PRA) methods and broad community participation have enabled researchers to identify children's needs and priorities. The role of children in social development must be strengthened and affirmed. Rachel Carnegie's working group report (4.7) recounts how participants were encouraged to recall and reflect upon proverbs from their own culture relating to children, the qualities which are valued in children, and the activities in which children are allowed or not allowed to participate.

Part 5
Priya Coomaraswamy (5.1) demonstrates clearly that in the crisis situation currently existing in Sri Lanka children can make a significant contribution through participation in research and programme development, though the security situation can slow down project development and create concern among children and adults about their continued involvement. Vesna Dejanovic (5.2) provides a lucid account of the way in which programme development can be reoriented toward child participation in the post-war situation of the former Yugoslavia. She focuses on two programmes: one to promote child fostering, and one concerned with the needs of disabled children. The need for cultural contextualization is highlighted, and child empowerment needs to be promoted in a non-threatening way.

Part 6
This part is divided into four sections:

Young people and institutions
The potentials of participation for children and young people are represented in papers and workshop examples from UK, Grenada, South Africa and the Philippines. They speak with a common voice of how children's interest in inclusion is tempered not only by the institutions around them, but also by their own self-image. They recognize that motivation to participate is com-

14

plex, a young person may be happiest doing her or his own thing, while also wanting to contribute to society and be valued. Amy Kaspar (6.1) describes a range of adult-defined frameworks through which youth have to climb before they can express their own interests and proposes that young people need to be involved in determining the contextual factors which will best promote their capacity for participation. Denise Allen (6.2), in her example from a project in which children conducted research for the national Tourist Board in Grenada, notes that participation can be superficial if care is not taken. She also illustrates, however, how children gain self-esteem, learn to work with one another and with adults and how they begin to produce valuable information for the Tourist Board.

Julia Gilkes (Box 6.1) reports from Palestine how understanding and pride has grown in parents through a programme of seminars and workshops, coupled with active child-to-child projects. In Uganda, Ben Osuga (Box 6.2) points out that the entire course of a child's life can be influenced by disputes between parents or discrimination between girl and boy children. Gill Gordon (Box 6.6) outlines experience in East Africa of a participatory community project dealing with sexual health, in which children and young people, among other community members, develop new means of communicating among themselves and with one another on a difficult and vital subject.

A report from Peace Child (6.3), an NGO run by children and adults in partnership, tells us how power-sharing, once developed according to a set of principles, can be straightforward and mutually reinforcing. It is candid about difficulties among the young people in sorting out the division of responsibilities and rewards, showing how they found a solution that allowed for co-direction by a whole team.

Schools
There has been considerable debate on the subject of children's role in schools, to which this section adds some significant insight. Amanda Saurin (6.6) in the UK, identifies the tremendous power that lies in the hands of school heads and teachers to promote or deny participation. She describes an environmental project that linked parents, teachers, local community members and authorities in creating a wildlife area, ascribing its failure to inadequate incorporation of child participation into the ethos of the school. Joanna Hill (Box 6.7) writes from Nepal with an example of children's educational options that have been increased with the introduction of extramural child literacy classes which are themselves able to involve children in the process of curriculum development and teaching in a way that is often more difficult for more formal institutions. From the United States, Mary Ellen Lewis (6.7) provides an example of the evolution of a children's environmental project in an inner-city area of New York over several years, while Lucy Harris (6.8) in the UK reports on an alternative approach to primary schooling that involves the full participation of each child.

Non-governmental Organizations
This section concentrates on the context of fostering a more favourable setting for children's participation in international and local non-governmental organizations.

15

The development of trust on both sides is described in examples from Jamaica, Tanzania and Ethiopia. In Jamaica, Denise Allen (6.9) reports on a nine-year-old project that started by offering choices to street children and got no contribution in return. Moving to a feedback stage, the project elicited children's opinions, then moved to shared decision-making and, in its most recent stage, to child-initiated decisions, resulting in increasingly responsible behaviour by the children in the project and in their homes. In Tanzania, Esther Obdam (6.10) tells us about a children's magazine written and edited by children and distributed all over the country. She describes how initial hesitancy is followed by increasing self-confidence and then quite often by boredom. New children then come in to take over the tasks and go through the whole process again. Finally, Abebaw Zelleke (6.11) from Ethiopia reports on the process of change in an outpost of the Save the Children programme. He describes the transition from relief to development among Somali refugee families and from NGO control to participation, emphasizing the role of child-specific indicators and child-led evaluation as ways of cementing their presence in organizational policy and practice.

Government and international agencies
The final section of Part 6 concentrates on the changing vision of children within the context of local and central government and looks at how the UN Convention on the Rights of the Child and associated conventions has made its mark on the processes of decision-making at national and local level. Mark Feeney (6.13) describes how a local council in the UK made use of the convention to underpin the principles of a process of public-service planning that incorporated children's views. Despite arguments that children should be left to be children, the local authority decided that children were already important social actors and should be included in decisions.

Amy Kaspar (Box 6.8) provides an insight into how emerging democracies can be crucibles of tremendous intellectual ferment where to review and critically assess democratic processes is a daily occupation that can challenge the indolence of the more established political systems of the West. Back in the UK, Barry Percy-Smith (6.14) reviews the children's participation scene and identifies barriers and issues from a number of sources, which provide a counterweight to Mark Feeney's (6.13) progressive example. He emphasizes the need to challenge existing forms of local decision-making and provide positive examples of successful experiences of involving children in local governance.

In tackling the great difficulties that pioneering researchers have faced in incorporating children into the agendas of tertiary education institutions, Rob Bowden (Box 6.9) points out that participatory research has grown phenomenally in recent times and this has led to changes in the modes of operation of the academic world. These changes may begin to extend to children, once the formidable barriers presented by academic rigour and compartmentalization have been surmounted. From Ladakh, in northern India, John Parry-Williams (6.15) describes how child-sensitive local government structures emerged and engaged with children's representative bodies by forming local children's committees of different age groups from both sexes and from in and out of school. In Rajasthan a children's parliament has helped children

16

review their education, develop skills and understand how democracy can be above gender, caste and creed.

Berry Mayall's chapter (6.16) on children as partners with adults outlines the usefulness of the 3Ps in the UN Convention on the Rights of the Child: protection, provision and participation, in order to discuss how we can enable children to work with adults.

The scene of a hushed auditorium in which young voices call for children's rights in six languages introduces David Woollcombe's (6.17) critique of international children's conventions and councils. Using children as token performers in events helps to explain why youth participation in bodies such as the UN has had mixed results. The paper ends with an example where children wanting to participate on their own terms with local government came up with a solution – a group entirely run by children, to which adults have some access but no control.

Rachel Marcus (6.18) gives us a detailed account of children's attendance and participation at the 1997 Oslo Child Labour Conference, while Sheena Crawford (6.19) gives a positive account of how international agencies, government and NGOs work together on issues of social exclusion of children in Yemen.

Part 7
Imani Tafari-Ama's chapter (7.1) examines the dilemmas of and potential for children and young people to be catalysts for change in a violent and deprived urban neighbourhood in Jamaica. Adam Haines (7.2) provides us with a clear case-study of a young people's environmental organization in Brighton, UK, funded by the local council. There is also a box on useful methods used in participatory work in urban regeneration and Agenda 21 in Brighton and Sutton. Andrew West (7.3) then explores some of the issues around participatory research, in the UK, with children and young people and looks at principles for further developing children-led research. The dilemmas of research with children are clearly delineated. Recent work in Bangladesh is also described which illustrates children's own concepts of social exclusion. This is compared to the children's concepts of social exclusion in the UK context.

Grace Mukasa and Vera van der Grift-Wanyoto (7.4) examine the dilemmas and strengths in giving children a voice, drawing on the experiences of working with communities in Uganda. Some of the problems that have ensued are described. Rob Bowden's chapter (7.5) focuses on the problems of gaining academic credibility for research with children. Using a proposed piece of research in Uganda as a case-study to demonstrate the legitimacy of child-generated data and analysis, he provides a comprehensive overview of some of the methodological problems of research and analysis with children. Donald Kaminsky (7.6) shares his experiences of approaches to peer education and youth advisory council experiences in Honduras, and gives us some insight in young people's views about the perceptions of participation and at what age participation can and should begin.

Part 8
Some conclusive strands from the book are discussed as a contribution to the continuing debate on the 'way forward'.

PART 2

Building Blocks and Ethical Dilemmas

Editor and co-author: VICTORIA JOHNSON

Co-authors: EMMANUELLE ABRIOUX, EILEEN ADAMS,
JONATHAN BLAGBROUGH, FARHANA FARUQUI,
ROGER HART, SARAH McNEILL, CLARE O'KANE,
MELINDA SWIFT

Summary

Part 2 explores some of the communication issues and ethical dilemmas that face us in addressing children's participation. It provides the building blocks that are needed when planning practical approaches and research with children and young people. Issues discussed include the following: understanding the political and social context within which one is working; children's varying capacities to participate; communication strategies; and key ethical issues, such as informed consent, confidentiality and the use of information. There are contributions from Afghanistan, South Africa, the UK, and a study that worked with child domestic workers in Bangladesh, Haiti, the Philippines, Indonesia and Senegal. The experiences offered range from working with girls on health promotion in Kabul to school classrooms in the UK; working with children in the slums of Johannesberg to establishing codes of practice in the international media networks.

Key issues raised in Part 2:

- One of the most important principles with regard to ethical issues is transparency in all interactions with children, young people and adults involved in any project.
- It is crucial that levels of confidentiality are transparent to all participants from the outset of the project. Strategies and legal positions to be considered in case sensitive issues are unexpectedly revealed, such as abuse or crime.
- Ethical matters, such as informed consent, need to be clarified and renegotiated at different stages in a time-line of a project or research process.
- In the early stages of planning, motivations for participation should be understood and unrealistic expectations avoided.
- Children should always have the option to have information withdrawn or modified.
- The way in which information is analysed and disseminated is an ethical issue. Even if information is collected in a participatory way, in translating its meaning misinterpretations can be made if children themselves are not involved in the analysis.
- Incorporating adults in the process is critical. Power relations will evolve only with time.
- Evolving power relationships and elements of risk to children must be fully considered throughout the project decision-making process and beyond.
- Children's participation requires adults who are willing to listen, relinquish certain elements of control and power, and allow children to develop their skills and capacities.
- Project staff and researchers must look at their own ideological baggage, including preconceptions about children's abilities and roles.
- Differences between children, such as age, gender, disability, ethnicity, religion, must be acknowledged and understood.

- Methods need to be planned and modified; matters such as informed consent, confidentiality and access will need to be addressed in varying ways to reach different children and young people.
- Universal concepts of childhood are misleading and deny the differences between children in different countries and communities, and those within the same community. Start from children's perceptions and develop with them appropriate processes and methods.
- Abrioux's spherical model can be used to assess the degrees of participation possible considering the starting point of people and the legal, political and social context (Emanuelle Abrioux, Chapter 2.1).

2.0 Introduction

VICTORIA JOHNSON

This part of the book aims to provide the building blocks underlying children's participation in a practical and theoretical context. It discusses practical factors that can influence children's capacities to participate, e.g. addressing adult attitudes, communication strategies and choice of methods in different contexts. It also seeks to address fundamental ethical questions and dilemmas that must be considered and acted upon throughout the lifetime of any project process and beyond. Questions of informed consent, confidentiality, access to children, the benefits to children of different processes and the implications of changing or threatening fundamental power relationships are discussed.

A review of relevant literature is first given. Virginia Morrow and Martin Richards provide a useful overview of ethical issues related to social science research with children. They reach three main conclusions: 1) children's competencies are different, with implications for the process of gaining consent and for the selection of methods and the interpretation of data; 2) children are vulnerable, and the day-to-day responsibilities of adults need to be fulfilled; and 3) adult researchers have the power to interpret data as they please. (Morrow and Richards, 1996). They discuss the tendency for adults not to respect children's views and opinions: the challenge they pose is 'to develop research strategies that are fair and respectful to the subjects of our research' (Morrow and Richards, 1996: 91).

In a summary of a workshop on children's participation in 1996 (Johnson, 1996) key ethical issues were raised that need to be further clarified and examined throughout the processes of research and participatory action, amongst them: informed consent; confidentiality; transparency of processes; access to children and appreciating issues of difference; piloting methods in different cultural and community contexts; and making sure research is fun and that children have the choice to opt out. Power relations and their changing nature are identified in both the above papers (Morrow and Richards, 1996; Johnson, 1996) Understanding evolving power relationships

Figure 2.1: *Opting Out*

is central to understanding the context of participation and the implications of increasing children's participation.

Judith Ennew (1994) offers suggestions on planning research and projects with street and working children. She raises issues regarding researching children as opposed to adults, for example how to approach informed consent, and addresses children's attitudes to 'being researched'. Young people are not a homogeneous group, and differences should be recognized in every aspect of programme planning. Ennew assists us in understanding the lives of street and working children and talks about the relevent ethical issues involved in improving their situations. As she points out, often the main barrier is the attitudes and preconceptions of the adult researchers.

Martin Woodhead, in his recent study on children and work for Radda Barnen, challenges the universal accounts of child development that are based largely on Euro-American contexts and values and tend to make statements about the 'nature, needs and best interest of children during successive stages of their lives'. Such sweeping statements are being 'rejected by researchers in favour of a more cultural, contextual and situated framework for child development' (Woodhead, 1997: 3). A principal message of Woodhead's work is the necessity to understand the context within which one is working. The participatory approaches referred to in different case

Figure 2.2: *Bright ideas*

studies seek to develop methods of working which suit children with different capacities to participate, determined not only by age but by a range of factors including gender, religion, ethnicity, wealth, and disability. It is essential not to have preconceptions about children's abilities and boundaries but to develop approaches with them in order to understand their views and opinions.

Participatory appraisal tools can be used to bridge culture and literacy gaps that often exist between professionals and members of the community, particularly young people (Garratt *et al.*, 1997). The Department of Public Health at the University of Hull has used participatory techniques to explore sensitive issues of domestic violence and adolescent sexual health (Garratt *et al.*, 1997; Sellers and Westerby, 1996). Lessons can be learned about the effectiveness of these techniques in communicating with adults and children. Ethical questions are raised in the context of this work, such as police checking of facilitators and trainers, confidentiality, and ensuring that young people can opt out. Sellers and Westerby point out, as does Judith Ennew, that on the street young people can just walk away! The situation in a classroom would be very different. The Barnados publication on 'Children, ethics and social research' (Alderson, 1995) was cited as useful in raising and thinking about some of the ethical issues in their work.

It is important to learn from other people's ideas and thinking on the ethical dilemmas that have arisen though the course of their work as then one can plan approaches accordingly from the early stages of a project. Part 2 cites a number of practical project-based examples which raise questions on just such dilemmas and provide a range of solutions or suggestions to some of the problems.

2.1 Degrees of participation: a spherical model – the possibilities for girls in Kabul, Afghanistan

EMMANUELLE ABRIOUX

As increasing attention is paid to the potential for the participation of children in research and in project activities, appropriate methods are sought which encourage their genuine collaboration. The variety of these methods and their respective applications are strongly determined by the particular context within which one is working. Socio-economic, political and cultural factors all play a role in determining the degree to which participation is possible and more specifically the degree of children's participation and clearer definition of methods which can be used. This is particularly pertinent in working with children in areas of conflict and in countries that have discriminatory laws. The girl child in Kabul City, Afghanistan faces many constraints as she lives in area which is constantly in conflict in a system which, due to her sex, denies her the opportunity to share or contribute to her own development. Among the concerns that arise from working with girls in Kabul are three main points that must be addressed if one of the aims of a programme is to increase their participation: (i) the ethical concern of whether the potential harmful consequences of girls' increased participation outweigh the benefits of their involvement in a project; (ii) the need to consider and create new types of participatory learning methods that are possible within the restrictive context of Kabul; and (iii) the need to develop an adapted model to gauge the extent of the girls' participation in this particular situation.

The consequences of increased girls' participation

During 1997, I had the opportunity to conduct health-focused participatory learning activities with girls attending the Ashiana Day Centre for street and working children in Afghanistan. In Kabul, girls are denied access to formal education, and after the age of twelve their participation in the public sphere is severely limited as they are not allowed to interact (in the widest sense of the word) with males. There are restrictions in terms of education, as well as participation in their own personal development and that of their society. Such severe restrictions have specific implications for programmes working with girls. A primary concern of any project must be for the safety of the girls. Merely to attend the activities that they are offered is potentially dangerous for them and for their families. The aim of integrating participatory learning into a health-promotion programme is to increase individual control over health and to allow people to effect changes in their own health and that of their environment. Inevitably this becomes a political issue in a country where questioning the factors which negatively impact on health can prove dangerous for those involved. The question is, therefore, can we and should we encourage the girls to make a choice to participate in programmes and how can we be sure that they are fully aware of the risks that this choice entails. In addressing this concern, the health-promotion activities have chosen to focus

25

on girls aged between ten and twelve. This does not, however, solve the larger issue of the security of the girls, nor provide a clear indication of when it may be necessary to suspend the health promotion activities.

Methods in restrictive contexts

Taking into account the context, it has been necessary to design new participatory health-promotion activities with the girls. As it is illegal to display any form of human or animal representation, many of the more common participatory learning activities cannot be used. The problem is further compounded as girls cannot learn how to read or write, making the use of written material inappropriate. One of the ways in which we have been able to circumvent this is to have girls bring objects to represent their ideas/thoughts on health as opposed to either writing or drawing them. There are occasions, however, when it proves impossible to avoid the use of pictures, and a decision must be taken either to transgress the law or limit the effective participation of the girls in the programme. It is important regularly to evaluate the possible risks of using participatory activities (the tools and methods used) with girls.

Effective participation is also limited at the centre due to staffing laws that prohibit the employment of women. An important consequence is a lack of role models for girls and the difficulty of having males conduct health-promotion activities. While the benefits of having some health-promotion activities with girls outweigh the negative aspects of having male facilitators, the degree of participation is definitely affected by this staffing issue.

Degrees of participation – a spherical model

The concept of degrees of participation is largely interpreted as a quantitative and qualitative measurement of children's participation. A commonly used tool for this is the ladder of participation (Hart, 1992), see Appendix 2 which describes various steps from 'non-participation' to 'child-initiated' programmes. In acknowledging the variety of contexts within which we work, I would argue that there are situations when this model is insufficient in representing the path of children's participation. In situations where individual rights are restricted, any activity or discussion encouraging children to express themselves is a considerable step towards their genuine participation. Basing the degree of participation on a ladder scale may result in certain activities seeming to have achieved a minimal level of child participation. I believe that within Kabul's formalized 'non-participatory' context, a model showing degrees of participation as a spherical process is more appropriate – each programme activity constitutes a different stage of participation. The decision of the girls to come down to the centre and attend an activity would, therefore, be a considerable way along a spherical process, taking into account the starting point (although not necessarily high if rated on a ladder scale).

While the girls attending the Ashiana Centre may not be able to change the wider issues which affect their health in the near future, l believe that each discussion and meeting is a step in the direction of improving their health and their lives. Health and participation are integrally linked and it is necessary to consider the potential of children's participation in any child-focused health programme.

2.2   The developing capacities of children to participate

ROGER HART

It is with some hesitation that I summarize the theories of developmental psychology as a guide to involving children of different ages in research and programming. The history of the application of theory from the field of psychology has not been a good one. For decades the emphasis has been upon universal accounts of the development of children as individuals and what they could not do at certain stages in their life rather than on the social contexts and supports that might further their development. Many contemporary developmental psychologists are now, however, critical of this history and are conducting research and developing theory that emphasizes the contexts of development and the processes by which children collaborate with and learn from others. I shall attempt to summarize some of this recent thinking.

Another potential problem in using theory from developmental psychology in an international context is that it has been constructed largely in North America and Europe. It should not, therefore, be borrowed wholesale by other cultures. Great mistakes have been made in the past in generalizing about children's intellectual development to other cultures, and the danger is even greater with social and moral development. Most writing on the application of developmental theories relates, furthermore, to the problems which these particular societies are facing with their children. For example, we in the West, have the problem of children's alienation from their families and communities but this does not seem to be the case in many other countries; also, while many children in developing countries face daunting hours of exploitative work many in the industrialized Northern states are denied the opportunity of ever experiencing meaningful work or participation in their communities. Many of these kinds of variations differentially affect girls and boys and so gender is another important consideration in the design of participatory programmes.

The story grows more complex as globalization brings many of the problems of the industrialized nations to the rapidly urbanizing countries of the South and a growing number of poor children of the North face poverty. Without the social safeguards of the past, these children have to work long hours after school. The conclusion, therefore, must be that we should not hope to establish universal developmental schemes for children from different cultures or even for children surrounded by very different social and economic circumstances within a culture. The children's rights movement is leading to an awareness of the importance of children having a voice as a way of both expressing their needs and protecting their rights. There is, then, great value for those who work with children in different cultures to reflect on the latter's development in order to be aware of the support that children of different ages and living in different circumstances need in order to participate.

The importance of play

While we may often think about children's participation in programmes with adults, it is worth noting how important play with peers, with minimal adult interference, is in the development of young children's social relations, empathy, sense of belonging and skills of self-control and co-operation. Play is an important training ground for participation. There is a role for adults here in creating safe places with a diverse physical environment and an uninterrupted time frame to enable children to develop these skills. One of the workshop participants (Ernesto Cloma) reminded us of the continued importance of play: getting adults as well as children into a playful frame of mind is critical for all participation projects at some time. At this point I think he informed us that we should all jump on our chairs because a mouse was running around the room!

The development of the capacity to think

A great deal of research has been carried out in constructing theory on the development of children's capacity to think. Until recently, Piaget[1] dominated theory on children's intellectual development but his writing, and even more importantly the way he was interpreted, tended to understate what children could do. The sequence of development he described from a state of egocentric thought where children think of things from their own perspective at the moment through a gradual process of co-ordinating their different perspectives remains relevant, but this theory seriously under-recognized the social character of cognitive development. While it has long been argued that empathy from adults is crucial to the social and emotional development of children, it is now realized that adults are also in various degrees attuned to signals from children regarding their cognitive development. They variously interpret their children's behaviour and stimulate more mature patterns of thinking through dialogue and joint action with them. Of great relevance to those of us working with children's participation is the recent research which reveals that children learn best in mixed age and ability groups. Peer relationships allow for greater flexibility than adult–child relationships because of the more horizontal nature of their power relationships to one another. By working together in groups with a wide age range children can adopt different roles with regard to one another, at one moment as a teacher and a few moments later as an attentive apprentice. There is also the realization that children have different kinds of strengths and modes of engaging with the world, or different 'intelligences' as some academics have called them. The implication here is that for the maximal involvement of all children, at all ages, a wide diversity of media should be used.

Social and emotional development

It has been known for a number of decades now that children with a positive sense of self, that is with feelings of self-esteem and a sense of control over their environment, can more easily manage stressful experience and can show initiative in new tasks and in forming relations with others. For children coming from a difficult family background, a single close reliable relationship with an external adult can make a great deal of difference to their capacity to work with others in groups and to form a more positive view of themselves and the world. It is therefore important to find adults to work with children who are sensitive to these developmental dimensions.

One can generally recognize two broad age ranges for which there are different benefits of participation. Pre-adolescent children (up until about 12 to 13 years of age) seem to need opportunities to be useful, to throw their energy into projects in order to develop and test their sense of competence. Broadly speaking, adolescents (beginning from about 12 to 13 years of age) need opportunities to experiment with different social roles as they struggle to form an identity through their engagements with their peers. While participatory projects with other children can be extremely important to children in both age ranges, the younger children seem to be more outward looking while the teenagers are more inward looking. These broad differences have important implications for the kind of engagements children might wish to have with each other and with the world, and implications also for the different roles of adults in relationship to them.

It is important to consider the ability of children to take the perspective of others, for it influences their ability to work in groups and to engage in dialogue where they balance their own views against the views of others. While three-year-olds may be able, in a limited way, to take the perspective of another, they find it extremely difficult to do so. Gradually, through the preschool years and into the beginning of primary school, children increasingly recognize that different people have differing perspectives. Developmental psychologists argue that it is usually not until sometime after they enter primary school that they are able to engage in reciprocal perspective taking, that is recognizing how others might simultaneously view their own thoughts and feelings. Later, sometime in the upper years of primary school, neutral perspective-taking develops in which a third-person perspective is possible; a child is now able to understand that people may have mixed feelings about something. They are able to form more cohesive group relationships because of common interests and beliefs, though this concept of a group may sometimes lead to an expectation of unanimity which suppresses difference of opinion.

With the continued development of their capacity to take the perspective of others, adolescents are able to reflect on what is good for society and develop a legal or moral perspective. This improved perspective can, however, also lead to heightened self-consciousness of how they are seen by their peers. How well facilitators working with adolescents can help them deal with this phase of development as 'young philosophers' can influence whether they become isolates or participants.

Adolescence is an important period for moral development. It was thought by developmental theorists that morality could be stimulated through abstract

29

discussion of values with children. It is now recognized, however, that opportunities to participate and the nature of children's participation with one another and with adults is more important than the abstract discussion of ideas (Damon, 1977; Kohlberg, 1984). From this perspective, democratic organizations for children and youth are extremely important for their moral development. This is especially so because schools all over the world tend to be autocratic expressions of the *status quo* and are hence much less likely to be able to offer the opportunities for participation that are called for.

The development of communication skills

It might be thought that at this time I would launch into an account of the limited language abilities of pre-school children and the gradual increase of their vocabulary. This is not the most important issue to consider. Certainly young children do have lesser verbal skills than adults and for this reason we should use as wide a range of possible media as we can in order to involve children of all ages, but more important than differences in language skills are all the subtle cultural rules about who one can talk to, when and about what. This is something that each of you in your own culture needs to reflect on and debate. All over the world, in settings where there is a lack of trust, children learn that it is safer to be quiet, especially about difficult emotional experiences or issues of shame or guilt. Rather than developmental capacity, then, we need to be aware of power relations within the culture and to use all our talents to try to put children in a position where they are comfortable and in modes of communication with which are familiar. For example, enabling children to re-enact disturbing issues in their lives by returning to the socio-dramatic play modes they knew with each other as children often offers great potential.

A strange aspect of discussions on children's participation is that they almost always seem to be about children's participation in something adults wish to foster in or for them. We need to be equally interested in observing and listening to children in order to discover how to help them achieve what they are themselves initiating. There has been too much emphasis on improving children's freedom to speak and not upon adult's abilities to listen.

Some implications for adult facilitators

This paper has argued that the development of children's sense of self, of independence, autonomy, responsibility, social perspective-taking skills, co-operation and personal sense of identity, do not develop spontaneously through social maturation but require adults who will allow them to develop these skills. These adults do not operate as teachers but as facilitators of development. They are caring, liberating persons who work hard to develop the skills of animating without directing, of being available and caring but not over-protective and, while encouraging children to think for themselves, are also willing to be true to their own values and standards.

During the pre-school years and early childhood adults are needed as facilitators of play. When they enter kindergarten and engage in more group projects, adults may be able to help children with the skills of rule-making that are so important in social relations. As children proceed through the primary school years, adults need to be good listeners and supporters, open to the spontaneous design of projects by children while also occasionally suggesting some themselves. As children enter adolescence adults need to be aware of the hyper-sensitive nature of social relations. They must be aware of the often inconsistent ways of behaving as young teenagers test out their alternative identities, including with the facilitators themselves! Standing on the side-lines there will be times when they are brought into partnership as a friend, at other times needed as a caring parent and at other times resented as a leader with responsibilities leading to limits and constraints.

Developing the ability to do these things well is a life-long task. All of us who work with children need times when we can discuss with one another our understanding of their developmental struggles. The better we can understand the processes by which children are trying themselves to develop, the more we shall be able to become useful partners in this development.

2.3   Child participation: ethical values and the impact of mass media

SARAH McNEILL

Much has been written and expounded on the subject of protecting children and on the protection of child rights but there is as yet little to be found on the subject of children's participation, yet it is participation that is central to current thinking on implementing the United Nations Convention on the Rights of the Child (UNCRC). In the convention, rights of provision and protection underpin the concept of participation. It is recognized, however, that these rights reside in the power and control of adults (parents, local authorities, governments) and therefore place the child in the centre as a passive beneficiary. The child's right to participate aims to enable the child to play an active role in the community s/he belongs to and also aims to make the community aware of children as active and participating members.

As research initiatives that involve children as participants multiply in urban and rural projects north and south of the equator, east and west of cultural dividing lines, the compilation of a valid body of knowledge on child participation to counterbalance the already weighty documentation on child protection becomes possible. New information drawn from participatory research projects involving children will make an important contribution to the adult's perception of the child as a valued member of society. Research documents validated by universities around the world and available through their libraries and on the internet can inform guidelines and codes of practice for professional organizations. Implementation requirements of the UNCRC are likely to cascade down to those groups involved in working with children. Print, television and radio media will need to be able to draw upon the latest and most up-to-date research practice. Until now such information, particularly with reference to ethical issues, has not been easy to find.

31

Figure 2.3: *Unlimited productions*

Global satellite television now reaches into homes and villages in the remotest parts of the world. Radio has an even greater outreach (an estimated 500 million radio receivers in developing countries compared with about 50 million television sets). It is important to consider what image of children is portrayed on the screen. It is also relevant to ask whether the voices of children are heard as part of the speech output on radio, or does this medium reflect an exclusively adult world? How much do the media have an effect on the status of the child?

A glance at news headlines during the year 1996–7 reveals stories of war, environmental disaster and landmines as well as reports of paedophilia, child prostitution, child labour, child soldiers and street children. It is the nature of 'news' to sensationalize and dehumanize. Viewers respond to this approach in a subconscious way: the more sensational the news, the bigger the audience. Isolate the pictures of children that appear on the screen and it soon becomes apparent that they are habitually represented as passive victims, as problems or as a threat to the community. Few television or radio reporters have the time to talk with children or to include their views in news reports.

How does this affect our perception of the child? Do we need to take account of the effect upon television audiences of seeing large numbers of children without families, homeless, in prostitution or murdered by clean-up squads in cities where their presence on the streets is a nuisance to the authorities? The larger aid organizations tell us that the numbers of children involved in these news stories is a tiny proportion of the total figures for improving child health and infant mortality world-wide. The good news is not on the screen. These are certainly factors that impact on the culture of social groups targeted by research projects.

Similar questions might also be raised about the way children are represented in television commercials. The happy, good-looking, eager-to-please personae that children are shoe-horned into by advertising agencies make for very successful marketing. This must interface with the aspirations and ambitions of parent-viewers. As television expands into new markets, its advertising values present another aspect of culture of which the researcher needs to be aware.

What is clear is that the involvement of children in participatory research projects is enabling small groups to have an active role, a shared responsibility and a voice in their communities. Even such widely scattered initiatives can start to reverse the negative trend of the mass-media portrayal of children.

At present there are few, if any, guidelines for the journalist. Articles 12 and 13 of the UNCRC state the child's right to hold an opinion and to have her/his views heard, together with the child's right of access to the media. The implications for broadcasters and print journalists are clear but their understanding of what is involved in enabling children to voice an opinion is as yet unsupported by training or preparation. Hence the letter that appeared in a recent issue of the ECPAT (End Child Prostitution, Pornography and Trafficking)[2] newsletter, from a reporter who was taken with a group of others to interview a teenage girl rescued recently from a Bombay brothel:

> Geeta had been repeatedly interviewed by the press, by foreign researchers, by individuals. She had walked four hours from her village to tell her story to us again. Did she willingly do so? Was she forced by the other committee members? Maybe she had a sincere hope in help from outsiders. Her reluctance and her tears during the interview pointed, however, to the fact that she did not appreciate repeatedly telling her story. My participation in this irresponsible, unethical, invasive fieldwork unnerved me and made me think seriously about ethical issues.

There are already in existence in Latin American countries, in Eastern Europe, in South Africa, Senegal and some other parts of Africa projects that enable children to own and control their own radio or television productions. Some of the radio projects have acquired airtime to broadcast their programmes on their national networks; some broadcast on small community stations; several make recorded shows just for the fun of it and to share with their local community. But these initiatives are not set up as part of any ongoing research. Their aim is to build capacity and to be sustainable. They are enlightened examples of a participatory approach that enables children's voices to be heard and gives them access to the media. In the long term this could produce journalists experienced in working with children and young people. In the short to mid-term, the problem of how to make important, relevant research available to today's journalists and broadcasters remains to be addressed.

The more participatory research involving children can define, refine and make available information on what is being achieved across such a wide spectrum of project work, the sooner results might filter through to the other professional groups involved in working with children. Ethical issues such as the implications of intervention, cultural values, informed consent, exposing children to risk, issues of ownership, power and control, and − central to all research documentation – credibility, all need to be analysed and explained. Project-evaluation indicators can then become common currency for those working with children. Academic endorsement will add weight to an area of research that has the potential to impact on professional codes of practice well beyond the framework of its initial remit.

2.4 Collecting information from child domestic workers: some ethical issues

JONATHAN BLAGBROUGH[3]

It is essential in any action-oriented research on the situation of child domestic workers to collect information from the children themselves in order to persuade others to take action, but there are also a number of ethical matters to consider before talking to the children concerned. Summarized below are some of these key issues faced by non-governmental organizations (NGOs) working with child domestics, along with the practical experiences of a number of them.

Child domestic workers are often extremely isolated inside their employer's households and talking to them there is likely to make them feel constrained and fearful of the consequences of upsetting their employers. In-depth interviews with children should, therefore, be conducted in a setting outside their place of work, preferably a place where the child feels safe and comfortable.

Even if the interviewer is experienced in interviewing children, it will be necessary to build up the child's confidence. Thus, interviewing children in depth is best done over a period of time in a relatively unstructured and informal way. The ideal setting is an existing project in which child domestic workers are participating; for example, a drop-in centre or an education programme. If no such project exists then any attempt to collect in-depth information from the child workers should be postponed until it does. Here is how some NGOs have done it:

In Bangladesh, Shoishab (an NGO) persuaded employers in certain vicinities of Dhaka – such as a large apartment block or a street network – to permit their young domestic workers to attend an educational class several times a week. During the course of learning to read and write, opportunities were used to encourage the child domestics to talk about their situations. Drawing and story-telling were used for self-expression. When confidence had been built up, in-depth interviews could be conducted.

In Haiti, the NGO Foyers Maurice Sixto has set up 'family centres' for restive children. The children may be sought out by enquiry among the local church congregation, or recommended by their parents. The centre provides a caring environment for the child domestics where they can rediscover their childhood, develop their talents and self-esteem. This setting is suited to in-depth research into the children's predicaments.

Who's that young girl in your household?

Woman: 'Who was that young girl I saw in your household the other day?'
Man: 'She's someone my wife has taken in. She comes from my wife's village – her family is very poor.'
W: 'I thought you were deeply opposed to child labour?'
M: 'Of course I am! She isn't child labour – we don't pay her to work! My wife took her in out of kindness.'
W: 'But I thought I saw her in the kitchen doing the washing up?'
M: 'Naturally she helps my wife about the house.'
W: 'And does she go to school?'
M: 'Well, no ... '

Figure 2.4: *Who's that young girl? (Source: Anti-Slavery International handbook. Illustration: Clive Offley)*

In the Philippines, Visayan Forum NGO in Manila made contact with young domestic workers in the park where they went on their day off. This led to the establishment of an Association of Household Workers. Visayan Forum conducted interviews to analyse the domestics' situation, and brings together those in the same ethno-linguistic group so that they can share their problems and give each other support.

Interviewing child domestic workers can often be highly stressful for the child. Some researchers have found that an interview can make a child depressed, or cause him or her subsequently to run away. Therefore, in-depth interviewing should be considered only if the researcher is prepared to provide help for the child concerned – either from an NGO with whom the researcher has links, or from another source – if it is sought.

In-depth techniques that elicit information from children without subjecting them to the rigours of questioning, such as drawing, painting, acting out and story-telling, are also revealing methods of eliciting information. They are especially useful in cultural settings where people are not used to being bombarded with questions.

Many NGOs use these kinds of techniques within non-formal education programmes. In Indonesia, drama and role-playing are used as a strategy for 'breaking the silence' when working with children and young people social-ized not to speak up in front of adults.

Another technique is the focus-group discussion. This is normally a semi-structured session with 6 to 12 participants picked for their special knowledge of the subject. These could be child and adult domestics, split into two sepa-rate groups, each with a facilitator trained in creating the kind of atmosphere which helps people speak with confidence. A set of questions can be explored in depth.

In Senegal, ENDA, a local NGO, conducted a research project with young women domestics by focus-group discussion or *entretiens participatifs*. Each group discussion was treated as a social event – a *thé debat* (tea debate). Around 50 participants attended, mainly girl domestics but with some of their 'aunties' (informal guardians) and some older women workers. The latter automatically saw it as their role to dominate proceedings and act as a con-trolling influence, which constrained the children involved. The facilitators divided up the groups, therefore, putting the youngest domestics together. In a position of peer solidarity they were able to bring out their intimate prob-lems, including sexual abuse by employers.

2.5   Children and decision-making: ethical considerations

CLAIRE O'KANE[4]

The 'Children and Decision-Making Study', carried out by Nigel Thomas and Claire O'Kane, University of Swansea and on which this paper draws, has been a 21-month project exploring the way children participate in de-cision-making when they are looked after by local authorities, focusing on children between 8 and 12 years of age. Stage one of the study focused on the most recent decision-making meeting, gathering information from social workers on 225 children in seven local authorities across Wales and England. The second stage involved interviewing 45 children and young people (aged 7–13 years), to listen to their views about the sorts of decisions that were important to them, as well as ascertaining their views and compre-hension of formal meetings, largely attended by adults. Most children took part in two interviews and two-thirds attended a Children's Activity Day. Social workers, carers and some of the birth parents were also interviewed. Throughout the study attempts were made to enable children to participate in meaningful and interesting ways. In particular, a focus on the development of participatory techniques and the process of reflection became central to our approach.

Adults' perception of children and ethical considerations
Our perception of children influences the way we talk to them, explain things to them, and choose to include or exclude them from decision-making, in

36

both their daily lives and research. In the past, children were largely invisible in social science investigations (Qvortrup and others, 1994; Alderson, 1995; Morrow and Richards, 1996; Butler and Williamson, 1994). An underlying belief in adults' abilities to explain on behalf of children prevailed (Fine and Sandstrom, 1988). The past decade has, however, witnessed a quiet revolution in the way children are viewed (Van Bueren, 1996), and there has been an increasing interest in listening to their experiences and viewpoints. In addressing ethical issues which arise when conducting research with children, the depth of our perceptions of children needs to be explored (see James, 1995).

'Ultimately the biggest ethical challenge for researchers working with children is the disparities in power and status between adults and children' (Morrow and Richards, 1996: 98). Relations between adults and children are regulated by power and interests. Adults' power over children 'means that merely in relation to adults' praxis ... children have no claim on equal treatment because they are not old enough' (Qvortrup and others, 1994: 4). Thus, within a context in which children's voices have been marginalized, questions concerning strategies to create a culture in which children's voices may be both facilitated and heard need serious consideration.

A culture of not listening to children

> *Interviewer:* Do you think adults listen to children the same as they do to adults, or differently?
>
> *Girl aged 10:* Most people – I am not saying all, but most people listen to adults differently, I think. I think they like to show off in a way, and just say 'oh well she is only a child – who cares. We can do what we like because we are bigger'.
>
> ('Children and Decision-Making Study', 1997)

Addressing the power imbalance: enabling children's genuine participation

The remainder of the paper outlines aspects of our approach which helped to redress the power balance between the child participants and adult researchers, enabling children to participate on their own terms. The sections are broken down as follows: preparation and guidance; participatory process; informed consent and access; choice of participation; confidentiality; communication strategies; and use of participatory techniques.

Preparations and guidance

A broad exploration of ethical issues and perceptions at the outset of the research project is fundamental to good practice:

- The researcher's perceptions of children and the implications for the research design were explored (see Box 2.1).
- Use of existing guidance helped identify potential ethical dilemmas (e.g. Alderson, 1995; Socio-Legal Studies Association, 1995; The British Psychological Association, 1995).

Box 2.1: James's (1995) Fourfold Typology

Through an exploration of social researchers' perceptions of children, the social anthropologist Allison James has provided a useful four-fold typology, illustrating how the way we see 'the child' informs our selection of methods and techniques, and our interpretation of the information collected. James identified four ways of seeing children which combines notions of social competence and status. These she identifies as the developing child, 'the tribal child', 'the adult child', and 'the social child'. The developing child is seen as incomplete, lacking in status, and relatively incompetent. In contrast, the tribal child is viewed as competent, part of an independent culture which can be studied in its own right, but not part of the same communicative group as the researcher. In this way both of these constructions imply that children are unable to have the same status as adults. The adult child and the social child do, however, have the capacity, but whereas the former is seen as socially competent in ways comparable to an adult, the latter is seen as having different, rather than inferior, social competencies. The social child sees children as social actors who often choose to communicate in more varied and creative ways.

- Ethical choices need to be situational and responsive, thus, research support in the form of supervision and consultation with an advisory group, practitioners and young people with experience of the care system were utilized.
- Lessons from literature regarding good practice in participation (e.g. Thoburn, Lewis and Shemmings, 1995; Treseder, 1997) and lessons from consultations with two groups of young people with experience of the care system further enhanced our research design.

Participatory Process
Approaching the whole study in a participatory manner is recommended. Furthermore, facilitation skills and sensitive questioning are central to the successful use of participatory techniques.

- By consulting groups of young people with experience of the care system at the outset of the study, we were able to construct the research framework from their definitions of reality.
- Ongoing reflection upon the research process and relationships allowed us to learn from the participants and become more responsive to their needs and agendas.
- We sought active collaboration with adult gatekeepers in order to facilitate contact with children and adults' encouragement of children's participation in the study. A range of opportunities for consultation, information-giving and feedback to social workers, foster-carers, parents and young people (via leaflets, telephone communications and meetings) were used.
- All participants were thanked, at meetings and by letter, for their participation and were kept informed about the progress and outcomes of the study.

Access and informed consent

In challenging prejudices about children, efforts need to be made to reach and involve youngsters in different situations with differing abilities. Against a tradition which maintains power in the hands of the adults, projects can seek the direct consent of children, whilst also acknowledging the need to respond to any concern from adult caretakers.

● All the research authorities were sent a copy of our police clearance forms prior to any contact with children.

Figure 2.5: *Meetings*

- Every child in the wider sample was given an information pack by their social worker enabling them to decide whether they wanted to participate in the study.
- The information packs, and consecutive letters, were addressed direct to the child. They included: a children's information leaflet (and/or tape), two activity sheets, a self-addressed envelope, and both a carer's and a parent's information leaflet.
- The leaflets were designed to be child-friendly and informative.
- The study required children's active consent to take part whilst also responding to any concerns of the adult caretakers.
- Efforts to explain important aspects of the study were maximized in all communications, via telephone, letters and at the outset of meetings.

Choice of participation
Children's choice of participation was central to the study:

- They could choose to: not take part; send back the activity sheets back (with/without meeting us); take part in one or two meetings.
- It was made clear that they could opt out at any stage.
- Many children were given the choice of attending a children's activity day to share their views and ideas with their peers.
- They were given choices about how the research meetings were conducted.
- Having given their permission to record meetings, the children were placed in control of the tape player, so that they could halt the recording when they wanted to.

Confidentiality
Matters concerning privacy and confidentiality are significant when attempting to break down the power imbalance between children and adults. Factors such as when and where interviews take place, who is present and who will be told are all likely to have an effect on what the child will talk about. Researchers need, furthermore, to think carefully about their strategy of response to any disclosure by children of abusive or dangerous situations. In some contexts, laws, policies or procedures may oblige adults to pass on information concerning any disclosures of abuse (see Box 2.2).

- Children were involved in planning when, where and at what time interviews would take place.
- They were given the choice of speaking to the researcher on their own or with someone else present.
- They were assured of confidentiality.
- Where a child disclosed abuse the researchers would not break the limits of confidentiality. They would talk to the child to inform her/him of the available options and to support the child (in her/his own time) to confide in another trusted person who would be in a better position to offer ongoing support. Only in extreme situations where such a strategy seemed ineffective would the researchers pass on information without the child's consent.

Communication strategies
A central focus of the meetings was on engaging with the child or young person to build a relationship where respect, openness and a genuine intent to listen by the researcher was evident, thus creating an atmosphere which placed value on children's communication.

- Creative forms of communication were used to engage children in more meaningful and interesting ways.
- The development and use of a range of participatory activities drew upon lessons regarding effective communication with children: they allowed children and young people to shape the agenda; drew upon real-life concrete events; and involved handling things rather than just talking.
- With an awareness of time constraints and the importance of a trusted relationship in facilitating communication, attention was given to getting to know children through the arrangements of meetings, as well as giving them greater control over the research meetings.
- Personal style and humour were also significant in enhancing equal and relaxed discussions.
- Varied opportunities for communication enhanced the building of relationships as children took part in individual meetings and activity days.

Use of participatory techniques
The development and use of a range of participatory techniques including the setting up of children's own decision-making charts, a pots and beans activity, diamond ranking, time-lines, drawings, and others, enabled children to discuss decision-making matters that were most relevant to their lives.

The use of participatory techniques greatly assisted in breaking down the barriers between children and adults as they:

- gave the children greater control over the agenda
- created a situation in which there were no right or wrong answers
- gave children more time and space to talk about issues that affected them
- made the meetings more interesting and fun
- didn't rely on literacy or writing skills
- enabled children to interpret and explain their own data.

With a belief in children's creative abilities to voice their own concerns, efforts can be made to break down the barriers between adults and children, giving children and young people space to speak and be heard.

2.6 The challenge of keeping participatory processes on track towards the achievement of practical goals

MELINDA SWIFT

Growing Up In Cities[5]

Growing Up In Cities (GUIC) is a research project initiated within the Children and Environment Programme of the Norwegian Centre for Child Research, Trondheim, Norway in 1994 which aims to extend a classic 1970s UNESCO project of the same name.

The goal of GUIC now, as in the 1970s, is to document some of the human costs and benefits of economic development by:

* showing how the use and perception of the urban neighbourhoods of young adolescents from working-class backgrounds affects their lives and personal development; and
* using young people's own perceptions and priorities as the basis for participatory programmes for urban improvement (Lynch, 1977).

The original sites in the 1970s have been replicated in Melbourne, Australia and Warsaw, Poland and will soon be replicated in Salta, Argentina. New sites have been established in Beunos Aires, Argentina; Johannesburg, South Africa; Bangalore, India; Northampton, England; Oakland, California, USA; and Trondheim, Norway (Chawla, 1997).

Growing Up In Cities, Johannesburg, South Africa
The first site in Johannesburg is Canaansland, also known as Kanana, a squatter shack settlement on the edge of the city centre with a high degree of unemployment. The project's primary goal has been to create space for the children to voice their thoughts, issues, needs and solutions and to ensure that city authorities act on these requests.

While the GUIC project planned to replicate the Lynch study, many of the attitudes and methods in the 1970s' study as well as amongst current researchers in all country teams could be viewed as participatory. The GUIC Johannesburg group decided to reconsider the overall approach of the project and its methods, and to embrace a more extensive participatory approach.

Approach
The Johannesburg approach to participatory methodologies is both systematic and flexible. In rejecting purely extractive research, a lot of emphasis is placed on not only the methods but the approach and attitude of researchers and the outcome of the research which will result in action. The overall approach to the GUIC project is outlined in Figure 2.6.

A first step was to identify a multi-dimensional team of people with varied experience, ranging from anthropology, architecture, geography and communications to diverse work experiences with and without children. The team underwent training in the approaches and attitudes underlying participatory rural appraisal (PRA) as well as in some participatory research methods.

The GUIC research had two defined aspects: (i) objective space information resulting in a scale lay-out plan of the squatter settlement and interior drawings of some of the shacks; (ii) field research with the children and adults in Canaansland. In the spirit of participatory research, all team members played a role in planning, reviewing and identifying clear roles for themselves within the research process.

In embracing participation as a fundamental base for the GUIC project work, the team accepted a framework of principles and attitudes widely accepted in PRA approaches (Singh, 1993) as outlined in Figure 2.6.

Different methods (listed in Figure 2.6) were used in order to maximize participation by the children and to allow for the cross-checking of information through the triangulation of the findings. Attention was also paid to separate information gathering for girls and boys.

The approach to sampling entailed inviting all children in Canaansland in the age group 10–15 to participate in the project. This invitation was extended at a community meeting held with the adults of Canaansland where express permission was obtained to work with the community's children on Saturday mornings. Due to high enjoyment levels, our main problem was dealing with high numbers of especially younger children who presented themselves for what they perceived as 'Saturday school', even when personalized invitations were delivered to the homes of specific children who were a part of the research project. A few children's decisions not to attend were respected.

Our emphasis was on group work and activity-based exercises, combined with open-ended interviews (in non-threatening situations) to cover issues that fell through the gaps or which required one-on-one discussion. The interviews were limited to critical questions, those of personal identification and to short periods of time.

Meetings and workshops were held with the adults and parents of Canaansland in order to keep them fully informed of the progress of the project, reaffirm their permission to work with their children and to discover their views of their children's needs. Numerous meetings were also held, with assistance from UNICEF South Africa, with city officials and the mayor's office.

In order to fulfil the social-change and words-into-action aspect of participatory research, a planned output of the project was the organization of a workshop hosted by the mayor of Greater Johannesburg, Isaac Mogase, 'Mayor of Peace' and 'Defender of Children'. The primary objective of the workshop was to facilitate the sharing of information between city leaders, planners, professionals and the adults and children of Canaansland. At the workshop, adults listened to the issues identified by the children and presented by their elected representatives. Plans of action to address immediate concerns raised by the children as well as to influence policy for children's participation in the city were drawn up and accepted by all as resolutions from the workshop.

Ensuring the implementation of these plans of action has presented a great challenge in a city with limited budgets and acute needs for across-the-board poverty alleviation and service delivery.

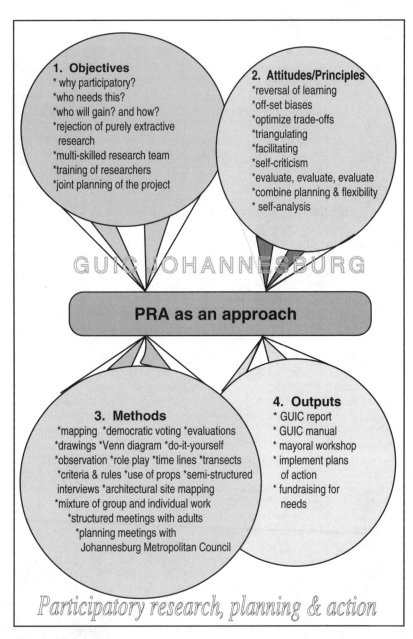

1. Objectives
* why participatory?
*who needs this?
*who will gain? and how?
*rejection of purely extractive
  research
*multi-skilled research team
*training of researchers
*joint planning of the project

2. Attitudes/Principles
*reversal of learning
*off-set biases
*optimize trade-offs
*triangulating
*facilitating
*self-criticism
*evaluate, evaluate, evaluate
*combine planning & flexibility
* self-analysis

GUIC JOHANNESBURG

PRA as an approach

3. Methods
*mapping *democratic voting *evaluations
*drawings *Venn diagram *do-it-yourself
*observation *role play *time lines *transects
*criteria & rules *use of props *semi-structured
interviews *architectural site mapping
*mixture of group and individual work
*structured meetings with adults
*planning meetings with
Johannesburg Metropolitan Council

4. Outputs
* GUIC report
* GUIC manual
* mayoral workshop
* implement plans
  of action
* fundraising for
  needs

Participatory research, planning & action

Figure 2.6: *Growing up in cities*

Challenges

A participatory approach presents many challenges, one of the most difficult being consciously to integrate well-planned processes and flexibility, something that can be achieved only through well-trained researchers committed to children's rights and able to embrace their errors. The tension between embracing a fully-fledged participatory research approach versus the undertakings made by all GUIC national teams to stick to agreed methods (having a large emphasis on the questionnaire tool) was an additional challenge. Participatory processes are also more difficult and require hard work throughout every aspect of the project.

The problem of multiple languages spoken by the children was overcome by the use of multilingual research assistants. The non-existence of local organizations in Canaansland and the desperate situation of the community as a whole remain challenges for the project.

We have attempted to create the space for children's voices to be heard. In this process our behaviour and assumptions as researchers and activists continue to be challenged. Our work in enabling the children to make a significant impact on the city has only begun.

Ethics and approaches: some questions raised by the research

The GUIC Johannesburg raises many issues. Participatory approaches and methodologies remain a relatively new concept for South Africans and parameters for interventions such as the GUIC project require ongoing debate. Issues worth exploring are:

- The GUIC Johannesburg team has found that direct beneficial impact of such a project on the lives of participating children is fraught with difficulty but remains a prime objective of our work. *Is it enough to have engaged with children in a participatory manner or is direct beneficial impact on the lives of children involved in research processes imperative?*
- The immense goodwill felt towards children often does not translate into a more fundamental recognition of their rights to participate in decision-making. We should not allow this to limit our attempts to encourage participatory processes but rather see each process as a step towards children's greater decision-making. *Does the diversity of adults' initial motivations for participating with children matter if at least it ensures their participation? What are the implications of these different motivations?*
- The GUIC Johannesburg team's experience has been that children have never been asked their opinions. As a result, they find it extraordinary that they should now be asked their views. The day-to-day difficulties they face dominate their thoughts. Consequently notions of establishing a process, seeking not only to empower children but also to promote opportunities for other children to participate in city decision-making, are unrealistic in the short to medium term. The team concluded, therefore, that any further involvement of children in the research process would have been overwhelming for them. These findings highlight the following questions: *When working with children do the fundamental participatory principles about joint process design, self-analysis of data and joint strategizing still need to be strictly applied? Are there conditions that make children's participation unachievable, or is this a view that results from preconceptions and biases about their abilities?*

2.7   Dealing with change: issues arising from young people's involvement in educational research and curriculum development

EILEEN ADAMS

This paper focuses on some ethical issues that have emerged in my research and curriculum development work involving children and young people, teachers and other professionals, based on experience of three projects: *Front Door* (Harahan, 1976), *Art and the Built Environment* (Adams and Ward, 1982) and *Learning through Landscapes* (Adams, 1990a), involving pupils in schools in the UK aged from 5 to 18, teachers and other professionals such as artists, architects, landscape architects and planners. All projects were a form of action research to bring about change in the school curriculum and in the school environment (Adams, 1990b).

Action research

Action research requires practitioners to engage in developing a fuller understanding of their work through systematic enquiry, careful evaluation and the testing out of possibilities as a basis for action and possible change (Bassey, 1983, 1991; Bell, 1994). Kemmis identifies four reasons for developing action research in schools:

- a strong interest among educational researchers in helping practitioners deal with problems of practice;
- a broad methodological interest in interpretative methods;
- a growth of collaborative work in curriculum development and evaluation; and
- an explicit ideological commitment to addressing social and political problems of education through participatory research carried out by practitioners (Kemmis, 1990).

Our involvement in action research started in 1974, nearly 20 years before Kemmis wrote that, before any of us involved had heard of the term 'action research'. On reflection, it was informed by the following principles:

- seeking improvement by intervention;
- involving the researcher as the main focus of the research;
- being participatory and involving others as researchers rather than informants;
- a rigorous form of enquiry that leads to the generation of theory from practice;
- requiring continuous validation by educated witnesses from the context it serves; and
- a public form of enquiry (Lomax, 1994).

Central to the notion of action research is the idea of change. The researcher not only seeks to understand existing situations or practices but actively to change them. The practitioner/researcher does not merely record the impact of change but is an agent of change,

> the researcher plans an active role in becoming a change agent by informing, encouraging and supporting the community group and studying and interpreting their actions in the light of his own interventions. (Uzzell, 1979)

Roles and relationships

Teachers, design professionals and young people were seen as partners in the research and development process. The teachers were experts on pedagogy, the designers had a professional expertise in relation to design and the environment, and the pupils had an expert knowledge of their local area. They were each dependent upon the other. The partnership was not equal. Power and control changed from time to time. Teachers were involved in generating different ways of thinking, devising experiments, trialling and testing ideas and introducing different ways of working. They embarked on systematic

Figure 2.7: *Pupil's skills develop to participate*

47

enquiry of their practice, and opportunities were created to discuss the work in progress. The development of the work required them to modify attitudes, teaching practices and working relationships. Artists and designers lent support, helping teachers reflect on, evaluate and change their practice; they also helped formulate the research questions and plan the research programme. They suggested techniques for observing and documenting evidence and contributed to its analysis and evaluation. Pupils were able to generate ideas for study, articulate their environmental perceptions, contribute to the development and testing of study methods and teaching strategies, and contribute to the evaluation of learning experience and teaching programmes. They did not control the research process but were active partners in influencing the research (Elliott, 1991; Dadds, 1993).

Issues

Many of the issues arose because the context for research was educational practice and because the researchers were acting as educators.

Action research: illuminative, qualitative research

The research methods were those familiar in action research. Those issues that apply to qualitative, illuminative research also apply here. The fact that some of the participants were children did not make a significant difference. There was a clear and supportive framework for the research activity but participants were encouraged to follow their own lines of enquiry. Young people's inputs were welcomed, though these usually focused on the content rather than the conduct of the research. An issue here was how far the pupils were active in the research as instigators, taking control of the process, and how much control they had in determining how their work was used.

Respect for children's experience, values and opinions

Participants, both adults and children, treated each other in the same ways as adults would in research activity. The work was based on children's experience of the environment. The intention was to extend their experience and deepen their understanding. Children's perceptions and opinions were actively sought and their views taken seriously. An issue here was that the work was concerned with ideas rather than action, though some of the projects did result in environmental change. It was made clear to the children that this was all to happen in an educational context and that the results might remain at the level of ideas rather than change on the ground. It was important not to raise their expectations that their views would have any impact on the environment. The researchers were prepared to engage in an exploration of ideas, although with younger children, it is not always clear what is for real and what is simply an exercise. However, pupils were accustomed to art and design projects in school where the outcomes were expressions of their thinking, which might not be acted upon.

Choice, compulsion, permission

Pupils did not have any choice as to whether or not they wanted to be involved in the research, which was viewed as part of their normal educational experience. Many of them were aware, however, that this was the case. Where necessary, parental permission was sought for children to participate in street-work activities and visits outside school. The issue here is permission. Pupils' permission was not normally sought for their ideas or work to be used in the development or the dissemination of the research results. Many of them knew they were involved in a curriculum development project and welcomed the opportunity to participate. For many, it increased motivation and excitement and they were pleased that the results of their efforts would be shared with others. For some, it improved the quality of their work to know that it would come under public scrutiny.

Experiment, testing, risk-taking/'at-risk', trialling
Although young people were put in experimental situations in the sense that teachers were testing ideas and methods, they were not put at risk. Educators have a duty of protection. There was the expectation that both the young people and the teachers would learn from the experience. In an educational context, it is a duty of the educator to ensure that pupils meet with some measure of success and are able to learn something from the experience. This is different from the scientist's view of testing to destruction. Where an approach or a study had not worked out very well, teachers might have discussed it with other teachers in terms of success or failure. However, analysing and evaluating experience of failure was also seen as a positive contribution to the research. Pupils' efforts were more likely to be considered in terms of learning outcomes, satisfactions, achievements and difficulties experienced. Young people were not made to feel that they had failed.

Partnerships, tensions, roles and relationships
Although adult roles were meant to be complementary, there were inevitable tensions (Adams 1990b). It was not always easy for some pupils to work with inexperienced and unfamiliar adults. Some artists and designers found it difficult to collaborate with children and young people and tended to take a patronizing or over-directive stance, or else had unrealistic expectations of pupils' knowledge and abilities. It happened from time to time that some children would play off one adult against another in order to gain more control. It was sometimes very difficult for young people to take the initiative and to generate ideas and working methods themselves with little adult direction. They expected the adults to tell them what to do, to direct them, to give them the answers. They wanted an answer or a solution. They were sometimes disturbed when the expected role of the teacher appeared to have changed. When the teacher emphasized more the role of researcher than educator, the pupils sometimes saw this as a withdrawal of support.

Communication
It was not always easy for adults other than teachers to communicate with young people in schools; at other times, children welcomed an unfamiliar person in the school situation and found it easier to communicate with a non-teacher. Often teachers acted as interpreters. This might have meant that teachers' perceptions were particularly influential.

Identification, acknowledgement, ownership, appropriation
Although pupils labelled their work in publications, results were not usually identified by name but by age and, perhaps, school. Where there was evidence of success, there was an attempt to identify schools but not when there was something negative to report. In some instances, where artists or designers have worked with pupils to develop art works or designs, the issue of ownership has arisen. Sometimes there have been problems of adults appropriating young people's ideas or work or else presenting as children's work something that is the result of a collaboration between adults and children.

Interpretation and evaluation; subjectivity, objectivity
As part of the intention was to develop critical thinking, children and young people were involved in critiquing their own work and that of others; likewise, they were encouraged to take a critical stance towards the ideas, study methods and working relationships that formed the focus of the research. Their feedback and evaluations of courses and projects were an important part of the research material. Criteria for judgement were negotiated between them and the adults, with the intention of sharing subjective perceptions and opinions of the environment and of learning and teaching experiences. Everyone was expected to try and explain or justify her/his views.

Documentation and dissemination
As part of the work in school, children would be asked to respond to an analysis, interpretation or critique of their work. At times, they were interpreters and offered explanations to their peers, to teachers and to other adults. Sometimes, this had a greater impact than adults' explanations, as young people's views were perceived as being more authentic.

Power and control
The research and development was not so much *about* as *with* children. It is not possible to divorce a study of learning in schools from a study of teaching. The intention was to encourage the stance of the reflective practitioner in both teachers and taught. All those involved were not so much the subject of research as collaborative partners in the investigative process. All levels of Hart's 'Ladder of Participation' were represented (Hart, 1997).

Summary

It is likely that the issues identified above may emerge in other action-research projects. They referred to the nature of collaborative partnerships, the necessity to have respect and regard for colleagues, both adults and children, and to understand the contribution that each could make. They acknowledged the practical constraints and limitations inevitable in a large-scale, loosely-controlled and long-term study. They recognized difficulties in communication, ownership of intellectual property and working relationships between individuals and groups. It must be acknowledged that in this study power and control over the conduct of the research were primarily in the hands of the adults. The children and young people were, however, able to exert influence on the content of the research by means of their ideas, attitudes and behaviour. Collaboration enabled everyone to change the ways in which they perceived the environment, leading to modification of the learning and teaching process in schools. Their example set in train a development programme aimed at improving the environmental quality in schools and extending educational opportunity.

Box 2.3 Building blocks and issues to carry forward

Since the mid-1980s, the development sector has increasingly seen children brought into the development discourse, into policy and practice. It is argued that children, together with poor and powerless adults, must be accepted as active social agents and responsible members of civil society. As a social entity in their own right, children form a distinctive category in the development process, representing characteristics, perceptions, capacities, concerns, needs and interests which are different in both definition and ranking from those of adults.

Despite the reality that children may form one social category, our experience at the grassroots provides evidence that this category is far from homogeneous. As in the case of adults, children, too, have competing and conflicting interests and divisions along the lines of gender, age, class, ethnicity, health and other social realities. It is, therefore, critical that development practitioners recognize and accept the different childhoods represented by different groups of children. Failure to do so has serious implications for the kinds of strategies and programmes that are developed to ensure children's well-being and to protect their rights.

Important issues arising from my experience include:

- attitudes of some groups of children towards others;
- attitudes and behaviour of adults, including our own, towards children;
- selection and application of participatory methods and tools (lack of process, sequencing, etc.) and how this affects children's well-being;
- cultural contexts and biases (recognizing issues of access, varying childhoods, etc.);
- the exploitative nature of adult–child relationships inherent in most cultures;
- lack of organizational commitment, support and prioritization, and how this affects children; and
- the lack of strategies to institutionalize children's participation and what this means for the processes used.

Farhana Faruqui

2.8   Ethics and approaches

WORKING GROUP REPORT

The main objectives of the workshop were:

- to facilitate the sharing of participants' experiences of ethical issues that arise when working with children; and
- to share ideas on approaches for good practice in order to address these issues.

The main areas of concern discussed were:

Preparation and guidance

There is often no framework within institutions for involving children in all stages of a project, even in those organizations that claim to be child focused. Training in children's rights and participatory approaches, developing communication skills, research support and supervision, and regular consultation with an advisory group of young people can be helpful. It is critical, however, to be clear about ethical issues such as consent and confidentiality from the outset of a project, and to review these issues regularly in the light of new developments and the learning processes of researchers, field staff and young people involved.

Values inform the research, but whose values? Project participants should be clear that they need to understand and address their own attitudes and preconceptions about childhood, adulthood and the transition between the two. The cultural and political context in which one is working also needs to be considered in order to plan a project which starts from where people are and builds a participatory process with them, without allowing local moralities which may be damaging to children to dominate.

Expectations

Expectations are often raised when embarking on research and project planning and implementation. The level of resources that an organization will make available for follow-up should be reviewed and clarified to those involved in the project when starting a participatory process. Changes in plans and funds can be made clear as the project progresses. Communities should be empowered to challenge supply and to express their own demands.

Recognizing and respecting differences

Children are not a homogeneous mass. Issues of difference affect their lives and their participation, for example age, gender, disability, wealth and ethnicity. Projects will target different children, but unless the visibility of marginal children is raised, it will always be the more articulate and affluent who chose to participate and are heard.

Some organizations seem only to involve youth to discuss children's issues, but different age groups will have different agendas and if work is being done about younger children then they too should be involved. There will be different ethical considerations for particular groups, for example for girls and boys. Disability often seems to be invisible in much work on participation and the same is the case for children's participation.

Not all children get on well. There are power relationships and jealousies amongst them, just as there are amongst adults.

Informed consent

The issue of informed consent has been raised in the following examples:

Woollcombe and Olivier — Information about the play is given to children, and they are given the choice of going to the audition. They can choose not to attend. In another example, producing a book 'Rescue Mission Planet Earth', consent for a group of children was obtained through the teacher. Furthermore, the teacher signed a disclaimer on behalf of the children that passed all the information made by the children to the Peace Child. If explanations are good this could be OK. But the position and power of the teacher can be negative. The children and adolescents were sent a copy of the book.

Faruqui — It is extremely important not to undermine adults' authority. Therefore, a lot of negotiation with adult caretakers is needed. Initially, the adults wanted to be present, but they usually gave more access to children. There is a need to feedback issues around confidentiality. There is some fear from children about adults finding out what they have said, so their identities need protection.

O'Kane — A children and decision-making study with children who are in care in Wales and England. In consultation with such a group of young people information packs were produced (in tape and leaflet form) which were sent to every child via their social workers. The packs were addressed directly to the child but included information leaflets for the parent or foster carer. It was the child's choice to take part and s/he could opt out at any stage.

Obdam — Access to children is via schools with which the Kuleana Centre for Children's Rights is already in contact. Teachers are asked to inform children about the children's magazine, *Mambo Leo*, and whether they want to be involved (they usually say yes). If so, they are given information and a letter to gain consent from their parent. The influence of the teachers may be a problem, as they select particular children.

— A child-centred community-based organization, with open and free membership. Children take home a form and ask their parents for consent. Follow up with children.

When seeking consent:

- fully inform children and adults of the objectives, process, expected outcomes and how the information may be used;
- gain support from adult gate-keepers;
- try to gain full consent from children;
- ask children to repeat what you have told them;

- renegotiate consent as the process continues and where necessary;
- demonstrate that participation will be worthwhile and fun;
- build trust in order to gain consent;
- give different children opportunities to take part; find ways of reaching children outside schools and children with differing abilities;
- children may say yes to please adults; give them more space to opt out.

Also consider the following questions:

- to whom do you give information and in what form?
- are children free to consent?
- do children understand what they are consenting to?
- in schools, consent is filtered through teachers; and head teachers; is it then the children's choice?
- is it easier to gain access to children who are already part of an organization?
- how can more excluded and marginal children be accessed?

Confidentiality

One end of a 'confidentiality line' represents 'no confidentiality', the other 'total confidentiality' – projects may be placed at either end of the spectrum or at any point in between. For example, there may be total confidentiality in a research project talking to children in care compared to one which aims to give children the space to stand on stage, perform and speak up about their issues.

It is legitimate for work in different contexts with different aims to be at different points on the line. The issue here is to be clear and transparent about confidentiality from the outset. When deciding on confidentiality, consider the consequences for different participants of their views and concerns being heard. It is imperative to be clear about the strategy to be pursued when there are disclosures of abuse or crime.

Communication

'Recognize the full spectrum of ways in which children can participate and communicate – how about just asking them?'

Participants were asked to write on cards approaches that had assisted their communication, and on the other side approaches that did not help (see Table 2.1).

How information is used

A key issue is the ownership of the information derived from a participatory process. Who has interpreted the information and how this has affected the action which may follow?

Children should have the right to review and block or withhold any data they wish at any stage of the process, and to have some input on editing and

Table 2.1:   Approaches in communication

Approaches that helped communication	Approaches that did not help communication
• good explanations • clear framework • being friendly • really listening • flexible and varied communication • choice of venue and time to speak • choice of time when children can come • build relationships through arranging • place child in control of tape player • choice in participation • participatory activities and methods • partnership – treat as equals • give children ownership • peer explanations • games, songs, icebreakers • theatre, music, dance, puppets • radio and video can be used in imaginative ways • talk about self • meet as a group • use child's first language • make information culturally appropriate • make information appropriate to age and situation • make it fun • talk about general topics before personal ones • be aware of child's perception of who s/he is • be more relaxed • be aware of potential risk factors – use this to inform sequence and methods • careful sequencing of who speaks • include children as facilitators and interviewers	• questions that are not easy to understand • shyness • limited time • one-off discussions • jargon/adult language • patronizing language/tone of voice • too much reliance on written information • just asking 'your' questions • censorship • adult-written 'kiddy' books • formal meetings • shouting • verbal abuse • no private meeting space – people walking in and intruding • pre-set ideas or agenda set by the adults

on presentation of results. In some situations information may not even be fed back to the children who have been the subjects of an investigation, or media drive to show their plight as victims, or the destructive behaviour of youth on the streets.

My house is full of many shapes

Henry

Figure 2.8: *Be careful not to over-interpret!*

In evaluating how we respond to children's rights to express their views and opinions as expressed in the CRC process must be included: consent for use of information and whether the process of gathering and presenting it has been participatory. There is often little accountability of who has control of the data and how they are used. Innovative ways of gathering and presenting information can be followed in consultation with children and young people, and their help can be sought to find new ways to disseminate ideas. Children can be involved in all stages of information collection, editing, interpretation and dissemination, and can help in determining how they ultimately benefit from action resulting from any investigation.

Motivations for children's participation

The diversity of adults' motivations and how these may impact on children's participation should be recognized. Although most adults' intentions may be honourable, there is an underlying and disturbing threat that some of them might try to use children's involvement as a way of getting close to minors. There is, therefore, an argument that children should be protected in research projects, just as they are in the provision of children's services where adults may be screened.

Do some adults develop research projects merely to find out how better to control children rather then to improve their quality of life? Children may also be seen as a resource in community development rather than as active participants who can help to shape their own development and become involved in decision-making.

Participation may be seen as an end in itself rather than a means to improving the lives of girls and boys. It can also be seen as a bandwagon for adults to further their careers. It is important to understand the starting-points of adults involved in the project and also to understand children's motivations for participation. Do children take part in order to please adults? Are they pressurized, not consulted, or do they actively and willingly participate and enjoy themselves?

Payment

There are many ethical problems when considering payment or rewards for participants in research. Clare O'Kane gave examples for and against payment:

For:
● it shows children's time is valued;
● you are treating them seriously; and
● you are treating them like adults (although this depends if you would pay adults for research).

Against:
● payment can be seen as manipulation;
● participants feel under pressure to say what they think the researcher wants to hear; and
● children may take part in something that doesn't interest them to get payment – can this really be genuine participation?

There are many concerns about payment amounting to bribing people to become involved in research and activities they are not interested in – it is sometimes referred to as economic coercion, especially when working with poorer members of the community. Researchers who disagree with financial payment may offer refreshments or help with tasks and work in return for participants' time; where do you draw the line?

Roles, relationships and power

Power and control relationships, and how participatory mechanisms change power relationships within groups and communities where projects take place, must be fully investigated. It is important to acknowledge the fundamental power relationships between adults and children to which increased children's participation may pose a threat. Those in power should be honest about when participation is or isn't possible but allow children to take control when appropriate. The different perceptions about 'when is appropriate' may change through the process of a project and may be continuously negotiated by different stakeholders with different agendas. Every scheme should allow for a process and forum whereby this can happen. Changing adults' perceptions of children and children's views about adults need to be understood within the context of a project process and beyond. Children should be allowed to develop and their skills grow over the lifetime of a project, as indeed should be the case with the adults involved. Roles will change over time and people will learn how to participate by taking part.

Awareness-raising amongst adults can enlighten them to the value of the views and opinions of children, especially young children. In some contexts, however, trying to increase minors' participation may put them at risk. Conflict maybe created by their increased participation and existing power structures and relationships threatened. Projects should be flexible enough to modify courses of action and we cannot afford to experiment casually with children's involvement.

There are successful examples of children and young people as researchers although, as with their involvement in participatory processes in other capacities, their time should not be overburdened and willingness to be involved exploited.

How to measure success

How can we measure success? Successful things are often seen as being influential or powerful. Here, however, we are looking at adults giving up power and at the incremental ways in which children's lives are changed and hopefully improved. We must find ways of measuring the changes in attitudes and power relationships, considering people's initial starting points. What happens after the event, after the researchers leave and after the participation has been achieved in the initial stages of the project process? Parents may fear a loss of control when children are seen as partners. What is the attitude of parents or guardians throughout the project process and beyond? Have researchers selected out those bits of what children tell them that suit their agendas or have children been involved in the selection of information to be presented? Has a piece of research with a high level of child participation retained important elements of credibility and reliability? Have only certain children benefited and if so which? How do other stakeholders feel they have benefited or do some of the adults still feel threatened? Do they close up to children's participation in any kind of decision-making after the researchers have gone? Is information given by children in a participatory process later used to manipulate and hold control over them? How has a project affected a child's own self-image and self-esteem? These are just some of the questions to evaluate the relative success of a process and to take into account the impact on the lives of young people in the longer term.

The final questions must be: (i) how to involve different children in the evaluation of projects that affect their lives; and (ii) whether adults' development projects are evaluated in a way that specifically examines their impacts on children's lives.

Figure 2.9: *'In pairs, we role-played interactions between adults and children showing different power dynamics'*

2.9 Conclusions

VICTORIA JOHNSON

Building blocks and ethical dilemmas discussed in Part 2 raise questions that are considered at points throughout the rest of the book. One of the most important principles is transparency. If we look at confidentiality as an example, we can accept that certain factors, such as project objectives and the legal and socio-political context in which children are living, will have a bearing on the level of confidentiality that may be desirable both for the project and the children. The crucial rule regarding confidentiality is that it is transparent to all participants from the outset of the project. Researchers and field-staff should have considered their strategy in advance and know their legal position if sensitive issues are unexpectedly revealed, such as abuse or crime. Transparency is also important in the use of information and the process that has been employed to reach a certain end-point when disseminating findings. It is important to aim for participation by children when information is interpreted and edited. Children should always have the option to have information withdrawn or modified if, on reconsidering its implications, they are unhappy with what they have said.

Ethical considerations need to be taken into account throughout a project or research process and beyond. If we think of a time-line of a process from the planning stages, through to the information gathering, analysis, information dissemination and action, ethical issues, such as informed consent, need to be renegotiated and explained at different stages. It is always important to extend the time-line as far back as you can to include all the ethical issues raised in Part 2 at the early stages of planning, such as understanding motivations for participation and not raising expectations too high. It is also important to extend the time-line forward to ensure that the long-term implications of participation are considered after the life-span of the project or research. Issues of changed power structures and relationships and elements of risk to children must be fully considered throughout the project decision-making process.

Issues of difference between children must be acknowledged and understood. Their recognition will inform choices to be made from the outset of the project. Which children will be involved? Which children will benefit? If issues of difference, such as age, gender, disability, ethnicity, religion etc. are not taken into account in planning the project objectives and process, it will always be the more articulate children who will be heard. Different ethical decisions will also affect different groups and individuals in varying ways. Methods will need to be planned and modified to reach different types of children. Issues such as informed consent and access will need to be approached flexibly, depending on whether children have parents or guardians, whether or not they are at school, whether they are part of a group or gang, are girls or boys, and their age. It is, however, also easy to fall into the trap of using the Western models of child development to determine the abilities of children at different ages. Differences between children in different countries and communities and differences within the same community need to be appreciated and understood by starting from where children are and developing appropriate processes and methods with them. Project staff and researchers have their own ideological stance and values, including preconceptions they hold about childhood, we can move on from perceptions and learn from situations of the particular children with whom we are working to inform their decisions and action.

The benefits of a project cannot be celebrated without fully evaluating its long-term positive and negative impact on children's lives. There are evolving power relationships throughout the lifetime of a project and beyond. Adults should be involved in participatory processes to ensure that their attitudes towards children develop through the project process and so that they can see the benefits to all stakeholders of increasing children's participation. As Hart (2.2) concluded, children's participation requires adults who are willing to listen and to allow children to develop capacities and skills. In altering

Figure 2.10: *Issues of difference*

the fundamental power relationships between adults and children, the long-term risks to the latter must be understood and evaluated. It is also important to recognize that change is not always immediately beneficial and that a longer time-frame than is often allowed for in projects may be needed to evaluate longer-term consequences.

The context in which one is working will make a difference to the type of participation that can be promoted. Emanuelle Abrioux, disscussing the participation of girls in Afghanistan (2.1), raised ethical issues about the degree to which girls in such a non-participatory context can participate without a project endangering them. She puts forward a complementary model to the 'ladder of participation' (Hart, 1992; see Appendix 2 to this volume). The spherical model that she puts forward can be used to assess the degrees of participation which are possible considering the starting point of people, and the legal, political and social context within which one is working. Abrioux's spherical model represents better the value of small steps that can be taken to improve the lives of girls in Kabul City through participation, which on the ladder of participation may be interpreted only as tokenism. Her model can be used in contexts that are more open to higher levels of participation and would still be challenged to achieve a greater degree of participation (Figure 2.11).

This spherical model can be used in conjunction with the concepts of increasing involvement on the ladder of children's participation. The disadvantage of a ladder is that people tend feel that they should have reached the top and that they have not achieved much unless they get past the first few rungs. With the spherical model, the degrees of participation achieved can still be significant even if the starting point is at a different point on the circle

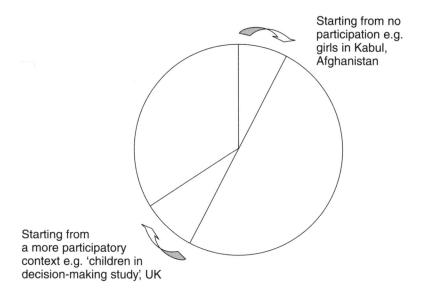

Starting from no participation e.g. girls in Kabul, Afghanistan

Starting from a more participatory context e.g. 'children in decision-making study', UK

Figure 2.11: *Diagrammatic representation of Abrioux's spherical model showing degrees of participation*

in terms of the different attitudes of stakeholders involved and the context within which one is working. It is the process and the incremental effect on children's lives which will be the measure of the degrees of participation achieved and the measure of success. The methods of participation and the objectives of a project may be different depending on the starting point on the model. Abrioux's spherical model is important in the consideration of the overall ethics of participation and what is possible in given situations.

Notes

1. For a fuller discussion of Piaget's theories of children's developing environmental competence see Hart (1997) or refer directly to Piaget (1954).
2. ECPAT (End Child Prostitution, Pornography and Trafficking) can be contacted on: Tel: 0171 924 9555; Fax: 0171 738 4110.
3. This paper is based on the Anti-Slavery International publication, *Child Domestic Workers: a handbook for research and action* (1997) by M. Black with additional material by J. Blagbrough.
4. 'The children and decision-making study' was funded by the Nuffield Foundation and was conducted by Nigel Thomas and Claire O'Kane, University of Wales Swansea, from April 1996 to December 1997.
5. The South African 'Growing Up In Cities' project was part-funded by UNICEF, UNESCO-MOST and the HSRC (SA). The views in this paper are not necessarily those of the above-mentioned donors.

PART 3

How To: the process

Editor and co-author: GILL GORDON

Co-authors: RACHEL BAKER, ERNESTO CLOMA,
JULIAN FAULKNER, MAHFUZA HAQUE, JOANNA HILL, RACHEL
HINTON, ANDY INGLIS, ALICE LAMPTEY, CHARITY MANYAU,
THABANG NGCOZELA and JOACHIM THEIS.

Summary

Part 3 explores issues related to the process and methods used in participatory research and planning with children. Contributors from Zimbabwe, Bangladesh, South Africa, Vietnam, Ghana, Nepal, Scotland and the Philippines share their experiences of working with children as a separate group and with children and adults together, and provide examples of good practice and approaches to overcoming difficulties. They describe innovative methods, including the use of video, photography and theatre, that enable children to record and present their own realities without adult interpretation and distortion.

Key issues raised in Part 3:

- A high degree of flexibility in methods and process is needed for participatory research with children, especially with working children.
- The process and methods should:
  —enable less-confident and marginalized children to participate fully in all stages of research;
  —build the skills and confidence of children so that they become more capable of participating in democratic processes and advocating their rights and needs;
  —enable children to own, plan, analyse, document and present their work to others including those in power and their peers; and
  —stimulate creative ideas, new visions and options for the future.
- Sequences of methods, including visualization, drama, ranking and focus-group discussion, used with children and adult groups can reveal very different perceptions of problems and solutions by different stakeholders.
- The micro-environment where activities take place is an important consideration. Participation will be more enjoyable for children in a friendly atmosphere, and at a time and place that suits them.
- Using the local vernacular can help people communicate ideas more fully.
- Tools and skills are needed to record power relations and interactions during a participatory process. This is at least as important as the data themselves.
- The relative lack of power of children means that facilitators of PRA activities must moderate biases and disperse barriers to open participation by children with adults.
- Facilitation has a major influence on how children participate. They may be more comfortable with facilitators of their own age.
- When groups of children meet regularly to participate in research, planning, awareness-raising, advocacy and evaluation they develop confidence and skill.
- Visualization encourages participation and avoids the problems of adults taking additional notes or adding their own analysis.
- Photo appraisal and participatory video are innovative methods that can enable children to document and communicate their own reality across

geographical, literacy, age and status barriers. Giving children a voice rather than a message is potentially transforming.

- Theatre pedagogy is a powerful process for enabling children to explore and understand their reality, generate solutions to their problems and communicate their learning to others. Those involved gain confidence and can become leaders and educators of other children and adults.
- Children can advocate for their rights by producing hard-hitting general-audience television programmes for national networks.
- Monitoring and evaluation indicators should be disaggregated to make visible the impact of development programmes on children's well-being.
- There is a need to work for the rights of poor and disadvantaged adults alongside those of children. Where adult participation is minimal because of powerlessness, it will take time for children's involvement to gain acceptance.
- There are advantages in involving children in mainstream development planning and rights' advocacy alongside adults.
- Researchers trying to increase children's participation may meet with the attitude that this type of research does not yield 'hard' data. These perceptions are changing as there is a growing body of successful examples and as decision-makers are convinced of the added value of using more participatory approaches.

3.0   Introduction

GILL GORDON

The use of role-play, drama, theatre, song and dance in participatory work with adults and children is becoming more widespread (PLA Notes No. 29, 1997). Building on the work of Boal (1974: 92), theatre activities are being used with community groups to identify problems, analyse their causes and consequences, explore and rehearse solutions, and evaluate change. In Kenya, Lenin Ogolla facilitates Participatory Educational Theatre (PET). He argues that Theatre For Development (TFD) is often 'like a wheel spanner which is then neatly tucked in the car boot before the journey resumes'. Rather than being a tool for development and *for* the people, theatre should involve open participation of the people from conception and problem identification to taking action, devising the programme, implementing it and monitoring and evaluating it (Ogolla, 1997). Stepping Stones is a training package on communication and relationship skills and HIV/AIDS that combines role play, games and other experiential activities to enable community groups of adults and children to identify their joys and problems in relation to sexuality, analyse causes and identify and rehearse solutions. This is based on the ideas of forum theatre and has resulted in the empowerment of young women and men to express their desires and practise safer sex (Welbourn, 1995; Mbowa, 1997).

Participatory video is an innovative method that shows great potential for work with children. Video allows for different actors to negotiate issues in a much more equal way than does written language. A video report can be narrated by the participants as a group with a minimum of outside interpretation (Johansson and De Waal, 1996). It is easy to translate and the same material can be understood readily by the different parties involved, from parents and neighbouring villages, to local and national authorities and donors. Video 'gives a sense of opening up space for public speech'. People take the opportunity to get their information across because they realize that their statements are not easily distorted once on tape. Knowing that everything will be replayed in their home villages and to the authorities, giving a true, fair and balanced picture becomes very important. Video can give children and young people a voice with which to articulate their concerns to parents, teachers and other adults. The children can create solutions and make demands of those in power.

The special issue of PLA Notes (No. 25, Johnson, 1996) and the Institute of Development Studies Topic Pack, PRA with Children (December 1996), provide background and context for many of the papers in this part of the book. In PLA Notes No. 25, Victoria Johnson highlights key issues in children's participation, which are also reflected in the report of the workshop in this chapter and in Part 2 on communication and ethical dilemmas. These include the need for informed consent, confidentiality, transparency and awareness and access to different groups of children. Methods need to be adapted for different age groups and cultural contexts, and the process should be fun. Power relations will affect the interaction between researchers and children and whether the latter's views are taken seriously. The use of creative, fun activities such as drawing, diagramming, games and role play can break down age and cultural barriers to children's participation and enable youngsters to express their own perceptions rather than trying to please adults (Duchscherer et al., 1996). In Ladakh, it was found that children were able to speak more openly to a child facilitator than to adults. Students were able to break through the shyness barrier very quickly and establish rapport and friendship.

The importance of encouraging less-confident children, particularly girls, to express their perceptions is a recurring theme in the following chapters. Mixed groups tend to be dominated by more articulate boys and adults. Sensitive facilitation, work in single-sex groups, discussion in pairs before presentation to the larger group and the use of games to develop trust can all help less confident children to participate. Johnson et al. (1995) describe work with children in Nepal. It was often difficult to talk to girls because they were frightened and shy. Songs formed an important part of the research process, particularly with girls, because they built up trust and understanding. Songs are used by girls, to express their perceptions of their present and future. Although it was hard to find women researchers, men tried to be as sensitive as possible and joined in activities such as collecting firewood with the women and girls. Girls in the area often did not speak Nepali and it was important to have friends or relatives acting as interpreters. Hart (1997) suggests that groups of four to eight children work best because they can work together and attain cohesion whilst also allowing for a diversity of viewpoints. Children can generate creative solutions by working in pairs and writing ideas on separate pieces of paper before brainstorming in the larger group. This maximizes their ability to identify their own ideas and have them expressed.

Drawing offers even non-literate children an opportunity to portray life as it really is or has been for them. In Durban, street children were able to express their feelings through self-portraits (Bedford, 1995). The 'draw and write' technique is fun and enables children to express detailed information on issues such as the reasons for good and bad health (Pridmore, 1996). It is important, however, to adapt the type of drawing to the experience and culture of the children. Kumkum describes the reluctance of girls who had only recently come out of their village to draw with paper and pens. When they were pushed into drawing, they drew only the designs used to decorate the walls, floors and ceilings of their houses. If the facilitator had asked them to use the medium they used for decorating their homes, they may have been less inhibited in expressing their views.

The flexible use of sequences of methods can bring out the different perspectives of boys and girls. Sey and VanBelle-Prouty (nd) use a sequence

Figure 3.1: *Listening to smaller voices Johnson, Hill and Ivan-Smith 1995 – From a photo by Ana-Cecilia Gonzalez, Peru*

of PLA visualization techniques with schoolboys and schoolgirls to explore their different experiences. Seasonality calendars, daily-routine diagrammes, pie charts and matrices helped children and teachers to analyse factors that had an adverse effect on girl's performance, attendance and participation. In the Gambia, similar methods used in single-sex groups enabled girls to speak out at full community meetings and give their suggestions for actions that would enable them to attend school and perform well (Kane, 1996). Sequences of methods can include the use of drama techniques linked to visualization methods (Gordon, 1997). This allows for more creativity and variety in working with children. For example, role-plays of problem situations can be analysed by flow charts to find the causes and consequences of the problems. Creative solutions are then developed using the Margolis wheel and role-plays. In a training workshop for street educators, particip- ants were asked to be creative in selecting methods enjoyable to children. Flipcharts were discouraged, and pie charts and the like were soon overtaken by puppet shows, role-plays, video, maps and cartoons (Henk van Beers, 1996).

The Child-to-Child programme is an important approach, with its six steps representing the active participation of children at all stages of planning. Using their personal experiences as a starting point, children are enabled to investigate why and how events occur, using a range of participatory methods including drama, storytelling, games, observation, mapping and dialogue (Bonati and Hawes, 1992; The Child-to-Child Trust and UNICEF, 1993). The Child-to-Child approach is explored fully in Part 4.

3.1 Situational analysis with children living in difficult circumstances in Zimbabwe using participatory rural appraisal

CHARITY MANYAU

An initial situational analysis was carried out in Zimbabwe with secondary school pupils living as squatters around the school because of the lack of accommodation. These children are referred to as 'bush boarders'. Participatory rural appraisal (PRA) techniques, questionnaires and focus- group discussions were used with community groups, including children and bush boarders. The objective of the situation analysis was to identify the main problems of the bush boarders.

The situation analysis revealed:

- a high incidence of sexually transmitted infections;
- an increase in the number of school pupils leaving before completing their education;
- an increase in marriages with young girls; and
- an increase in reports on child sexual abuse and child labour.

These results prompted SCF Zimbabwe to carry out a specific study on bush boarders using PRA methodologies.

Background to the current bush boarder situation

Mola Secondary School, in Kariba district of Mashonaland West Province, draws its pupils from primary schools as far away as 140km. The school has no formal boarding facilities, making the walking distance very long. Boys who live long distances from the school often live as bush boarders, squatting on land near the school during term-time, a situation considered too dangerous for girls. Many girls walk for up to four hours daily to attend school or drop out of the school system prematurely.

Camfed, an international NGO, has provided hostel accommodation for girls who live far from Mola Secondary School. The community provided the land, building materials and labour at low cost. This has enabled more girls to go to school and live in safety out of school hours. Save the Children Fund (UK), has been supporting Camfed's initiative.

This intervention could provide a model for Zimbabwe. However, there is need to take a closer look at the situation, with the involvement of the children going to Mola Secondary School. As insiders know their own situation better than anyone else, a participatory, action-oriented approach was selected.

The pilot study

The objective of the pilot study was to test the PRA methods in a peri-urban area at a squatter camp in Dzivaresekwa with approximately 50 school children aged 10–17 years and a youth group aged from 16–18 years. A women's group was also involved to promote their participation and test the methods with a low-literate group. Most of these women had mobile lifestyles between the camp and the rural areas. The games and exercises that were employed worked well and the women expressed their gratitude for having such a free and relaxed platform to air their views.

Preliminary findings

- Children know more about HIV/AIDS than young people.
- Children know more about child abuse than women and young people.
- Child labour is more evident after school, for example, in grass cutting and farm labour.
- Some children have abandoned school to work in farms.
- Forced early marriages are encouraged by parents.
- The community is operating below the poverty line, resulting in some community members engaging in prostitution.
- Poor sanitation leads to the spread of diseases.
- Ill-treatment of children by stepmothers is prevalent in the camp.

Lessons learned on methods for working with children

- It takes time to build up children's trust, but when this is done their information appears to be less constructed than that of adults.

Table 3.1: Positive and negative aspects of methods used

Positive aspects	Negative aspects
Children enjoyed comparing experiences, action-oriented, participatory techniques, and representing their experiences visually	Limited time factor Sample was not entirely representative of the wider squatter population
Children like attention and acting as rapporteurs and communicators to their peers	Children reluctant to discuss their sexuality
Children, young people and women valued each other's opinions	The more reserved adolescent youths took time to unfreeze; they did not appear fully to appreciate energizers
The planning team comprised of PRA team, 2 women, 2 school youths and 2 school children	Community groups not involved in data analysis

- Children thrive on exploratory, open-ended exercises. It is their inquisitive nature that influences them to venture into the unknown.
- The use of pictures as a medium enhances participation. Children enjoy writing and drawing. Some end up showing more of their artistic prowess than the issue at hand.
- Drama was one of the favourite activities. Most times they prefer action to dialogue.
- When children are working, such as producing a picture, it is essential not to disturb them because their concentration will be lost and they are likely to tell you to be quiet.
- Singing is also another form of play that motivates children to continue afterwards, even when they are getting tired.
- Games and energizers are necessary to refocus children and bring the group back together. Energizers should be not just for pleasure but a learning tool, they are likely to remember analogies.
- Children need to feel that they are always learning.
- Children like active listeners and become easily dejected when they feel that they are not receiving due attention.
- Separating girls and boys after an initial induction period is essential. It will induce more debate for some contentious issues.
- Six is about the ideal group size, anything bigger is too difficult to handle for a single trainer. A team can handle much more.
- Asking children to work individually and then display their work to the group is successful.
- Children differ from adults because they do not bother to fabricate interest or pretend to listen, they may even leave the room or lie down.
- Children often want to take their work home with them but vital information can be lost.

- Children may enjoy the exercises so much that they do not want to stop. Trainers should be diplomatic in halting the process for the day.
- Trainers need to be sensitive and empathize with children to respond to their various needs.
- Incentives that are given out to reinforce good behaviour and performance keep the children motivated.
- Children shape their worlds and characters by emulating what they see or hear. Trainers need to be careful how they handle conflict amongst the children. Strong rebuke or violent behaviour gives younger children permission to behave in a similar way.

Objectives of the bush boarder study

- to identify problems faced by the students and formulate possible solutions together with them using PRA;
- to assess the appropriateness of the girls' hostels as a solution to the bush boarders' problem; and
- to identify the community's problems and felt needs in relation to the bush-boarder issue and their motivation for change.

Methodology

The study lasted for five days and included groups from three home communities of the bush boarders: the Rural District Council and Department of Social Welfare and Education; the general Mola community – bush boarders, boarders in new structures and those who live at home; and primary and secondary school teachers. The number of participants per group was around twenty.

Students, compounds and communities were selected using purposive sampling. From a total population of approximately 250 pupils within eight compounds, three compounds with distinct features were selected, including: distant places where children had a choice of school but chose to attend Mola secondary; relatively distant homes with no alternative schools; and immediate neighbouring communities that were strong feeders to the school.

Participatory rural appraisal: key issues and methods used

Mola community
This group began with diagramming and mapping to look at social structures and socio-economic profiles. Focus group discussions (FGD) were used to learn about the attitudes of the general Mola community to bush and non-bush boarders. Problems and priorities were identified through brainstorming and ranking. Social mapping showed the water and sanitation situation, including breakdowns.

Parents and guardians from Negande community
A number of PRA methods were used to identify the perceptions of the parents and guardians. These included FGDs, picture codes, pie charts, wealth

and well-being ranking, seasonal charts, brainstorming and ranking, and a helping diagram.

Bush boarders from Gokwe, Negande, Mayovhe and Marembera
A range of PRA methods was used with bush-boarders from three compounds, with sequences building cumulatively on the knowledge gained in each. The bush boarders analysed their existing situation, identified problems and their causes, prioritized and looked for solutions. In all, 120 students participated.

Boarders in new structures
FGDs were used to find out this group's attitudes and ideas on the advantages and disadvantages of the old and new accommodation, teacher-pupil relations, attitudes of primary school children to secondary school and the bush boarders' attitudes to school. Pocket charts, bar charts and seasonal charts helped to explore issues of school performance, study habits, reasons for dropping out and absenteeism.

Pupils living at home
FGDs were held with pupils from the Mola community living at home to compare and verify the information collected from other groups.

Teachers
Semi-structured interviews were held with primary and secondary school teachers to elicit their ideas and attitudes on the problem, possible solutions and their role in assisting the bush boarders. Statistical data on numbers, ages and gender of bush and non-bush boarders, together with absenteeism, study habits, performance and drop-out rates were collected.

Stakeholders from Kariba and Siakobvu districts
Semi-structured interviews and FGDs were held with key informants from the Nyaminyami Rural District Council on policy-related issues. They discussed their perceptions of the problem, its causes and possible solutions, and the role of their agency, external agencies and the bush boarders themselves in solving the problems.

Synopsis of findings

All groups used words such as squalid, derelict and poor to describe the bush boarders' accommodation. Huts leaked, leading to the destruction of books, and mosquitoes result in malaria being a 'number one killer'. In the holidays, huts were destroyed or used as toilets and parents paid extortionate prices to builders. A lack of toilets and clean water resulted in diarrhoea and children were harassed if they tried to use community boreholes or firewood. The new structures, on the other hand, were safe and provided safe drinking water and toilets.

Theft was said to be rampant among the bush boarders, although parents blamed the Mola community for stealing their children's belongings. There is no security; if children report each other outside the camp, they may be

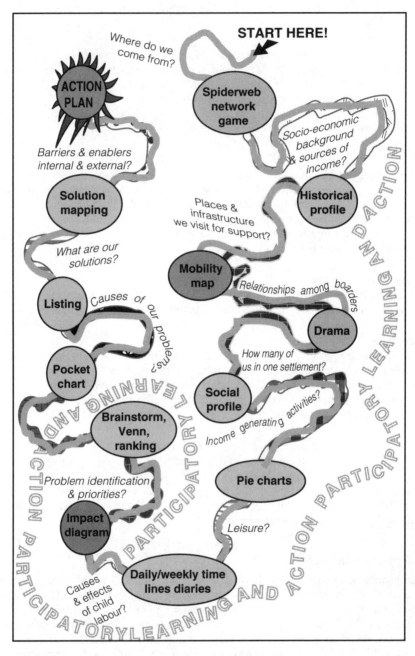

Figure 3.2: *Bush boarders: sequence of PLA activities*

punished for breaking a code of solidarity and police show a nonchalant attitude to their problems.

Poverty results in a high level of drop-outs, absenteeism and girls providing sexual favours for school fees. Parents face escalating expenses for food, hut building, fees and transport. There is a dire shortage of food for bush boarders, reinforced by a lack of draught power for agriculture. School fees are the primary concern of bush boarders, and children drop out of school to do piece-work to pay their fees. Some parents believe that Camfed sponsorship has to be repaid and so do not use the opportunity to send their girls to school. Many believe that it is a waste of money educating girls because they will marry or become pregnant. Children are kept at home to chase away animals. Some parents do not value education, preferring their children to work.

There is conflict between the local community and the children caused, according to the Mola community, by a lack of respect for and deterioration in Mola cultural values resulting from Western education. Mola people and teachers believe that children lack moral education. The non-bush boarders believe, on the other hand, that the forced marriage of young girls is promoted by the Tonga culture and 'will remain until there is a complete transformation with the advent of Western culture'. Bush boarders said that abuse by step-mothers causes some children to stay at school all the time.

Strong bonds characterize the interpersonal relations among bush boarders. They have a protective attitude towards each other in relation to external challenges. This manifests itself in their spirit of survival and development through appropriate coping mechanisms. However, some big boys bully and intimidate other bush boarders. There are normal adolescent sexual relations and 'mock marriages' where girls live with boys during term time. Beer drinking is only a problem if it is excessive.

A shortage of furniture, stationery and equipment at school was a priority problem for bush and non-bush boarders. Non-bush boarders have to walk a long way to school and are punished when they arrive late as well as having to sit on the floor.

The children living in the new accommodation are happy with the protection of a supervisor who gives them time to study, the toilets and safe water, and the lack of absenteeism except for illness. The bush boarders feel strongly that giving only girls rondavels is highly discriminatory; they should be given to all children. The non-bush boarders had negative attitudes also because the structure helped a negligible proportion of the pupils.

The bush boarders would prefer to improve the equipment and furniture at the school before their accommodation. Teachers and parents were both very concerned about the vulnerability of the bush boarders but felt helpless to assist in a sustainable way. The Mola community thought that more co-ordination between the Mola and home communities was needed to draw up the parameters for assistance.

3.2   Understanding with children: coping with floods in Bangladesh

MAHFUZA HAQUE

Riverbank erosion and flooding are recurrent hazards in the charlands of Bangladesh. Charlands are mid-channel islands and bankline areas. Periodic shifts in the river channels frequently result in extensive bank erosion, leading to loss of land, homesteads and assets, population dislocation and impoverishment of local communities.

We organized a participatory workshop in December 1996 in one of our rural projects to explore the issues that we would be addressing. The objective of the workshop was to bring together children's representatives from the project areas and a number of national non-governmental organizations (NGOs), in order to exchange their experiences and ideas and develop an understanding of the issues confronting poorer families, especially their children.

We selected five NGOs which had been working in charland areas and with whom we collaborated in implementing emergency flood-relief operations. Each sent two representatives to the workshop. We also invited seven children from the poorest families. Our project manager met these children with their parents and explained the purpose of the workshop. With the help of grassroots female workers, he randomly selected four girls and three boys, aged between 12 and 16 years and attending primary and secondary schools, who were willing to take part in the workshop. We thought that these older school-children would be able actively to participate in the workshop compared to younger, out-of-school children. We did not face any resistance from the families in allowing their children to participate, perhaps because of the mutual trust that we had developed through our work in their areas.

Workshop design and methodology

It was a residential workshop of three days duration with twenty participants, including three from Save the Children Fund (SCF). The participants were not involved in designing the workshop but were informed in advance about its purpose. In the preliminary discussions, we emphasized that the workshop may not lead to any tangible benefits but we would maintain contact and find ways of addressing the issues raised. The senior staff of SCF and one external resource person acted as facilitators. We thought that the child participants might feel isolated and ineffective working on their own so I acted as a co-facilitator. My role was to remain with them throughout the workshop and provide constant encouragement and support in obtaining and analysing information.

The children, especially the girls, were initially shy, distant, scared, hesitant and self-conscious. The girls were younger than the boys. I spent the whole evening helping them with introductions and getting to know each other and finding out about their family backgrounds, education, likes and dislikes. We played games and had fun. These helped the children to overcome their fears and develop good relationships between themselves and with me. It was the first time that they had participated in a workshop and none of them could explain its purpose properly. One of the boys told us that he had come to the workshop to listen to what *sahebs* (men wearing trousers and shirts) would talk about.

I explained that the workshop gave them an opportunity to talk about their own situations, that is their opportunities, problems and options. They should speak freely using their own words and terms to express their ideas and interests. After I had assured them that I would be present throughout and provide all the support they needed, they developed some confidence.

The methods used included lectures, group discussions and presentation. I realized that these conventional methods might not hold the children's interest and instead arranged dancing, singing, role-plays and rehearsals. I thought the liveliness of such events would hold their attention and release their creative energies.

After the welcome and introduction of the participants, the first day started with a lecture on the likely opportunities, threats and options in the charland environment. This was delivered in standard Bangla mixed with English, at a pace and in a style that was not fully understood by the children. I observed that the children were not finding the lecture at all interesting and two of them fell asleep. I asked one of the boys to tell the facilitator that they were having difficulties following his lecture and that he should speak slowly in simple Bangla. This helped only a little.

We did not mix the children with the adults for group work. Initially, the children were confused about how to proceed with their group work. After more explanation and help with providing and assessing information, we generated a collective process of discussion of the issues. The children sometimes rehearsed before presentation in the plenary.

As the workshop progressed, the interest amongst the children grew and they participated actively and presented their views more freely. The boys talked more than the girls. In the culture of Bangladesh, girls are less exposed to the outside world, which makes them reluctant to speak at gatherings. However, they asked for clarification of the issues discussed and once they understood them well, they were able to express their views.

In the evening, I helped the children to review the issues discussed during the day and the difficulties they encountered in understanding and communicating them. They wanted more frequent breaks to relieve the pressure of work. However, the workshop's designers found it difficult to allow these because of the extra time needed to finish the workshop.

Recreational events were organized each evening for the children, who enjoyed the opportunity for recreation, cultural productions and inspiration. Issue-based play mixed with singing and dancing provided answers to the issues raised and a means for expression of feelings and analysis of major problems confronting charland-born children.

We observed that the problems raised by the children were far removed from the thinking of the adults. They identified issues that affected their daily lives during floods. One boy said that education was a problem. One girl said she found no raised ground where she could play. Another said she had to take a long walk through the flood water three or four times a day to collect drinking water from wells and she caught fever on several occasions. One boy said that the local government and other agencies provided plenty of relief materials in the past flood but most of these went to the rich families which did not need them. The same boy said that his family members had to spend nearly a month on the road and cover themselves with plastic because their house was washed away. One girl spent many sleepless nights in a tent with her family because of the fear of snakes, following the death of one her friends from snakebite in the last flood. She described the difficulties that she, her mother and sisters faced without adequate toilet facilities during the floods. They raised other problems which adults never considered.

The girls identified several issues relating to the disposal of dead bodies, problems during the menstrual cycle, difficulties in giving birth, and so on, which boys did not mention. The girls were hesitant to raise sensitive issues like menstrual problems. This was natural, given the sensitivity in our cultural context of discussing the issue in the presence of males.

Lessons learnt

- Participatory work with children requires patience, perseverance and careful probing by the adults.
- The purpose, issues and methodology should be spelled out to the children very clearly before the start of the workshop.
- Strong rapport-building is essential to stimulate and encourage active participation by children. Understanding and mutual trust between the facilitators and children can help the latter overcome their fears and develop self-confidence.
- Children can express their views if they are provided with information and assisted in analysing that information in a way they can understand.
- Workshops with children need to be conducted in a language they can understand and at a pace and style that is appropriate to their lives.
- Lectures do not encourage children to participate.
- Children are not satisfied unless recreation for the restoration of their energies and creativity is provided at workshops. For example, dancing, singing, role plays and fun.
- It is necessary to adopt flexibility in the methods and processes that seek to promote children's participation.
- Children's participation requires recognition of the time they are able to give and the pressures they can cope with.
- Mixing children with adults in identifying and validating issues, problems and solutions might work, provided the latter are empathetic to the former.
- The children are more likely to feel happy and honoured by having responsibility and scope to express their views with adults. Participating with adults in discussions and debates makes children feel equally valued.
- For the representatives of NGOs, the most important lesson was that children were able to express their views in discussions.

3.3 Key issues in children's participation – experiences of the Ilitha Lomso Children and Youth Organization

THABANG NGCOZELA

Needs assessment

A key aspect of children's participation is an initial needs assessment. This helps to identify their immediate needs and sets a good beginning for a participatory programme. It helps children to identify with each other in seeing common problems, needs and experiences, and assists the facilitator in understanding the children's backgrounds and developing a programme tailored to their needs, rather than a top-down, blueprint approach. Children's participation in the process is an ideal. The question is, how can this be achieved?

Expectations

Children's expectations about the learning process in which they are to participate are of vital significance. Although a needs' assessment may have been completed, it helps to allow children to share what they expect to learn in the particular programme of the day. This makes participation much easier for them and helps the learning process. Sometimes it is found that children's expectations differ from those of the programme. Knowing the children's expectations helps the facilitator to explain what the programme can and cannot provide for the participants. It also helps the participants and the facilitator to agree on what each could and could not do in the process of the learning experience. The facilitator would then conduct a preview about the actual programme of the day or module. He or she would introduce the programme, from the first to the last session, outlining the intended activities. Participants then ask questions about what is to be done and what activities will be involved in each session. The important question in this session is how will the expectations of the children be handled in the course of the programme?

Setting, environment and subsistence issues

The kind of setting and environment in which the programme is to take place needs to be looked at carefully. Dangerous objects, harmful people, things to play with, enough food and water, and toilets are among the matters to be considered. These may be thought petty by some people, but I believe that for any effective participation from children, these need to be properly organized and explained clearly before the learning process begins. This would include an explanation of the schedule, with details about lunch and other intervals.

The seating arrangements during the different sessions contribute to the children's learning environment. They affect the interpersonal relations within the group, which are influenced by the group's listening, hearing and seeing capacity. A circle, semi-circle or small group helps to speed the learning process because participating children can share and learn from each other in a structured and supported system. The question to explore is what would be the results of an unplanned learning venue for children?

Methodology

The methodology employed in a child participatory programme determines everything concerning the programme, from the needs' assessment to the programme itself, up to its evaluation. Balancing the participatory learning process with different activities is essential for children's effective inputting and outputting. The different activities may involve games, dialogue, group discussions, big-group brainstorming and presentations or reporting. This allows for capacity building in different areas; for example, communication, sharing and listening, which are so crucial for children's development. The question to explore is, what will happen to the process if the methodology does not take into account some of the aspects that are mentioned here?

Facilitator

The facilitator of the programme has a major influence on how children participate, and thus a self-critical facilitator is ideal. Sometimes children are not critical or confident enough to raise objections with the facilitator, so balanced facilitation is not achieved and an effective programme does not develop.

As important as the children's mutual respect is the respect of facilitator for the children's individual views and background, and vice versa. This makes everyone comfortable and eager to participate and observe. The facilitator must be democratic and accountable to the participants during the learning experience. S/he must be in a position to respond positively to inquiries by the children not pertaining the programme. The facilitator is mainly responsible for setting the mood, guiding, commenting and summarizing discussions by the participants. The empathetic role of the facilitator and extension of that empathy from her/him to the participants is important as it helps to develop sound interpersonal and intergroup relations. What are other important issues that the facilitator should remember to integrate in terms of facilitation and its planning?

Supporting resource materials

Other resource materials to be employed in support of the children's participatory learning process are vital to a successful, effective programme. These could include books, leaflets, videos, and posters which could be used in different ways in various sessions of the participatory experience. The supporting materials should be pertinent to the theme of the programme. They must be easily understood, taking into account the children's backgrounds, including cultural differences and practice, for example, language. How could the extra resource materials help to accelerate and stimulate critical learning?

Evaluation

Sometimes the impact and continuity of the programme is not influenced by whether or not the evaluation was carried out but by how it was done.

Children need to evaluate their learning experience, and it must be clear to them how and why they should evaluate themselves. Written evaluation would be ideal at times, so as to avoid confrontation between the participants and not to interrupt the new understanding that has developed. Also, it could be carried out more openly or verbally with a minute-taker. If guided by the facilitator, this kind of session may be useful and beneficial to everyone. What is the importance of carrying out evaluation with children?

Conclusion

I would like to stress that everyone involved with facilitation and participation has her or his own views and values of the process, depending on the environment in which facilitation takes place. But children have their values and personal views and they are learning, therefore the process should not infringe on their participation in any way. The age of the children also determines the approach, and everything going in and coming out of the programme. That is why flexible, democratic and open-minded facilitation is a key to effective child participation for their capacity development and enrichment. What could be the children's conclusion in a participatory learning process of this nature?

3.4   Participatory research on child labour in Vietnam

JOACHIM THEIS

A new concept of childhood in which children are regarded as social actors rather than as passive beings on their way to adulthood is gaining popularity. This new perspective requires child-focused development organizations fundamentally to reassess their assumptions and rethink their approaches.

Over the last two years, the Save the Children Vietnam programme has begun a series of studies in order to redirect existing projects and to make them more child-focused. New information is collected about children, from children and by children themselves. The primary objective of these efforts has been to improve our understanding of children's lives, their interests, capacities and needs. Children are researched in the context of their family, community and society, rather than in isolation, and locally collected data are linked to country-level statistics. A secondary objective is to demonstrate children's ability to participate in research activities.

Research on rural child labour

Between December 1996 and March 1997, Save the Children (Theis and Huyen, 1997) carried out research on the situation of working children in rural areas of Vietnam in order to inform SCF's programme of a better

Table 3.2: Household labour contribution matrix

Name, sex and age of informant: Oanh, female, 16

Interviewer: Huyen **Date:** 28 December 1996 **Village:** Thanh Cong

	Household members						
Name	Binh	Tam	Oanh	Cuong	Hong	Van	
Age	37	35	16	13	8	4	
Sex	–	–	–	–	–	–	Total Score
Heavy agricultural work	•••••••	••		•			10
Light agricultural work	•	••••	••••	•			10
Subsidiary crops		•••	••••	••	•		10
Tending buffaloes/cows				•••••••	•••		10
Pig & poultry raising		••	•••	••	•••		10
Cooking and cleaning		•••	••••	•	••		10
Child minding		•	•	•	•••••••		10
Food processing		••	••••	•	•••		10
Trade		••••••	••••••				10
Fuelwood for sale			•••••••	••••			10
Fuelwood for home use			••	•••	••••••		10
Migration	•••••••••••						10
Local wage labour		•••	••••	•••			10
Construction	•••••	•	••	••			10
Fishing	•••			•••••••			10
Who works hardest?	••••	••	•••	•			10
Who works longest hours?	•	••••	••••	•			10

Note: Use ten counters for each category of work.

understanding of the extent of child labour. Specific topics included: typology and causes of child work, conditions and effects of child labour, children's contribution to household livelihoods, income and food production, and children's own views on their work.

The research involved children in the process of data gathering through a range of participatory research methods, including semi-structured interviews and discussions, diagramming, listing, scoring and photography (see Box 3.1). In order to facilitate children's participation, research methods were developed that were tailored to children's capabilities, disaggregated by age, to the topic of the research and to the conditions in each research location.

Box 3.1: Research plan for each community

1. General commune information (from People's Committee, Women's Union and Peasants' Association)

- Demographic statistics
- Seasonal calendars by men, women and children
- Labour contribution diagram
- What work at what age?
- Definition of labourer
- Wage rates by age and sex

2. In schools

- School records: boys and girls in classes, drop-out, enrolment, boys and girls aged 6–17
- Work with three classes (3rd, 5th, 7th grade) and with kindergarten class:
    listing of children's activities
    which activities are done more by girls, which more by boys (reasons)
    likes and dislikes: reasons and attitudes
    seasonal calendar
    daily time use (school days and non-school days)
    mapping

3. Work with children of different ages: (work with children who attend school and those who dropped out or never attended and with children from a variety of socio-economic family situations):

- Socio-economic household data
- Children's daily time use
- Household labour contribution
- Likes and dislikes: reasons and attitudes
- Mapping
- Listing of children's activities
- Which activities are done more by girls, which more by boys (reasons)
- Observation of children working
- Photography of children working – pictures taken by researchers and by children themselves

Work profiles: especially of work that is unique to the location; children doing wage labour

Discussions with adults, teachers and children:

- Attitudes towards child labour
- Changes in children's work as a result of economic changes

Migration: commune migration records, migration case-studies

Accidents: commune health-station records on children's work-related accidents; case-studies of children who had accidents while working

Sale, trafficking and abduction of children: general information from commune officials; case-studies

Research tools and sources of information were triangulated to develop a more detailed, comprehensive and in-depth understanding of children's work and to avoid over-interpreting data collected from only one source.

Children participated enthusiastically, especially in the listing, scoring and diagramming exercises. Their active involvement provided a new perspective on the lives of working children and helped the research team to adapt the tools for children of different ages. Involving children in the research process demonstrated to adult community members and researchers that children have important experiences and opinions to contribute, which differ from those of adults.

This is an easy tool to use that generates information about the work of male and female household members at different ages, and about the labour contribution of different household members to different types of work. It is problematic to use the data to calculate average contributions to the overall household labour budget, since the figures represent a relative rather than an absolute value. Different types of work are also not weighted. Nevertheless, if used carefully, this is a useful tool to gain an understanding of the distribution of work in the family.

Children's active participation was, however, largely confined to data collection and did not extend to developing the research plan, analysing data or presenting research results. Accordingly, children's participation was deprioritized whenever it competed with the primary objective of generating research results.

The research neglected to explore children's own coping mechanisms and survival strategies. It is ironic that this research project which expressly tried to involve children overlooked their abilities, capacities and ingenuity. The research team found itself caught between two contradictory concepts of childhood and unconsciously still perceived children as helpless victims in need of protection, rather than as social actors in their own right. This experience also demonstrated the need to involve children more actively in developing and revising research plans.

Research on urban child labour

To complement the research on rural child labour, SCF carried out research on child labour in Ho Chi Minh City between June and August 1997. This study focused on children involved in money-earning activities. It required a complete revision of the original research plan, given the differences between rural and urban work conditions and the complexities of labour arrangements in a metropolis of six million people. Involving children in the research proved much more difficult than in the rural areas. Children working in factories were under the constant supervision of their employer and were not able to take breaks to participate in discussions or participatory exercises. Many children lived far away from their place of work that made it logistically difficult to track down factory workers at their place of lodging. This part of the research therefore relied largely on informal interviews with children at their work place and on the direct observations of working children. More participatory methods, such as daily routine diagramming, could only be used with working children attending evening classes and with children at their place of lodging.

Photo appraisal

In order to overcome some of the limitations to children's participation inherent in conventional participatory research methods, SCF has begun piloting the photo appraisal approach in Vietnam (see Hubbard, 1991). This method equips community members, including children, with cameras to document their lives. The photographers then comment on the photos and select pictures for presentation in exhibitions and publications. In this way children can be involved in the collection, analysis and presentation of information. Moreover, visual images reach audiences who would normally not read a research report. This is a powerful way to change adults' perceptions of children's capabilities and to communicate children's views.

During the rural child-labour research SCF did some rudimentary trials with the photo appraisal approach. A few children in the communities received disposable cameras to take photos of other children working. The children responded enthusiastically to this opportunity. Initial results were mixed, but encouraging enough to carry out further experiments with this method.

Currently SCF is supporting one of its partner organizations in Ho Chi Minh City in piloting photo appraisal with a group of street children. Much time was spent on acrimonious negotiations between SCF and its local government partner concerning the ownership and control of the negatives. This issue demonstrates how sensitive children's participation is when taken seriously, especially in a country that does not have a tradition of freedom of expression. It also raises ethical issues regarding children who are encouraged to express their views openly and critically. SCF will pursue this experiment cautiously while at the same time nudging its partner towards a more open-minded and whole-hearted approach towards children's participation.

Children as researchers

Over the coming years SCF plans to push further the limits of child participation in research. Experience has shown that it would be difficult for children to work in the same research team alongside adults. In order to involve children more fully, conditions have to be created which make it conducive for children to assume greater responsibility for the entire research process. Towards the end of 1997, SCF intended to train a group of children in Ho Chi Minh City to carry out research on street and working children in their own community. This project aims to empower children and to raise the awareness of adult community members about children's capabilities as researchers. Collecting good quality data will be important, but will be done as part of the exercise and not at the expense of children's participation. The process of children's participation will be given priority over a glossy report.

3.5   Children creating awareness about their rights in Ghana

ALICE LAMPTEY

Ghana was the first country to ratify the UN Convention on the Rights of the Child (CRC) in September 1990. The Ghana National Commission on Children (GNCC) was selected as the main co-ordinating and policy-making body for promoting the welfare of children and publicizing the convention widely. In 1997, seven years after the ratification, there is still little awareness among Ghanaians about the CRC.

Working as partners within existing structures

A number of government agencies and NGOs are working to protect children's rights, and recognition of these rights is slowly gaining ground. However, we have a long way to go in promoting understanding of these rights and how they can work to guarantee them among policy-makers. The SCF Ghana Programme works closely with the GNCC, the ministries of Health, Social Welfare and Education and national NGOs. Our work with GNCC seeks to build the capacity of the commission to monitor effectively the status of children in Ghana and report to the UN Monitoring Committee. Training on the CRC is a major activity to create awareness of its existence and familiarize participants with its principles. A first training-of-trainers course was held in April 1997 and a number of follow-up workshops are planned by the Child Rights NGO coalition.

Children are seldom consulted for their views in Ghanaian culture, so their participation in consultation and planning is a new concept that will have to be promoted alongside the responsibility of publicizing the CRC widely. SCF Ghana is trying to persuade people that children's participation is relevant to Ghanaian society.

Beginning with the children themselves

Children's participation must begin with their needs, interests, capabilities and concerns. Article 12 of the CRC stipulates the right of children to express their views in matters that concern them and to have those views taken seriously. On the basis of this principle, we are encouraging and facilitating children to express their interpretation of the convention in words, art, drama and other culturally appropriate means. We are hoping to create awareness among the children themselves about their right of participation, whilst creating the environment for recognition of those rights by adults.

Children producing their own media

Children have taken the initiative to design and develop a weekly television programme on national TV designed to draw attention to issues affecting them. They interview other children and adults on specific issues. For example, they produced a programme about neglected children and another about girls who do not attend school. The programmes included interviews, drama, songs and visits to street children, and interventions designed to support them. This programme is produced by, and reaches predominantly, urban children because rural children do not have access to TV sets. Reaching rural children is a challenge that SCF wishes to address. Around 90 per cent of the population has access to radios so this medium could be used. A campaign on sending girl children to school was carried out through the use of audiotapes on long-distance buses.

The video was positive in several respects. It showed children talking as equals with adults in authority, and the programme was aimed at a general audience, not just children. The national broadcast network had made space for a children's production and it was home-grown television showing local images that children could relate to, rather than an outside culture being imposed by satellite. Although adults assisted the children with technical aspects of film production, the children designed the programme themselves. Public notices were used to advertise for potential filmmakers and presenters in Accra, and the children selected the presenters. They selected the children most articulate in English and there was a lack of disabled children or those who did not speak English. SCF is hoping to include a broader mix of children in future programmes.

The video showed that even in a society where children are supposed to be seen and not heard enormous progress can be made in children's participation.

The way forward

A great deal of sensitization and advocacy is needed at all levels to dispel misconceptions and obtain commitment from children, staff, partners and the general public if children's participation is not to be seen as an imposed Western concept. We need to identify specific target groups and their needs; this is a slow but rewarding process. Our commitment to including children in programming must be in the best interest of the child. At all times we need to ask the familiar planning questions in relation to children (see Box 3.2).

Box 3.2: Planning questions for children's participation

What kind of activities can children participate in?
Why should children participate in these activities, how will it benefit them?
Which children should participate, considering age, gender, urban/rural, capabilities and experience?
How will the children participate?
When can they participate effectively?
Where will they feel safe and comfortable to participate?

3.6   Participatory video-making in Brazil

JULIAN FAULKNER

This paper describes my experience in using participatory video (PV) in Brazil for the purpose of research, though I believe it can also be applied to planning and evaluation. The concept of participation is understood and applied in many different ways. Video can be a very powerful instrument to enable different forms of participation. Johansson and De Waal (1996) talk about 'giving people a voice rather than a message'. Unfortunately, video has traditionally been used for participation that is instrumental, that is giving a message, rather than transformational, which means giving people a voice.

Why participatory video?

When adults invite children to participate in their actions and children accept, adults should hope to learn from the children and vice versa. Participation is essentially dialogue, which is central to any learning process. Ideally, those watching the video should be where the camera is, in order to interact with those producing the video. When dialogue is not feasible, PV is often the most appropriate alternative. Therefore PV is essentially a learning tool, which involves people in the documentation and communication of their realities. By sharing different perspectives and experiences, PV can challenge knowledge and values. This may result in a change in attitudes and behaviour.

Evaluating participatory video

We can divide the criteria for evaluating the merits of video into the quality of participation and the quality of the research, planning or evaluation (RPE). There are three pillars to participation:

- children's interest in participating – perceived benefits;
- adults' willingness for children's participation – whose reality counts; and
- enabling factors – ability and feasibility.

There are two distinct stages in the use of PV whether for research, planning or evaluation.

- recording/documenting; and
- communicating the information.

Quality of participation
Enabling factors include feasibility in terms of time, money and energy. Many argue that video is too expensive; however the costs are dropping rapidly and the equipment is becoming more user-friendly. A child can often participate more readily in making a video than in writing a report, especially as the former does not require the child to be literate. However, it is important that adults and children agree on what they are able and not able to do, to avoid arbitrary judgement by adults in order to justify exclusion.

88

Willingness of adults: Video equipment is usually in the hands of adults, therefore children's ability to participate in its use depends on the willingness of adults. When adults are in control of video-making, they can easily manipulate the voice of children. When children are in control, it is a powerful tool for questioning and challenging authority. The camera becomes an unforgiving witness of adults' lack of co-operation or attempt to sabotage the process. They can only escape the camera by regaining control. There is a danger of confrontation, leading to a breakdown of dialogue, although if this does happen, it is likely that the dialogue was not genuine. One hopes that adults can recognize this as a chance to learn rather than as a threat.

Interest of children: Video gives value to work, as it is an instant audience of inestimable numbers. Children were more willing to show me around or answer my questions when I had a camera, as they were not being disturbed just for my sake but getting something for themselves. Many, particularly younger children, were interested mainly in the novelty of seeing their face and those of their friends on TV. For many, it was just fun. For others, it is a chance to communicate their wish-list to people outside. PV can unfortunately exclude children within the community because the dominant children will to some extent control access.

Quality of research, planning or evaluation
Video is not the only means of recording and communicating information, so what are some of the advantages and disadvantages of PV as opposed to other media?

Recording: Video can be used as a tool, a means to recall the maximum amount of information, like a Dictaphone or notepad. However, Braden (1996) points out that 'community information in even the most participatory of PRA processes is not always retrieved and represented before it is transformed.' When community information is recorded in text form, adults usually organize the empirical data of children into their epistemological framework; in other words, 'it is transformed'. With PV there is less selection, no codification and therefore less potential for bias. The reality of children can be captured through their eyes and ears. Additionally, as the information remains in a more primary form, others can lend their own interpretation to its meaning. The process of analysis is more open to participation.

Many people have expressed a concern about children 'playing up to the camera', which I think is certainly no more worrying than a researcher 'playing up to a report'. I found that some of the children, mostly the girls, would play up to the camera because of vanity rather than mislead the viewer on any fundamental piece of information for the sake of vested interests. More importantly, we have the final say on the video as the children no longer exert any control once we take the video away. We can denounce a child's statement as misleading but the child is not able to denounce our representation as misleading. This raises important ethical questions.

Communicating: There are many situations where PV is more feasible or more appropriate than dialogue. It can facilitate dialogue across barriers, for example geographical distance, conflict, language, culture, generation gap and people who refuse to listen or intimidate others. Video can reach adults in situations when it is not feasible for a child to meet with decision-makers, give a public lecture or communicate horizontally with adults. Video enables children to communicate their perspectives and reality in their preferred format, in their own environment and clothes, rather than in an office, wearing adults' clothes. However, experience has shown that children often prefer to appear like adults when given a 'voice'. Their video becomes their *porte-parole* as opposed to an unaccountable and subjective representative, who is usually an adult. The adult cannot interrupt or intimidate the child but instead is forced to listen.

The main drawback is that communication flows one way. Those who produce the video do not get immediate feedback from those watching it. Johansson and De Waal (1996) have overcome this problem by filming the decision-makers' reaction to the video and showing it back to the community to create an 'evolving narrative'. I attempted this with two groups of children and found it was difficult because for them TV is for fun and relaxation, not thinking. With time, though, this barrier can be overcome.

How is it done?

I don't believe that the more participation the better. I believe there is an optimum level of participation that is determined by the three pillars of participation mentioned earlier. There needs to be transparent communication between children and adults so that they can determine what is the best level of participation according to the demand, supply and resources (see Box 3.3).

If there is little potential for participation, video can be used as a tool in adult hands to recall processes such as PRA exercises, discussions or the daily activities of children. It is also ideal for capturing artistic representations of reality: for example theatre, puppets, dance and music. Amongst disadvantaged youths, Rap has become a popular form of expression and was an excellent starting point for my work with a group of street children. Unless the adult has vested interests that are antagonistic to those of the children, there is no reason to believe that the adult will use the camera less objectively than they. In fact, children do not usually have the same concern for objectivity but prefer to do close-ups of their friends or things they personally find interesting. The idea is to capture the general picture and avoid close-ups. There remains much to explore in making PV part of the PRA process. There are interesting possibilities at the editing stage and this is made more feasible by advances in technology.

I was not able to put the camera in the hands of children, because of strict rules by the university that govern its use. This seemed a major blow but the children quickly developed an alternative. They always tried to emulate TV

Box 3.3: Market approach to participation

Children's interest – perceived benefits	Demand
Adults willingness – who's reality counts	Supply
Enabling factors – time, money, skills	Resources

---

and when I asked a group of girls to represent their lives in a sketch, they did a scene from a popular soap-opera about the wealthy. With the camera on them and a microphone in their hands, they chose to become news interviewers, a technique I call reportage. It is an interesting compromise, because the person controlling the camera has to follow whoever is holding the microphone, as that is the focus of attention. More importantly, the person with the microphone determines who speaks and what is heard. This can be a disadvantage as the dominant children with the microphone end up speaking the most. The camera person has the power to decide whether or not to film. In my experience, if the children had full control of the camera, they would only have filmed themselves rapping, playing football or capoera.

In order to put more camera control into the hands of the children, 'Rap-TV', a pilot project in Rio de Janeiro, linked the camera to a monitor so that the children could see what was being filmed and become interactive directors. I found this technique clumsy and unnecessary. The children were largely satisfied by being shown the footage later, usually at the end of each day. The most important problem was sound. We were forced to use a microphone and cable because the noise of the favela would drown voices on the camera microphone. Natural conversation was impeded because only one person could control the microphone at a time.

There are some excellent experiences where adolescents produced, directed, filmed, acted and edited their own film. The professional adult became a resource person at the service of the children. The time and money required for this is, however, considerably more than for the above. It is a long-term process that requires the children to be completely engaged in the research or programme agenda. The preliminary work where they learn to think critically about their reality is crucial. There is no point in giving them a voice if they don't have a message for which to use it.

Conclusion

PV facilitates a learning process aimed at generating better quality actions. Its main asset is to democratize RPE by giving the community, including children, access to the process of recording, interpretation and communication of a community's information. The hope is that children shift from being passive objects of RPE, with the adult researcher as the active subject, to a situation where they become subjects and objects of their own RPE. In this case, adults act as resource people, who participate actively in the children's learning and acting loop.

This paper is not intended to be a blueprint but an attempt to structure my experience and that of others in Brazil so that we can learn from each other.

3.7 Towards louder voices: ACTIONAID Nepal's experience of working with children

JOANNA HILL[1]

The use of participatory techniques with children in ActionAid Nepal's (AAN) programme areas has acted as a catalyst for encouraging adults in the communities and AAN to listen to and begin to change their behaviour towards children. Children's groups have been formed through which children have demonstrated their potential and confidence in articulating their needs.

AAN's mission is to eradicate absolute poverty through the empowerment of women, men, girls and boys. In 1993–5, ActionAid carried out research on children's lives using participatory approaches to enable children to share their experiences and opinions (Johnson, Hill, Ivan-Smith, 1995). These techniques were further developed during a child-centred participatory research (CCPR) project. This demonstrated that girls and boys must be active participants in development planning, with their voices heard and needs and rights considered, otherwise interventions could adversely affect their quality of life.

Getting organized: children's groups

The CCPR research brought children together to analyse their situations. This resulted in the formation of a group set up by children, motivated by the example of adults' savings groups in the area (Hill and Sapkota, 1997). Other children's groups have since been formed throughout the areas where AAN is working to enable children to develop confidence and gain more control over decisions that affect their lives. These groups have about 15 members between 11 and 15 years old, with fewer girls than boys. Most meet monthly with an elected chair and treasurer and carry out a range of activities. Local community development workers (CDWs) and child group advisers support the groups. Consultation with the groups has become an important part of AAN's planning process.

Involving children in evaluating change

Children's groups have been involved in evaluation in a recent mid-term review (MTR) in Nawalparasi and Sindhuli, where AAN has been working for the last four years. A short evaluation study was also carried out with children in the area where, in 1995, the first children's groups were formed. Girls and boys from the groups participated in the process. Participatory techniques included focus-group discussions about changes, diaries to record the daily activities of children, and social maps to show which children went to school. The rapport already established between children and facilitators was a crucial factor in enabling children to participate in focus-group discussions: if a new CDW acted as facilitator, the girls and younger children in particular hardly spoke at all. After discussions, the children compiled their own reports.

Findings: how are children bringing about change?

By forming groups, the right of children to have a space to discuss their issues has been formally acknowledged. Adults in the community and AAN are beginning to listen to the children's groups, and participation in these groups has allowed children to develop skills, knowledge, experience and confidence. The Lahape group in Nawalparasi reported, 'One lesson is that any kind of work can be done by being in a group' (Development Area 2).

Increased schooling

A key problem identified by the groups was children being sent for wage labour, which prevented them from attending school. Their groups have raised awareness, for example through street drama, about girls' rights to education. They have directly persuaded male household heads to send girls and women to school, CLCs and ALCs. Some groups have supported children who cannot afford to pay school expenses, from the proceeds of group savings.

The studies also indicated a change in attitudes. Instead of saying 'Girls are meant for mending the walls of others' houses, so do not need to be educated', women now say 'If we educate our daughters ... they need not remain under anybody's domination. They would have support in case of difficulties' (Waiba, 1997: 12).

In comparing the past and present situations, Mahadevstan children's group said: 'In the past we were innocent and no one would listen to us, and they (adults) sometimes used to scold and dominate us. Now the situation has

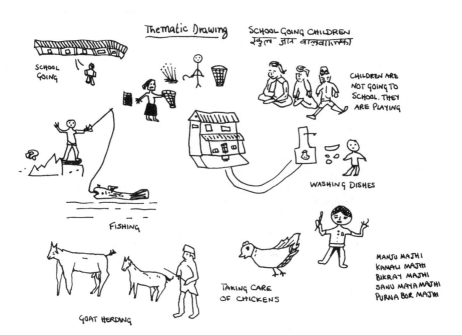

Figure 3.3: *Thematic Drawing*

93

changed: we are able to read, write and speak after completing the CLCs. We are able to solve our problems by ourselves because of the CLC' (Development Area 3).

However, AAN needs to help communities to work out ways of mitigating a negative impact on women's work-burden when children go to school by, for example, encouraging men to share the extra labour. The groups are having a positive impact, as shown by new children's groups starting in nearby villages after seeing the activities of children at Ghata. These groups are networking informally and sharing their ideas. Lahape children's group suggested, 'AAN should take children's groups to visit other children's groups, so that we can learn something new and become more active'.

Relations between children and adults
Relations between adults and children are critical in enabling children to participate: adults must be willing to share power and play the role of facilitating children's participation (Johnson *et al.*, 1995: 72). The review study in Sindhuli attempted to understand children's and adults' views of each other.

Children said that adults supported them but that they would appreciate more advice about their ideas. They had to work hard to convince adults that their activities were worthwhile: 'When we start any work, they oppose us at the beginning, saying that we will do damage, but when they start getting some benefit from whatever we have done, they say that we have done a good job!' (Waiba, 1997: 9).

Parents acknowledged that children had influenced them to adopt better personal hygiene and sanitation, and to vaccinate their children. Women said that children had become more confident. 'They were unable to speak and now they can speak ... We are fortunate they have changed in this way. We are hopeful that our children will have a better future from now on' (Waiba, 1997: 11).

Learning from working with children

Enabling factors
In-depth research reported in Johnson *et al.*, 1995 and the CCPR project led to a heightening of understanding about children's lives and views.

Work with the children's groups has enabled adults in the community and AAN to realize that children can plan and make decisions about their lives, that they can influence adults in the home and the community, and that their opinions are worth taking seriously.

A child forum of AAN staff has been set up to mainstream children's issues in AAN programmes, to ensure cross-programme learning and capacity building. Sponsorship officers have been sensitized on working with children, including child rights, and involved in a review of the outcome of AAN's work with children.

Challenges
AAN's experience shows that working for children's rights must be done alongside work with the rights of the poorest and disadvantaged adults. In

94

places where adults' participation is minimal because of their powerlessness, children's participation will take time to gain acceptance (Singh and Trivedy, 1996: 28). This has been vividly demonstrated in areas of Sindhuli where Maoist insurgency and the response of the authorities to it regularly interfere with human rights. The studies have shown that teachers are key players in enabling children's participation because they have status and respect from parents.

Another issue is the physical abuse of children. Whilst children report that parents more frequently express remorse over beatings inflicted when drunk, increased awareness of the importance of education has, ironically, led to greater acceptance of teachers beating their pupils. Children have a right to be free of any kind of physical violence and such power relationships need to be challenged.

A further challenge concerns girls' and younger children's participation which is hindered by shyness. Forming separate groups for them may enable them to build up their confidence.

Children's groups have to some extent encouraged a separate focus on children. There is still a need to involve children in the planning of the mainstream livelihood, savings and credit programmes with the poorest households. A review of this programme shows that success in increasing the income of a household as a whole (for example through goat-rearing) can have adverse impacts on the quality of life of girls, boys and women, for example, a greater work burden. AAN is beginning to make children visible by disaggregating all programme monitoring and evaluation indicators by age and gender to assess their impact on children's lives.

Integrating participatory approaches into formal and non-formal education can build up children's capacities to take part in decision-making and to convince adults of their capabilities. A programme using participatory techniques with children in literacy has been successfully piloted in Sindhuli (Sharma, 1997).

AAN's work with children has illustrated the importance of advocating children's rights to participation at the policy level. Following its ratification of the UN Convention on the Rights of the Child (CRC), the Nepalese government passed a wide-ranging Children Act in 1992. However, there is still no specific provision for children's rights to participation. There is potential to make a reality of children's rights, including their right to participation, through the Central Child Welfare Board and the District Child Welfare Committees (DCWCs) created by the act, but these have been largely inactive. One of the first responsibilities of the DCWCs is to analyse the situation of children and formulate policies and actions. As children's group networks develop, they will have the potential to lobby the DCWC to represent children's needs. AAN plans to play a role in facilitating such linkages.

A major focus for AAN in the future will be to work with partner NGOs to overcome some of these challenges to enabling children's participation.

3.8   Using matrices for health research with children

RACHEL HINTON AND RACHEL BAKER

This account looks at research with children in Nepal. It draws on work with refugee children in Jhapa, South East Nepal (Hinton, 1995) and street children in Kathmandu (Baker, 1996). These children were concerned with the health issues that affected their everyday working lives. During the course of the research, children contributed as both facilitators and participants. One way they explored health issues was through the use of matrix diagrammes. Both Hinton and Baker were conducting research as part of Ph.D programmes. They were also affiliated to NGOs which wished to learn from their research results. It was hoped that participatory methods would give children a chance to facilitate the research process and to have ownership over the results for use with policy-makers. The following account explains the context, scope and limitations of working with the children and highlights two variations of the matrix tool: a comparative rating of illness in Bhutan and Nepal over the year and a rating of illness and source of treatment amongst street children in Kathmandu.

Matrix rating as a seasonal calendar with refugees

The process of conducting participatory exercises with refugee children
The participatory exercises were carried out by a group of self-selected refugees, brought together after school hours. They were trained for several weeks, practising different exercises amongst themselves before trying out activities in the community. For each exercise, the tool to be used was discussed prior to going to the community. The students usually brainstormed the possible issues that might arise, such as different types of illness that might be chosen but left the selection of categories (such as illnesses) up to the community.

Matrix rating is a method for prioritizing issues. Rating can usually best be displayed through a simple scoring table with choices across the top and situations down one side. It can be carried out successfully in many situations, but often becomes complex with more than five choices. When matrix rating is conducted using months of the year or groupings to look at changes over the seasons, it is commonly referred to as a seasonal calendar. It shows information which varies with time in a repetitive (often, but not necessarily) seasonal way. Seasonal calendars indicate types of activity, when these activities occur and the relative significance of simultaneous events. They are a means of diagramming to show the distribution of activities or features such as the prevalence of illness, rain, food, expenditure or work-load. They were a good way of highlighting how seasonal activities had changed for the Bhutanese as a result of their becoming refugees. The calendar in Table 3.3 shows the occurrence of different illnesses as experienced by Bhutanese refugees in their camp compared to the situation in Bhutan. It indicates how the occurrence of diarrhoea, malaria and vitamin deficiencies varies through the year in Nepal and Bhutan.

Using visual tools with children

Seasonal calendars, as with other PRA tools, lend themselves to a participatory approach because all participants can contribute their particular knowledge and can represent it easily by drawing on the ground. Locally available tokens can be used symbolically.

When the diagram was shown to the whole class, participants noted that this method allowed the information to be presented in a report or discussion in a way that people can quickly understand. They pointed out, however, that the illnesses in the camps and in the surrounding villages may be quite different, and seasons rather than months might have been more appropriate time periods to put across the top of the chart. They believed that it gave a full and clear account of this group's opinion, which could easily be compared to the opinions of other groups.

Power and authority

Participatory research raises issues of empowerment and it was felt important that these were discussed with the children before they facilitated sessions. In Nepalese society, many people adhere to clearly defined cultural rules of hierarchy and lines of authority. Discussions with the children around these issues of power were, therefore, animated. Community reactions to the young people acting as researchers were mixed. In Nepal, status correlates closely with age, and this was sometimes reflected in the low priority discussion with children had on officials' agendas. However, in a refugee situation where days were empty of many regular livelihood activities, community members seemed ready to share their knowledge and understanding of health matters.

Understanding the PRA process – interpreting the results
The community members' motivation for involvement was also discussed in small groups and with individuals who had taken part in the PRA activity. It became evident that expectations had been raised by past stakeholder analysis and aid programmes. This resulted in biases in the information provided. However, the women argued that, with the children as researchers, the biases generated were moderated by the perception by both researcher and researched that this was a learning exercise, not an aid-project assessment.

Through these discussions it became clear that participants also had their reasons for an interest in health. It is important to understand why people want to be involved and the background to their knowledge and interest in the topic under discussion. Women noted their particular concern with the issue of well-being. It was of paramount importance to them as they were responsible for the health of the entire family. One woman vocalized her opinion: 'Seeing these symbols on the ground makes it clear the [range of] illness we suffer here – I learn from the others' (Heema, aged 26). The older members of the community seemed to enjoy the interest the young students were taking in their knowledge, lamenting the demise of what they considered significant medical knowledge: 'Here so much is in the modern world. In Bhutan we used the home medicines, the learnt remedies – but the young ones don't

Table 3.3: Matrix rating (seasonal calendar) of illnesses experienced by Bhutanese in Chirang, Bhutan and Beldangi II Camp, Nepal.

Illness	Nepalese month											
	Vaishak	Jestha	Ashadh	Srawan	Bhadra	Ashwin	Kartik	Marga	Paush	Magh	Phalgun	Chaitra
	English month											
	Apr/May	May/Jun	Jun/Jul	Jul/Aug	Aug/Sep	Sep/Oct	Oct/Nov	Nov/Dec	Dec/Jan	Jan/Feb	Feb/Mar	Mar/Apr
Diarrhoea			γγγ γγ	γγγ γγγ γγγ	γγγ γγγ γγγ γ	γγγ γγ						
	ςςς ς	ςςς ςς	ςςς ςςς ς	ςςς ςςς	ςςς ς	ςςς	ς	ςς				ςςς ς
Malaria	γγγ γγγ γγγ	γγγ γγγ γγγ	γγγ γγγ γγγ γγγ	γγγ γγγ γγ	γγγ γγγ γ	γγγ γ	γγγ	γ				
			ςςς	ςςς ςςς	ςςς ςςς	ςςς	ςς					
Vitamin B deficiency	γγγ γ	γγ	γ									
	ςςς ςςς ςςς ς	ςςς ςς ς	ςςς ςςς ς	ςςς ςς	ςςς ς	ςςς ς	ςςς ςς	ςςς ςςς	ςςς ςςς	ςςς ςςς ς	ςςς ςςς ς	ςςς ςςς ςςς

March 1994, Nepal. 'γ' in Bhutan, 'ς' in camp. PRA Participants: Dhan Maya Luitel, Heema Biswa, Madan Kumari Giri, Prabha Gurung, Dhan Maya Baral, Renuka Devi Nepal.

learn that nowadays' (Renuka, aged 56). The sharing of traditional know-ledge, even in a more formal manner, was valued as an activity in its own right. One indication of this was the way in which the research output was kept and displayed by the community members.

Example of a matrix rating with street children

Background
The matrix rating technique gives more information than a simple ranking table. It shows the extent of the differences, not simply their order of importance (see Table 3.4).

Discussion

When exercises are conducted in groups, individuals may be influenced by the presence of more vocal members, so while facilitating this research the age and status differences of group members were noted. These affect inter-personal relationships and discussion. Some children may also shape their responses to please the facilitator, particularly when the adult is associated with the NGO programme they are involved with or when it is aimed at bene-fiting them. To try to reduce these biases, children rather than adults can con-duct the exercises and act as facilitators. The exercise can also be adapted so that participants are each given a certain number of counters which they can place in boxes according to their own preferences. It is a vital part of participatory research to encourage discussion of the process, and to record any concerns. The way the data are collected, and the comments made, are at least as important as the data themselves. It is clear that a matrix exercise carried out by different groups and different facilitators within the community may produce very different results.

Pitfalls and potentialities of using PRA with children

Documenting the process – whose voice is represented?
Documentation of the process has been neglected as the focus on 'how to do' dominates data collection. Group exercises are seldom created with equal contributions from all present. The presence of external actors, interpersonal relations and power differentials all affect the information offered. How such data are then read and translated, and whose voice they represent, are rarely reflected by knowing who is present. All too frequently lists of members exclude the posts, relative positions and contributions made by the contributors. The skills and tools required to take note of the power relations and interactions moulding information generation require considerable attention. Table 3.2 provides a basic trigger for the recording of process during a PRA activity. The older children became good at critical awareness and observation; the younger students were, however, more interested in obtaining a result and in joining in the visual game. It was also culturally inappropriate for them to be critical of elders and to record this on paper.

Table 3.4: Impact of illnesses and action taken, compiled by street children who rag-pick and live in a junkyard

Illness	Boil	Dog bite	Wound	Scabies	Diarrhoea	Hit by vehicle	Cold	Fracture	Hunger	Fever	Total
Frequency	4	5	5	3	5	2	5	3	5	3	40
Degree of pain	5	4	3	3	3	5	2	4	5	5	34
Effect on earning	5	3	1	0	5	3	2	5	2	5	31
Treatment sought at/with	Free homeopathic clinic	NGO clinic/state hospital	NGO clinic	Non; friends	Non; friends	NGO clinic/ junkyard owner	None	NGO clinic/ state hospital	Friends/ junkyard owner	Homeopathic clinic	

Source: Hinton (1996).

100

Transparency
Particularly when working with children the issue of making objectives, aims and purpose transparent is not necessarily an easy one. Children are skilled at interpreting what is said to find a hidden meaning. Explanations given are, therefore, sometimes not taken at face value. One way of clarifying what children believe the research to be about is for them to explain to a third party the purpose of what they are doing. Understanding of complex issues may be revealed through open discussions around the topic of hidden agendas and cultural confusions. Such transparency may make apparent reasons for local people's involvement that were unexpected and previously unspoken.

Working with schoolchildren
Children who are socialized in a school environment often find an intrinsic value in participating in PRA research. They have been taught to rate highly the acquisition of knowledge, and learning new skills is prioritized and valued. However, they may also have been taught to feel Western values are more acceptable than local ones, as was made evident with one PRA activity undertaken in Jhapa. A group of schoolchildren conducted a seasonal calendar amongst a group of refugee women. That evening they presented their findings to the other students. In writing up the two divisions of the year drawn by the women, the children had translated these wet and dry seasons into 12 Western months – creating completely new categories. Interestingly, children in the camps often choose to use the more mathematical PRA tools, such as bar charts and pie diagrams, than transect walks and sociograms. Such experiences remind the researcher both of the diversity of experiences within a community and that assumptions, biases and expectations are not always dispelled just because the importance of using local descriptions has been explained and discussed. Constant checking and presentation back to the community itself is necessary for a valid understanding of a situation.

Ethical issues and the validity of data
In many contexts, children stimulate support and co-operation from adults. The research environment is no exception. Children's ability to elicit assistance moves beyond domestic boundaries. Their ability to act as the facilitator and discuss issues in an informed and constructive way often surprises the observer. 'When talking with children people adopted a more open manner – they did not seem to draw boundaries'(Suk Maya, 42-year-old Nepalese facilitator). The concern and hesitance to speak freely to adults was further reduced when children took the leading role in the research, since they were both junior and insiders. Children's perceived subordinate position in the community and relative lack of power results in a dispersal of many of the barriers external facilitators encounter when conducting participatory research; however, their relative lack of power also makes exploitation of their involvement a real possibility. Children often feel an obligation to be helpful or are inhibited from voicing their true feelings. Many of the children made their interest explicit. Some spoke of improving their English by working with a *bideshi* (foreigner), some of learning how to interview with pictures (Susma, refugee aged 14). On occasions the researchers provided material incentives such as snacks after the activities. Others enjoyed the reversal of

roles, from student in the classroom to facilitator in the community. The children enjoyed comparing their experiences and being able to represent them visually (Baker, 1996: 57).

Lama aged 15 stated simply: 'We enjoy meeting and learning together'. Despite preparatory discussions, some children retained high expectations of immediate further action. Baker (1996: 60) notes street children's expectations of full health examinations and treatment. Time and space to allow children the free choice as to the extent and nature of their involvement is essential, but it may be argued that research will always lead to unmet expectations. However, attempts to understand children's motivation for involvement is important, as is providing them with the necessary tools for meeting their own health needs. The ethical implications of children's involvement in research is an issue of considerable debate (see Baker and Hinton, forthcoming). Researchers have a responsibility to assess at every stage the ethics of children's participation. Informed consent is a term that could be applied equally to the community respondents as to the children themselves.

3.9   Involving children as equal participants with adults in community-wide participatory planning and research

ANDY INGLIS

Most discussion about children's participation seems to concentrate on processes involving children only. This may be desirable or necessary for some areas of research, or in planning children-only facilities. However, when the objective is to involve children in issues that affect the whole community, there are many advantages in using processes and tools that enable children to be equal participants with adults; for example, in the setting of the agenda, the generation of ideas and preferences and the analysis of outcomes.

These processes have the universal objective of Participatory Rural Appraisal (PRA), that of enabling what Robert Chambers (1997) calls 'lowers' (usually meaning disenfranchised, less-confident adults) to have input on an equal basis with 'uppers' (dominators, powerful few). My experience has shown that processes which enable less-confident adults to participate also empower children.

Some examples of joint children and adult processes with the above features, which I was involved in designing, training or facilitating, include:

- an economic revival strategy evaluation and development process in the Welsh valleys;
- the development of neighbourhood plans for a Greenway system in Ottawa;
- participatory planning and monitoring and evaluation in Somalia and Albania;

- the analysis of present situations and development of plans for the future in urban and rural Scotland, and
- participatory land-use planning in South Wales.

Visualization of analysis and outcomes by participants

Objectives for the outcomes of any participatory event should be established and agreed on before designing a process and selecting or inventing visualization methods to reach these objectives.

All methods should result in all of the outcomes being transparent, and in the handwriting, drawing or other presentational form of those who made them. If some participants cannot write and it is important that things are written, they should be asked to select a trusted friend to write for them. If it is not important that the inputs are written, then drawing their meaning is fine.

Copies and/or photographs are taken of the outcomes. These form the basis of any report with typed text describing what the participants were asked to do, why and what is said on the map, diagram, post-its and so on.

If the facilitators feel that the verbal discussion generated is more important or pertinent than what it being put on paper, this is usually an indicator that the visualization method needs to be modified or redesigned, or a different method used or invented to reach the objectives.

No note-taking or analysis by facilitators
Note-taking by the facilitator introduces a number of opportunities for bias, distortion or error. The initial notes may not record the words of the participant(s) but their interpretation or adaptation by the facilitator. The potential for bias, distortion and error is high when adults are taking notes of what children are saying, as they may change the phrasing, grammar and even words. The notes may even be unreadable later on.

It is difficult to enable participants to read all the notes taken. This means that they cannot be checked and verified *in situ*. It is therefore impossible to obtain permission to show them to others or to publish them, unless a traditional, and not very empowering, draft reading and clearing process is undertaken some time later.

Box 3.4: Features of processes that enable less confident adults and children to participate

- facilitators should attempt to have 100% visualization of analysis and outcomes by participants;
- facilitators should not take notes or analyse *in situ*;
- the planning and facilitating of an effective outreach strategy to reach all sections of the community, and to enable people to work in small groups or as individuals, in places where they can be secure, comfortable and relaxed; and
- not giving any scope or opportunity for confident public speakers (adults or children) to dominate any event.

It is especially important not to bias or distort what participants in conflict or post-conflict situations say. Misinterpretation or misquoting could lead to serious consequences for the individuals involved, particularly the local person but perhaps the facilitator, too.

Planning and facilitating an effective outreach strategy

Many societies are divided into two types of people: those who go to public meetings and those who do not. In some countries, the latter group is bigger. If processes that intend to enable local participation are based only on meetings, then these people, adults as well as children, never get heard. Even some of those who do go to meetings never say anything, as the agenda and inputs are dominated by a few confident, vocal and often powerful individuals.

It is important to reach all sections of a community, especially 'lowers', and to enable those involved to work in small groups or as individuals, in places where they can feel secure, comfortable and relaxed. Depending on the local context, examples of such places include: street corners, clubs, play areas, pubs, shops, arcades, under shade trees, gang huts, doorsteps, kitchens or front rooms in houses, mothers' and toddlers' groups, hairdressers, waiting rooms, cafés, libraries and common rooms.

When working with children, schools may not be the best places to hold participatory planning or research events. They tend to be formal, adult-controlled settings, with an underlying culture of children trying to give adults the answers that will impress or please them, rather than expressing what they are really thinking. In addition, only a few pupils, typically the most confident, can be selected and put forward for the event by teachers, who want to put the school and/or their class in a good light. In extreme cases,

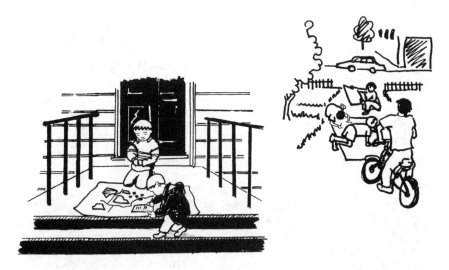

Figure 3.4: *Source: Outreach – Edinburgh Greenspace appraisal, Scotland, Susan Guy*

this has resulted in middle-class children, who live elsewhere, being involved in planning for poor inner-city neighbourhoods.

In many ways, the micro-cultural aspects of the participatory work setting need to be taken into account more than the external cultural norms, when designing participatory research, planning and evaluation processes. In other words, the culture of the micro-environment can be a greater determinant of whether participation will happen effectively and productively than the culture of the wider community/society.

No scope or opportunity is given for confident public speakers (adults or children) to dominate any event

After going to the trouble of getting all outcomes visualized and not dominated by a more confident or powerful few, it is important to allow the sharing and interpretation of the outcomes to be as enjoyable and accessible to as many people as possible.

Both children and adults who do not normally get involved are happier describing and discussing something they have produced, rather than purely abstract verbal interchanges. These sessions should be as informal and as comfortable as possible. Focusing feedback on the visualization outcomes reduces the risk of any individual dominating the discussion or hijacking the process.

The design and process of further analysis of outcomes will also be most effective if it has the features described above.

Where there is not a good reason to keep children and adults separate, it can be far more enjoyable and productive, in both the short and long terms, to design participatory processes that allow both to participate as equals. If processes are designed well, children of most ages are definitely capable of taking part as equals in community-wide participatory planning. This has more value than the use of processes designed specifically for children.

3.10 The Children's Theatre Collective of the Philippine Educational Theatre Association

ERNESTO CLOMA

The Philippine Educational Theatre Association (PETA) was founded in 1967 with a vision of the role of Philippine theatre in the development of people and society. Over the period of Martial Law (1972–86), PETA was actively participating in the emergence of a people's theatre committed to social change, lead by artists, teachers and leaders. From 1986–7, it embarked on a world tour, 'Oath to Freedom', to share the people's triumph after 14 years of martial rule.

Through its repertory company, PETA has performed over 200 productions. The School of People's Theatre has provided training and developed curricula for amateur, community and professional theatre groups. Theatre in Education, Children's Theatre Collective, (CTC), Women's Theatre Collective and the Metropolitan Theatre League have initiated theatre organizing and networks, giving birth to hundreds of drama groups in schools, parishes, communities, sectors, regions and migrant groups. This experience has been shared locally and globally through PETA's library, archives and publications, film and broadcasting, and participation at conferences. It is active in a national theatre movement inspired by the ideals and vision of nationhood, global understanding, respect for persons, democratization and greater participation of the people in theatre, culture and social change. At present PETA has 40–50 active members, from the ranks of media artists, writers, musicians, dancers, teachers, other professionals, students, workers and out-of-school youth.

The CTC is a group of artists and teachers who specialize in children's theatre geared towards the development of the Filipino child. It works closely with many other agencies with similar objectives. Its activities include workshops and training for child advocates, child-care workers, teachers and children, and the production of children's plays acted by children from community groups.

Some examples of PETA–CTC experience

In 1988, PETA-CTC began a partnership with Salinlahi Foundations Incorporated (SFI), an alliance of children's organizations working for the Rights of Children. CTC organized creative workshops with children on issues that concerned them, including rights, situations of armed conflict, street children, child labour, sexual exploitation and children with special abilities. Most of the participants were aged between 10 and 16 years and had various degrees of experience of the issues. Large gatherings of children's groups and organizations were held, including Children's Solidarity Day (1989–93), Children's Art Camp (1991–7) and the Children's Theatre Festival (1992–6).

Bahay Tuluyan (BT) runs a drop-in centre for street children in a tourist area. CTC's work with BT gave birth to a group of street children who were more confident, analytical and able to express their thoughts to other children in the streets. These children have become street educators who hold discussion groups and play activities with other street children. Themes range from personal problems to life experiences, families, rights and eventually an invitation to the children to join groups or institutions which will help them to give meaning to their lives or reunite them with their families.

CRC offers therapy to children traumatized by war. The psychologists have learned from CTC how to use art processes and techniques for healing children caught in armed conflict. Now older children who have taken part in workshops assist the therapist to heal others.

SFI lobbies for laws beneficial to children, who make presentations in front of the congress building and talk to law-makers. Children gain understanding of the real issues, and their perspectives are forwarded to the lawyers.

CTC worked with children from Smokey Mountain, a notorious dump-site where hundreds of families live and collect items for recycling to earn a living. The children breathe in the toxic fumes from the dump, which affect their health. CTC collaborated with three organizations working with children to produce a piece of theatre, which was performed on the top of a 16-wheel truck. The following year the group toured refugee centres to perform the play and run workshops for displaced children.

The Metropolitan Teen Theatre League is composed of 20 young people between the ages of 15 and 20 years at school or college. PETA has trained these young people to organize schools and communities to produce theatre and the annual Youth Theatre Festival where plays written and produced by young people on issues relevant to them are performed.

These CTC experiences reveal the immense potential of children to discover more about themselves and their society and to do something to improve the existing social conditioning.

Children's participation using theatre pedagogy

It was natural for PETA-CTC to use theatre pedagogy in its training and partnerships. The experience over the years of working with the Salinlahi network of institutions followed a cyclical pattern of activities with adults and children (see Box 3.5). Some groups have undergone the whole cycle of activities, whilst others went halfway and then took their own course of action to meet their institutional objectives. Most groups gave birth to a core of child leaders aged 14 to 18 years who lead and implement activities for play groups, supported by their institutions.

Consultation and studies

This stage usually starts with an organization feeling the need to solve a problem or reduce the burden caused by an issue that affects children. Children are also consulted about their thoughts and feelings on the issue. This is followed by two or three study meetings to gather relevant materials and facts, and reach a common understanding for developing the work programme. The studies help to build modular activities for children to deepen their understanding of the issue in the follow-up workshop.

The study workshop for adults and children lasts for one or two days and use various artistic approaches, amongst them visuals, movement, drama,

---

Box 3.5: Framework for children's participation using theatre pedagogy

1. Consultation and studies
2. Programme of activities
   a) workshops and skills training
   b) production
   c) educational package
   d) junior trainers' module
3. Children leading other children
4. Institutional initiatives

---

songs and games. The outcome is usually a list of activities that children would like to take part in to help raise consciousness of the issues, particularly among other children. Since the fun, camaraderie and analysis of the issues were done through theatre processes, these are usually what they recommend.

Programme of activities

Workshops and skills training
These last for one or two weekends. The children are exposed to creative drama, writing, music and sound, movement and visual arts, all carried out in dynamic, participatory and evocative group processes. The story is woven from the sharing and creative improvizations of the children. The drama facilitator or adult playwright guide the older children, or those who wish to be involved, to write the creative products as a cohesive scenario. The resulting storyline is dramatized and presented in theatre styles chosen by the children, usually involving singing, dancing and visuals.

Production
The theatrical production is usually presented at the end of the workshop. If the children want it to be shown to other groups, it is polished with the same cast guided by a theatre director. The children receive additional skills training, including how to facilitate group discussions for the educational package.

The educational package
This is usually a performance followed by a workshop. The performance usually lasts for 45 minutes to one hour, followed by a one or two hour workshop in which the performers lead activities on the issue.

Junior trainers' module
This process is for institutions that want to use art processes with their junior street educators, facilitators or play-group leaders. Children are given training in communication, planning and organizing skills. The module is capped by the actual conduct of workshops or discussion groups with street children or other children's groups with an interest in the specific issues or objectives of the programme.

Children leading other children

This stage may come straight after the workshop, or after a production for more children or the junior trainers' module. Children may organize play groups, or activities that they wish to implement with other children.

Institutional initiatives

These are activities programmed by particular institutions to enhance the participation of children and give them the space and time to develop themselves further by conceptualizing and initiating new developments.

Box 3.6: Case study: tackling the problem of pollution

A theatre advocacy workshop was held with children from the Subanam tribe. Children identified mercury pollution in the river from gold panning as one of the key problems in the area. They interviewed old people in the community and then came up with a story and drama ideas about the issue. The theatre artist developed a drama from the story and taught the children theatre skills. The performance was shown in the village where the children had interviewed the old people. The children then decided to show the drama to a municipal board meeting.

The main objective of the process was to increase children's confidence and skills so that they can express their opinions and be more articulate. The theatre by itself may not change society, but more articulate children and adults provide hope of change.

Last thoughts

As children enter the world, they discover the extent to which they are able to influence events by cries and movement. In infancy, they discover the extent to which their own voices influence the course of events in their lives. But this is also influenced by the culture in which they live. The same culture that helps children to develop themselves and chart their destiny may also stunt their growth and development and trap them so that they are powerless to change things. But when children come together for a creative workshop, a reservoir of creative energies is drawn out; inner resources are tapped and minds are opened, helping children to find both exciting alternative solutions to problems and inner visions to pursue. Children become resourceful and sensitive, so that they can lead and participate in change.

3.11   Workshop to share experience on children's participation

ANDY INGLIS

The day began with an icebreaker, in which participants were divided into regional groups and invited to introduce themselves to each other using the greetings typical of their culture. Participants then formed a circle and each person described themselves with three words and one gesture: their name, country and an action depicting something they enjoyed doing. The rest of the group then repeated together the words and action.

The objectives of the session were outlined: to share our experiences of working with children only and with children and adults together; and to consider examples of good practice and lessons learned from working with children. Participants were asked to break up into small groups according to the month of their birthday. Three groups discussed question one and the others discussed question two, as follows:

Q1) In thinking about research with children, share one example of good or any practice of working with: children and adults together; and children only.

Q2) What difficulties have you had involving children in research and how were these difficulties overcome?

Participants shared examples of good practice and lessons learned from around the world, using post-its. Key points, outlined below, were written on flipcharts and displayed for viewing:

- Children and adults must be given full and honest information both about who is initiating the research and its objectives, process, end results and potential benefits before the research starts. Only then can they decide whether to commit time and energy to participating and give informed consent. They must also feel free to opt out of the process or parts of it at any time.
- Children's motivations for participating may be different to those of adults.
- Children should be involved in planning the research agenda, questions, methodologies, analysis and action planning.
- Children may reveal problems or issues that are denied by adults, put them in conflict with adults or are not reflected in the research or programme agenda.
- Concepts of childhood vary and this affects children's level of participation. In cultures where children are to be 'seen but not heard' or seen as helpless victims, it is difficult for adults to accept that they should participate in decision-making. Adults need to change their attitudes towards children and realize their capabilities at different ages.
- The question of which children participate in research is critical, both in terms of being present and taking a positive part in activities. Gate-keepers, female gender, young age, heavy workloads, poverty, disability, low literacy, remote homes and lack of confidence can all act as barriers to participation.
- Gate-keeping by adults in the private and public sphere can form barriers to children's participation. This can be protective of the children or reflect authoritarian attitudes or fears of children disclosing sensitive information.

Figure 3.5: *Gate-keeping*

- Participatory research can expose children to risk if they are encouraged or pressured to reveal sensitive information and confidentiality is not assured. This is difficult to achieve in public group settings.
- Considerable time is needed to access and establish rapport with children, involve them in planning research and enable them to work at their own pace. However, time is a scarce resource for donors, researchers, families and children, particularly poor working children.
- It is important to find places where children feel comfortable, relaxed and secure to work individually or in groups.
- Methods should be designed to reflect the age, capacity, culture and literacy of the children, the issue concerned and the context. They should be enjoyable and ideally designed by the children themselves.
- The personal qualities of the facilitator and the level of rapport established are key factors in enabling children to participate actively in research. Gender, age, culture, language, empathy, and communication style and skill are important.
- Adults often organize the empirical data of children into their own epistemological framework, beginning with a transformation of children's words during note-taking. This outsider interpretation introduces serious bias.
- Trustworthiness of data may be a problem if peer pressure or a desire to please adults prevents children from expressing their real thoughts and feelings.
- A belief in the value of children's participation and their right to be involved in planning that affects their lives needs to permeate institutions at all levels.
- Participatory research and planning with children can create more equal relationships between adults and children, so that adults value children's knowledge, skills and experience and children become more confident, aware of their rights and able to take part in the democratic process.

Working with children and adults together
Critical elements include the importance of ownership by children and their involvement from the planning phase of the research. Adults should support children but also allow them adult-free space. Adults often dominate when children and adults work together. This can be overcome by working with separate groups of children and adults before bringing them together. Children's confidence and skills need to be built before working with elders, and adults need to become more sensitive to children and less impatient with them.

Graphics, video and photographs are good ways of enabling children to express themselves. There is, however, a risk of manipulation of the final product.

Working with children only
If children's skills are not developed sufficiently, they may be unable to cope with feelings such as anger that arise in facilitating discussions or to prevent some children dominating others.

Figure 3.6: *'We divided into continental groups (Africans, Asians, Europeans, Latin Americans, etc.) and each group greeted the others using the words and gestures of their culture.'*

3.12   Conclusions

GILL GORDON

Many different processes and methods for participatory research with children are described in this part and the importance of flexibility in their use is emphasized. The authors identify a number of key factors to consider when processes and methods are designed for work with children. These should:

- enable less-confident and marginalized children to participate fully in all stages of the research;
- build the skills and confidence of children so that they become more capable of participating in democratic processes and advocating for their rights and needs;
- enable children to own, analyse, document and present their work to others including those in power and their peers in other places; and
- stimulate creative ideas, new visions and options for the future.

The additional effort required to create processes and methods that achieve these objectives is worthwhile in terms of research and empowerment outcomes.

Less-confident and marginalized children may include girls, young children, non-literate children, ethnic minorities, poor working children, those living in remote areas and the disabled. The papers in this part have given a range of suggestions on process and ways of achieving this.

The age and sex, credibility, skill, patience and empathy of the facilitator are crucial in enabling less-confident children to express themselves. Shy children talk more easily with people they know than with strangers and time must be spent building rapport, explaining the purpose of the activity carefully and getting to know each other through games. Children may relax and express themselves more freely with child facilitators and without adults.

It is easier for children to participate in small single-sex groups of around six children of similar ages. Work in pairs or individually before presentation to the whole group gives every child an opportunity to express her/his own views. Sharing ideas with a partner enables shy children to rehearse their thoughts before presentation. Creating individual drawings before combining them in a group visual is less intimidating than drawing in front of the group. Role playing in pairs builds confidence for presentation to others. The children's own language should be used. If some children speak only minority languages, some way of translating needs to be found.

The methods used must take into account the age, sex, culture, literacy, experience and abilities of the children. Children are able to design their own methods if they are given the opportunity and these are likely to be more appropriate than those of adults. Even very young children can participate actively using play and methods suited to their stage of development. Girls and boys may prefer different methods of expression. If some children in the group have never held pen to paper, those who have been to school are likely to dominate the discussion. Drawing pictures and diagrams on the ground and using local materials such as sticks and leaves as symbols ensures that everyone understands and uses the same medium of expression. This will help people communicate their ideas more fully. Song, dance, role-play and the use of local arts such as clay modelling and cloth painting may work better than unfamiliar drawing conventions.

On the other hand, shy children who have been to school may prefer to write or draw their ideas on a square of paper than speak about them. This has been the experience in exploring issues of sexuality in some communities. Disabled children can also participate in activities that use their strengths. For example, deaf children could create tableaux or body sculptures without words. Video and photography have the potential for enabling less-confident children to select images that are important to them. The facilitator would have to ensure that the camera is handed over to quieter children and that more dominant children do not set themselves up as directors.

The micro-environment where the activities take place is an important consideration. Many children feel intimidated by public meetings or those held in school. There is a need to reach children more informally in places where they feel relaxed, comfortable and secure, for example a play area or place where children meet. This requires an outreach approach rather than waiting for children to come to a central venue, often a school. If children are given disposable cameras they are free to use them at their own pace in places they consider significant.

Figure 3.7: *Children as social actors*

In terms of presentation, it is often easier for less-confident children to describe and present a visualized outcome of their work or to present an idea through role-play than just to express themselves verbally. The level of participation of different children will determine the outcome of the research in terms of validity and empowerment. This makes it as essential to record the group process as the content. Video allows for this and for subsequent review. This is a powerful way to demonstrate group interactions and power dynamics. Without the video, a check-list can be used to record who speaks and for how long, who 'holds the stick' and who is listened to. If children act as observers, they become more aware of the importance of group dynamics and can help the less-confident children to participate.

Different processes and methods build the knowledge, skills and confidence of the participating children. This is an empowering process that equips them for planning, decision-making and the articulation of their ideas to important people. Different methods build specific skills. The process generally has the potential to build communication skills such as listening, questioning, empathy, conflict resolution, negotiation and the expression of ideas. The facilitator can optimize this process by inviting the group to make ground-rules for their work, suggesting activities that develop communication skills and empathy, and drawing attention to the dynamics of the group. Drawing, literacy and performance can all be enhanced by participatory activities. Children who make their own video or take photographs gain new technological skills. All of these can empower children in their daily lives. In this way, the children who take part can benefit from the process quite apart from any other outcomes. Children who participate in analysis, documentation and presentation of their work acquire a range of new skills in these areas. Presentation to a wider group in particular can greatly increase confidence. Taking part in this participatory process will increase self-esteem.

When groups of children meet regularly to participate in research, planning, awareness-raising, advocacy and evaluation, they develop confidence and skill. Especially if they meet over a long period of time, they are likely to gain far more confidence than those who participate in a one-off PRA event. This can have an important impact on adult-child relations and finding solutions to local problems

There is need to pay more attention to children's participation in the analysis, interpretation, reporting and presentation of outcomes. Too often, children engage in participatory activities that enable adults to take notes on their ideas and analyse, document and present them to others in their own epistemological framework. This can seriously distort and bias the children's perceptions of reality. It also deprives them of an opportunity for further skill development and empowerment and for sharing their learning with family, peers, community and others with an influence on their lives.

Total visualization of analysis and outcomes of the research is one way of ensuring that children are the owners of their work and enabling them to present it to others. If the method used is well designed, there should not be any need for an adult to take additional notes. Performance methods allow children to present their analysis and outcomes to others. However, there may be constraints of distance, time and cost if they wished to show it to a range of people from neighbours to policy-makers. This problem can be overcome by making audio or videotapes for wider dissemination, even on national networks.

Photo appraisal can involve children in analysis, documentation and presentation of their reality. They comment on the photographs and select them for presentation elsewhere. Video made by children reduces the scope for bias because there is less selection and no codification. The children present their perspectives through the video. This opens up participation in analysis and interpretation. If it is necessary to edit video material because of time constraints, the children themselves should do this. The use of video for the presentation of reports of participatory activities in the field allows all the stakeholders, including the children, to see the same material in a much more equal way than the written word. Video has enormous potential as a process for empowering children to produce their own material and use it for advocacy, negotiation or influencing their peers to take action. It makes it possible for those in power to hear the views of the normally invisible and silent. This can create a feedback loop if the response of this audience is also filmed so that the short- and long-term impact of the process can be captured.

Children can advocate for their rights by producing hard-hitting general audience television programmes for national networks. The challenge is to enable less literate, poorer rural children to take part in producing media that reach their communities with their own problems. Radio and drama are two possibilities.

Visuals, photographs and video all have the potential for manipulation by adults and endangering children in closed societies. Ethical issues relating to the ownership, analysis and use of information must be brought to the attention of children, discussed and agreed; these should be reviewed as the work progresses in case new issues arise.

The importance of creative solutions to problems, alternative options and new visions is increasingly recognized in planning and management. The surfacing of new perspectives is empowering in the situations of many children, who may feel trapped by difficult circumstances. Different processes and methods may stimulate varying degrees of creativity. Experience will show which methods offer the greatest potential. Theatre and the performance methods appear to allow the imagination more freedom than the more mathematical diagram techniques. Brainstorming practices, such as the Margolis wheel, allow everyone to suggest options, however crazy, without editing.

There are programmes that may be specifically targeted to improve the lives of children, but monitoring and evaluation indicators developed to track progress in broader development projects should be disaggregated. In this way, the impact of all development programmes on children's well-being will be made more visible. Participatory techniques are key to determining the most important criteria in the lives of girls and boys of different ages.

There is a need to work for the rights of poor and disadvantaged adults alongside those of children. Where adult participation is minimal because of powerlessness, it will take time for children's participation to gain acceptance. There are also advantages to involving children in mainstream development planning and rights' advocacy alongside elders. This can be achieved by using processes that enable children and less-confident adults ('lowers') to participate.

Researchers may wish to collect high-quality data by enabling children to carry out their own research, but may meet with decision-makers and funders who do not perceive this type of research as yielding hard facts. There is, however, as shown by the examples in this book, a growing body of positive examples where decision-makers have taken research *with*, as opposed to *for*, children seriously and have started to value this type of participatory research more broadly. This part has provided a lot of exciting and sound ideas for developing our work in a way that optimizes its value for the children who participate, and the programmes which are striving to enhance the quality of all children's lives.

Notes

1. With many thanks to Pashupati Sapkota, Krishna Waiba, Krishna Hari Paneru and Krishna Ghimire who provided information for this paper and to Chris Murgatroyd for editing.

PART 4

Culture: Attitudes and Perspectives

Editor and co-author: PAT PRIDMORE

Co-Authors: RACHEL CARNEGIE, KATE HARRISON, SAFA
HALASAH, CHRISTIANA OBENG, BARNABAS OTAALA, DAVID
STEPHENS, MARTIN WOODHEAD

Summary

Part 4 explores the interrelationship between culture and children's participation and challenges the acceptance of cultural norms which are contrary to the articles of the Convention on the Rights of the Child (CRC). It acknowledges the way in which the globalization of communication has facilitated the worldwide debate on children's participation and argues that, because culture is dynamic, cultural norms need to be constantly revisited and re-evaluated in relation to children's own lived experiences. Furthermore it argues that culture has been a neglected dimension in research and programme development and considers the way in which children's participation can serve both to promote their individual development and to facilitate adult education. It includes papers from Jordon, Ghana, Uganda, Namibia and Zimbabwe, and also has a paper including cross-cultural work conducted in Ethiopia, the Philippines, Bangladesh, El Salvador, Guatemala and Nicaragua.

Key issues raised in Part 4:

- Culture exists at both the personal and social level, being concerned with what particular individuals think, learn and do and also with what society approves of and considers important or meaningful.
- Increased sensitivity to cultural context needs to examine both the positive and negative aspects of culture.
- Culture is dynamic in nature and not static; it is strongly challenged by the forces of modernity.
- Account needs to be taken of not only the power vested in dominant cultures but also the issues of difference relating to sub-cultures within communities.
- Particular western constructions of childhood masquerade as scientific knowledge about children's 'nature', their 'normal' development and their 'universal needs'. These constructions render working children invisible or pathologize them.
- Within the school, culture operates at a number of levels and between the individuals and groups concerned. School culture can act as a barrier to children's participation.
- The way in which children's rights are conceptualized is relative to the specific context.
- Participatory learning and action (PLA) can influence positive change in street children's attitudes and their willingness to participate in socially useful activities.
- How youth see themselves within youth cultures needs to be understood as do the ways they can be enabled to be agents of change within subcultures and in the wider community.

4.0   Introduction

PAT PRIDMORE

Past failures in programme planning and implementation underscore the need for a systematic approach which fully acknowledges the importance of local contextualization. The key to such contextualization is a detailed and sensitive understanding of the cultural context. The term 'culture' can be defined most simply as the ways and reasons why people act. The need to understand the cultural context has been eloquently expressed by Francis (1993: 19):

> (Programme planning) should never be seen as the turning of a single key – rather, it involves finding out about the nature of a wide variety of locks and knowing how to make appropriate keys .... while we may know something about the keys, we are unsure of the nature of the locks in different social and cultural settings.

The challenge is how to identify and involve talented 'locksmiths' who understand both the nature of the locks and how to work sensitively with families and community groups. The innovative child-to-child approach to health education believes that children, together with their teachers, can become these locksmiths.

Figure 4.1: *'What is child abuse? ... hitting or hurting a child to relieve your own frustration.' (Redd Barna, Uganda)*

Four of the contributors to this part make reference to the child-to-child approach, which has been rapidly adopted and used in more than 80 countries over the last two decades. In common with the United Nations Convention on the Rights of the Child (UNCRC) adopted by the General Assembly in 1989, a central principle of the child-to-child approach is the right of a child to participate as a subject and not merely as an object of development. The approach stresses, however, the need to balance rights with responsibilities: 'Just as adult citizens have rights and duties towards health, so do children' (Hawes and Scotchmer, 1993: 16). Clearly the nature and degree of moral responsibility in childhood is a large and complex issue but child-to-child is surely right in recognizing the growing capacity of children to take responsibility for themselves and for others.

The child-to-child philosophy respects but at the same time challenges traditional attitudes to children's participation: it builds on a cultural tradition of children helping each other and their families and sharing their ideas but rejects the low position traditionally occupied by children in the social hierarchy; it supports the tradition of children as partners in child care and child development but also promotes them as partners in decision-making processes; it acknowledges that children should never be put in a position where they are openly confronting the attitudes and values of their elders but aims to empower them as communicators of innovation in health and nutrition to families and communities; and it promotes traditional pedagogy in using song and dance but rejects traditional didactic teaching.

It has been argued (Pridmore, 1996) that this balancing of respect for tradition with commitment for change is in reality a sophisticated approach more easily understood in theory than applied in practice. Although child-to-child ideas are sufficiently flexible to be adapted to local cultural contexts there is a risk that in their adaptation the essence of the approach may be compromised or lost. It has been noted that concern for children has not always been evident in practice (Feuerstein, 1981). We shall see later in Part 4 that programmes may lack an understanding of the child-centred methodology promoted by child-to-child, which challenges children to think and to solve problems for themselves. It remains to be seen how far child-to-child can overcome traditional resistance to the principle of children as agents of change by those who do not share its ideas about children and their status in society.

The attention given to participation in Part 4, reflects a growing international interest in the concept. This interest has been strengthened by an explicit endorsement of the concept in the World Declaration on Education for All (WCEFA, 1990), Article 4 of which states: 'Active and participatory approaches are particularly valuable in assuring learning acquisition and allowing learners to reach their fullest potential'. While the authors acknowledge the obstacles to be overcome in its implementation, their thesis is clear: participation should be a key concept in development strategy. We can start by acknowledging the dynamic nature of culture and by re-evaluating cultural norms.

4.1 Culture, education and development

DAVID STEPHENS

We are reaching the end of the UNESCO-inspired World Decade of Cultural Development (1988–98). The observance of this decade is evidence of a growing awareness around the world of the vital importance of the cultural dimension in any human, societal or developmental effort (UNESCO, 1991).

The decade had four aims. To: enrich cultural identities; broaden participation in cultural life; promote international cultural co-operation; and acknowledge the cultural dimension of development. This fourth dimension – the relationship between culture and, in this case, *educational* development – provides the fundamental underpinning of this paper.

The concept of culture in education and development

Given the obvious centrality of culture in our daily lives, it is a little curious to find it being referred to as 'the forgotten dimension' (Verhelst, 1987) and the 'neglected concept' (Smith and Bond, 1993). Culture in education and development seems to have come on to the stage rather late and to have emerged at a time of crisis in the world of development theory and educational change. Robert Klitgaard (1994) in his paper, 'Taking culture into account: from "Let's" to "How"' puts it well:

> If culture should be taken into account and people have studied culture scientifically for a century or more, why don't we have well-developed theories, practical guidelines and close professional links between those who study culture and those who make and manage development policy?

Two major reasons seem to be: the predominance of economic theories of development; and the narrow focus on developing the education system and concomitant dominance of 'school effectiveness' in educational thinking. This has left little room for any consideration of the interface between school and society and, more importantly, the life of the child who is both shaped by and shapes the culture in which she/he lives.

A cultural focus, we would argue, would assist us in recentering attention on what actually matters: namely the child and the community that sustains him or her. But if we are to use culture in this way it is important to have a workable definition. Much of what has been written about the term (and there has been an awful lot) seems to agree that there are two dimensions to the concept: first, that culture exists on both an individual and a social level, being concerned with what particular individuals think, learn and do and also with what society considers important or meaningful; second, that culture as a concept has come to relate to both the desirable and the descriptive, current 'value-free' use of the term much in favour with sociologists and anthropologists.

If culture is about individuals and societies and the way such people and groupings are described and evaluated, it is surely concerned also with ideas and beliefs held by those individuals, personally and collectively. Culture is therefore concerned with two things: the knowledge and ideas that give meaning to the beliefs and actions of individuals and societies; and the choice of method of enquiry which can be used to describe and evaluate that action. Culture is, then, both about what people think and do and how we describe and evaluate those beliefs and actions.

Culture as a means of improving children's educational experience

Desiring to place the child at the heart of the educational and development process is, therefore, a cultural decision. It is based both upon knowledge and ideas stemming from particular educational and philosophical traditions and the promotion of these views, particularly in diverse societies such as Britain. Early examples from the 1920s and 1930s of the success of child-centred participatory learning include the work of Maria Montessori's 'self-education' in Italy and John Dewey's 'teamwork' in the USA. This is eroding the practice of child-centred education in many so-called developing countries which accord traditional importance to hierarchy and deference to age.

Let us start with the first area of cultural knowledge and ideas that shape our understanding of children and the worlds they inhabit. Data are actually very close to hand. We all have a rich store of experiences about our own childhood, and many of us are brought into daily contact with children. What we need to do is to learn to listen to what they can tell us about their lives and to look to ways of building a store of knowledge and ideas grounded in the experiences of children past and present.

On a societal level much can be gained from examining literature (songs, proverbs and stories written by and for children) and from more qualitative educational research which puts the focus on understanding the processes rather than solely on the outcomes of schooling (Stephens, 1994). Such processes are intimately bound up with the experiences of the child and constitute the arena in which culturally- and child-sensitive development can occur.

The second area is bound up with what we want to achieve and how we propose to evaluate our actions. In exploring what can be achieved by schools it is useful to draw on conceptual models which can explain and offer guidance on ways forward. Per Dalin and colleagues (1993) (adapting Hodgkinson, 1983) suggest that schools can be viewed as operating on three levels:

- *the trans-rational*, where values are conceived as metaphysical based on beliefs, ethical codes and moral insights;
- *the rational*, where values are grounded within a social context of norms, customs, expectations and standards, and depend on collective justification; and
- *the sub-rational*, where values are experienced as personal preferences and feelings which are rooted in emotion and are basic, direct, affective and behaviouristic in character.

The researchers suggest that few schools are clear about their cultural values at the trans-rational level, though there are exceptions such as the Steiner and Montessori schools that consciously set out to educate a child in a particular way and articulate their ideology clearly. It is at the rational level

123

where most schools express their values through curriculum objectives, norms, rules and daily practices. If we are to ask schools to take a more child-centered approach to schooling we would need to analyse how decisions taken at this level impact on the experiences of the child.

At the sub-rational level individual teachers can play an important part in mediating values and norms at a personal level. Efforts to raise awareness of the child's perspective, the development of child-focused pedagogies and the importance of holistic teaching approaches that attempt to bridge the world of the school rest on teachers' reflexive understanding of the aims and objectives of their teaching and how their subsequent behaviour impacts upon the child.

Culture in the world of the school and the child: a new language of debate

In summary, it seems useful to identify a number of key facts when considering the incorporation of culture in education and development work. First, that any consideration of culture must acknowledge both the descriptive, i.e. what people think and do, and the normative, i.e. what values are attached to that description. Second, that data about children and schooling must come from children past and present and from sources sensitive to the worlds of children past and present. Third, that at the school level culture operates at a number of levels (the trans-rational, rational, and sub-rational) and between various individuals and groups concerned. The current concern with school effectiveness or improved assessment procedures is as cultural as is the context in which the debate occurs. Fourth, that in using culture we must be alert to the difficulties in both clarifying the complex and yet avoiding the oversimplification of what is a major yet potentially rewarding task.

4.2   Child work and child development in cultural context: a study of children's perspectives in selected countries in Asia, Africa and Central America

MARTIN WOODHEAD

A neighbour . . . took me away from the village to Dhaka . . . I didn't want to go . . . but . . . my mother forced me. The night before . . . I cried a lot. (Girl domestic worker, Bangladesh)

Our parents make us work. They tell us that we must go picking. That's what we're here for . . . to help with the work. (Girl farm worker, Guatemala)

We work to have food, if we stop working we will starve to death. (Boy lead miner, Guatemala)

No one forced me. I learned myself, out of curiosity . . . I had some friends, they went to get the material with their mother, I went with them and saw how they did the work, since then I've been working in my house on my own. (Boy making fireworks, Guatemala)

To work is a natural thing to do. Our friends do it. My parents work. My brothers work so why shouldn't I work? Even schooling is not an excuse not to work. (Boy fishing, the Philippines)

These five accounts are amongst many hundreds recorded as part of a Rädda Barnen (Swedish Save the Children) study into children's perspectives on their working lives (Woodhead, 1998a, 1998b). They illustrate the diversity of perspectives, from those who feel they are forced to work to those who believe they have made the choice to work.

This issue was addressed by the Rädda Barnen study alongside other key questions about the circumstances of work, the relationship of work to school, as well as the place of work in parental expectations and children's own self-esteem. Three hundred children (mostly aged 10-14 years) participated in the study that was carried out by local fieldworkers in four regions of the world (Bangladesh, Ethiopia, the Philippines and El Salvador, Guatemala and Nicaragua).

There are three aspects to the study:

- the background debate on child labour and child work;
- the case for a participatory study of children's perspectives; and
- the research methods used, especially the Children's Perspectives Protocol.

The Rädda Barnen study has been carried out against a background of international debate and policy-making about the detrimental effects that work can have on child development, especially work that is hazardous, abusive or exploitative (UNICEF, 1997). The UN Convention on the Rights of the Child (UNCRC) requires signatories to protect 'children from performing any work that is likely to be hazardous or to interfere with the child's education, or to be harmful to the child's health or physical, mental, spiritual, moral or social development'. Most recently a new Convention has been proposed by the International Labour Office (ILO) designed to 'Target the Intolerable' (ILO, 1996). These trends raise fundamental issues about what harms and what enhances child development for working children, as indeed for all the world's children, and how this knowledge should be used to inform interventions that are sensitive to local contexts. The case for protecting children from hazard and exploitation in every area of their lives (at work, in school or in the family and community) all too often becomes distorted by focusing on particular issues that offend modern Western sensibilities. The net outcome of context-insensitive intervention can be to damage rather than enhance their prospects, as in the case of Bangladesh garment workers thrown out of factories in order to satisfy consumer pressures for child-free products (White, 1996).

Natural childhoods, cultural childhoods?

I have been particularly interested in the part played in this process by 'expert knowledge' about what is normal and natural in child development. In an earlier study, I explored the possibility of reconciling universal assumptions about quality practice in early childhood with the relativistic diversity of contexts and beliefs (Woodhead, 1996, 1998c). My starting point for the project on children and work was a similar awareness that textbook accounts are based largely on the specific contexts and child-rearing values of Western childhoods. Play learning and schooling are staple topics, while work is rarely mentioned. Exclusion of working children as subjects for study cannot be justified even within the context of European and North American societies, where many more children work than is officially recognized (McKechnie *et al.*, 1996). In global terms their exclusion is absurd, given that according to UNICEF (1997) estimates, at least 190,000,000 children aged ten to fourteen years are working; 75 per cent of them the equivalent of six days a week. The consequence of expert myopia is that particular cultural constructions of childhood masquerade as scientific knowledge about children's 'nature', their 'normal' development and their 'universal' needs (Boyden, 1990; Burman, 1996; Woodhead, 1990, 1998d, 1998e). Working children are at best rendered invisible, at worst pathologized as living outside the definition of childhood. Rarely is explicit recognition made that the modern childhoods of which working children are said to have been deprived is a relatively recent and far from universal cultural arrangement for young humanity. That its dominant status now regulates childhoods throughout the world is a curious phenomenon.

If progress is to be made enhancing the lives of working children, it is essential to acknowledge that the 'child development' that the UNCRC, Article 32, seeks to protect is as much cultural as it is natural. Every child's development is constructed within a particular economic, social and cultural context. The definition of children's needs, and the process of meeting those needs, as well as protecting children from harmful influence, is profoundly shaped by beliefs and practices through which children are incorporated into their families and communities and which gradually become part of their own identity and self-esteem.

A rationale for context-appropriate interventions

The sociocultural status of child development is increasingly being accepted within the mainstream of the subject (e.g. Cole, 1992; Woodhead *et al.*, 1998). But there is a long way to go in recognizing the wider implications. A cultural, contextual approach to child development does not undermine strategies to reduce childhood poverty, increase educational opportunities and promote social justice, nor does it challenge international efforts to combat child labour in circumstances of exploitation and hazard. What it may do is alter the character of those interventions and the images of childhood that sustain them: it opens the door to more context-appropriate strategies and more creative solutions to the problems that face today's working children; it recognizes competing pressures and priorities for child development, especially in contexts of rapid social change which demand constant reappraisal of what is in children's best interests, for present and future generations; it acknowledges multiple stakeholders in the child-work debate, each with distinctive beliefs and goals for childhood; and it recognizes that children are the principal stakeholders, seeking to support their own efforts, in concert with families and communities, to improve their well-being and prospects, in their everyday struggle to survive, learn, and develop a sense of self-respect.

126

Children as participants in the child-labour debate

As the principal stakeholder, children are most affected by work that is hazardous and exploitative, and by any interventions designed to regulate or abolish the place of work in their lives. Taking account of their perspectives is important in at least four respects:

- Children have a right to be heard about matters that affect them. UNCRC Article 12 requires that signatories 'assure to the child who is capable of forming his or her own views the right to express those views freely in all matters affecting the child, the views of the child being given due weight in accordance with the age and maturity of the child'.
- Children are not affected passively by their work (too young and too innocent to understand what is going on). They are for the most part intelligent, active contributors to their social world, trying in their own way to make sense of their circumstances, the constraints and the opportunities available to them.
- Children are capable of expressing their feelings, concerns and aspirations within a context that respects their abilities and is adapted to their interests and style of communication.
- Children are an important source of evidence on how work may harm their development, in the particular economic, family, community and cultural context. While they may not be aware of certain detrimental effects (e.g. long-term health hazards) they may be acutely aware of others, and their concerns may be an important indicator, especially of the psycho-social effects of work.

Despite the overwhelming case for children participating in the child-labour debate, the adult world is not always eager to hear their voice. Notable exceptions during 1997 include the invitation made by the Dutch government for eight representatives of movements of working children to attend a meeting in Amsterdam, and the attendance of working children at a major international conference in Norway.

The Rädda Barnen study was designed to complement such initiatives. Fifty local workshops were organized where groups of working children were able to share their experiences, opinions and concerns. A feature of this study was that most of the young people had no direct involvement with child workers' organizations. A parallel study has focused specifically on the perspectives of working children who are involved in or supported by programmes in Bangladesh, El Salvador, Ethiopia, Peru and Senegal (Tolfree, 1998).

The Children's Perspectives Protocol

A specially designed Children's Perspectives Protocol, adapted to local circumstances, guided the groupwork to encourage young people to represent their feelings and beliefs in whatever ways were most meaningful to them, including drawings, mapping, role play as well as group discussion. At the heart of the protocol was a series of semi-structured activities and games focusing on key themes in children's lives. Many were based around locally produced picture-cards which participants were asked to compare, sort and rank, yielding a combination of individual and group responses. In brief, the activities were as follows:

'*My Day*' invited young people to describe their daily lives orally and through using drawings and mapping techniques.

'*My Work*' explored the circumstances of children's work and the detail of the activities they undertake.

'*Who matters?*' asked about young people's social networks, parental expectations, as well as their own self-evaluation.

'*Work and school*' asked what participants consider are the bad as well as the good things about their work, and then repeated the activity for school.

'*Which work is best?*' asked participants to rank children's occupations (including their own) in terms of relative desirability/undesirability, and explored the criteria on which young people base these judgements.

'*What is a Child?*' explored young people's own views on child development. They were asked to chart a wide range of work activities in terms of age appropriateness.

'*What if?*' presented young people with common dilemmas facing working children and invited them to comment on what might happen next.

'*Life-stories*' provided an opportunity to explore these issues with a particular child, in order to enrich the level of detail provided from group work.

While the fifty groups participating in the Rädda Barnen study cannot claim to be representative of the world's working children in the statistical sense, they do represent a wide range of working situations, with equal numbers of girls and boys, in rural and urban settings. Their occupations included lead mining, fireworks manufacture, weaving, brick-chipping, domestic work, market work, porters, street vending, shoeshining, fishing and associated trades, plantation and other types of agricultural work. Just as their experience of becoming child workers varied for each of these groups, so did their view of the place of their work in the future:

(We will be working on the farm) until we are very old and can no longer work nor grab the sickle . . . we will work until we die . . . until we are stiff.
(Boy farm worker, El Salvador)

My husband will say 'go break bricks. Work and feed yourself.
(Girl brick chipper, Bangladesh)

It cannot be the way it is now, it must be better. You know, when you are little, you think one way . . . but when you grow up (you realize) you don't even know what is going on.
(Street vendor, Nicaragua)

I've been doing this work for five years and I want to stop. When I leave here I'm going to the capital city to work.
(Boy making fireworks, Guatemala)

Figure 4.2: *'It's OK, the young people haven't gone crazy, it's just their sub-culture.'*

4.3 Using participatory approaches in schools: the experience of child-to-child in Uganda

KATE HARRISON

Child-to-child is an approach to health education based on the belief that children can be actively involved in promoting good health for themselves, their families and their communities. The approach links school and community through a series of activities known as 'the 6-step approach' (Bailey, Hawes *et al.*, 1992). In this way, school health knowledge is combined with finding out more from the community, with planning and taking action, and with evaluating its effectiveness.

The use of the child-to-child approach in primary schools is part of a wider movement initiated by the Uganda Government and non-governmental organizations. This includes promoting the use of more child-centred, participatory approaches in schools and community development, reassessing the nature of partnership between children and adults, and the role children play in society (Government of Uganda, 1992).

Child-to-child activities have many similarities to the methods used in participatory rural appraisal (PRA): visualization techniques such as mapping, small-scale localized research, and a commitment to shared decision-making, with the aim of giving children a greater voice in their community. However, child-to-child differs from PRA because it grew out of a very different discipline. While PRA was developed in non-formal, often agriculturally-oriented rural development, child-to-child grew out of more formal, school-based education, with the emphasis on health.

The study

In order to investigate the way in which the approach is conceptualized and practised by teachers and children in primary schools, a small-scale study was conducted in Uganda in 1997. The study used qualitative approaches, such as focus-group discussions with teachers and children, the draw-and-write technique, and in-depth discussions with teachers and co-ordinators of the child-to-child programme in Uganda (Harrison, 1997).

The findings of the study suggest that there is a wide gap between the ideal or rhetoric of child-to-child and the reality as practised by teachers and children. When co-ordinators were asked to describe how the approach works in schools, they described it in terms of children's empowerment, with children participating actively in their own learning:

> You will find a lot of initiative from the children themselves . . . you will find an atmosphere where teachers and children are working together, and the teacher is working as a sort of facilitator to help children think out ideas and activities.

> When you look at the child-to-child school, children initiate some of the things that take place in the school, and they go to the teachers and inform them.

However, teachers explained the problems they face when adapting to this new attitude towards children in schools:

> Teachers see children as people who receive information; children have the concept that they're just supposed to be filled and filled with information and ask no questions.

> Teachers may look at the child as somebody who can't do something without them, when they're not there.

Children described their concept of child-to-child in terms of their sense of duty and responsibility, using words like 'helping', 'caring' and 'advising', and drawing pictures illustrating children cleaning, cooking and fetching water. In contrast to the way the co-ordinators described child-to-child, children do not see the practice as a form of empowerment or joint decision-making.

It is clear that there is a wide variation in the way child-to-child is perceived by different groups. There is obviously a reality gap between the co-ordinators' idealistic view of how they would like it to operate in schools, the teachers' more realistic understanding of the problems they face, and the children's experiences of it on a day-to-day basis. This gap is not necessarily a bad thing. Idealism is an important force, and teachers who had worked with child-to-child for many years had gradually adopted many of the attitudes and beliefs shared by the co-ordinators. It is, however, important to be realistic about what is achievable in schools, which leads us to a consideration of school culture.

School culture

Schools have rules, written and unwritten, which taken together constitute school culture. This culture is created by the combined influences of education officials, head teachers, teachers, parents and pupils. Some aspects of school culture may support the introduction of innovative approaches:

- the institutional infrastructure;
- the existence of teachers as familiar and established figures in the children's lives (who are also trainable);
- the very fact that children are expected to come to school every day; which means in effect
- that they are a captive audience, available to take part in whatever new idea is being practised in school.

However, other aspects of school life may work against the principles underlying the use of participatory, child-centred approaches:

- school culture encourages task-oriented activity which fits into a predetermined lesson period;
- it encourages the idea that there is a right or a wrong answer to most questions, and that the teacher should define this;
- it is believed that the teacher should always be in control of what happens in a classroom; and
- there is a time-based element which pressurizes teachers – a lesson to be finished, a syllabus to be covered– which discourages the use of open-ended, exploratory activities.

Conclusion

The realization of the ideals promoted by child-to-child co-ordinators is, inevitably, a protracted process, an issue that is discussed elsewhere in this part. The fact that schools are well-established institutions, recognized by the community, with a deeply entrenched culture, may mean they are not the ideal place to try out techniques and approaches that may challenge long-held views about children. On the other hand, the potential of schools, as places where change may be initiated and supported with wide-ranging impact, means that their importance in community development should not be underrated.

4.4 Cultural relativity in Ghana: perspectives and attitudes

CHRISTIANA OBENG

This paper discusses some of the cultural values, views and attitudes that have helped to shape the lives of Ghanaians, and considers how these values could be modified by having children participate actively in community development. First, definitions of the terms 'culture' and 'cultural relativity' are offered.

Culture
Culture reflects the history and tradition of a people. It involves a set of guidelines for the management of recurrent problems, such as the need for food, shelter and clothing. It is also concerned with aspects of life such as religion, values and parenthood. In Ghanaian schools there is currently a strong emphasis on the teaching of culture as a subject to help pupils appreciate the country's cultural wealth.

Cultural relativity
Cultural relativists subscribe to an ethic of pluralism and in so doing seek to understand and appreciate cultures different to their own. In this view, no culture can be condemned in preference to another since the natural environment has a significant impact on the cultural adaptations of a society (Hess et al, 1988).

Cultural values: views and attitudes

Religious beliefs
Ghanaians are very religious. Most of them believe in the powers of lesser gods as well as in the supernatural God. The invocation of the names of these deities has to some extent prevented certain wrong-doings in the society. In the past, stealing or adultery were not even mentioned in conversation; it was believed that a guilty person could suffer a mysterious death. Modernization has diluted this value which had served to regulate people's actions.

Puberty rites
Puberty rites involve an initiation ceremony which ushers a boy or girl into adulthood. The Dipo custom of the Krobos in the Eastern Region of Ghana, for example, is an elaborate puberty rite for girls between 14 and 21 years of age. Its purpose is to provide preparatory training prior to marriage (Wellington, 1988). A teenage girl could be disowned by her parents if she became pregnant before the initiation ceremony. Parents feel a sense of shame for their inability to keep their daughters chaste before marriage. This is a very useful practice which controls teenage pregnancy and the general moral behaviour of youth. Some people, however, view this as backward, immoral and ungodly since girls, as part of the initiation ceremony, expose themselves (almost naked) to the full glare of all community members. These rites are

gradually losing their significance as some parents no longer choose to observe them.

Communalism

A high premium is placed on communal values by Ghanaians. This is because about one in ten households live in family houses or flats. Other people live in rooms or huts in compound houses (GLSS, 1995). These families share a common social life, care for each other and have a high level of interaction. A child in this society belongs to the whole community and therefore could be punished or rewarded by any member of the community for his or her actions. As a result of this communal ownership of children, a child can feel free to enter any household to discuss health issues with neighbours.

Children's role

Ghanaians consider children to be important because it is they who continue the heritage and name of the family. Despite this apparent importance of children both to the family and society, they have a subservient position and are expected to be humble, obedient and respectful of their parents. They are to be seen and not heard. Although many of these cultural values are positive, some destroy the initiative and creativity of the child, who is afraid to confront traditional norms and is thus unable to speak his or her mind easily. With the advent of modernization, some negative cultural values are gradually changing, especially in the urban areas.

Children's participation in research and programming

There is a Ghanaian maxim which states that 'A child breaks the shell of a snail and not that of a tortoise' (Gyekye, 1996). This implies that a child should behave as a child and not like an adult. If children do what grown-ups do, they will see what grown-ups see. With the existence of such cultural hindrances in Ghana, how are children going to maximize their God-given talents in the development of their nation? The child-to-child approach appears to provide an answer.

Child-to-child and children's participation

Child-to-child is an approach that seeks to bring children into partnership with adults to improve the living conditions of the community. It also initiates health action at the school level that is translated to the community. In order to address effectively the issue of children disseminating health information to their parents, education of the adult population is required. Awareness-creation programmes are organized for parents and members of the community, assuring them that their parental rights and responsibilities are recognized and would not be undermined as a result of the children's participation in activities. Child-to-child also involves children's participatory activities as individuals (I) or as a group (we). In areas, therefore, where it is difficult for children to advise, admonish or educate adults in a community as individuals, groups of children come together and give a presentation using activity methods.

This is an effective way for children to reach out to adults without fear of reproach. This approach was used recently at a community-awareness *durbar* (fair) organized by PLAN International – Ghana in Eyisam, a small community in the Mfantsiman District in the Central Region. In attendance were the entire Eyisam community and selected schoolchildren from six schools in six communities in the district. Representatives from the other five communities were also invited. The district ministries of health and education officials as well as PLAN staff were present. In all, more than 600 people attended. The schoolchildren educated the gathering on the causes and prevention of malaria and worm infestation. They used various activity methods such as role play, story-telling, songs, posters and recitals. The adults enjoyed this educational activity and the messages transmitted by the children were taken in good faith. Following the programme, some parents remarked 'We do not want children interrupting our conversation; however, we do not mind learning at their feet since they certainly know more about health issues than we do!' The knowledge, skills and the level of confidence exhibited by the children during the programme were testimony to the fact that children are effective change agents when given proper guidelines and supervision.

Exposure and children's participation
Children's active participation depends, to a large extent, on the level of their exposure to the world around them. Successful role models motivate them to improve themselves. Further, children in urban areas are open and speak their minds more easily than do their counterparts in the rural setting, without any fear of being reprimanded. This is because urban dwellers have access to modern technology (television, video and the Internet) and good schools with well-informed teachers. Rural children, are, by contrast more likely to be deprived of the basic necessities of life and are not abreast of developments in the wider world. Such factors should be taken into consideration when looking at children's participation.

Language barrier
Language is a powerful means of expression. Inability to communicate can suppress children's potential to play an active role in the developmental process. Recent studies by the Ministry of Education (1996) have shown that children cannot express themselves fluently in English. It is important, therefore, that the means of communication is familiar and understandable to children.

Programme content
In addition to the need for the content of a programme to be educative, cognizance must be taken of the norms of the society in deciding the choice of vocabulary. For instance, it is considered profane and deviant for a facilitator to mention sensitive words, like vagina, before one's elders during sex education. The question thus arises: How can children be involved in programmes that are difficult to broach without upsetting the sensitivities of the adults? The use of dramatic techniques to convey messages in a subtle manner may provide a solution.

Child motivation

Programmes should be fun and demonstrate sustainable benefits to the child. Recognition of success, through the awarding of prizes, can help to motivate children and inculcate a positive attitude.

Conclusion

Ghana is endowed with a vibrant culture that enriches the life of her citizens. In our quest as a people to involve children in the developmental process of the country, the inculcation of positive cultural values in children is vital. The potential of children to play a meaningful role in the nation's development must be affirmed.

4.5 Children's participation for research and programming in education, health and community development: selected experiences in Africa

BARNABAS OTAALA

Many critics of post-colonial Africa have not been complimentary in their observations on the education scene. In the area of educational research, for instance, they observe that the research has tended to have a replicative intent and an ethnocentric and particularly a Eurocentric stance (Otaala, 1995a). Much of the work done has been mainly for academic journals and has not been relevant to the solution of significant human problems of the day. For instance, child-rearing beliefs and practices in African cultures are extremely important in the growth and development of children, but not much account is taken of these in many of the programming activities on early childhood care and development in many African countries.

In the case of African and other Third World countries a number of international initiatives which have shaped thinking on children's issues include:

- the child-to-child movement which began in 1978, shortly after the Alma Ata Conference which launched the world-wide commitment to spreading the concept of primary health care, in preparation for the International Year of the Child in 1979;
- the ratification by the United Nations of the Convention on the Rights of the Child (UNCRC) in 1989;
- the Jomtien World Conference on Education for All in Jomtien, Thailand, March 1990; and
- the World Summit for Children, in New York, September 1990.

The CRC broadens the concepts of many civil and political rights to include children so that they may participate more fully, as appropriate, in decisions affecting their well-being (Articles 12–17, 30). The convention elaborates one of the central foci of this volume: rights of participation. It establishes several rights of participation for children, including the rights to:

- express opinions (particularly in official proceedings which affect them);
- free assembly and association;
- operation in culture and language;
- privacy; and
- access to information.

These rights are seen by many people as the most controversial guarantees in the convention. For some, the rights of participation are the most visionary and far reaching; for others, they go too far in the creation of rights without responsibility of adults to provide direction and guidance to inexperienced young people. Those who are wary of participation rights fear they could usher in an era where children could go as far as to take their parents to court for insisting on the completion of homework. At present, perhaps the greatest advance has been to consider, on its merit, the concepts of child participation in decision-making, and to broaden the discussion about the way issues affecting children should be addressed.

This paper examines some of the investigations conducted and reviews done in selected African countries, particularly since the inception of the international initiatives referred to above. Specifically we examine:

- child-to-child approaches in Namibia;
- preliminary studies on early childhood education and development in Namibia;
- investigations relating to children's rights;
- interpretation of 'the best interests of the child'; and
- children's views on children's rights and on teachers.

On the basis of this discussion there will be a brief exploration of strategies to improve the present situation so as to involve more active child participation in both research and programming.

Child approaches in Namibia

Child-to-child started as an international programme designed to teach and encourage older children, especially schoolchildren, to concern themselves with the health and general development of their younger brothers and sisters and of younger children in their own communities. The programme has grown from a few health messages to be spread by children into a world-wide movement in which children are considered as responsible citizens who, like their parents and other community members, can participate actively in the community, including in its developmental affairs.

The approach emphasizes that children need to be accepted as partners to promote and implement the idea of the health and well-being of each other, of families, and of communities. In so accepting them, they are helped to develop. The approach enhances their own worth both in their own eyes, and in those of adults. There is, therefore, a strong link with the idea of children's rights. One respects and works with them as partners.

The parallel between child-to-child and the CRC may not be immediately obvious, but the philosophy and work of child-to-child is in fact a practical expression of the convention's many provisions which seek to ensure children's survival, protection and development. Articles 5 and 14 of the convention speak of the evolving capacities of children; Article 12 refers to children's right to express views freely in all matters which affect them; Article 24 obligates governments to 'ensure that all segments of society, in particular parents and children, are informed, have access to education, and are supported in the use of basic knowledge of child health and nutrition, the advantages of breast-feeding, hygiene, and environmental sanitation, and prevention of accidents'. These extracts from the convention read like guidelines for a child-to-child project.

In Namibia, child-to-child was introduced formally towards the end of the first year of independence in 1990 (Mostert and Zimba, 1990) at a major workshop held in Windhoek, with participants coming from the health and education sectors, non-governmental organizations and communities. More recently, a series of workshops was held in both northern and southern Namibia (Otaala, 1994a, 1994b). During the workshops teachers and health workers have been provided with selected health messages which they have been able to pass on to older children who in turn have passed them on to their younger brothers and sisters, other children, their parents, and their communities. Selected child-to-child activity sheets such as 'Playing with Younger Children', 'Preventing Accidents'; 'Road Safety'; and 'Immunization' have been translated from English into Oshidonga for use by primary school teachers and children in Owambo Land, one of the most populous parts of Namibia.

Currently there is a pilot project to examine the workings of the child-to-child approach in colleges of education and selected nearby satellite schools. The monitoring of this project over a period of time would make it possible to assess better the potential of the child-to-child approach in health education, the potential of colleges of education in promoting such an approach, and the value of health education as a model for promoting more active, learner-centred, relevant and community-related learning in other areas of the curriculum, and within the school as a whole (Otaala, 1995b).

Child-to-child projects have also been conducted in other parts of Africa including eastern, southern, and west Africa, with positive outcomes. These have been summed up aptly by Vanistendael who observed that it was interesting to note that the methods employed in the child-to-child approach originated in Africa, in the Third World, where they are part of the educational tradition. He comments:

> For the first time, the experience of the South has been used to formulate an educational concept which is valid for both North and South. The immediate success achieved by this method in Africa is due to the fact that it is derived from practices already in operation there. (Vanistendael, in Tay, 1989: 3–4)

A more recent review of child-to-child programmes by Lansdown (1995) points to their achievements in many parts of the world. However, Lansdown indicates a need for in-depth case-studies, placing the activities into the wide, social, cultural and economic context of the community. A similar observation was made by Otaala, Myers and Landers (1988) with a plea for multidisciplinary approaches to identify the effectiveness of culture: specific rearing practices, patterns and beliefs.

Preliminary research in early childhood education and development in Namibia

A brief outline of the work done by Zimba and Otaala (1991) is provided here.

A study by Zimba and Otaala entitled 'Child Care and Development in Uukwaluudhi, Northern Namibia', was completed in 1991. It was undertaken to illuminate our understanding of traditional, child-rearing practices and beliefs among the people in Uukwaluudhi. This was the initial step in the implementation of a UNICEF child development project, the general objective of which was to create optimal conditions for early childhood development and care at the household and community levels. In order to do this, UNICEF staff felt it was important to undertake research that would provide background data for establishing developmentally stimulating household-based child-care. More specifically, the purpose of the research was to assess the extent to which qualities of a developmentally stimulating environment were provided by the Uukwaluudhi community.

The findings indicate that, in Uukwaluudhi, parental and community goals for children are centred around social and human values which include respect, self-reliance, helpfulness, co-operativeness and obedience. Children are regarded as gifts from God and have a special role to play in perpetuating the family and culture and in providing care for elders.

There is an expectation that a variety of community members will support the child's growth and development. This begins with traditional birth attendants; it then includes extended family members, older brothers and sisters, and extends to the community at large, including the elderly. There is little understanding of the value of interacting with infants and young children. Adults don't 'really' play with children, at least until the child reaches pre-school years. Goals which parents have for their children centre around the development of appropriate social skills and humanistic values. Parents want their children to respect elders, and it is also important for the child to be co-operative, helpful, hardworking, and to participate in work at home and in the field. The need for the child to be educated, obedient and believe in God was frequently emphasized.

Significantly, the results from the study fed directly into the UNICEF Report on the Situation of Children and Women in Namibia (UNICEF, 1991) which formed the basis of UNICEF programming activities in the first three years of Namibia's independence.

Investigations relating to children's rights

Some investigations have explicitly addressed the question of specific children's rights or specific legal aspects, such as the interpretation of the 'best interests of the child'. Others have sought children's own views on a number of specific rights, and their views about what makes a good teacher. We cite briefly investigations by Zimba and Otaala (1995), the discussion by Armstrong (1995) on the legal interpretation of 'the best interests of the child', and views of children sought by the Ministry of Basic Education and Culture, Zimbabwe (1989) and UNESCO (1996).

Preliminary study on children's rights

A main objective of the study by Zimba and Otaala (1995) was to examine Nama child-rearing practices associated with selected articles of the CRC. Using structured and unstructured questions, representatives of 71 families were interviewed, *inter alia*, about children's rights, child survival, protection, development and education. I refer specifically to our findings on children's rights. The conceptualization, promotion, nurturance and development of Nama children's rights could, from the results, be discussed from three vantage points. First, there was some consistency between their conceptions of children's rights and those widely accepted elsewhere. Children's rights to education and good health were, for example, valued by Nama parents in ways similar to those expressed by concerned parents all over the world. However, the Nama families faced considerable hardships in providing for their children's education and medical care. These were attributed to unemployment, lack of stable incomes and affordable medical schemes. Income-generation activities and community-development initiatives appear to present possible solutions to the problems.

Second, by contrast, some of their conceptions of children's rights were inconsistent with current global formulations. Nama parents' conceptions of corporal punishment present a good example. In many parts of the world it is widely acknowledged that the use of corporal punishment in the home and at school constitutes physical and emotional abuse. According to the Nama, this interpretation would be inappropriate. To them, corporal punishment is one of the tools available to parents for socializing children into honest, well-behaved, self-disciplined, obedient and reflective individuals. In addition, it helps to develop individuals who fear and respect authority. To the Nama, this is important for the maintenance of regulated and ordered social relationships. The question is to what extent those who uphold the CRC should take into account the context in which the Nama of Namibia sanction corporal punishment.

Third, our data revealed contextualized conceptions of children's rights. These were displayed when the consideration of the freedom to make choices and decisions went beyond the literal meaning of children's rights. In most cases, the conceptualization of the Nama children's freedom to make their own choices and decisions regarding entertainment, spending money, friends, schools and churches to attend implicated not only the social-cognitive developmental needs and welfare of the children but also involved matters of safety, security, protection from harm, custom, tradition and social relations with peers and adults. For example, whereas more than half of the respondents thought that adolescents were old enough to exercise the freedom to choose their own friends, more than a third considered this to be in error. These respondents felt that the youth required advice, counselling and guidance from their parents and other adult family members to protect them from alcohol and drug abuse, anti-social behaviour, the misuse of sex and other negative influences. According to the Nama, the exercise of children's rights to free choice and decision-making should take into account their contextualized best interests. These interests should reflect Nama custom, tradition and contemporary social-cultural, social-economic and community-development realities.

Interpretation of the 'best interests of the child'
In examining the Shona in Zimbabwe, Armstrong (1995) indicates that in their custom, which is typical of many African ethnic groups, the custody of the child usually rests with the paternal family rather than the individual. This, together with other customs, such as deference to elders and authority, and acting in 'male' and 'female' ways, raises the question: 'to what extent is it in the best interests of children to be raised to change parts of their culture, or to create a less hierarchical, less authoritarian, less gendered world?' Moreover, in contrast to the traditional custom, Armstrong points out that the concept of the 'best interests of the child' is also influenced by Western values enforced by the state. For instance, according to the law, custody rests with an individual, usually the mother, rather than the family group. This creates conflicts with the interpretation provided by 'culture'.

Armstrong indicates that if law is to be used as a practical tool to improve the lives of children, it will be necessary to develop a better understanding of the ways that decision-makers at formal and informal levels interpret the best interests of the child in different contexts. The author concludes by emphasizing the need for soliciting children's views, involvement and participation.

Similarly, more must be learned about children's opinions of what they do, want and need. It is necessary to begin looking at childhood from the perspective of children. In the same way that feminists began challenging the way 'people' thought and acted by pointing out that the 'people' being studied were almost invariably males, it is appropriate to challenge studies of 'children's rights' which rely only on the views of adults. (Armstrong, 1995: 33).

Children's views on teachers and children's rights
In 1989 the Ministry of Basic Education and Culture in Zimbabwe (MBEC) invited children in every part of the country to indicate what they believed to constitute their rights. These were expressed in essays, poems, paintings, drawings and posters. In order to help them address the issue, the following sub-themes were suggested: children's rights to life, to health, to education, and to shelter and security.

The purpose of the ministry in undertaking this exercise was to 'challenge parents and all the guardians to evaluate their children's rights and services which are provided for children of all ages from zero to eighteen' (MBEC, 1989: 4). The results obtained indicate the ability of children to articulate their views and needs on a range of matters germane to them.

The view of one ministry official sums up succinctly children's contributions:

We sought to tap something of the children's changing perceptions of the link they made between their own activities and their view of being and

140

staying healthy. What was revealed to us was much more than this. Far from being 'empty vessels' waiting to receive a measure of health education, what the children brought was a wealth of information, often filtered through their own unique explanations. (MBEC, 1989: 3)

Finally we also refer to children's views of 'what makes a good teacher' as sought by UNESCO (1996). In this respect we can do no better than let the children speak for themselves:

> A good teacher should treat all pupils like his own children. He should answer all questions, even if they are stupid. (Fatoumata, 11, Chad)

> A teacher must not have any favourites and does not separate the poor from the rich and the not-so intelligent from the intelligent. (Zandile, Sandra, 12, Zimbabwe)

> A good teacher loves the job; good teachers are well-prepared to do their work, and are proud of teaching their pupils! (Tapsola, 12, Burkina Faso)

> A good teacher answers the needs of the pupils and not only the needs of the chosen programme. (Omar, 12, Morocco)

> A good teacher doesn't come drunk to his classes in the morning and doesn't hit his pupils or sleep in the classroom. (Maurice, 15, Gabon)

> I like a teacher who helps me think and get answers for myself. (Bangani Sicle, 9, Zimbabwe)

The views expressed by children have been published by UNESCO (1996).

Children's participation in research and programming: future directions

From the above descriptions of various investigations, projects and programmes and from other available evidence it is evident that nations are beginning to collect and share information about early childhood services, and the role children play in the provision of those services, in order to expand educational opportunities. New research should focus on the strength of programmes and successful initiatives at a time when government funding or international aid is often limited. Such studies would be at the cutting-edge of current research in alternative education strategies. They should address issues relating to the global concerns for the rights of the child at the beginning of a new millennium. Successful strategies initiated by local communities in both cities and rural areas should be documented.

Many previous studies have focused on the needs and deficiencies of people (Myers, 1992). Studies are needed to document the strengths of local communities as the foundation upon which to promulgate their successes to other communities and regions. Research indicates that innovative and traditional strategies, such as those in the child-to-child programmes, in poor countries, may be applicable to settings in more prosperous nations.

The studies of young children should be situated in a social, political, economic and historical context. They should pay particular attention to the following topics, among others:

141

- traditional and local practices of child-rearing;
- local and traditional perceptions and understandings of the child and his/her place in society;
- exploration of kin and family structures and the position of the child/children within them;
- the impact on children of social conditions such as poverty, sexual exploitation, abuse, and armed conflict; and
- local and traditional forms of art and culture (stories, songs, puppets, poetry, pottery, weaving, games and dances) that reflect and transmit children's values.

An important part of a new research agenda in African countries will be the need for active involvement of children. The children need to share views of the state of the world and what they feel is required to enable their generation and future generations to attain their full potential.

Engaging children in participation, both in research and programming is, of course, fraught with pitfalls that are, nevertheless, not insurmountable and which, in any case, as some authors (Alderson and Mayall, 1994) have indicated, are no different from the pitfalls encountered in conducting research with adults. The main intractable problem seems to be the inequalities in status and power as between the researched (children) and researcher (adult). The best that can be done, as suggested by Thorne (1993), is to recognize these inequalities at all stages in the research (and programming) process and, with the participation of children, address strategies for mitigating them.

In undertaking the activities referred to above it is important to underline the need to build on people's strengths. The Bernard van Leer Foundation (1991: 7) states:

In Africa ... there are strengths that are universal yet rarely recognized by outsiders and even by those inside ... Within communities there are people who are helping others – what can we do to support them? There are early childhood programmes that are having a positive impact on communities – let us identify why they are having such an impact. People co-operate and share for their mutual benefit – can we extend this sharing and co-operation into other areas of their lives? Traditionally, children are prepared for adult life from a very early age by participating in household and family duties – how can this be adapted to prepare children for the next century while still retaining the best of their traditions? How can we develop an instinctive ability to listen to the community and interpret its strengths so as not to impose our agendas but build on what the community already does and knows?

4.6 Participation with Jordanian children to understand and improve their role in local neighbourhoods

SAFA HALASAH

Jordan is a country experiencing a rapid rate of change as it develops a modern, urbanized population. In the late 1950s and 1960s, movement from rural areas to growing towns began as people sought jobs with regular salaries. After the 1967 war, a large influx of West Bank families settled in Jordan and resources in the country were expended on improving the living conditions of these people. In the 1970s the Lebanese civil war brought about economic growth in the country, as Lebanese private capital was invested. In the 1980s the overheated economy and overvalued dinar led to currency devaluation, which has been reflected in increased prices and low incomes for much of the populace in the 1990s.

Such rapid urbanization and increased costs of living have meant that people moving from rural to urban areas, or rural people caught in urban growth, face an uncertain future. The job market requires skills that many people do not have, people live in high-density communities and access to effective institutions is difficult to obtain. As a result of this situation, families raising children are confronted with urban pressure of which they have had little experience. In the recent past, urban neighbourhoods were places where children related to the wider social community. The neighbourhood was a safe place where they could play. Families knew each other, and through neighbourhood relations they experienced a kind of solidarity, as each family knew other families, and children were well-known to everyone. The situation of children in urban areas is different now. As modern cities grow, institutions begin to have a more active role than parents in raising children. A child may spend more time in school, on public transport and in street-play than in the family home. The institutions in a rapidly urbanizing city are overwhelmed with demands for services. The roles of parents and local communities are shrinking at the same time that institutions are not yet prepared for playing effective roles in the lives of urban children.

The situation of children is also affected by the traditional Jordanian social structure that is based on a system of clans. In this social system, the family is not the heart of the traditional community; an extensive set of relationship ties form the identity of a family and its children. This relationship structure, in a modern city, is not geographical but is embedded throughout the city and the country. The child is a member of a family that is a part of a clan, which is the 'neighbourhood' of the child. The child is also considered to be under the authority of the father, which is deemed to be higher than that of the state. The unfortunate outcome of these combined influences is that children are left without anyone to listen to them. No one is prepared to engage children in serious discussion of their viewpoints.

143

Research project

Questscope, a private British voluntary organization, has initiated a participatory research project to obtain a better understanding of children's circumstances and ways of improving their quality of life. In this research, participation is not to be viewed as a method imposed on children, it is not a product to be delivered, but emerges out of effective interaction of neighbourhood groups. A neighbourhood is a complicated network of autonomous and semi-autonomous bodies which have an interest in what is happening to the children.

In one of the communities in which we work, children spend most of their time on the street; the family home is the site of violence directed against them. These children have created a kind of street family among themselves that meets their social, emotional and economic needs. A child may have access to a house, often shared with a parent, siblings and grandparents, but the child lives effectively on the street and the significant supportive relationships come from among his peers.

There are constant fights among these children to maintain status in their social hierarchy. At the same time, this hierarchy of one or two dominant children means that needs for affection and protection of the children can be met. The role of such leaders is to protect children from outsiders. Each dominant child has her/his own way of protecting their gang.

The research site is one of the busiest places in Amman. There are 10 000 to 12 000 residents in one square kilometre. High population density, large family size and low incomes characterize the area. Children play and work all day in the streets without adult supervision.

As a first step in establishing contact with the children, we went to their street to learn how to describe the place through their words. We spent a lot of time observing and listening to them. But when we visited the social centre the children reacted violently. They broke all the windows of the centre, threw rotten vegetables and stones at us and set small fires around the building. In subsequent interviews with the children we learned that the location of the building had been the only play area for them. They were angry that it had been taken from them. The children in the street were outside the scope of interest of the centre: no programmes existed for them. They were even denied access to the building. In order to build trust with the children, we invited them into the centre for discussions about it, the area and their problems. We initiated activities with them such as kite flying, painting, etc. We also invited the children to join us for a special lunch.

As we introduced ourselves to the children, we started to design our research topics. Our goal was to study the stress on children regarding economic, social, health and institutional factors by participating with them in participatory rural appraisal (PRA). We held many discussions with them describing their situation, problems, economic pressures and personal needs through the use of PRA tools (semi-structured interviews to collect information and ranking exercises to set their priorities). In one case we interviewed adults about children's needs in the area. The adults' first priority was to provide children with a playground. When we asked the children the same question, their answer was entirely different. Their priority was the problem of children who carried switchblades, knives and leather belts. They explained that if a playground were built, the fights between children carrying weapons would move into the playground. The only change would be moving the problems to a new place.

Results gleaned through the PRA indicated that children are expected to provide an income to the family on which most families depend. The school system is unable to have an appropriate role in educating children because of large class sizes and few resources. The social centre limits itself to providing services to women, such as sewing and hairdressing classes. It does not provide assistance to families, such as counselling and helping them in raising children. We also observed two types of children in the neighbourhood: those who live in the street ('causing problems') and those whose families keep them indoors, away from street influences. The neighbourhood is therefore split into 'actors' and 'retreaters'.

During group discussions, the children mentioned that they wanted their neighbourhood to be a place of which they could be proud. They wanted to clean it up because it was dirty, smelled bad, and garbage was piled where they wanted to play. We helped them organize a special clean-up day in which they divided themselves into groups, each with a leader and responsibility for one of the alley-ways between the houses. The effect of this day on the children was very positive, and they began to ask themselves how they could do this on a regular basis.

The centre building had been constructed in such a way that the alley behind the building (out of sight from the front) was used by adults for drinking alcohol, sex, fights and other dangerous activities, that took place at night. The children again expressed anger towards the centre and towards those associated with it. In order to create a safe place in the area and to improve the reputation of the centre among parents and children, they asked for a two-metre high wall to be built around it and a gate to control access.

In the interviews with the children we observed that almost every child over the age of three had noticeable scars on his/her face, neck and arms. These marks of physical violence were the result of aggression from adults and from other children. Most of the time we found that violence among children is a way for the child to establish his/her presence: to be acknowledged and listened to.

One of the children was the passive recipient of aggression from other children. He was given a role in the clean-up day and through our interaction with him we found that he did not know how to socialize with others. The only language he knew was violence, and his only role up to that time was to be the recipient of that language.

In order to create a safe atmosphere where children would like to talk about their issues in depth and to interact with other children, we organized a five-day summer camp in the countryside to learn from children about their lives and how to co-operate with them. We wanted to understand their violence in a different environment, and to see if they would respond to new ways of communication in a new environment that did not require violence.

The camp activities were designed to absorb their aggression through sports and to build their self-confidence. We involved outsider speciality providers for personal counselling and behavioural management. During the camp we created space for the children to interact with others in non-violent ways. One child often became upset during camp activities. He would change back into the clothes he wore before the camp and run away. Each time we would follow him and bring him back. If we did not see where he went, he would shout, 'I am over here in the tree'. After becoming aware of his strategy, we ignored him. He then came back and participated in activities with other children. He started to be aware of his self-esteem not by our chasing him, but by our listening to him.

One of the results of this camp has been that the children developed the idea that they are our partners. They have come to visit our office and initiate more discussions regarding their situation. They visited the juvenile authorities as visitors, not criminals, arranging appointments by phone. This is not always a comfortable partnership. The children are pushy. They want to be included in planning for their needs, and they want things to happen quickly. However, their desire to be treated as people, not as projects, is a positive development. The change in their behaviour is remarkable as they become more aware of their role in the community. They are spending more time in the centre, helping the staff organize activities. Now we are in a new stage with the children as we design together their new roles as participants in their neighbourhood.

While we have been working with the children, we have also addressed the structure around the children: the neighbourhood. We visited many families to explain the purpose of our presence and to communicate the need to have them participate with us in the project. Eventually ten volunteers (two men and eight women) from a variety of backgrounds joined us. For three weeks they were trained in PRA skills in order to conduct their own assessments. They learned how to carry out open-ended interviews, rank responses, create diagrams to convey data and establish a map of the area of the study. They used these skills in teams to gather information from families, children and individuals working in the area, and they analysed the resultant information.

The volunteers' awareness of the needs of their community and its children was heightened through these experiences. When they submitted their priorities for the next action steps, they included the children. They formed a committee to continue work for the benefit of both kinds of children in the neighbourhood.

Conclusion

Children's participation with social researchers is itself a form of social development. As awareness of issues is created with children, new roles can be envisioned by and for them in a neighbourhood or community. These new roles will require that adults in the community reflect on the changes that could result in adult roles and in the responsiveness of adult-mediated structures and institutions that constitute the social environment of children. Participatory research ultimately, therefore, creates a dynamic for initiating actions based on understanding children's viewpoints. These actions will have community-wide implications and can create the social space for constructive impact that will affect all the members of the community.

Participation with children in research and action is a complex phenomenon. It requires that adults listen to children and take them seriously, and then respond to their viewpoints by giving them roles as significant actors in their own lives.

The challenge for effective participation with urban children in Jordan will be to link community consensus on children's issues with local experts who will assist in problems (such as youth violence, school leaving, etc.). It will also be important for children and their urban neighbourhoods to articulate the need for changes to improve access to resources and increase the responsiveness of institutions' policies and practices.

4.7 Workshop on culture and children's participation

RACHEL CARNEGIE

Proverbs about children

The participants were asked to think of proverbs about children and childhood, either from their own culture or from a culture they knew well. They wrote their proverbs on cards.

The participants then formed an outer and inner circle, of equal numbers. The two circles rotated in opposite directions, starting and stopping with

Figure 4.3: *'It is the young trees that make a thick forest.'*

music. At each stop, each participant discussed the meaning of their proverb with the person standing opposite.

The proverbs were then clustered on boards by region. In the discussion that followed, it was noted that proverbs may reflect obsolescent cultural values and that culture is dynamic and evolutionary. For example, the proverb 'Children should be seen and not heard', may no longer be regarded as acceptable or reflective of current attitudes. The collection of proverbs listed below makes for thoughtful reading!

ASIA

- The diplomatic calf takes milk from two cows. (Uzbekistan)
- The egg should not be smarter than the duck (Vietnam)
- Girls are for making the walls of others' houses. (Nepal)
- If your son is born every year your store will be full of crops. (Bangladesh)
- The son of a duck is a floater. (Arab)
- Give them a morsel of gold, keep a lion's eye. (Pakistan) (Give the best you have to your child, but also ensure that it does not spoil the child.)
- The childhood shows the man as morning shows the day. (Philippines)
- A (small) child's contribution in the fields will not bring anything home. (Sri Lanka)
- Children are innocent like angels; they can't do any harm. (Pakistan)

AFRICA

- Children are an investment in the future. (South Africa) This has positive and negative applications. Children are expected to provide a pension for their parents.
- Children should be seen and not heard. (South Africa)
- A tree should be bent while it's still young. (South Africa) (If a child is not taught when young it will not be possible to teach him or her new behaviour when older.)
- A child who does not allow its mother to sleep will itself not get any sleep. (Ghana)
- Children are different from each other, therefore they should be treated as individuals. (Zimbabwe)
- He who never saw his mother when she was young, wonders why his father wasted dowry on her. (Uganda) Children always have questions about the actions of adults, so we need to be ready to explain.
- When a child knows how to wash his hands he eats with the elders. (Ghana)
- He who despises traditions/culture is a slave. (Kenya) (We need to retain cultural values to keep families and moral values intact.)
- A child breaks the shell of a snail and not the shell of the tortoise. (Ghana)
- A disobedient child will get his ear pulled by thorns. (Ghana)
- *Mtoto sio Mtoto tu.* (Tanzania) (A child is just a child and as such is not important.
- Nothing for us, without us. (Morocco, a disability group)
- You don't put a child on the roof and remove the ladder from under its feet. (Ghana)
- What children prepare will not be enough for dinner. (Ethiopia) (Only adults are capable.)

Figure 4.4: *'Children should be seen and not heard.'*

EUROPE
- Little birds in their nest agree. (UK) (Children in the same family should not argue.)
- Children should be seen and not heard. (UK)
- Don't teach your gradmother to suck eggs. (UK)
- Don't be childish. (Wales)

AMERICAS
- Idle hands make for the devil's work. (USA) (Children should not have free time.)
- Children should be seen and not heard. (USA)

The negative nature of most of the proverbs recalled by the participants was surprising and we need to recognize that there are also many positive proverbs about children. For example 'It is the young trees that make the forest thick' (Uganda); 'Children are the wealth of the Nation' (Tanzania).

The qualities of childhood

Working in the regional groups identified through the proverb exercise, participants worked on the following task: each participant identified a child known to them. Details of name, age, sex, and location were given. Three questions were then discussed:

1. What does this child's culture value in a child?
2. What activity/ies is this child allowed to participate in?
3. What activity/ies is this child prevented from participating in?

The groups then presented their discussion using cards on pin boards. The results, illustrated in Figure 4.4, show the creativity of the responses. Some of the examples demonstrated how a child may also find him/herself pressured

Jo, 13, residential care, Scotland

"If I was with my family trouble wouldn't happen. I would have more of a normal life. I idealize my family. I don't have to go to school and I have leisure activities if approved. I'm allowed to go out with permission. I can go to meetings to make choices about my life. I have to be in by a certain time. i can't have friends around. I get punished physically. I can't cook or go into the kitchen. I can't see my family when I want. If I'm late, the police get involved."

"Jo is a bad example, a scapegoat and the cause of the family split. He is marginalized and he should grow up.

The public think he's dangerous. Not a good friend. A bad influence. Disruptive in school, lazy, a health hazard."

Malisa, 10, rural Africa

ALLOWED:
to do domestic work
to eat after the boys
to join women's activities and go through inititation rites.

QUALITIES:
Caring, pretty, chaste, hard working, balancing multiple roles, respectful, obedient small mother, physically strong.

NOT ALLOWED:
to interrupt adult conversation, socialize with males, to be a tomboy, to have full-time education, play too much, look straight into men's eyes, inherit parents' property, to have a choice on initiation rites.

Hassan, 12, urban Jordan

NOT ALLOWED:
Play with girls, stay at home during day, initiate conversation with father, drink alcohol.

ALLOWED:
To smoke, have social activities, go to school, work for money, make decision about leaving or staying in school, play with boys, initiate conversation with mother, stay out late.

VALUES:
Obedience, silence, protecting sisters' honour

Sameena, 10, Pakistan

She has opinions with boys and girls, but...
No challenging adult males!

I'm allowed to play with boys and girls. I'm not allowed to go beyond the village. I'm not included in decisions relating to big expenditures.

I must help with harvesting, weeding, cleaning animal shed, household chores, I must go to school, and be a substitute mother when required.

Halima, 11, refugee, Ethiopia

QUALITIES & VALUES:
Accept the traditional beliefs, be quiet and respectful to adults.

I MUST not marry outside the religion. I must not climb mountains, or cycle or play football. I'm not expected to be educated.

HOUSEHOLD CHORES:
Fetch water, collect firewood look after sheep and goats, support the family, cook, clean, look after siblings.

I MUST make henna on my hands, feet and hair, marry early by my parents' choice, make sure clothes cover all my body and eat after the men and boys.

Figure 4.5: *Children's cultures.*

150

by conflicting expectations, where the culture of parents and peers value different qualities and behaviour.

4.8   Conclusions

PAT PRIDMORE

The ideas and experiences presented in Part 4 have highlighted the way in which the study of the participation of children must be situated in a social, political, economic and historic context. A detailed and sensitive understanding of the cultural framework and of the child's culture is a key factor in determining programmes' effectiveness.

In the past, cultural contextualization in relation to children's participation has been a largely neglected area of study, with the exception of a few notable contributions to the literature that recognize the need for researchers to step back from their own experience of childhood and to allow children's voices to be heard. As James and Prout (1997) point out, childhood is now emerging as a significant area of study within sociology, human geography and anthropology. Reynolds (1991) offers a detailed and sensitive record to illuminate how boys and girls in Mola Village in Zimbabwe view their world and how their lives are affected by the cultural values, traditions and practices of the society in which they live. Ennew and Milne (1989) present case-studies to explore the reality of popular images of the lives lived by children in poor countries around the world which aim to avoid Eurocentric preconceptions of children and to provide new insights. Detailed, micro-level case-studies in diverse cultural contexts such as these are essential to the development of culturally appropriate programmes that aim to enable child participation and enhance the physical and psychosocial development of all children, including working children. There is much to be learned from successful programmes.

The agenda for action research can usefully combine both qualitative and quantitative approaches and draw on the tools and perspectives of diverse disciplines such as education, sociology, anthropology and medicine to enable child participation. We also need researchers to pay attention to the issue of sub-cultures. The perceived tendency for research to have a replicative and an ethnocentric, and particularly a Eurocentric, stance must be guarded against. The development and dissemination of research protocols to help illuminate children's perspectives that can be adapted to local circumstances is an important step forward.

Whilst acknowledging the importance of cultural contextualization, it is important not to use culture as an excuse to avoid challenging cultural norms which underpin harmful practices. In many societies, for example, the use of corporal punishment by adults against children in the school and in the home is widely accepted; in other cultures it is considered to be an unethical use of adult power. Bearing in mind that culture is dynamic not static we need to consider the long-term benefits of change and to approach such conflicting views from an ethical as well as a cultural view point.

If the rhetoric of children's participation is to become reality more adults need to develop the special understanding and skills required to work with children in different cultural contexts. Children are especially vulnerable and adults must be sensitive to the fine line between participatory approaches that involve children actively and those which manipulate and coerce them. Including children in research and programme development requires professionals to work with children as partners. Partnership with children is important because partners are people whom you respect. Accepting children as partners helps them develop and enhances their feelings of worth not only in their own eyes, but in those of their elders.

However, the notion of partnership with children is complex and can be problematic. If children's participation as partners is not to be mere tokenism, adults need to be flexible and willing to trust children and to work alongside them. Working with children as partners requires that adults open their minds to the notion of partnerships with children, stop to listen to children and take note of non-verbal communication. The real challenge, however, is for adults to let go of the control traditionally exercised over children and to learn how to work with them as partners without imposing participation on them or expecting tireless devotion to task. Adults need to find the right balance between giving too much and too little guidance and to learn when to follow and when to offer practical advice and support in a culturally appropriate manner. Although children's participation in the work of the family and particularly in child-care is traditional, the notion of children as partners in the decision-making processes is both new and radical, and some would argue that it is neither desirable nor achievable. It remains to be seen how far institutions will ever overcome traditional resistance to admitting children to the decision-making process in societies where they are traditionally the least-powerful members.

Training adults to develop appropriate attitudes and skills is important but its potential cannot be fully realized without adequate follow-up and support. We need to ensure that trainees have regular opportunities to share their experiences of working in partnership with children and to continue to develop their confidence and skill in the use of participatory approaches. When considering appropriate methods for involving children, it is more effective to use ways of communicating with which they are already familiar and which they use themselves, before introducing new methods. In many situations children's experience and skill in the use of song, dance and drama is a rich resource which has yet to be fully tapped.

Practical questions raised by field workers are: 'Who participates?' and 'Why participate?' We need to ensure that marginalized children are enabled to take part alongside their more élite peers whilst at the same time being sensitive to their needs and putting these before our own. In providing children with the right to choose whether or not to become involved, we need to take into account the disparity of power between them and their elders in settings such as the classroom which makes it difficult for youngsters not to agree to participate. Similarly we need to recognize the extent to which not only the cultures of the community and of the child but our own personal culture and that of our organizations influences the capacity of children to participate.

The child-to-child approach to health education has enormous potential for promoting child involvement. The rapid spread of its ideas around the world shows that it is sufficiently flexible to be adapted to different cultural contexts and to be owned by those implementing it. However, in common with the UN Convention on the Rights of the Child (CRC), the philosophy underpinning the approach presupposes a frame of mind about children and their status in society at variance with received attitudes in most non-Western cultures. In the process of contextualization, the nature of the child-to-child approach or of the CRC may, consequently, be changed beyond all recognition. The question is how best to bridge the gap between rhetoric and reality. One way forward is for national governments to initiate a much overdue dialogue between the national and local levels within their countries in order to enhance understanding of what child participation means to mothers and to fathers. Such a dialogue would serve to illuminate the extent to which the rights of children to participate can be assimilated within non-Western societies.

It is widely acknowledged that to facilitate child participation we need actively to raise the status of minors within the community and increase their credibility as development workers in the eyes of their parents. One way of achieving these goals is to involve children in local radio programmes at the community level, where the child's voice is rarely heard. The Child-to-Child Trust in London has recognized this need and produced an audio-tape titled 'We're on the radio'. The child-to-child approach is also being used increasingly to address issues such as drugs, violence, poor sexual health, bullying and environmental concerns. These issues are often addressed in informal educational settings such as youth groups and church groups, but the tension between local and institutional cultures remain to be resolved.

PART 5

Children's Participation in Situations of Crisis

Editor and co-author: PAT PRIDMORE

Co-authors: PRIYA COOMARASWAMY,
VESNA DEJANOVIC

Summary

Part 5 explores what participation means for children living in the especially difficult circumstances of social, economic and political instability and war. It recognizes that whilst emergency situations are not homogeneous they are dynamic, having both peaks and plateaux of crisis which allow for the use of more child-centred approaches. It calls for the identification of strategies to build trust and promote resilience in children and argues that we need to make full use of the opportunities for positive change presented by crisis situations.

Case-studies from Sri Lanka, Yugoslavia and different parts of Africa demonstrate how a more child-focused approach to programme design and implementation can be developed. They confirm that even in situations of crisis, progress can be made if the Western paternalistic model that treats children as victims is rejected and replaced by a model which accepts children as social actors. The case-studies illustrate the way in which crisis situations can present opportunities for positive change alongside efforts towards cultural reintegration.

Key issues raised in Part 5:

- We need to identify factors that enhance children's resilience in the face of adversity and to design programmes that promote the development of resilience.
- The security situation can frustrate regular extended interactions with children but there is a strong argument for increasing the level of children's participation in programme design, implementation and evaluation in these settings.
- Even in crisis situations programmes can be successfully introduced in a flexible manner, bearing in mind the reality of the situation and the different levels at which children can participate.
- It is important to be aware of the ethical considerations around informed consent and to provide adequate support to traumatized children.
- There is a need to monitor carefully how participation affects children's workloads.
- Participatory learning and action (PLA) methods yielding visual data help to avoid the need for note-taking, which can arouse suspicion. Involving children in recording and sharing their life history and finding ways of investing in their own future can be especially useful.
- Child-fostering programmes and child-disability programmes need to have children's participation as a central and explicit objective and to create opportunities for children's views to be heard, respected and taken into account. The first step is to help adults to listen to children.
- There is much to be gained by agencies working together to promote the concept and the practice of child participation and to improve child-related services.

- It may be best to avoid the political implications of children's empowerment and to start presenting the benefits of their participation in terms of children and adults trying to make child-related services more relevant to their needs.

5.0 Introduction

PAT PRIDMORE

Despite the magnitude of the disruption caused to children by situations of crisis, the participation of children themselves in such situations remains a neglected area of study. It might in fact be reasonable to question whether child participation has any role to play in situations where the emphasis is on saving lives in as short a time as possible. However, as we shall see in the case-studies presented in this chapter, crisis situations are often protracted and mortality rates may remain high for many months.

Under the pressure of such situations it is generally assumed that the more traditional top-down approach to programme development, which frequently has a narrow focus on service delivery and transfer of health information, is the only feasible strategy, even though research has shown that this approach is relatively ineffective (Baric, 1996: 17). Moreover, in crisis situations such an approach may do harm by undermining the coping capacities of individuals and communities (Ferron and Pridmore, 1998).

Muecke (1992) highlights the way in which the prevailing approaches view children in crisis situations as victims rather than survivors. This is surprising in view of the fact that conflict frequently results in an increase of child-headed households in which children are essential social actors responsible not only for their own survival but also for that of their siblings. Baden (1997) reflecting on the post-conflict situation in Mozambique points out the need for gender analysis to be better integrated into policy and planning and for increased understanding of the way in which people are active agents in creating and responding to conflict rather than passively allowing it to impact on their lives. Van Damme (1995: 361) argues that the way in which displaced persons' camps are administered, positively 'encourages passivity (and) the lack of autonomy engenders hopelessness'. This is important because studies have shown that having some control over one's environment has a significant impact on health (Rodin and Langer, 1977, Naidoo and Wills, 1994). Consequently adopting a child-focused approach has the potential to improve health and even to save lives.

In recent years there have been calls for development workers to adopt a more people-centred approach to their work, to be more accountable to the beneficiaries and to increase participation in the planning and execution of activities which affect their well-being (Cuny, 1994; Walker, 1996). The UN (1989) Convention on the Rights of the Child has highlighted the need for greater participation of children and provided a framework for policy development. Despite such calls for reform, capacity building has not yet been widely accepted as a goal amongst aid workers in crisis situations. However, a debate has started within some of the major aid organizations about what constitutes ethical practice in working with children in such situations and there is growing recognition of the need to share experiences and to develop guidelines for programme development. This chapter is a contribution to this debate. It presents case-studies of innovation and change in response to the call for greater participation of children in research and programme development.

The need to build trust and promote resilience

Baden (1997) highlights the way in which conflict can lead to increased neglect and abuse of children and to their becoming much more visible in a range of survival strategies, such as sex-work and begging. Moreover the way in which trauma caused by crisis can have profound and long-lasting effects on psychosocial development has been well-documented, and the special vulnerability of children to damage has been recognized (Garbarino and Bedard, 1996; Jensen, 1996). Trauma challenges children's understanding of the meaning and purpose of life and their identity formation can be damaged. As Jensen (1996: 418) points out 'healthy identity formation can only be built on basic trust and a secure, social base for their personal and collective development'. When trauma has shattered a child's sense of trust in the world, an important first step in the healing process can be to involve the child in culturally sensitive activities that help restore basic trust and identity. In some traditional societies there are rituals such as medicine dances, healing circles or dialogue with elders that enhance the healing process and it can be argued that we need to explore and adapt such alternative strategies more widely. However, it needs to be stressed that building trust between adults and children takes time and requires adults to have special abilities to listen to children and to empathize with and respect their views. This also has implications for the continuous training of field workers.

Involving children in recording and sharing their life history and finding ways of helping them invest in their own future can be especially useful in crisis situations. This approach draws on the perspective developed by Frankl (1993) in his classic work *Man's Search for meaning*. Cohler (1991) contends that we can see support for this perspective in the growing body of evidence linking the ability to tell a coherent and meaningful account of one's life to the crucial variables of resilience exhibited by children in the face of adversity. Furthermore Garbarino and Bedard (1996: 469) argue that 'this evidence offers support for the proposition that the emergence of this ability in children and youth is the most important foundation for resilience'.

The need for a positive attitude

Times of crisis in society can effect rapid cultural change and it is important to recognize that this can also present opportunities for positive change. This point is endorsed by Jensen (1996: 420) who contends that in crisis 'we not only witness the mobilization of hate, prejudice, brutal soldier socialization, etc; we also witness the mobilization of care, love, sacrifice and solidarity'.

159

watoto wana haki ya

kulindwa na madhara
ya vita

Figure 5.1: *'Children have a right to be protected from the effects of war'*
Source: *Kuleana Centre for Children's Rights, Tanzania*

Here, then, is an opportunity for relief and development workers to work in partnership with children building on the positive aspects of change in order to develop a counter-movement based on solidarity, love, care and compassion for each other.

Box 5.1: Promoting resilience in children

The Rädda Barnen (1996) report based on case-studies from 26 countries (including 10 from Africa) indicates how deliberate recruitment of children for action in combat has dramatically increased. The report finds that the vast majority of child recruits are from impoverished and marginalized backgrounds, particularly those without families or with disrupted family ties. Although the majority of child soldiers are boys, many girls are recruited by armed groups not only to perform the same roles as boys but also to be forced into sexual service. The physical and psychological impact of this experience has led to concern for promoting resilience in children.

Resilience is a universal capacity which allows a person, a group or community to prevent, minimize or overcome the damaging effects of adversity (Grotberg, 1995). It may transform or make stronger the lives of those who are resilient. This universal capacity for resilience is developed and nurtured from factors of external supports and resources, inner personal strengths and social interpersonal skills.

An international project (co-ordinated by Grotberg) set out to examine actions taken by parents, care-givers or children that seem to promote

---

resilience. An attempt was made to devise ways to promote strength in children as they mature. Thirty African countries (including Namibia, Sudan and South Africa) participated. The instruments used to assess resilience were:

- 15 situations of adversity to which adults and children were asked to respond;
- a checklist of 15 statements that indicate resilience in a child;
- three standardized tests; and
- actual experiences of adversity reported by respondents together with their own reactions to these situations.

In the case of Katutura (a relatively impoverished suburb of Windhoek, Namibia) the six major external problems the family experienced within the preceding five years were, in rank order: robberies, war, fires, earthquakes, floods and car accidents. The six major internal problems the family experienced over the same period were: death of a parent or grandparent, divorce, separation, illness of parent or siblings, poverty and the family or friend moving.

According to Grotberg (1995) the findings suggest that each country in the study is drawing on a common set of resilience factors to promote resilience in children. She concludes that it is clear that there are relationships between resilience and culture. Some cultures rely more on faith than on problem-solving in facing adversity. Some are more concerned with punishment and guilt while others discipline and reconcile. Some cultures expect children to be more dependent on others for help in adversity rather than becoming autonomous and more self-reliant.

Barnabas Otaala

5.1   Exploring child participation: the Sri Lankan experience

PRIYA COOMARASWAMY

Why child participation?

In late 1995, the Save the Children Fund (SCF) (UK) programme teams in Colombo and the district offices came together to undertake an information-gathering exercise which for the first time would include obtaining children's own thoughts and perceptions of their lives. Our learning from past experience pointed to a need for a greater understanding of children's lives, experiences, needs and issues, particularly from the perspective of children, if we are to understand the impact of programme interventions on children's lives. While work in the past had been designed to help children, there was little evidence of the benefits, if any, of our interventions. Project planning and management,

161

with limited community participation, had not included child participation nor responded to specific needs of children.

In our efforts, therefore, towards achieving more effective children-oriented programmes, SCF (UK) in Sri Lanka has been developing and testing a child-focused approach to programme development. Child participation is an integral component of this approach. It is also one of the general principles of the UN Convention on the Rights of the Child (UNCRC), which provides the framework for the planning and development of our child-focused work.

This paper summarizes the practical experience of SCF in Sri Lanka as we have attempted to integrate the participation of children within the programming process, especially in areas affected by the conflict in the north-east.

Our experience and learning have evolved through various phases. Our first steps led us to incorporate children's views and observations into data gathering and analysis. We have continued this approach with efforts to include children as partners in the programme development process.

We began by talking to children in areas affected by the conflict. Information was gathered from men, women and children through the adaptation and use of tools within the participatory rural appraisal (PRA) approach. Other pieces of research/needs assessments have followed. Lessons have been learned but questions remain to be clarified.

Participatory research – the learning and the issues

The PRA tools used proved to be effective in stimulating children's participation in the research process. Their flexibility made possible some modifications in their application to suit group characteristics and the information sought. Discussion around the PRA exercise created entry points for in-depth discussion with children.

- How effectively are we using the PRA tools? What information is sought? What do we mean by 'listening to children'? What are the underlying reasons for the data on the maps, diagrams and matrices? In talking/listening to children, is the analysis in terms of the UNCRC? Are nuances (body language, facial expressions, etc.) properly recorded? If not, significant analytical insights may be lost.
- It should also be recognized that this phase is just the beginning of a process. As we build a relationship of trust, children and adults should start to communicate and share their thoughts more freely.
- The children enjoyed the games, the singing and the PRA activities, which helped us build a rapport with them. These also provided a sense of normalcy in conflict-affected areas.
- It is important to be sensitive to culture, power structures and divisions, and gender issues, as these can dictate how children participate.
- Children are not always willing to take part. Concerns raised by adults about children's issues could not always be explored with older children because some of them, especially the boys, did not join in the exercises. While children were forthcoming when providing general information, we encountered difficulties in eliciting their opinions and feelings. This raised a number of questions: could children's inhibitions be attributed to the fact

that they are not often encouraged by adults to express opinions?; could their reticence be indicative of a possible closing of minds to past thoughts as a way of coping with unpleasant experiences?; does the lack of privacy in group sessions coupled in some instances with a large group size impede in-depth dialogue? We found that there was increased communication when a child was alone with us.

- Our work has highlighted that working with children calls for an investment in time. Security considerations restrict time available with communities in most conflict areas. The inability to spend a full day or days with them during the research process delays rapport-building, and valuable information obtained through observation is lost. During the school term it is difficult to meet with children as they have little spare time.
- The importance of ethical considerations was recognized. To what extent should sensitive issues be pursued? Probing could trigger memories of fear and pain and produce reactions to which the research team may not be able to respond. How do we assess 'informed' consent? Before undertaking research, both adults and children were 'informed' about the purpose of the research work and the dissemination of the findings. While their consent was obtained, the extent of understanding among the (younger) children needs to be reviewed. Age and maturity of children must be considered in efforts to involve children.

Programme development and children

Participatory research has been followed up by child participation in project planning, implementation and monitoring. The Women Headed Households (WHH) Income-Generating Project in Eachchantivu, Trincomalee District, is a child-focused pilot project undertaken in collaboration with a local partner organization, the Trincomalee District Development Association. While the main objective of the project is to assist project participants in establishing viable income-generating activities, the project is being studied in terms of its impact on children, with attention to their participation.

Children have been involved in the project process since the needs-identification stage. The older children in particular have actively assisted their mothers in setting up and helping in various tasks related to their small enterprises. An older children's group has been formed, with one child from each of the WHH families. As a possible method of monitoring the progress of the family activity, these children, with the exception of one eight-year-old, began maintaining diaries. This ended when children lost interest and the process became cumbersome. It has been found that older children are now consulted by mothers during decision-making and are taking on more responsibilities in managing activities. Changes have occurred to time/leisure activity allocation. The children do not appear disturbed by such changes and they continue to take pride in their varied contributions. School attendance has not been affected by the project. Table 5.1 shows the SCF indicators for this income-generating project.

SCF Anuradhapura, in collaboration with the Sucharitha Women's Society in Etambagaskade, is supporting a sanitation project in Etambagaskade, a border village. Children's participation in problem identification led to

Figure 5.2: *We lost our coconut tree*

discussion about health practices and the problems caused by the non-use of latrines. The children offered ideas on ways to promote the use of latrines.

Adults have worked on the construction of latrines. The children provide family support by assisting with small tasks. Their main association with the project is in the health-education component. A group of children have received training from the government health worker. Health messages were conveyed through child-to-child and child-to-adult communication. The children have also used puppetry to raise awareness. Some of the children are part of a team that has received training in puppetry and child rights.

Table 5.1: SCF indicators – income-generating project

Portion of profits used to meet children's needs.

Children's savings started.

Changes in mother-child relationship. Older children's participation in the family business activity, especially in decision-making.

Impact of family income-generating activities on the daily lives of children: changes in time/daily activity allocation, school attendance.

Participation of children's club in recreational and community activities.

Level of participation within process of project activity.

Informal discussions and requests for participation in the sanitation project indicate a greater awareness of the importance of improved health and hygiene practices. Parents of children who had received training expressed pride in the confidence and ability displayed by their children. A project-monitoring exercise is ongoing. The children are also participants in this exercise. Table 5.2 shows SCF indicators for this sanitation project.

Working with partners
In our plans to take forward child-focused work, SCF is developing and strengthening relationships with partner organizations. We recognize that SCF can have only a limited impact on children's lives given our capacity and spatial coverage. By encouraging partner organizations to adopt a child-focused approach to programme development and use the UNCRC as a programming tool, attitudes towards child participation are being examined. In workshops held with NGOs and government agencies with whom SCF is establishing programme collaboration, the debates and discussions reflected an encouraging interest in pursuing the child-focused concept. Their interest has prompted some partner organizations to consider ways of putting their learning into practice. Our work has raised the following issues:

- Possibilities exist for children's participation in different forms and at different levels. Children demonstrated that they could be involved actively in the main project activity or could make important contributions through associated activities.
- Why/how are they participating? Who decides? How will the effects of their involvement be monitored? What indicators should be used?
- Organizations promoting child participation need to consider the time children can allocate to project activities. Distance, transport and tuition classes lengthen the school day.
- Will the promotion of child participation add to children's work time? The impact of children's activities will require careful monitoring with appropriate indicators.
- Children have shown that, given the opportunity and encouragement, they can contribute to developmental initiatives. The nature of their involvement could be an indicator of their increasing self-confidence and self-esteem.
- In facilitating participation through group formation, how should inclusion or exclusion of children as members be decided? Would exclusion lead to divisions? Who decides?
- It is important to understand the diversity of children's lives and adult–child relationships and adapt projects to suit the particular conditions within a project setting. The demonstration of children's capacities could lead to attitudinal change and a respect for their views and contributions to

Table 5.2: SCF indicators – sanitation project

Better health practices among both adults and children.
Reduced disease.
Level of children's participation in health-education activities.
Level of participation within process of project activity.

community-development initiatives.
- What are the implications for community social/power structures? How would adults perceive possible changes?
- The security situation in conflict areas frustrates regular extended interactions with children. It delays project development and creates concern among children and adults about their continued participation for project completion.
- Other organizations are also willing to explore child participation. The main hurdle is the attitudes of individuals.
- Our experience has underlined that this child-focused approach with its child rights perspective requires a different capacity of staff and a continued training input to develop the skills necessary for effective implementation.

Conclusion

The major thrust of our child-focused work has been to make children visible within the policy and practice of development initiatives. In SCF Sri Lanka, our work has created opportunities for exploring child participation. Our practical experience has shown that, while the process has its challenges, children can make significant contributions through participation in research and programme development. Our learning will help develop further child-focused work in Sri Lanka.

5.2   Children's participation – past experience and future strategy[1]

VESNA DEJANOVIC

The ratification of the UN Convention on the Rights of the Child coincided with a serious political, economic and social crisis in former Yugoslavia. In the Federal Republic of Yugoslavia (FRY) it was followed by war, an influx of 650,000 refugees and displaced people as well as by isolation from the international community through sanctions. The present time can be described as a post-war, politically and socially unstable period. There is increasing poverty and family breakdown, as well as transition processes characteristic of the central and eastern European countries. This very complex situation can, however, be considered in a positive light. It should be seen as a time of changes and challenges, both in the economic, social and political sense, and in terms of challenging attitudes, thoughts, behaviour and relationships which can be a basis for the improvement of child-related policy and practice.

To introduce a discussion on the concept of children's participation in a society in crisis, which is greatly influenced by both transitional processes and tradition, I will summarize Save the Children Fund's (SCF) concrete work in FRY from 1994, with regard to the involvement of children and young people. The aim of this approach is to present the development of our strategy to promote children's participation as concept and practice.

What has already been done?

When the progamme 'Separated Children in Exile' was initiated in June 1994, it was refugee and emergency focused. Child-participation wasn't recognized as a significant issue and consequently it wasn't set as an objective. As part of the United Nations High Commission on Refugees' Operation 'Reunite', the programme aims were to:

- identify, register and document all children living in FRY separated from their parents because of the war;
- ensure help regarding reunification;
- ensure the best possible interim care until reunification became possible; and
- long-term solutions for children who may never be reunited with their families.

When analysing the methods of work that were applied, it becomes clear that child-participation existed on a practical level despite the fact that it was not established as a concept intentionally. The methods used were as follows:

Interviewing   In a process of registration and ongoing assessment every child was interviewed, together with their carers. In this way, project workers gained insight and developed opinions regarding the issues they considered important.

Informing   Every person who was to be interviewed (carer and child) was informed in detail about the aims and subject of the interview before it began. Everyone had the right to accept or to refuse the interview. This is still the case.

Contact-card   After the interview, every child was given a contact-card (with the address and phone number of SCF and the interviewer) to encourage them to contact us whenever in need of assistance.

Consultation   In every activity that has been offered, initiated and/or carried out, the child has been consulted and his/her opinion has been taken into account. The programme continues to monitor and reassess each child's situation.

Because child-participation wasn't an explicit objective, no evaluation indicators and methods were established.

Phase 2, in March 1996, was planned using the conclusions from our regular reviewing procedure and in the framework of SCF's global-strategy approach. In an attempt to move beyond individual casework towards a more developmental approach, while still working on durable solutions for individual children, the concept of child participation has become an important subject in our seminars and publishing activities.

What are we working on?

In attempting to achieve a balance within our country programme between available resources, contributing to overall SCF strategy and meeting real needs in FRY, child participation has become more explicit in this phase of our work.

The promotion of fostering programme
This programme aims to improve fostering services, the objective being: 'to act in order to give the children opportunities to be listened to and to encourage them to take part in activities and decisions regarding foster service proceedings'. This aim is central and explicit in the programme.

The first phase concentrates on increasing the number of foster-carers and improving assessment procedures through media promotion and support to professionals in the Centre for Social Welfare. Both these methods (below) encourage children to share their view on fostering and help adults (potential foster carers) to listen to their own children:

- video tape – presents foster-children's insights on fostering at fostering evenings organized to inform and encourage people to become foster parents;
- interviews with potential foster-carers' own children within the assessment procedure. Teams at the Centre for Social Welfare have been already trained.

When evaluating the fostering evenings the level of influence of the children's views on participants will be assessed. New documentation will be designed for the assessment procedure to take into account views of children in the potential foster home.

Within the second phase (improvement of the follow-up procedure) a workshop will be developed to create opportunities for the views of foster-children to be heard. They will be encouraged to share their opinions on living in foster families. Based on this, the foster-child diary will be developed. This should be a guide for a foster-child to talk about important issues with regular follow-up procedures. The follow-up documentation will be a means of verifying action taken on issues raised by children.

The disability programme
This programme aims to promote a non-institutional system of care, improve professionals' skills and encourage parents' associations to act on behalf of children. According to its aims, the programme targets professionals and parents directly. Once again, child participation has not been an explicit objective but the stated aim: 'to work on making services more relevant to disabled children's needs', included a child-participation approach. It was more explicit on the level of activities:

- individual work-plan for each child based on an assessment of his/her needs and abilities;

- competition to choose the names for toy-libraries;
- establishment of local toy libraries where children and parents can interact positively and expression of opinions is actively encouraged; and
- training and publications for parents in relation to their child and disability which includes communication and interaction with children.

The next child-participation phase has explicit objectives: to develop a child-led group which will demonstrate the inherent value of disabled children as individuals, their potential as positive and independent members of society, the value of participative methods of research and work with disabled children, and the reality of institutional and public responses to disability.

What next?

In considering joint work and the influence achieved through local agencies, we are developing a comprehensive strategy for the next period. Together with local partners, SCF established a local NGO, the Yugoslav Child Rights' Centre, one of whose specific objectives is to promote the concept and practice of child participation. The centre is working on a distinct Child Participation Programme that aims, together with the other programmes within the centre (Resource Base, Advocacy Programme, NGO Development), to promote the UN Convention on the Rights of the Child. Our contribution is focused especially on creating the programmes that specifically facilitate children's participation and improve child-related services. The promotion will include:

- child participation in all centre activities and programmes (as appropriate); and
- specific child participation programmes, projects and actions.

The following principles are established as the basic ones:

- taking into account children's needs, views and interests (e.g. including them in the initiating, planning and realization of programmes);
- taking into account cultural and social realities; and
- a practical action approach in all types of activities.

A developmental approach, active-learning techniques and development of appropriate models comprise the methodological frames of our activities. The multidisciplinary working group that is creating a strategy for the next two years has suggested the following activities:

- *Research* – on children's knowledge and understanding of their rights, on adults' attitudes towards children's rights and participation, on children's contributions in life and comparison between legal regulations and practice;
- *Education* – for different targets (e.g. different age groups, youth leaders, parents, professionals, volunteers, specific groups like scouts) by using two strategies, depending on the subject: (i) education only for children or adults; and (ii) education for children and adults together
- *Participation models* – e.g. support to a joint decision-making board within institutional care and support to a jointly organized conference on child participation;

- *Child-led work* – supporting existing child-led organizations, actions and initiatives; and
- *Informing* – supporting the establishment of a children's news agency/newspaper, influence through an existing magazine for children.

There is a significant emphasis on programme monitoring, evaluation and the assessment of expected outcomes.

We have moved from a situation where children's involvement in programmes was not recognized or structured as participation and the concept seen as alien and threatening to many professionals, through explicit recognition and inclusion in project objectives and activities to recognition of the need for a comprehensive, separate programme established as joint work between SCF and a local NGO to promote and develop children's participation as a concept and a practice.

What have we learned?
Even when it seems (for example, in war or crisis) that child participation is not a priority, it can be introduced in a flexible manner, having in mind the context and the different levels of participation, but, if we want to act in a developmental, long-term way to make visible impacts and assess effects, our work must be methodologically based. That means that, at the very beginning, we have to:

- start with a situation analysis regarding child participation issues in society;
- define indicators in order to be able to evaluate programmes and to assess impacts; and
- develop a step-by-step action plan which takes into account not only possible constraints but also existing capacities.

What about cultural specificity?
The methodological rules are more or less universal, but the implementation strategy should be discussed in local cultural terms. A situation analysis means obtaining culturally based attitudes towards children in order to disclose the barriers to participation, together with other data. Common statements like 'this society is traditional, frightened of participation' and so on have to be translated on an operational level in order to create a strategy to deal with them. One way of taking into account cultural specificity is to work together with local agencies and to extend influence through them.

What about historical (transitional, post-war) issues?
There is no correct answer to this question. There is only our belief that the present time should be seen as an opportunity for positive change. Because of this we have decided to start with broad action that includes advocacy, lobbying, research, education, informing and, above all, promoting models of child participation. When we look at the components of the participation process (to listen, to respect and to take into account) we can consider them as phases of children's empowerment. In an attempt to be realistic about our work, we have decided to define as the first step: 'to help adults to learn how

Figure 5.3: *'We will rebuild...'*

to listen to children'. Further, in order to avoid political implications, a sensitive matter in FRY, we should start by presenting the benefits of empowerment on the level of the child and encouraging adults to make child-related services more relevant to children's needs.

5.3 Conclusions

PAT PRIDMORE

The experiences presented in Part 5 confirm that even in situations of crisis[2] there is a need for agencies to reorientate policy towards a child-focused approach. Children should be recognized as active agents in creating and responding to conflict, they are not victims passively allowing the situation to impact on their lives. Where agencies have grasped the crisis situation as an opportunity for positive change and accepted the need to implement such approaches, children have been able to make a valuable contribution to research and programme development. The challenge now is two-fold: (i) to work with children to define qualitative indicators in order to evaluate programmes better and assess impacts more efficiently; and (ii) to encourage partner organizations to follow suit.

Reorienting policy has wider implications for the training of project staff. There is a particular need to develop ethical strategies to support traumatized children and to train staff and local people to develop the skills needed for working with children in a truly participatory way. Training is needed in the counselling skills required to enable field workers to support the healing process. Adults have to learn how to listen to children and involve them in activities that help develop the trust and rapport which often become eroded in the face of trauma. We need to bear in mind that researchers, too, must develop these special skills. Resource materials focusing on the use of participatory approaches in crisis situations and refugee camps have been compiled by Attwood (1996) and Hanbury (1993). These make a valuable contribution to the growing pool of ideas and methods for increasing the participation of both adults and children in crisis situations.

Further research is needed to increase understanding of the way in which children's resilience can be strengthened in specific cultural contexts. This understanding can then be used to develop more relevant programmes that aim to build inner personal strengths and interpersonal communication skills. Such programmes can help to prevent, minimize or overcome the damaging effects of adversity. Feedback of research findings to the child participants has often been neglected and needs to be prioritized.

There is a need to identify field methods which are fun for children and which minimize the risk of people becoming suspicious of 'outsiders'. In situations of social and political instability it may be better to avoid note-taking, and to use visual methods which allow the information generated from activities and discussions to be displayed for all to see. Special attention must also be given to the micro-culture of the setting where programme activities take place. This is of paramount importance because the micro-culture can allow for successful participation even when the macro-culture is in an unstable state. The notion of participation as 'child power' can also be threatening and it can be more valuable to focus initially on ways in which listening to children and trying to understand their viewpoints can help to resolve problems and to increase the relevance of services provided to the community.

Notes

1. Paper 5.2 has been extracted from paper 4.5, written by Barnabas Otaala.
2. For many participants in the workshop the special issues around children's participation in crisis situations provided valuable new insights into the factors which help and hinder children's involvement.

Figure 5.4: *'I'm going to tell you a story. Every time I say "roach!" stamp on the floor, every time I say "snake!", jump on the chair and hiss, and when I say "lion!", hide behind the chair and growl!'*

PART 6

Institutions and Power

Editors and co-authors: VICTORIA JOHNSON
AND PATTA SCOTT

Co-authors: DENISE ALLEN, SHEENA CRAWFORD, MARK FEENEY,
JULIA GILKES, LUCY HARRIS, AMY KASPAR, MARY ELLEN LEWIS,
RACHEL MARCUS, BERRY MAYALL, ESTHER OBDAM, AMANDA
OLIVIER, BEN OSUGA, JOHN PARRY-WILLIAMS, AMANDA
SAURIN, BARRY PERCY-SMITH, DAVID WOOLLCOMBE,
ABEBAW ZELLEKE

Summary

Legitimizing children's participation raises challenges for people who try to change the web of power relationships between adults, children and institutions. A thread running through Part 6 is how personal behaviour and attitudes towards children are central to achieving positive outcomes within different institutional contexts. Part 6 is split into four sections: section 1 addresses institutions from the perspective of young people's roles and motivations and also looks at young people's organizations and the family in its many forms; section 2 explores the role of the school; section 3 the role of non-governmental organizations; and section 4 the international and tertiary education institutions, whose policies often seem beyond our reach. Power relations within and between institutions are examined, and successful strategies and processes to increase children's participation suggested by contributors from many parts of the world, including Ethiopia, Tanzania, Palestine, Jamaica, South Africa, countries of west Asia and various parts of the UK.

Key issues raised in Part 6:

- There are numerous examples that demonstrate the value of children's participation in policy, research and community programmes. Despite this, there must be closer evaluation of the positive and negative impacts of participation for children and young people, and children must be given the option to opt out of adult-initiated schemes.
- Issues of difference, e.g. gender, class, ethnicity and disability, lead to children's exclusion from institutions and their broader society.
- Children's participation poses a fundamental threat to adult/child power relationships, which makes its institutionalization a great challenge.
- During the lifetime of a project, adult attitudes towards children's participation change. Adult decision-makers can gradually become convinced of benefits to all parties and may start to relinquish an appropriate amount of power and control to children.
- Young people can gain confidence and self-esteem through the process of a project offering genuine participation.
- Capacity-building of all adult stakeholders, including staff and parents, may hold the key to a greater understanding and acceptance of children's participation.
- Institutionalizing child participation is likely to be successful only if built upon the values and experiences of young people.
- It is vital to understand children's and young people's own informal networks and groupings, and their personal motivations for participation. It is important to support and fund youth groups, set up and directed by young people themselves.
- Funding agencies need to be aware of the time needed to achieve more meaningful and effective participation of children and young people.

- Young people can be in a special position to contribute to social change. They may not have such vested interests, and such responsibility as adults; but possess insight, courage and the inclination to bring about change.
- Participation can be capacity-building for children, in the sense of sustaining their lives, communities and environment, and also for institutions which, in the long term, are infused with greater legitimacy and energy.

6.0   Introduction

VICTORIA JOHNSON and PATTA SCOTT

The image of a child at the centre of a series of different institutional levels that affect her/his life is an important starting point. These layers of influence affect the ways in which a child can become involved in family, street, and community life and in the broader context of service provision and policy decision-making.

'The PRA experience is that the institutional challenge is formidable' (Chambers, 1997: 221). Two recent publications are relevant here (ed. Blackburn, with Holland, 1998) and (ed. Holland, with Blackburn, 1998). The first contributes a range of experiences from the field, exploring the opportunities and challenges of institutionalizing participatory approaches. The editors note that participation has become a central theme in development and that as it becomes institutionalized new sets of challenges arise. They identify three major areas of change: scaling-up, 'an expansion [of participation] which has a cumulative impact'; organizational change, 'a change not only in the way projects are implemented but also in the procedure and processes by which development decisions are made'; and behaviour and attitudes, 'the question of "who changes?"'. Holland, with Blackburn (1998) explores the relationships between participatory research and policy. It highlights initiatives that have challenged power structures to recognize heterogeneity in society and foster greater inclusion of the poor and marginalized groups in policy decisions. In the case of children's participation, it is clear that not only do institutional processes and power structures need to be assessed critically, but that the fundamental power relationships between adults and children need to be analysed and challenged.

The 'universal' model of childhood, dominant in the development psychology literature, has imposed on the developing countries a notion of a 'good childhood' from the industrial world. This approach is clearly evident in policies of NGOs, governments and international organizations that have a mandate to work with children (Edwards, 1996a: 818):

Traditional welfare approaches based on sentimentalizing children and Western models of childhood have given way to arguments about children's central role in development, though couched mainly in terms of good economic sense (investing in a future workforce) rather than political participation. The next stage in the evolution of agency approaches is to incorporate the challenge of treating children as social actors.

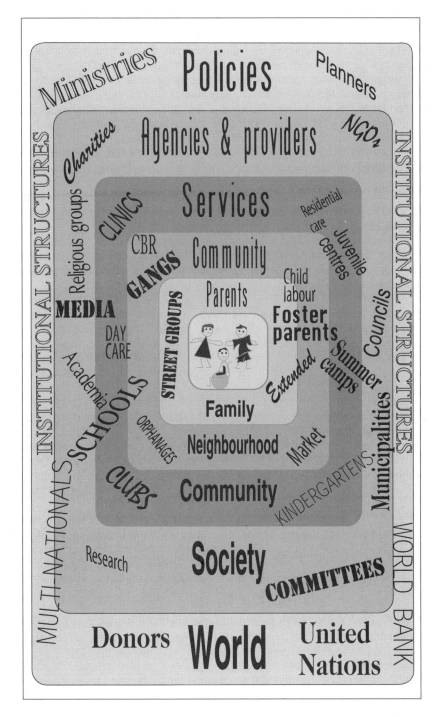

Figure 6.1: *Institutional structures*

177

Although some agencies are moving in this direction, as is shown in this part, many are still at the stage of treating children's views as inferior and irrelevant to decision-making regarding their own development or that of their society.

In order for the outcomes of participatory approaches with children to influence policy and action, active institutional support is needed (Edwards, 1996b; Niewenhuys, 1996). Training and continual reflection throughout a project process can build the skills necessary to draw the best from children's participation, primarily by changing attitudes and behaviour. This applies to all levels of programme and policy staff and to other adults involved in projects with children, including parents. Training is often the most visible aspect of institutionalizing participatory planning, but holding a few initial participatory workshops may not be adequate to achieve more than a superficial and temporary change. Organizations often find it hard to go beyond this stage as they have not only official rules and policies, but also unspoken rules and value systems (Guijt, 1996). Changing an organization means addressing fundamental human relationships and taking risks with people and resources. This type of assertion is starting to become central to the broader participatory debates – a South-South workshop was held in India in 1996 by ActionAid India and SPEECH on the 'ABC of PRA: attitudes, behaviour, change'. In this workshop it was recognized that there needs to be transformation of organizational cultures along with changes in personal attitudes and behaviour. 'At a personal level, practitioners and trainers have found that the problem in development is not with "them" – local people, the poor and marginalized, but with "us" – the outsider professionals,' (Chambers, in ActionAid; SPEECH, 1996: 3).

We should recognize that there is a great difference between children's organizations and the adult bodies that make decisions about the communities in which children live. Hart (1996) promotes a concept of 'children's democratic socialization' that calls for new kinds of institutional structures. Innovation can also arise from revision of existing organizations. However, he also states that we have to understand links between children's groups and adult institutions, such as local community organizations, local governments and local environmental-planning agencies (Hart, 1996: 56).

Many of the chapters in this part examine the ways in which adult organizations can foster greater children's participation and support children's initiatives and young people's organizations. However, the importance of understanding children and young people's own informal networks and groups is also acknowledged and discussed. In each context, young people's motivations for participation need to be clarified and their right to opt out of participation respected.

Part 6 shows the importance of understanding the inter-linkages and power relationships within and between institutional structures and levels. Children's and young people's own informal networks and groupings are as vital to understand as the more formal organizations in this regard. Despite its tendency to generate conflict and uncertainty along the way, the participatory process can have a tremendously beneficial effect on these relationships. This may be one of the primary reasons why increased participation by children is desirable for a child as well as for a broader set of actors. There is a call for closer examination of the impact and desirability of participation for all involved. The need for progressive learning about the benefits and pitfalls of participation through a gradual process of involvement is acknowledged, particularly to understand how children themselves feel about it in different contexts and how they could benefit from different types of involvement. Children and young people already play important roles as social actors and agents of change, and the future of their participation can build on this foundation; developing partnerships and celebrating diversity and innovation.

6.1 Patterns for the future: knitting reflection into the practice of children's participation

AMY KASPAR

While interest in children's participation grows, there is concern that broader implications of its practice deserve deeper reflection. Issues need to be resolved before young people can realize their full rights and international mandates (such as UNCRC, Agenda 21, and Children's Rights and Habitat) are met. Children's participatory rights must be advanced with the assurances that (i) children are actually benefiting through growth, development, and realization of citizenship; (ii) that families, communities, societies and cultures are benefiting; and (iii) that the dangers, pitfalls, and *naïveté* of practice have been planned for to prevent negative repercussions in children's lives. Discussed here are some implications of children's participatory practice that must be considered.

Institutional structures and capacity for participation

Institutions are the vehicles by which policies on children's rights and sustainable development are set in motion, yet existing institutional structures counter the realities of children's participatory projects and limit young people's capacity for participation. Funding, legal, and economic structures must be adapted to suit the needs of those working to implement participatory principles at the grassroots level.

Current international aid structures demand deliverable projects. Those which receive funding and continued support are the projects which can deliver results within specified constraints of financial budgets, time-frames, indicators, reporting mechanisms and predetermined agendas. Participatory projects are, however, time and human resource intensive. Typically, the more autonomy which young people develop in the project, the more unpredictable and lengthier the process has been. Outgrowth activities often result from the deep involvement of young people in decision-making processes. Short-term funding structures limit projects' evolutionary capacity and children's longitudinal development.

Marginalized by laws, young people are restricted from full involvement in adult society and are kept away from political and economic arenas. Adults' protective efforts limit their access to space, activity, productive duties, responsibility, ownership of their own ideas, and interaction with adults and other children. Until voting age, their concerns are overshadowed legally by the voices of adults. Until they gain employment with substantial economic benefits, they remain economically dependent on others and/or at the margins of survival. This is clear in the lives of working children, and is also apparent in the increasing emphasis on the attainment of higher levels of education away from the job market. These protective measures actually limit children's ability to develop self-protective skills, identity, responsibility and constructive assertions that are vital to their functioning as citizens. Here lies an inherent conflict between protective and participatory principles.

Power relationships associated with young people's participation

Power dynamics influence children's capacity for participation through roles and relationships. Adults influence young people as facilitators and parents, and children influence each other through peer relationships. The degree of young people's 'real power' is one determinant in the type of genuine participation which can be achieved.

As facilitators, adults determine how projects are presented to children, how children are guided through the process, what information is presented to them and how informed consent is handled. Each of these duties can influence the choices that a child makes.

As parents, adults set limits on children's capacity for involvement, provide support, contradiction, advice or reinforcement to projects. Advancing children's participatory roles in society may be contrary to the expectations of the family unit. This conflict may be acutely felt in the lives of girls in developing democracies where family units have experienced dramatic changes or where parents are limited in asserting their own rights. Intergenerational difference may be exacerbated by the perceived 'empowerment' of children.

Because children are not independent entities, facilitators must not only work with the family unit but must also consider the influence of peer groups in young people's lives. Youth are as diverse as adults in their characteristics, talents, interests, and chosen role models. Youth sub-cultural norms can influence how adult-initiated participatory projects are perceived and implemented by young people.

If they are to realize their rights and citizenship, young people need to have 'real power' (Woollcombe, 1996) to negotiate and work in partnership with adults. Beyond voting, children need to be involved in working through decisions, taking responsibility for actions and learning from outcomes. Despite adults' protective notions of childhood and uninformed fears over loss of power, young people need to be owners and partners of ideas, space and process management. With their own space, children can have a sense of control over their environment and freedom to explore ideas. With developed skills, young people can share in responsibility for financial and resource decisions. Not involving young people in this process gives adults the 'final word' in how funds are spent, how resources are used, which projects proceed and the process by which projects develop.

Contexts of participatory practice: institutional and informal

In participatory practice, there exists a strong dissonance between institutional requirements and youth perspectives. In order to establish projects with youth, there must be in place legal, financial and logistical frameworks.

181

Without these supports, adults are limited in their accessibility to young people and management of projects. With these protective constraints, most participatory projects occur in formal settings. Within the contexts of institutions, young people are often told to participate through classroom exercises or in community-development programmes. Projects initiated and sustained by youth are less common in formal settings. Such approaches may limit the genuine level of involvement which young people may achieve.

In order to bridge the gap between institutions and youth perspectives, young people need to be involved in determining the contextual factors which will best promote their capacity for participation. It may be that youth actually engage in more genuine participatory roles through informal contexts. While young people learn significant skills in formal settings, one questions whether this is the type of participation that will encourage the long-term development of citizenship. Informal settings may provide more opportunities for youth to communicate in their own language, to develop competency in working with their peers and negotiating with adults, and for young people to exercise greater autonomy in the growth of projects.

Defining and measuring genuine participation

Policy-makers, funders, and project managers need standard definitions, models, and monitoring structures to quantify participatory projects in budgetary decisions. Without models that consider multiple variables and contexts, participatory projects cannot be adequately planned for, funded or evaluated. Relying on current definitions, the 'measurement' of children's genuine participation is highly subjective, yet developing contextualized definitions and models, which account for infinite variables, is an extraordinarily complex task. Children's development, cultural context and forms of participation are fluid factors that melt into infinite possibilities of interaction stretched over time. In both the immediate and the long term, the development of participatory skills affects a child's, family's and community's holistic being. While participatory rights may be universal, their interpretation, meaning, inferred agendas and roles are socially and culturally constructed.

The meaning and motivation for participation for young people

Perhaps listening more closely to young people will solidify meanings of genuine participation. Current literature explains the adult-perceived benefits of participation, yet adults may not know how their notions of participation are perceived by children. Real participation does not feed answers to children but rather provides questions to fuel personal growth and an understanding of their world. If not told to be involved in projects, then why do youth choose to become involved, and what benefits do they perceive? Participation may be a means to an end: the hope that, by becoming involved, basic needs may be achieved. For instance, for children in urban slums, is participation about attaining appropriate sanitation or about developing skills and knowledge to help them break the cycle of poverty?

If support is to be given to children to develop their participatory roles and skills, then adults must know what the process means to young people. To connect with youth and to create appropriate spaces for its exploration, adults need to understand what inspires and bores young people about participation. Understanding the factors that motivate them into action can improve programme design, accessibility, reach and support. It may also help build bridges between young people and parents, communities and funding institutions.

The relevancy of political will as a motivator also needs to be explored. The development of citizenship is not devoid of political meaning or effect. One questions if, especially in situations of economic, political, ethnic or racial oppression, the need to participate is inextricably linked to political willpower. Examples of students and young people aligning with other societal groups abound in the twentieth century. While broader social changes may be an ideal of participation, democratic movements involving young people have both triumphed over and been crushed by dictatorships within the past decade. Such history may support the relevancy of a link between political will and the acquisition of participatory skills. The potential political consequence of this link implies heavy ethical responsibility for critical awareness on behalf of promoters of children's participation.

Longitudinal impact of participation in young people's lives

The long-term hope of participation is that young people may grow into citizens capable of sustaining their lives, communities and environment. So far, the effects of participation on children's adult lives are not known. Longitudinal studies are necessary to dissect experiences.

In the immediate time-frame there are several realities. Participatory projects are time-intensive and unpredictable evolutionary processes. To impose time-frames and pre-established agendas limits young people's ability to develop the project as an organic process. The consequences of projects that are unable to meet specified (budgetary) criteria are rarely reported. For adult facilitators, a failed, incomplete, or mismanaged project is chalked up to experience; for young people, however, the consequences can colour their perceptions for a lifetime. Youth, who may already be marginalized, may become further disillusioned.

Over the long term, young people are both put at risk and benefit by involvement in participatory projects. In cultures that are resistant to participatory activities, the risk arises simply by their involvement. Enabling young people to develop alternative thought processes can render them vulnerable over a lifetime. An idealized outcome is to enable them to question dominant values, issues and paradigms in their cultures; but without appropriate support, they may become isolated in their ideas, weakened and, in the worst scenarios, threatened or punished.

Hope appears in the experience of individuals who have learned participatory skills as youth and who are now, as adults, reinvesting that awareness in the next generation. Such individuals have developed an inherent knowledge of effective participatory practice. If the positive impacts of participation on children's lives are to be realized, then both positive and negative outcomes need to be evaluated and incorporated into programming.

Cultural resistance

The practice of participation introduces new ways of thinking about oneself, the world, and one's relationship with that world. Many cultures are resistant to this type of change, and some may even perceive it as a threat to their society's foundations. Intergenerational conflict, strained facilitator–parent relationships and restrictions on children's involvement can be symptoms of this resistance.

In each situation, the legitimacy of cultural resistance needs to be determined. As the long-term outcomes of participatory actions are unknown, promoters must tread cultural boundaries with great ethical responsibility. Issues of power relationships, adequate support and longitudinal impact are interrelated. How much should cultural resistance be heeded, and when (and how) should its boundaries be pressed?

The role of participation within cultures which are resistant to its methods and ideals needs to be evaluated. Culturally specific meanings of children's participation must be explored if young people's capacities and needs are to be met effectively. Theoretical approaches to participation need to be contextualized into various cultural bases.

Knitting reflection into practice

International organizations work hard to sell certain mandates, ideals, philosophies and methodologies. It may, on the one hand, be necessary for adults to market the concept of participatory rights in order to obtain alternative spaces, institutional support and appropriate environments in which to nurture, practice and learn about participation; on the other hand, there is concern that without appropriate reflection, adults may be inadvertently marketing participation to children without knowing the ramifications of the product's effects. As promoters of young people's rights, there is an ethical responsibility to resolve these implications if children are to realize their potential as citizens. As reflective practitioners, such discussions need to bridge continents and experiences, including the wisdom of those who may not usually be involved.

6.2 Children's participation in research: the Paradise Project in Grenada

DENISE ALLEN

Oliver's Story

Oliver displayed low literacy and expressed his need for glasses. He is eager to learn and exhibits much interest in the project, though his educational level sets him at a disadvantage. Oliver, like the other boys, entered the project a month after the girls and he is younger than most group members. He is punctual and helpful. A relatively quiet but an active listener, Oliver is shy and seems the least likely person to lead any group session.

During the preparation phase other children were taking the questionnaire they designed to their own areas where they could test their skills among their peers with whom they were comfortable. Oliver was reluctant to do this work and seemed a little more comfortable using the recorder for his questioning.

The first opportunity for data collection came when the interviewers met 29 children from a rural community called Belvedere. At this point Oliver surprised everyone by standing up before outspoken Jessie and addressed the group. He introduced himself, outlined the aim of the project and our reason for visiting, smiling proudly throughout his presentation. This was a significant achievement for a young man who, seven weeks earlier, had had great difficulty expressing his views in a small, intimate group. Oliver's actions on this occasion spoke volumes on the kind of advancement made in building self-esteem, confidence and skills. Oliver further took the initiative to ask for the tape cassette as he was 'manning' the tape recorder seriously. He also asked for brochures on the UN Convention on the Rights of the Child (UNCRC) and sought permission to share them with the children in Belvedere. Oliver's blossoming may be attributed to many things: exposure to a team environment, the older girls' role modelling, continued support and encouragement from the co-ordinators, and somewhere, a decision within himself to trust himself and take a risk. It seems to be paying off. (Dorsey Precht, Paradise Project Co-ordinator)

Background to the Paradise Project

GrenSave approached Save the Children (SCF) to support a research project that sought to ascertain how tourism affects children. SCF agreed, but requested an approach whereby children's views were more accurately represented and also one where they would be more closely involved in the process.

Oliver typifies most of the children who enlisted as co-researchers for the Paradise Project. The original research conception did not have Oliver at the planning and implementing end of the project. Instead he, like others, was to be a simple respondent whose views would be gleaned and examined completely from an adult perspective. This approach seemed undesirable when we recognized that children have a developing capacity for fostering, analysing and promoting their own perspectives on issues that affect national life. Consequently, we abandoned sophisticated statistical tools and used the resources to buy lunches and pay bus fares for 15 youngsters to participate in redesigning, preparing and carrying out the research project. An additional challenge was added as we recruited children not for their academic abilities or talents but their interests. As a result, children like Oliver entered the team.

The Paradise Project is the name of a research project that examines the effect of tourism on Grenada's children. It uses an approach which involves children fully in the process. The research is qualitative in nature and will therefore use techniques that the children believe best receive and convey their views. Consequently, in addition to more traditional data-collection methods such as interviews, more participatory methods, including drama,

185

social-mapping exercises and calypso (a popular Caribbean music form), have been introduced. The project is currently in progress and the children are gathering data for analysis and presentation.

Challenges of child participation in research

Team building

> In the afternoon, Sister Ann Celestine, principal of the Grand Anse RC School, brought with her six young boys to join the group ... First deciding on the interview questions, we broke the group up into three, to conduct their own interviews with each other. With only three girls present, we put one girl with each group. We discovered that three of the six boys could not read or write above a 'Dick and Jane' level. The girls had the opportunity to be leaders in their groups and were very good with the boys, challenging the boys' shyness and encouraging them. (Dorsey Precht's journal on the preparation phase of the Paradise Project).

Unlike adults, a few years' difference in age meant significant differences in capacities and interests amongst the children, while gender differences affected the children's inclination to work as a team. The co-ordinators discussed their experience in this kind of work and the expected outcomes of the project. Although team-building exercises were unnecessary for the girls from the same school and grade, it became crucial when the boys entered the project a few weeks later.

Before introducing new information about tourism, we established what the children already knew about the subject. Encouraging them to recognize the knowledge they already had, the co-ordinators began blending confidence-building exercises into the activities. For example, everyone was given an opportunity to address the group on an aspect of tourism about which they knew. Through these exercises the group members learnt the value of listening to each other, exchanging ideas in an open and constructive fashion and how to support each other.

Literacy and education

There are differences in educational levels between the girls and boys. The co-ordinators conducted the activities, none the less, making allowances for the youngsters to develop at the tasks, and adjusting their own expectations of the children. Academic limitations were a potential problem but offered the co-ordinators an opportunity to confront important issues that arise when adults seek to increase child participation in any work. They came to the conclusion that patience, flexibility and acceptance are fundamental values that must accompany interaction with children. Experience so far suggests that child researchers need lots of freedom to express and experiment. The challenge lies in how well adults are prepared to accommodate their unconventional methods as legitimate and important. Dorsey Precht noted that:

> Bringing children into an adult arena, to gain their input in decision-making processes does not mean that the child enters that arena as anything

other than a child. Too often adults select more articulate, mature children to represent children's views. This in part happens as these children blend into the adult world better than a child who is playful, energetic and spontaneous.

Keschey (a child researcher) made note of the evaluation question regarding any disappointment she may have had at the camp. Her concern was over the superficial nature of many of the children's response to the exercises. She hoped that they would go deeper, considering the economy and the negative effects of tourism rather then offer pat answers. Keschey said she was not surprised by the lack of understanding or ability really to examine issues, she was accustomed to this problem at her school. (Dorsey Precht's research journal).

Keschey's problem with her peers speaks to a common problem that dogs the Caribbean education system. Children's school learning does not appear to stimulate critical thinking. Instead they learn by rote. A passive approach coupled with a strict adherence to good behaviour and observance of rules seem to hinder many children's natural creativity, curiosity and critical thought processes. Genuine participation in this project necessitated that the co-ordinators assisted the children to break through these restrictions to become more creative in their thinking and confident in their own internal sense of responsibility and humanity. The UNCRC proved very useful in helping the children to appreciate how special they are in society and there-fore how crucial it was for them to have their own perspectives on what was happening around them.

Data-gathering methods
After experimenting with a few data-collection methods, the young researchers met to decide what methods were most effective:

They felt the group discussions were the best way to bring out ideas and then to go with them into the TOURISM, job-ranking, article and UNCRC exercise. I was glad to hear they wanted to include the CRC in the work. . . saying the kids would not know their rights and should. They felt that other children would be interested to hear that there was actually a document to support them. (Dorsey Precht's journal on the preparation phase of the Paradise Project).

Practising data-collection methods was a central part of the preparation phase before the children began. They were allowed to select the most appropriate methods with minimum direction from the co-ordinators. The collection tools were worthwhile, first if the children felt they could use them, and second if they elicited the information adequately. Since the selection is critical for the next stage the co-ordinators thought that the children ought to have as much room as possible in making those choices.

The research methods pose challenges for us in safeguarding the credibil-ity of the results while at the same time ensuring that children remain genuine partners in the process. At this stage the wider Grenada community is intrigued with both, and awakening to the fact that children have views and thoughts that are important to understand. The authorities are slowly waking up to this realization. One tourist official who was opposed to the project initially is now giving it his full support and has offered a short plane trip for the children to visit a tourist site on a nearby island as part of their orientation and training.

Next stage

The Paradise Project has strong potential for work in advocacy with children as the primary actors in its development and execution. SCF's Caribbean Programme is currently working closely with partners including GrenSave on developing methodologies around children-led advocacy projects. Both the child researchers and research findings could form an integral part of this next phase of work. The national advocate group on children's rights is already poised for fostering the youth arm.

6.3   The Peace Child rescue mission experience

DAVID WOOLLCOMBE AND AMANDA OLIVIER

The story of Peace Child is one of increasing responsibility by children. It started with a musical play in which the dialogue, characters and story were drawn from children through improvization and workshop techniques. It moved on to the creation of books which were written, designed, edited and illustrated by children drawing on a minimum level of professional adult support. It also included the design and building of the student hostel from which the organization is run. Having proved themselves capable of exercising their responsibility most effectively in these roles, it was a natural progression for them to take on the responsibility for running the organization, again in partnership with adults, not instead of adults.

The structures put in place to enable this to happen are fairly straightforward: a board of directors was set up, composed of representatives of the major Peace Child groups around the world along with key adult advisers. Young people form the majority on the board and can, theoretically, hire and fire the project director because ultimate responsibility for all activities of the project rests with them. This fulfils a key principle of children's participation, that they should have real power. In South Africa, the new School Act makes great noise about the need to set up student councils in every school. The new councils will have a substantial advisory role but no real power, for example, to fire bad teachers. They stress that this provides them with citizenship training, but the experience of being on a council with no power might confirm only that citizens are powerless, which is not perhaps the lesson the authors of the strategy had in mind.

In South Africa, there is a colossal divide between the black schools, where children have never had any real participation and probably never will, as the whole culture of black schools seems to resist it, and the white schools where there is more readiness to accept it. Even so, Rescue Mission in Amanda's school is the first group ever to be set up and run by students. This is in a liberal, go-ahead school, which again emphazises how rare the idea of children's participation was in the apartheid years. There will have to be much greater leadership and surrender of responsibility from the top to enable children's participation to take root in South Africa.

Interestingly, the only problem encountered in the Peace Child/Rescue Mission institutional structures has been how to divide responsibility amongst the young people, not the division of responsibility between the adults. If the principles of respect, communication, ground rules, time alone, support, etc. are adhered to, there are few tensions between the two groups as there is much positive experience of what each generational group can offer to the other. Also, as explained above, the institutional structure demonstrates that real power lies with the young people, so adults can only do things with their express approval.

However, at an early board meeting, the adults present felt that it would be a good idea to have youth and adult co-directors so that the organization would be perceived by outsiders as being run by adults and youth in partnership. Without consulting the full youth membership, an appointment was made, and a youth co-director started work. Some of the adults argued that she should be paid the same as the adult co-director, clearly absurd as she had no responsibilities, no family to support, etc., but it was agreed that she should be paid a salary, where the other young people working at the headquarters were volunteers. This immediately created tension, as did her position. 'Why?', the young people asked, 'should she have any more power in this organization than we do. Many of us have been connected to it for longer than she has!' The backchat and arguing went on, making life extremely difficult for the co-director until finally, at the next board meeting, the young people proposed a different administrative structure. A group of 5–10 young people at headquarters took collective responsibility for co-directing projects, thus empowering the whole group of young people working there rather than just one. This decision was painful for the young co-director as she felt she had failed. She got over it, however, and the new arrangement works well, she having taken over the co-directorship of several key projects.

The other main problems we have encountered are related chiefly to finance and cash flow. This is not a specific concern of a group that practises children's participation but it may be illustrative of the fact that, in the funding world, there is no particular benefit that is perceived to have been derived from working in partnership with young people. However, the benefits to the organization in terms of the quality and freshness of the materials produced, of the ideas generated, projects started and strategies fulfilled is indisputable. A youth-directed organization like Peace Child shows that young people should be engaged to do more co-teaching in the classroom; granted more responsibility in the development and running of community structures; and given a seat at the table in the running of all organizations that affect their lives.

Box 6.1: Raising awareness of children's rights to opinions and participation in decision-making in Palestine

During the last 10 years, SCF in Palestine has worked with partners in child-focused NGOs and with staff from ministries in the National Authority through training and programme development. Recently the focus has had two key aims:

(1) to strengthen relationships and partnerships between parents, the community and programme providers through workshops, seminars and parent committees;
(2) to raise awareness of the potential and capabilities of children to share their opinions on issues of interest and importance in their changing lives.

The child-to-child approach has introduced teachers, club leaders, parents and the wider community to new insights of children's views of the world around them. In societies where children have little opportunity to voice their opinions, parents have developed great pride and listened to children presenting their ideas on the television, in newspapers and in concerts, surveys, demonstrations and posters. Activity sheets are now being drafted with community-based rehabilitation (CBR) workers and teachers for promoting inclusive education for children with special needs.

In the kindergartens, some children with disabilities and special needs have been included in a pilot scheme in Gaza. Teachers and CBR workers, together with parents, are working to ensure that all the children have a fair start in their pre-school years. Children are being involved in monitoring and evaluating the scheme. At the ages of 5 and 6 years, young children are quite capable of commenting on activities and situations that affect them, and can work with adults to develop indicators of impact on their kindergarten experience. It is hoped that at the end of the first year of this scheme, the voices of the children with and without special needs will contribute to the evaluation of this stage and comment on the expectation of inclusion in the transition into school.

Julia Gilkes

Box 6.2: Reflections from Uganda: the household

From my experience, the household is the first institution. Here, a child's potential to participate in influencing decisions and policy is often overlooked. Power at a household level affects children's welfare. The power dynamics between adults and children, and between male and female must be understood. In disputes between the father or the husband, and the mother or the wife respectively, children are often caught in the middle. Understanding issues of difference between the male and female child is also important. In the case of decision making, preference by adults in most families is for the male child.

190

Apart from power, one of the most important issue affecting children's participation is poverty. Poverty disempowers everyone, especially children. From my experience of living and working in East Africa, children from poor families, especially the girls, usually find it difficult to attend school in tattered and dirty clothes. If they do, they may be shy and unassertive. This affects their performance in school and they may also fear to go out in public.

Ben Osuga

6.4   Young people and institutions

WORKING GROUP REPORT

Young people's different values and cultures influence their perspectives on participation and their motivation to act. They need to feel they are getting something out of their involvement and that the activities they decide on are valued by adults. Their decisions are very much influenced by their relations with adults and the preconceived ideas of elders, youth and children about one another and their roles in their communities.

Children in the South African example identified with the political struggle by looking at the realities of their own circumstances and how these relate to the larger society. The same was true in the US and Europe in the 1960s and

---

Box 6.3: A South African experience

In the past decades, young people have played a substantial role in the political development of the nation. Students were and are still deeply involved with workers in a struggle to change the system. This was triggered for young people when they began to confront issues within their schools. From this, they got involved in community and NGO activities and as these are tied up with politics, young people moved into the political struggle. In one area, young people developed a programme based in two black communities working with 250 children and youth on the street, in schools and in youth organizations. Children formed committees, recruited members and met together regularly, creating child-centred community organizations; they worked together on environmental projects, life-skills, training, art and performing arts. Through their theatre productions they ran workshops that crossed racial barriers and explored the relationship between adults, young people and institutions. The children's groups looked at how they could make use of local cultures to get more young people involved and they developed networks between different groups, which created a truly multicultural enterprise.

Thabang Ngocozela, South Africa

in eastern Europe today. Young people's ownership of project institutions and their accountability to the membership helped them to build their identities and experience. Through their involvement, children have gained experience and have grown to run organizations more effectively than their forebears. In the South African example, this empowerment was based on a gradual devolution of power to young people, because even though adults made the initial contacts and were the ones with the power, the children took over when they were able. Initially it was adults who knew how to organize logistics and negotiate with other adults and local institutions, how to manage projects and how to be credible to donors. As time went on, young people started to make decisions and adults became advisers, endorsers and consultants. It was this transition that gave young people a sense that they were fighting for themselves and had a valid role to play.

Young people are particularly well placed to become actively and passionately involved in social change. They are often the only ones capable of standing up against their own system. They usually have no established way of life to defend, the only thing at stake is themselves so they often seek political change before they look for stability and careers. They have always been the breakers of convention and the ones to suggest new ideas. They enjoy being

---

Box 6.4: An example from the Philippines

As members of a theatre project in the Philippines, children analyse their situations and bring out important social issues through playwriting. They run all aspects of the plays and are members of the board of directors of the project. Their involvement with adults on the board helps to validate the children and adults to one another. Adults often run into dilemmas; for example they have been surprised by 'new' issues brought up by young people – children put on a play about incest in a nunnery school. The projects originated from the adult-defined sectors, but young people define all the projects and programmes.

Ernesto Cloma, Philippines

Box 6.5: An example from the UK

Rescue Mission in the UK shows how young people or adults come up with projects; after discussing them, each group will appoint a co-director. We learned how important it is to make clear the nature of the relationship between the children and the adults; transparent power dynamics and structure are critical. The group ran into some problems:

● Running the programme is not the only responsibility of young people; they also need to be involved in financial control and grant writing.
● There are often clashes among young people themselves because some do better than others.

Julian Olivier, UK

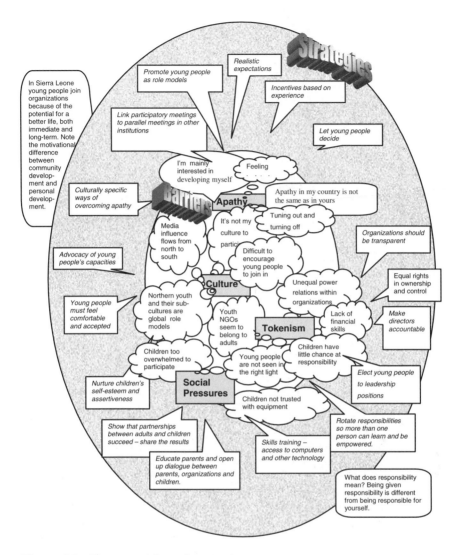

Figure 6.2: *Young people and institutions*

the torchbearers for change, and each generation continues to push forward, particularly in changing societies such as developing democracies. Where family life can stifle ideas, youth groups can be an opportunity to be involved in change, where young people can develop their individual and group identities and socialize. Part of the process of joining groups is to escape from being youngsters and to experiment with sub-cultures, so youth organizers and workers need to resist the instinct to interfere, sanitize and supervise.

The question arises as to how far young people should go in their political and experimental enterprises aimed at making a break with the system. Adults

193

often exaggerate young people's desire to rebel at all costs – youth are 'supposed' to break out and not be partners to adults. But when consulted, young people often show a considerable desire for partnerships; what they need, they say, are flexible institutions. Others say that we must recognize that young people cannot be both agents of change in an anti-structural sense and partners to adults at the same time. They may use existing structures as a way forward, but they also struggle against those structures in their search for satisfactory solutions to the issues they see as important.

6.5   The family in context

WORKING GROUP REPORT

Family is the first important institution in the lives of children. What does family mean to children living in different cultures? What does it mean for children in societies passing through periods of transition, affected by changing gender roles, increased urbanization, conflict and political and social change?

Children's Contributions

Moving into the twenty-first century, children are experiencing an increasing diversity of different forms of family life (Fig. 6.3). There is a wealth of evidence of children taking responsibilities and participating in the economic survival of the family, in the daily chores of home and child care, in animal husbandry, in the care of the sick and the elderly. Children continue to play a major role in the cultural lives of communities, and in family learning and development. They contribute with conversation, observation, song and dance, through myriad cultural events ranging from mealtime gatherings to community festivals. Children, especially girls, are making decisions at many levels, even when they are very young, as part of their role in supporting parents and other primary carers. These responsibilities and contributions are often invisible and undervalued by adults in the family or by policy-makers making decisions that will influence the family. Children with disability are less likely to be included in the various family tasks and activities and many have less opportunity to be allowed to contribute and to develop participation skills.

Adult Contributions

From an adult's perspective, there are a number of ways to foster effective participation and enhance family life. There are also many obstacles to children in achieving meaningful and more complex decision-making. These barriers are created not only by adults in the family, but also by the children themselves and by local cultural and religious practices and philosophies. In Fig. 6.4, the siblings voice important messages to the family and community. The adults respond by pointing out the roof that they intend to construct inside the surrounding fence of difficulties.

194

Figure 6.3: 'Different kinds of family'

Figure 6.4: *Barriers and solutions in the household*

Elders can positively influence the contribution of children by providing environments that increase understanding and raise awareness through innovative training, research, dialogue and experience. They need to start with themselves: creative and changing roles and partnerships between adults will most likely be reflected in changing expectations and partnerships with children. When adults become aware of both the resourcefulness and the different perspectives of children, they contribute to building awareness in children that their involvement in family concerns is valued and is their right. One way to build this awareness would be through gathering historical and anthropological examples of involvement of children in decision-making in family life, through literature, art, drama and poetry. Understanding the real contribution of children in different environments will help to break myths of children's participation; Do children in the North have greater freedom and decision-making power in the family? Are children in the South given no opportunity to participate in their own family settings? There is also a need to research and raise awareness of gender, considering gender-specific restrictions in family life, with appraisal of the division of labour between male and female members of the family.

Community Contributions

Community projects can also provide a useful contribution. They may offer dialogue and participatory training, helping develop communication and assertion skills that equip adults and children with increased abilities to debate issues. They may also, through increasing knowledge of child development (particularly of early childhood), help to ensure that the opinions of younger children can be heard and recognized. There are many allies in the community who promote and support this development and sharing of knowledge, including health workers, play staff, teachers, day-care and kindergarten workers, social workers, religious leaders and youth workers. Training of these support workers and community leaders needs broadening to become more holistic, so that the child's development is not compartmentalized. For example, health visitors who advise families on nutrition and immunization could be in a particularly sound position also to demonstrate the need for interaction between child and adult. Their training would therefore need to equip them with knowledge of play and other aspects of child development and participation, as well as covering the traditional aspects of the health visitor's work. In the course of their interaction with children, health visitors could become increasingly effective in their work with parents.

The Media

The message of children's right to participate can be shared in cultural and traditional ways as well as by taking advantage of the wider communication opportunities available through the media and new technology. The messages can highlight the positive capabilities of all children, including those with disability or special needs, and their right to be included in family decision-making. Such advocacy, however, requires that there is a legal framework to support child rights, so that raised expectations of the right to participate are not blocked or ignored. Families can explore the legal and social frameworks that exist and they can work together to lobby for their implementation or change.

The young still remain the least powerful members of the co-operative family team. For many children who are hemmed in by strong barriers of culture and tradition, it is only through change in the external environment that they may find the opportunity to change their own position. For those who are already participating in decisions, there is potential to explore strategies within and beyond the family, strategies that enhance the process of family negotiation and lead to mutual support and economic well-being.

Box 6.6: An example from East Africa

Situation: Community in a rural setting in East Africa
Entry Point: Unwanted pregnancies in adolescence
Initiators: Community members
Partners: Community members, local NGO with expertise in health, sex education and reproduction
Needs: Education between family and community members on sexual behaviour and reproduction, particularly with high concerns for HIV/AIDS
Methodology: PRA with children's groups aged 9–12 years, 13–16 years, girls' groups, boys' groups and mixed if permitted, Men's groups, women's groups with girls to ensure inclusion, mixed groups

The dialogues of each group were recorded and exchanged between them. They then explored together the similarities and differences of opinions expressed from the different view points of children, adults, men and women, elders, senior citizens and those with little power in the community, particularly the disabled.

Each group developed messages to be promoted within the community using traditional means, with storytelling by elders, by dance and drama performance by children and youth.

Gill Gordon

6.6   Participation within the school

AMANDA SAURIN

Rather than child participation being seen simply as a desirable consequence of schooling, it may be regarded from the outset as the heart of curricular planning and pedagogical development. Thus, whether children contribute to the planning of the theme or topic to be followed during the school day, negotiate the rules that govern classroom behaviour or create school councils where policy issues that affect children can be explored and decisions made with the opinions of children being sought and acted upon, their initial understanding forms the point of departure for curricular planning. Such participation gives children a sense of authorship and agency over some of the issues that affect their daily school experience.

The success of initiatives such as school councils is strongly dependent upon the skill of the teachers, head teachers and other adults working with the children's ideas and not altering them to suit their own agendas. However, just as the principle of child participation can founder on the difficulties of the teacher/pupil relationship, so too the principle of participation cannot mean an 'anything-goes' policy, still less a 'free-for-all'.

There are many options for children to become instrumental in the development of their school. More and more people, including parents, local community members and professionals are prepared to offer their time and skills to schools, either on a voluntary or paid sessional basis. Such sessions can be organized to meet the needs of the children rather than to fit into the constraints of the national curriculum; the specialist knowledge drawn upon also often augments the teacher's skills. This benefits the school in the long, as well as the short term. Additional specialist-support classes can be organized to accommodate small groups of children outside whole-class sessions. This allows children to feel less inhibited. It also empowers them to act and behave differently without the preconceptions and expectations of their class teacher affecting the outcome.

One such project was undertaken at a semi-rural school in Britain. A group of parents became aware that the school grounds were significantly underused, particularly at one end of a playing field. In negotiation with the then head-teacher and governing body, the group agreed to take on the management of an area approximately half an acre in size. The guiding notion for the parents was that the children should be the architects of the scheme. Following this idea, each member of the group went into every class to discuss what use could be made of the land. The children all wanted to establish a wildlife area. They visited the site, carried out surveys, drew up line drawings of the physical features they wanted to include, made lists of which creatures they wanted to attract after consulting reference books, journals and materials from relevant advice agencies. The parental group compiled the children's ideas and worked out, in collaboration with the children, a way forward. Part of the child–adult negotiations was to create realistic and viable plans; some children's hopes of attracting wild horses and iguanas could, sadly, not be realized. All these stages were important parts of the children's participation since they encouraged the children to research, refine and then to rationalize their plans.

At the same time, the parents were in discussion with all the relevant statutory bodies relating to health, safety, ground maintenance, school governance and wildlife advisory groups as well as the staff, the wider parental body and the village community. Even the village milkman delivered flyers to every house asking for donations, tool shares, plant shares and/or skills that could be offered in support of the scheme. There was huge enthusiasm from every quarter.

Once the plans had been agreed with everyone concerned and funding found, through grants, prizes and awards (the project won 5 major awards and attracted £3000 of prize/grants), the children, parents and community began to construct a large pond, a meadow, a pond dipping platform, a native species woodland, and benches made of chestnut and oak. Every child planted a tree for which s/he continues to be responsible. A newsletter was produced each term with children's ideas and comments on the area and how it could be further developed, and the group provided equipment, teaching aids and books so that the teachers and children could use the area effectively. Parents attended staff meetings to keep the staff abreast of developments.

Such a scheme demonstrates clearly the benefit of ongoing child consultation and participation. It also encourages children to think of themselves as being a part of, rather than apart from, their environment. In addition to the aims of the children to attract wildlife, a corresponding aim of the parent group was to create an environment which was diverse, sustainable and which drew attention to seasonality (something many children were quite unaware of, given the globalized food market).

This particular project has demonstrated that consultation and participation are both essential to the fulfilment of complex and multifaceted ambitions. In consulting with the children from the outset, the parents were able to facilitate the development of plans that were unique to that group of 150 children. During the construction phase, for example, the children were able to appreciate each stage and participate fully because it was their agenda and plans that were being followed.

It is essential that the teaching staff are both supportive and appreciative of the pedagogical benefits of schoolchild participation. In the case of the above project, the head teacher under whose auspices the scheme had flourished was succeeded by a head who neither understood, still less shared, the ethos of child participation and environmental sensibility. The resulting restructuring of power led to the breaking of lines of communication and participation that had been so well established between parents, children and the wider community. In consequence, the resource that the children were so instrumental in establishing is now itself under-utilized and relationships which were created with the wider community have now ceased.

From the above, one might conclude that for child participation to become a resilient practice, it is necessary for this ethos to become incorporated into the very fabric of the school at every level so that the culture of child participation is not jeopardized by personnel changes. Alternatively, and less ambitiously, there is scope for child participation in shorter-term projects with finite aims and objectives. The essential quality of this particular wildlife project was, however, its open-ended, co-operative nature that offered the possibility of evolution through continuous child participation.

Box 6.7: De-formalizing the formal system; making education in Nepal more relevant to children's lives

Education should be made relevant to the lives, work and aspirations of girls and boys. Children who have to work to survive need education that can be combined with working. This means education at times when they can attend and education in the workplace for those who cannot get to classes.

Realities of children's lives

ActionAid Nepal's experience of working with children shows that the difficult geographical terrain and engagement in household chores leads to a high drop-out rate from school of children, especially girls, from poor households. Son preference and the fact that girls leave their parents' household on marriage means that girls' education is often not seen as a worthwhile investment. These discriminatory attitudes obstruct the provision of equal opportunities for girls.

Obstacles to the participation of poor children in the formal system include: the need for uniforms; the uninteresting formal curriculum; language constraints to local-language speakers as the formal curriculum is in the national language, Nepali; and an education system biased towards the wealthy. Another barrier is the lack of time of the poorest children to attend formal classes, which are fixed by the national-level system.

Poor attendance of teachers in schools is another critical problem in rural areas. In many areas, teachers are untrained and lack the proper skills to teach and communicate with children. School facilities and teaching materials are minimal and of poor quality.

De-formalizing the formal system

The formal system needs to be made more flexible in terms of curricula, innovative teaching methods and timetables, to take into account the work of children. The experience of non-formal education has addressed many of these issues. It is important, however, to recognize that non-formal education should not be set up as an alternative to the formal system; rather that its innovative, practical experience should be integrated into the mainstream.

ActionAid Nepal has child literacy classes (CLCs) for those children who are unable to attend formal schools or have dropped out. Whilst these CLCs aim to enable children to join formal schools, they also enable children who are unable to attend school to obtain basic literacy and numeracy.

Timetables

Children often have to drop out of school, either temporarily because of the need for their labour at certain times of year, for example during harvest, or permanently, because of year-round heavy workloads. These children may, however, be able to attend CLCs because CLCs are usually for two hours early in the morning, before their work begins.

Centralized planning cannot produce school timetables that adapt to the different agricultural workloads in different regions. In Nepal there has been a positive attempt to timetable the school holidays with the peak agricultural seasons, but this is not sensitive enough to regional variations. Decentralization of school planning, including timetables, to village-level school-management committees (SMCs) could improve this situation.

Curricula

The curricula of the CLCs tie in with the formal classes so children can rejoin the latter. CLCs use primers, and the emphasis is to move away from the rote-learning system. An important innovation towards making the curriculum more relevant for children is the development by ActionAid Nepal of CLC curricula in two local languages: Tamang and Magarati.

ActionAid Nepal has also begun to pilot the use of participatory methods to generate the curriculum locally. For example, a social map of their village may be generated by children. Through discussion of this map, their situation, problems and priorities can be understood and this analysis enables them to identify follow-up actions and inform our programmes. The identification of specific key words from the map enables children to transcribe the reality into written form, developing reading, writing and arithmetic skills while at the same time learning to participate in their own development (Sharma, 1997).

Being local

Facilitators are selected from the local community by the community. They receive training from ActionAid, which covers such areas as child psychology. The facilitators have the advantage over the school teachers in coming from local community and, therefore, being able to speak the local language and having better trust with the children.

Attendance: not of children, of teachers!

Recent research in Nawalparasi, one of the areas in which ActionAid works, shows that a key problem in the formal schools is that teachers are not from the local community. Not only do they not speak the local language, they are often absent as they do not like staying in remote areas. Many children do not see the point of attending school when the teachers fail to turn up.

Curricula for formal and non-formal education need to be developed locally so that they are relevant to the area's children, even if throughout the country there are common main themes. It is also important to train local people, especially women, to become teachers in their own communities. More female teachers would encourage girls to attend school.

Parents
Whilst adult literacy is important in its own right, literate parents have proved generally more motivated and more likely to send their children to school. ActionAid Nepal supports adult literacy classes, and issues such as children's, and particularly daughters', education are discussed.

Parents are also involved in the SMCs, which make decisions about the running of the school. The SMCs tend, however, to be dominated by political leaders, and parents have little say. In order to improve their participation in these committees, ActionAid has held workshops with them and the SMCs to facilitate their understanding of education policy so that they can lobby the local district education officer for action on specific issues or complaints. It is also important to ensure that children's views are represented on the SMCs.

Joanna Hill

Thanks to Manvi Shrivastave for sharing some of the initial findings from the ongoing Nawalparasi primary education research with me.

6.7 Project Grow at the City-as-School High School in New York

MARY ELLEN LEWIS

City-as-School (CAS) was founded in 1972 as the first alternative high school in the New York City Board of Education. It was designed to serve students who had begun high school in traditional schools, but who were at risk of dropping out. Instead of the usual eight classes a day, five days a week for each semester, CAS's innovative design stressed experiential learning internships throughout the city, combined with classes and more individual attention than is possible in a large school. In our four-cycle a school year schedule (plus summer school), a student's programme might be different every day of the week, with new choices made four times a year. The programme also provides the student with the chance to explore interests in the world of work while earning high-school credit.

Project Grow, which began in 1992, is the CAS gardening, horticultural therapy, environmental science, landscape design, environmental art and entrepreneurship programme. The students, teachers and other staff, in collaboration with design professionals, greening organizations and others involved in experiential and service learning have undertaken a range of environmental projects over the last five years. Students designed and constructed a mini-park on the raised brick courtyard of CAS, including seating, trellises and small and large containers for ornamental plantings. They also painted culturally and historically relevant themes around the mini-park and other larger-scale environmentally themed murals on the courtyard's surrounding three walls. In 1996, a 24' x 25' compost-heated greenhouse was built on the courtyard by the students, assisted by teachers from the NYC Board of Education's School of Co-operative Technical Education. The compost is the product of organic waste collected from school and local sources and recycled by the students. In this greenhouse, the school has been running horticulture and science programmes, and the students are also learning how to design marketing strategies and packaging for CAS greenhouse-produced compost.

Outside the school, the students have collaborated with Parklands Partnership in a hands-on forest restoration project, involving research and fieldwork in natural areas of New York City parks. The same students also participated as co-researchers in a parallel study of the experience of older urban adolescents in green spaces in the city. Project Grow is currently putting together a design proposal for community use of Pier 84 on the Hudson River in collaboration with a museum educator and graduate students. Finally, students and staff have begun to design and create a Project Grow website and there have been a number of 'how-to' workshops for local, national and international education, horticultural therapy and environmental design organizations.

Working together on participatory action and research in the school setting has presented a number of challenges and issues to the students and staff. The big issues they face are balancing process and product, establishing and developing professional consultant/community partnerships and developing sensitivity to issues in working with different cultural groups (age, ethnic, racial, ability/disability) in the school and community. Whereas in a more traditional school setting the administrative and academic decisions are made for the students, in this case they have to work with the staff to gain school support for their projects, negotiate school politics and also develop appropriate academic goals and curricula. This also means addressing academic-skill improvement through project learning and determining how to document and evaluate student learning and growth. The groups work together to address ethical challenges, including resolving conflicts of interest regarding project and student needs, and community and school expectations. They are consistently defining and refining tools for students' informed consent regarding identification of themselves and their work outside the school community.

The adults have to deal with the challenge of such a flexible and unpredictable system. They need to establish and maintain effective working relationships among the team of staff, administration and community partners. They need to find on-going school time to plan, share and evaluate the project, to balance other teaching and counselling responsibilities and to obtain on-going professional development to support project learning. Their work with the students means shaping the adult facilitator role with the older adolescents, while meeting the academic and personal requirements of a wide range of students. Working in new ways that recognize adolescent personal and social strengths and challenges, and preparing teenagers to participate in the novel decision-making responsibility for the design, process and outcome of the project, is itself an enormous challenge. The groups find themselves dealing with adolescent resistance to new or challenging experiences while also negotiating youth autonomy needs and limits in the school and the field.

Practical details need careful attention. Safety and liability in hands-on working in potentially risky circumstances is a big priority, as is on-going maintenance of projects when the school is not in session. They have to cope with security and vandalism, transportation of students and materials to and from project sites and securing funding and non-traditional materials. As a model programme, the school is often called upon to disseminate project information, and available staff time has to be balanced with deadline-driven demands by funders and news organizations.

The work of CAS and Project Grow has already made a deep impact on students, staff and the local community. The project has made progress in raising environmental awareness and promoting remarkable community action for change. The school design has reconnected thousands of young people with secondary education by helping them to see its relevance to their present lives and future goals.

6.8   The Brighton Centre for active learning and amazing achievements

LUCY HARRIS

Our belief is that anything and everything is possible, that childhood is not merely a preparation for adult life but that children are themselves experts in living their lives fully in the present and contributing to the world in which they live.

Children are inherently confident, enthusiastic learners; our role is to provide them with a supportive environment in which they can explore their potential. At the Brighton Centre we are advocates of learner-directed learning. A learning experience which has been instigated by a child is a far more relevant and, therefore, a more valuable experience than one which has been imposed.

We trust that each individual is evolving fully, that each learning experience they choose for themselves is appropriate to their development. It is natural to progress in such a way. This is the only means of developing independent, free-thinking, confident individuals.

Opportunities for learning are everywhere. The centre provides a base for exploring the local environment and the world beyond. Visits, expeditions and external activities are undertaken in accordance with children's interests and needs; likewise, children may invite visiting experts to the centre to advise and contribute to project work. Community awareness is an integral part of the centre's ethos. This encompasses both the local and world communities as well as the centre community, which is democratically run, with each child contributing to the planning, organizing and running of the learning environment.

Every two weeks each child designs her/his own programme. This is an exciting time, with group discussion about possible projects and developments. The children need to anticipate what resources will be needed, what time-scale they will allow and what information they require. Children may develop individual and shared projects. The teacher's role is to offer support and advice as required, and the children themselves offer back-up and encouragement to each other during project development.

Each child keeps a photo diary that records progress and offers an opportunity for continual self-assessment. On completion of each project the children select suitable means for celebrating their work; for example a display or exhibition may be created, whether within the centre or in an appropriate local venue. Parents and visitors may be invited to attend a presentation, a book may be produced or a discussion may take place, thus allowing the children to share their experiences with others.

The centre is both for full-time and part-time participation. Full-time participants are in the care of a fully qualified and experienced teacher in a ratio

Figure 6.5: *Planning learning projects together*

of 1:6; part-timers are accompanied by their parent or carer and all participants have the opportunity to collaborate with each other on projects and
activities. Our commitment is to enable each individual to develop her/his
own unique abilities and talents and realize their potential. By offering children the chance to take an active role in designing their own learning experiences you give them the right to develop into self-motivated, flexible adults,
who have the confidence and skills to transform their dreams into reality.

6.9 Child participation in programme planning and implementation in the marginalized youth projects, Jamaica

DENISE ALLEN

SCF marginalized youth projects in Jamaica were developed as a non-institutional approach to reintegrating street and working children into society. The projects are nine years in existence and have experienced transition from a welfare to a developmental orientation. Equally significant are the initiatives taking place to give the beneficiaries (children, young people and parents) an increasing stake in programme planning and implementation. A primary constraint has been complying with donors' agendas, which demanded specific actions and results that were not always compatible with genuine participation. Programme activities have, none the less, gone through a transition.

Stage one: 'buffet style'

The programme activities were organized so that children had the option of choosing that which interested them. They were under no obligation, but it was hoped that by starting with the more interesting activities (such as lunch and snacks) they would gradually move toward those less attractive to them (English classes and individual counselling). The children had almost no input in the content and range of activities offered to them. Instead, the programme staff crafted activities in keeping with their professional knowledge of children's developmental needs and perceptions about the unique needs or interest of the population served. The result was that the children took several months to feel any loyalty or commitment to the scheme. This difficulty was most apparent with the street boys or other children suffering from extreme emotional difficulties, less so with the working girls. The parents also shared the children's perceptions of regarding the programme as essentially a welfare service from which they made demands but did not expect to give anything in return.

Stage two: 'feedback'

A shift in participation by beneficiaries gave parents a greater share in creating and carrying out some activities that required little technical knowledge or skills. Children were allowed to give their views on the activities without any commitment from programme staff to carry out their ideas. This opportunity served largely as a monitoring function. The parameters remained adult defined and limited children's views to safe areas such as the menu and preferences in recreational activities.

This kind of tokenism had a surprisingly energizing effect on the children, who customarily do not have much of an audience with adult authority figures. Opening this window in communication also gave the staff the chance to check their assumptions and programme plans. It also brought a realization that the children could be engaged more in planning and implementation.

Some adult members felt threatened by the fledgeling power of the children. Those most affected were parents who worked as volunteers in administering project activities. They were unaccustomed to listening to children and found it unsettling to recognize children's views. Labels such as 'rude', 'out of order' and 'troublesome' became commonplace among them. Measures were quickly taken to address this resistance. Workshops on the UN Convention on the Rights of the Child and its implications for adults' responses to children were valuable in enabling parents to appreciate both the changing world and internationally accepted standards. Along with sessions on child development and programme strategy, these parents became less resistant to listening to children, at least in the projects.

In many respects the children took participation to the next stage as they felt sufficiently empowered not simply to express their views but to demand that adults take them seriously.

Stage three: 'adult-initiated, shared decisions with children'

A new practice began to emerge in which programme staff constantly shared programme plans with the children for their input and support. The parent/staff management group that met frequently to plan and implement project activities now had new partners: children. It tried to have at least three children to ensure all special groups were represented and that these were sufficiently strong in numbers to avoid tokenism. Their peers chose these children based on leadership strengths.

Extra measures were taken to allow the youth representatives to meet their peers without adults present. The results were mixed, as most children had little appreciation of a child-initiated process. Consequently, these meetings were held irregularly and at times demanded that an adult be present to support the youth leadership in keeping order. In spite of these difficulties, both the youth leaders and children began displaying a new sense of confidence in themselves. They grew accustomed to being outspoken among adults and expected to be heard.

The children's commitment to project activities also became more apparent as they took on greater responsibility in starting and sustaining schemes. Increasingly, the programme staff relied less on employing additional adult staff or volunteers, as the older children developed skills and confidence in supervising their younger peers.

At a recent summer day-camp that focused on 'children's rights', children and young people played a leading role in designing and managing camp activities. Historically, the project would have hired or recruited several volunteers. This year only a nurse and parent volunteer were needed. A team of 25 children and young people ran the camp for approximately 200 children.

Although both projects have a higher ratio of boys to girls, there has been a reverse in proportionality in leadership. The girls have displayed more staying power in planning and project implementation that seems consistent with similar experiences in the English-speaking Caribbean islands. The term 'marginalization of boys and men' is commonly used as a label for the developing trend for males to perform academically below their female counterparts. This has resulted in a shift in the student population in tertiary institutions as more women are entering and completing higher education, thereby making them stronger candidates in the job market. Studies suggest that the long-entrenched institution of female-headed households with transient male figures contributes strongly to the problem. In addition, social mores seem to equip girls better for success through diligent work and application while boys are allowed to be free spirited and self-supporting from an early age. Consequently, far more boys enter street life than girls. In fact, girls on the street are usually there under fairly strict conditions and closely supervised by an adult, for example selling wares in the market or on the street corner. Parents make a greater effort to teach girls how to carry out household chores and send them to school more consistently. Girls are less likely to be victimized by a disenchanted mother who may think sons resemble their 'worthless' father who has abandoned them. In summary, the girl child has far more structure and guidance than do boys, especially in marginalized communities.

It comes as little surprise to the programme staff, therefore, that girls dominate at leadership levels. Much more motivation is given to the boys. The challenge we face is to increase gender equity. Retaining activities that are male-dominated seems essential. The staff have created avenues for adult males to share their skills and experiences with boys in a way that is both constructive and beneficial to both groups.

Stage four: 'child-initiated and child-directed'

A new thrust was taken in environmental work. A child's environment club was formed, initiated by programme staff and subsequently led by children. In many respects the Environmental Protectors' Club has the highest stage of participation on the internationally recognized 'ladder of children's participation' (see Appendix 2). However, the club did not start with a young leadership. The programme staff held a great deal of management control in the initial stages, gradually releasing that control as the children displayed increasing leadership capacities.

As the children gained some control over the club's finances they brought a new dimension to participation. The notion that power comes with the control of resources suggests that without it participation is insincere and possibly meaningless. Our experience with the children does not fully support this view. Instead it seems to suggest that power in the form of authority can genuinely change hands with little or no resources involved. That authority is given in a context where it is recognized and supported by all parties. Now the children control the club with project staff playing a consultative role in programme planning and implementation.

The resulting positive changes in the children, in terms of their confidence and maturity, did not go unnoticed by their parents. They reported that the children were behaving more responsibly at home and thereby won their

Figure 6.6: *A gradual process of inclusion*

respect. The 'Children First Project' now has a stronger basis for promoting children's rights among parents who have traditionally been resistant. The Environmental Protectors Club and other child-participation activities provide tangible ways of convincing adults that children's rights are as much in their interests as they are in those of the child.

6.10 Mambo Leo, Sauti ya Watoto: child participation in Tanzania

ESTHER OBDAM

In June 1996, the Kuleana Centre for Children's Rights began a new project within its publications department: *Mambo Leo, Sauti ya Watoto* (Swahili for 'Life Today, Voices of Children'), Tanzania's first magazine for children written and edited by children themselves.

The reasons behind the project were two-fold: the magazine would inform children about their rights and other subjects that affect and/or interest them in a way that is both fun and educational; and it would provide children with a forum to make known their thoughts, ideas and opinions.

Mambo Leo is managed by an editorial team of five school students, aged 12 to 15, with support from two adult facilitators. Articles and illustrations are sought from children all over Tanzania.

The magazine is produced in poster format and consists of four colourful pages. Themes and contents vary with each issue, but there are some regulars, like the boys' and girls' corner and the editors' introduction. The magazine is distributed to primary schools, libraries, teachers' training colleges, and centres and NGOs all over Tanzania.

After more than one year of producing *Mambo Leo*, we have learnt a few valuable lessons, perhaps the most important one being the realization that a theoretical discussion about child participation is quite different from practical implementation!

Voices of children

Tanzanian society, and especially the school system, teaches children that they are not important, that their ideas and opinions do not matter. They are to do as they are told without question. When a child disagrees or fails to do what is expected of her, she is punished, often beaten.

Children grow up believing that they are not worth being listened to. They find it hard to formulate their thoughts and opinions because they are never asked for their views; they are told what to think. They are reluctant to speak up out of fear of doing something 'wrong' and being punished for it.

The school system forces children to learn through memorization and does not give them the opportunity to think for themselves or to take part in decisions that affect them. Together with the harsh punishments for mistakes and any behaviour that is out of the ordinary, this crushes creativity and imagination.

For *Mambo Leo* this meant that the editors were usually hesitant to take any initiative and waited for instructions from the adult facilitators. In their choice of subject and writing they tried to do the 'right' thing by saying what they thought the adult facilitators wanted to hear, usually copying Kuleana's points of view. This was in complete contradiction to what we had envisioned when we started the children's magazine!

Figure 6.7: *Kuleana Centre for Children's Rights, Tanzania*
watoto wana haki ya kufikiri! – CHILDREN HAVE A RIGHT TO THINK!
watoto wana haki ya kusikilzwa! – CHILDREN HAVE A RIGHT TO BE HEARD!
watoto wana haki ya kutoa maamuzi! – CHILDREN HAVE A RIGHT TO MAKE DECISIONS!

212

As adult facilitators we spent a lot of time with the child editors, trying to make them feel more comfortable and confident about their own ideas, and more free to do things in their own way. To a certain extent, this was success-ful. The children liked coming to the office to share their experiences from school and home. But to make them feel as comfortable with the magazine, making it their own, representing their own ideas and tastes, is still a challenge.

With every issue that we produce, however, the junior editors feel more confident. Seeing their name in print and having people comment on their work makes them feel good about themselves. It makes them believe that what they say is important, and hopefully this will make them more confident about expressing their own views.

We have also noted that after producing one issue of *Mambo Leo* the chil-dren involved become less motivated. It seems that the initial novelty and excitement of involvement wears off and that the magazine becomes an oblig-ation. Inviting other children to join helps but means starting again to build a relationship with, and the confidence of, the children.

Mambo Leo is, however, starting slowly to inspire other child readers to write and send us their drawings, which gives us hope for the future.

Children as part of society

Launching and producing *Mambo Leo* has taught us how much children are part of society and how, in order to be successful, any project involving them has to include many of the people around them. To work with the children on *Mambo Leo*, we have had to get permission from both their parents and their teachers. Since Kuleana is an organization promoting children's rights, this was not always easy. In some cases parents and teachers feared that we would have a bad influence, making their children rebellious and demanding.

With regular communication and clear explanations about the project and its goals, we have managed to win their support. In the case of the teachers we have tried to involve them by eliciting their opinion on which students should be invited to join the magazine. *Mambo Leo* needs to be careful not to be too negative about parents or school because being too outspoken would probably do more harm than good, as schools would refuse to display it or deny their students the opportunity to contribute to it.

Schools are the main target for distribution of the magazine. To do anything in schools in Tanzania, you need the permission of the regional and district education officers. For *Mambo Leo* we not only got their approval but also their active support and co-operation. Without it, the distribution of the maga-zine would have been difficult, and without distribution *Mambo Leo* would have merely been produced but not read or used. The whole project would have been ineffective and the children involved in the its production discour-aged. Now, with the co-operation of the educational authorities, the magazine is distributed to schools all over the country.

Only limited time was needed to seek the endorsement of the people and institutions around the children, yet, without that backing, running *Mambo Leo* had been virtually impossible. Even better is that because teachers and the educational authorities are involved in the project they feel a sense of ownership and pride. Adults that were sceptical at the beginning, especially about the children's capacity to produce this magazine, are now advocating its use in schools.

Conclusion

After one year's production, *Mambo Leo* is still a learning project. In the past year we have realized that starting up a children's participation project involves the community around the children. The children are not only formed by that community, by the society around them; working with them, that background needs to be taken into consideration and be respected to support the children and allow them to play their part but also to make their work useful and credible. If we want to make children's voices heard and their opinions known, we have to find the people ready to listen to them.

6.11   Involving children in the project cycle: experience from SCF Jijiga

ABEBAW ZELLEKE

In Jijiga, Ethiopia, SCF has been working in refugee camps, with emergency feeding programmes. From 1993 to 1997 there was a transition from emergency to a rehabilitation and development programme, an integrated development initiative aimed at the facilitation of returnees coming home and reintegration into their pastoral, agro-pastoral or farming communities. The programme is characterized by strong involvement of local communities (mostly using PRA techniques), and by joint planning and capacity-building with local government.

Development of new activities meant there was a need for reskilling staff, who were formerly Somali refugees. They needed to change from feeding-programme workers, to rural community-development workers, with agricultural, credit, water, restocking and education skills. At the same time, SCF was calling for greater rigour in monitoring the impact of work on children and on exploring issues relating to the child focus within our programmes.

This paper aims to show how the Jijiga programme has tried to tackle these issues and has moved towards integration of children throughout the project cycle.

How did it start?

The catalyst to give greater prominence to children within the Jijiga projects came from the following two factors:

● A workshop was held in Jijiga in September 1995 to review the use of PRA skills over the previous year, to discuss problems in their implementation with a view to reviewing methodologies in the next phase of the project, and to refresh staff knowledge of both tools and approaches. A 'talking to

214

children' day, was included in the workshop, facilitated by two senior staff, and participants were sent out to interview children in Jijiga.

• During project visits and reviews, senior staff made a point of finding time to talk to children about the SCF projects and, inevitably, about other aspects of their lives.

These two factors led to a change in staff attitudes in the SCF Jijiga office. Whilst some remained sceptical, others discovered, to their surprise, the following about children's participation:

• children have a good understanding of the environment in which they live, and the causes of their own problems;
• they are anxious to be more involved in community meetings, decisions and discussions concerning community life; and
• they are sometimes more reliable informants than adults, and their views can be used to cross-check what adults are saying.

Incorporating children's views into needs assessments

Following this, the method of carrying out community needs assessment was adapted to ensure that, as well as women and men being consulted (which had been the case in the 1994 assessment), children were also involved. With time, needs assessments methods have improved. Determining how to prioritize needs articulated by different groups in the community, in order to come up with an action plan remains, however, problematic, and is limited in part by institutional processes and available resources.

From involving children in needs assessment we have so far learnt the following:

• children's priorities differ from adults, but have to be seen in relation to other differences, such as age, sex, wealth and other characteristics;
• whilst boys' and girls' priorities are discussed during needs assessment and the information can be readily incorporated into project activities, we lack a system for achieving consensus on priorities, or of confronting different groups within the community with the views of other groups.

The following questions still remain therefore: how do we act on information gathered with increased children's participation and how do we resolve or confront different points of view and priorities within communities?

Identifying child-specific indicators

SCF has carried out work to identify child-specific indicators, both by asking adults what benefits they expect to gain from a certain intervention and by talking to children. However, SCF in Jijiga has not tried to involve communities, or children, in collecting information on an on-going basis in a more participatory monitoring system. Examples of child-specific indicators include:

• Changes in workload and time available for Koranic school, formal school or recreation. For example, various interventions in the water sector freed children's time for other activities. Whilst this has not yet been measured,

215

children were asked to identify change in work and time for different activities, following implementation of *birkas*.

- Increased milk consumption for young children (under 6 years) following restocking of female-headed households with sheep and goats.

Involving children in review and evaluation

Obtaining children's views formed part of the methodology employed in evaluation work carried out in 1996. For example, children were interviewed as part of an education review and evaluation in order to assess the impact of teacher-training programmes on teachers' skills. Far more information was acquired than would have been obtained from other methods, as students were well placed to observe changes in teachers' attitude, skills and behaviour.

Students in rural primary schools identified the following changes in teachers' performance after short teaching-skills training courses, and these were then used to monitor changes in other schools:

- teachers' ability to explain concepts and information in the class;
- frequency of use of teaching aids;
- involvement of student children in teaching-aid preparation;
- teaching methods adopt dialogue, question-and-answer sessions; and
- improved organization by teachers (lesson preparation, text books, class attendance sheets).

From here, it was possible to develop with teachers a checklist of good and poor teaching qualities.

Case-studies of children's experience of reintegration, and how that was affected by SCF projects, were incorporated into evaluation work. This helped to illustrate issues such as increased work burdens, changes in roles, improved water quality and lack of access to services, particularly in comparison with what they had had when living in refugee camps. These highlighted, for example, the impact of food-for-work (FFW) on the activities of teenage boys. When the FFW projects began the adults were engaged in water-point excavation, so young boys replaced adults in cultivation. It was argued that work activities increased as a result of the FFW projects.

Problems and issues

Although much has been done to raise the profile of children within the project cycle, the Jijiga programme is still far from fully incorporating children and from knowing what is practical and feasible within the local Somali cultural context.

Issues that need to be addressed in the future include:

- Developing skills and tools to talk to and interview children, and developing rigour in such informal and PRA information-collection methodologies. Hand in hand with this, there needs to be a greater understanding of issues of difference: what do gender, age, disability, wealth or caste mean in terms of programming and implementation?

- Additional time needs to be built into field-work to take into account the need to explore and analyse the experiences and views of different groups in the community, whether of age, sex, wealth, caste or other factors. Pressures of implementation and project work mean that processes were often rushed and that not enough reflection was put into how information was used. In the future, more thinking needs to be put into the use of information, its analysis and how it is used in decision-making and programme direction.
- The water evaluation in Jijiga highlighted the need to explore the representation of young people on water or development committees at community level. How far this can be made practical, and more than tokenism, remains to be explored.

6.12   Non-governmental organizations – barriers and solutions

WORKING GROUP REPORT

The main barriers to children's participation were discussed in the context of international, national and local non-governmental organizations (NGOs) and of community-based organizations (CBOs). They fell into the following key areas of concern:

Organizational policies

Programmes are often designed under pressure to produce results. Decision-making in the field needs to be responsive to children's requirements and views; this is, however, often hindered by the demands and dead-lines of large bureaucracies.

Child participation may be supported in theory by an organization which, in practice, has found this difficult to translate into policy. There is generally a lack of flexibility in organizational policies in terms of resource allocation, reporting requirements and timing. Activities relating to children's involvement should be given more space in plans and budgets, and decision-making on day-to-day programme management should be more decentralized to the field to make it more responsive to the needs expressed in local participatory processes.

Programmes may also be designed to respond to donor priorities and schedules. Longer time-frames needed to ensure more genuine children's participation should be taken into account by donors. NGOs can express project plans in terms of log-frames that identify specific objectives, outputs and impacts for different stages of the project that can help to show how a scheme is developing over such a longer time-frame.

Mainstreaming or a separate structure?

Should children's participation be introduced into an NGO through developing a separate, or 'add-on' structure, or through mainstreaming? It may be preferable to do both simultaneously. Children's issues are rarely mainstreamed, but are more often introduced through a separate unit, but a contact person in each office can be a good place to begin the process of mainstreaming. Holding a child forum or working group on children's participation can help to raise the profile of the issues and provide a platform for discussion, including a contact person from each department and office.

A culture of experimentation with methods and approaches enables progress to be made more quickly within an institution. It is also an easier starting-point if, at least in theory, children are seen as central in the project rationale and if an organization (for example Save the Children UK) has taken on a child-focused approach, starting with gaining children's insights.

An important part of mainstreaming children's concerns is to have child-sensitive indicators for all development projects and programmes. There could be a demand by donors that all schemes evaluate their impacts on children. A further step would be to get children to plan and evaluate development projects themselves.

Working with partners

Supporting children and youth groups (especially those set up and directed by young people) is a particularly effective way to ensure more genuine and visible participation of children and young people.

Working with local partners in NGOs, CBOs and government can be an effective strategy as long as those partners are sensitive to gender and age issues. It is important to work with those agencies that prioritize children's involvement and show an understanding of their lives. Practice creates a better understanding of new approaches to children's participation for both adult and child. Networking and communication of ideas and practice can help to demonstrate the potential of children's participation. There also needs to be more rigorous research to prove the value of involvement and to lobby organizations to take children's issues more seriously.

NGO staff capacities and attitudes

It is in their attitudes that NGO staff often encounter the greatest difficulties. Despite a willingness to be innovative and a commitment to the concept of participation, staff may feel they lack the necessary skills, time and resources. It is important to allow them to go through a process of learning with children and gradually to recognise the importance of their participation. Much involvement seems to start on adult's terms. It is only through a process of learning that it can be built on an understanding of children's own varying perceptions and expectations.

There are several aspects of training for NGO staff and partners that can be useful:

- child-sensitive participatory approaches;
- ethical issues;
- facilitation/communications skills;
- listening to children and using their own methodologies;
- working with adults to change their attitudes and build their capacities;
- basic child development and its relevance in different cultural contexts;
- issues of difference in childhood;
- analysis of which policies impact practically on children;
- practical application of the UNCRC;
- understanding children's situations through field visits; and
- networking of ideas on children's participation among field staff.

A further practical barrier encountered in many of the development NGOs is the negative attitude of senior management. These often do not regard children's participation as serious or as real development work. They need lobbying within the organization to raise their awareness, and they would benefit from focused training to build their capacity to deal effectively with the issues of children's involvement.

6.13   Introducing participation by children and young people into local public services: first steps, early mistakes and lessons learned

MARK FEENEY

This paper seeks to examine the experience of one local area of the UK as it took its firsts steps to build children's participation into local public services, and sought to create the means and mechanisms to make these sustainable.

Why Kirklees?

Kirklees is a Metropolitan Authority in West Yorkshire in the north of England. It is a collection of mill towns grouped together more for adminis-trative reasons than because it forms a natural community. The population is about 390,000, of whom 12 per cent are from ethnic minorities.

In 1996 Kirklees local authority began to prepare its first children's plan. From the outset it was decided to take as broad a view as possible and to incorporate all public services for children and young people into the plan.

Having considered other possibilities, we determined that the United Nations Convention on the Rights of the Child was a particularly useful framework for our purposes and that it would provide a set of underpinning principles to which all agencies could subscribe. The aim of public services in Kirklees came, therefore, to be seen essentially as upholding for local chil-dren and young people the rights embodied in the convention. The right that caused the most discomfort was that 'children and young people have a right to have a view and to express their views in matters that concern them'. We had few, if any, mechanisms for inviting the involvement of children and young people, and no tradition of doing so. The draft plan had to be written without their involvement. It was decided that participation should be seen as the major priority for action in the plan's first year.

Barriers to overcome

The involvement of children and young people in planning and evaluating services inevitably brings into play some widespread stereotypes, not least because to some degree it involves handing over power. Those who wish to discredit the approach point to stereotypes of children and young people as not deserving the involvement and neither competent nor responsible enough to make use of it. They claim that children have a right to childhood, that they live in small worlds and in short-term time-scales that make their involvement problematic. The counter-arguments are that children and young people are a significant part of the community in which they live and influence that environment whether or not we invite them to. Involving them will produce better decisions and outcomes, and produce long-term benefits. If their experience is of being listened to and valued, they are more likely to grow up into adults who respect and value others, and play a full part in community life. There was a need to have these discussions out in the open before real progress could be made.

First steps

We gained significant support to base our services on children's rights, and to begin to involve them in those services as part of that approach, but some hesitation then followed because of our concern to get matters right. Issues were raised about which young people to involve, whether they could be truly representative, how we should involve them, on what agenda we should meet, and what would be a successful outcome in terms of long-term structures and processes. We were at risk of never getting the plan off the ground. It was agreed therefore, to start from where we were, and to learn from our mistakes. Much of the learning would be from children and young people themselves, provided that we were open enough to hear what they said about our first attempts. In the first year, two main activities were planned. The first was short term and time limited, and was about preparing a bid for government funding. The second was about creating long-term mechanisms to substantiate the culture change that we wished to bring about in our agencies. These two areas of activity were in many ways interwoven and interdependent, each feeding off the other.

Short term

It was decided that local agencies would jointly make a bid for regeneration funds from central government. The theme of the bid was 'Youth' and this was to be rooted in the concerns and aspirations of local children and young people. Essentially they would set the agenda. The first five months were therefore spent discovering their concerns. A variety of approaches were used. A series of focus groups was held. The concerns that emerged were used to devise a questionnaire which was targeted on 14–25-year-olds. A total of 1850 were returned. Young people aged 11–14 were consulted through two one-day events. The process was extended finally to the youngest age group, 4–10 years, approached using methods appropriate to their age but with essentially the same questions. Around 2500 children and young people contributed in some way to this exercise.

Armed with all this information about the major concerns and priorities of children and young people, two separate groups of 40 young people spent weekends away together talking through the issues raised, and identifying solutions. These became the focus of the bid. The preparation of this funding bid was a highly complex process. The priorities grew from a whole range of national agendas, and a whole new jargon had to be learnt to make sense of the process. Two-thirds the way through, a new government was elected with new priorities. The process became technical, fast-moving and involved compromises for adults and young people alike. Despite all of this, young people have been part of every aspect of the process, and will be part of the team that implements the work if the bid is successful.

Long term

At the same time as the involvement of children and young people was sought for the short-term funding bid, different processes were being put in place to bring about a long-term culture change in our organizations and to begin to build into those bodies the participation of children and young people as standard and routine. To this end a special initiative was set up, funded by the local authority, health authority and Save the Children (SCF). This was not about imposing change on organizations from outside but about targeting them from within. Existing agency staff were seconded to spend half their working week establishing the means by which children and young people could routinely influence what their agency did and how it did it. A total of six secondments of staff was established under the overall direction of a member of staff from SCF. Whilst the purpose of all secondments is the same, different approaches have had to be adopted to customize the approach to each participating agency. At the time of writing, this initiative has been under way for just over six months, and the first evaluations are about to be undertaken. It has been important in the process to have SCF as a catalyst and honest broker as we tackle the contentious issue of participation.

Initial impact

The impact of these two pieces of work has been substantial in the first year. Both of them have had the same intention, namely to take forward the commitment given to participation in the children's plan. They are both about public services changing their approach so as to view services for children and young people through the eyes of those for whom they are intended, and to do this by consulting the children and young people directly. The benefits of such an approach are considerable. It will attune services to the needs and expectations of users and potential users, and therefore ensure that we make the maximum positive impact from existing resources.

Lessons learned so far

The learning curve of those of us involved in providing services to children and young people in Kirklees has been steep. A number of lessons, many of them predictable, have been learnt so far:

- Participation by children and young people constitutes a major threat to the *status quo*, and will therefore erect barriers, particularly in settings where adults maintain control, e.g. schools, children's homes.
- It is important to have top-level support for a move like this. Local authority members and chief officers need to be persuaded of its potential benefits. Direct meetings with young people have done a great deal to assist in this.

- There is a tendency towards involving young people rather than children. This is something we have attempted to correct on a regular basis, not always successfully.
- There is positive value in aiming high. For example, we are attempting to build in early examples of young people handling their own budget, because this is seen as real power; if they can be seen to do it successfully a number of other myths can be dispelled.
- There is an issue about wanting young people to be representative, and to have a constituency. This can have the effect of shutting out those who are not engaged with organizations and from whom there is much to learn.
- There is a need to be prepared for the fact that young people are a population and move on as their interests change. Long-term structures that rely on the same individuals being present throughout are likely to be problematic.
- There is a need for a support system for young people throughout the process in order to bring about sustainability. Such support allows for constant renewal of the young persons' group, because not everybody has to be at the same stage together. It also reduces the risk of a small group of young people becoming professional consultees who are asked about everything.
- There is a need for clarity about expectations, constraints and time-scales so that young people are clear about the rules of engagement.
- The question of whether young people should receive some form of payment if they are involved in assisting public services to make decisions needs consideration.

Results and prospects

We have seen significant progress in a comparatively short period of time. Perhaps the two most important changes have been:

(1) A major change in the perception of young people and what they can offer. The experience of the last year has demonstrated enormous benefits in involving children and young people. They have been constructive, committed, and imaginative. Already, small things are happening which denote the change of attitude. A group of young people is involved in advising the leader of the council about a new government initiative which is likely to affect youth of their age. The appointment of a senior local government officer will involve a session in which young people will offer their views of the world to the applicants. A council-wide budget that is intended to benefit children and young people will be administered partly by the young people themselves.

(2) The other major change is in the perception that young people have of themselves. One young person involved in preparing the bid for government money described the weekend consultations and spoke of all the young people there as experts, experts at being homeless, experts in being without jobs, experts about being bullied etc. He was implying that their views and experiences had been valued and seen as relevant. Another young person, when asked what the involvement had meant to him, replied that he had grown two inches. On being pressed to explain this,

he said that he used to stand with a dejected air and his head slouched forward. He now stood proud, and as a result was taller than he had ever been.

With statements like that, it is not difficult to stay motivated and determined to develop further the involvement of children and young people.

Box 6.8: Transferring knowledge, learning from emerging democracies

The golden potential of participatory projects is that they may have profound impacts on all young people, regardless of their economic, social or cultural background. Citizenship skills and awareness of sustainable development need to be learned by all the world's citizens. To this end, practitioners may learn from each other's processes and methods across cultural boundaries. One questions where the most fertile land lies for this exploration and how these lessons can be transferred most appropriately. Deeper questions arise about the contextual meanings of participation.

Knowledge transfer is most often assumed to flow from industrialized to less-developed countries. An underlying bias holds that Western nations, which have prospered in democratic states for over two centuries, provide the best territory for exploring the meaning of children's participatory rights. In fact, many Western democracies have grown so blasé and stagnant that citizens participate only rarely. Democracy has lost its meaning, with too much rhetoric and few truth-seeking discussions. Civic education, in such climates, does not promote the realization of citizenship but weakens its youth to political mantra and patriotic superficiality. Most Western democracies are so well established that change concerning entrenched values and social concepts is seen as societal upheaval. Democracy is here no longer an evolving agenda in which norms are continuously re-evaluated; rather, any alternative models are perceived as fights against the established *status quo*.

Citizens in developing democracies experience on the other hand the harsh edges of the democratic governing philosophy every day. In these nations' living memories, struggles for freedom are fresh. The challenge of learning to live and function in a democratic state is a lived drama. Citizens must continuously carve out community structures and define democratic meanings for themselves. The potential for children to participate is ripe; an abundance of progressive participatory projects represents this (Hart, 1997; Chawla, 1997). With much less litigation and fewer formal institutional structures, certain barriers to practising participation with youth do not exist (Rich, 1997). The hope is that lessons learned in developing democracies may be transferred across historical and cultural boundaries to youth in all nations. Inherent in this ideal must be a conscious reverence for cultural specificity and consistent reflection on the appropriateness of lesson transfers.

Amy Kaspar

6.14 Children's participation in local decision-making: the challenge of local governance

BARRY PERCY-SMITH

Increasing concern for the well-being of children has given rise to unprecedented international efforts to elevate their interests on local and national agendas. The United Nations Convention on the Rights of the Child (UNCRC) has been one of the most important milestones in providing impetus to achieving rights for children. Implicit in the convention is the need for social policy to take full account of children's interests, needs and perspectives as equal citizens. In particular, Article 12 draws attention to the right of children to participate in decisions that affect their lives. This article is 'a powerful assertion of children's rights to be actors in their own lives and not merely passive recipients of adults' decision-making' (Lansdown, 1995: 2). In reality 'Children's interests are all too often neither seen nor heard in government policy-making and review' (Hodgkin and Newell, 1996: 15).

Despite the wide ranging sphere of activities that constitute their social worlds, children are rarely encouraged to participate fully in community affairs and local decision-making. At best they are limited to taking part rather than being involved (Matthews and Limb, 1998). Hart (1997) draws attention to the value of children's participation in community development. Hodgkin and Newell (1996: 17) noted, however, that 'without commitment from the highest level – including the support from the prime minister of the day – new structures are unlikely to have real impact'. None the less Article 4 of the UNCRC states that: 'States parties shall undertake all appropriate legislative, administrative and other measures for the implementation of the rights recognized by the convention' and that 'the state party consider the possibility of establishing further mechanisms to facilitate the participation of children in decisions affecting them...' (United Nations, 1995: 15). This means is that governments are obligated in providing the necessary structures to meet children's needs and encourage them to participate.

Article 4 is set within the burgeoning literature on child participation and is concerned with their involvement in local governance. It begins by reviewing the case for institutionalizing children's participation at the local-authority level. It highlights obstacles in the way and concludes by setting out principles for children's participation and suggesting a model for child-friendly local governance.

Children's participation and local governance

For many children local authorities are conceptualized as some kind of all-powerful abstract phenomena which affect their lives and provide services for them. Many young people appear resigned to the fact that local affairs are decided by someone else, somewhere else and that they have no part in decision-making. However, young people also frequently express a frustration about not being adequately provided for and not being asked what they think. As this 13-year-old boy said:

225

. . . people like politicians and stuff don't really know what we want to do . . . and just think we're, like, really stupid and a bit of a waste of time really, I suppose. Think we just stay in all day watching telly. They just think 'oh, he's just a little kid, what does he know'. (Percy-Smith, 1997)

Traditional structures are not conducive to the participation of children. Policies at national, regional and local levels have been slow in turning the rhetoric of the UNCRC into reality. So often the rhetoric of children's rights and participation that many local authorities embrace gives rise to a range of piecemeal responses which do not always lead to genuine opportunities for participation but remain at best on the fringes of local government, at worst tokenistic.

Initiatives in the UK that have been most successful in facilitating children's participation can be divided into five categories:

(1) participation in community social units such as schools, youth clubs and young people's advice and support services (Save the Children, 1997a);
(2) community-development projects (Hart, 1997);
(3) issue-specific groups, e.g. on environmental issues (LGMB, 1996);
(4) youth and Local Agenda 21 (LA21) initiatives (LGMB, 1996); and
(5) youth councils (Matthews and Limb, 1998).

The first three are important within the context of community-service provision and issue-specific objectives but they remain relatively powerless with regard to local authority decision-making. LA21 initiatives have provided a hopeful forum but in the majority of cases have not received the necessary political and financial commitment and have been set up without adequate community representation and support.

Matthews and Limb (1998) identified an incipient structure of youth councils/fora in the UK serving different purposes and therefore taking different forms. There are only a few youth councils which have been given genuine opportunities to work alongside local authorities (Devon Youth Council provides an exceptional example) in a meaningful way. There is a danger of tokenism with youth councils unless, as with the Devon example, there is an expressed political commitment to children's participation. Participation may also be restricted to an unrepresentative group of motivated young people, to the detriment of more marginalized or disadvantaged individuals, and views and decisions taken by the councils may not be taken seriously by adults, or indeed considered at all.

All the same, youth councils/fora and Agenda 21 groups provide useful frameworks for children's participation (if taken seriously by local authority officials) and act as important catalysts in raising the profile of children on local agendas. Indeed, enduring structures for children's participation are only likely to be successful if built on community initiatives (Hart, 1997). Other approaches, such as participatory research including techniques such as Planning For Real (Gibson, 1994), deliberative polls, using the Internet and use of the media, are alternative means by which participatory objectives may be achieved (SCF, 1997b). They act as educational tools in raising awareness, providing opportunities to learn the skills of participation, as a conduit for communication and consultation between local authorities and communities, and provide a stepping stone of opportunity into local governance. All too often, however, resistance to the participation of children restricts the development of suitable structures.

Barriers to participation

Reasons why young people tend to remain largely excluded from the local democratic process can be divided into three: those based on negative social attitudes towards young people; those relating to the structure and functioning of local authorities; and those associated with the low status of young people on political agendas.

Social attitudes

- Children are viewed as being immature, incompetent, irresponsible and irrational and therefore lacking the credentials for participation (James and Prout, 1990).
- Adults feel that because they have been children themselves they are in a position to act for them (SCF, 1995).
- Children are seen as by-products of families and as such are treated as passive dependants on parents (Jones and Wallace, 1992).
- Prevailing negative social attitudes of young people in many countries tend to give rise to ideologies that condemn and contain rather than encourage and empower young people. For many adults, allowing children greater power is seen as a threat to the power relations between adults and young people.
- In many countries a 'culture of powerlessness and non-participation' exists (Lansdown 1995).

Low political priority

- Government policy tends to be dominated by economic rather than social objectives and tends, therefore, to be reactive rather than proactive (Hodgkin and Newell, 1996).
- Children tend to be seen as unproductive members of society.
- Since children do not get the vote (until 16, or even 18, in some countries) their needs and interests are subordinated to those of voting adults.

Exclusionary structures and functioning of local authorities

- Paternalistic attitudes of bureaucrats are premissed on the supposition that as servants of the state they are given the legitimacy to take decisions for children based on adult rather than child perspectives.
- Entrenched bureaucratic structures simply do not have the facility to allow children to participate. Many social and political institutions are hierarchical, with little accountability to those they are serving (Save the Children, 1997a).
- Legislative frameworks prohibit participation (Franklin and Franklin, 1996).
- Children tend to be invisible in statistical accounting (Qvortrup, 1990).

There is a strong moral case as well as clear social and economic benefits in promoting children's participation. One of the aims of effective government structures for children is to encourage and prepare them for responsible participation in a democratic society (Hodgkin and Newell, 1996). This, however, involves challenging established social norms and values and implanting a new consciousness which gives a higher profile to children, places them at the heart of the policy-making process and creates new structures of local governance which are accessible to young people.

Such fundamental changes are unlikely to happen quickly or easily and as yet there is little evidence in the UK that local authorities have developed a fully coherent and comprehensive model for children's participation. Evidence to date does, however, suggest a number of guiding principles for promoting children's participation in local governance.

Children's participation in local governance[1]

The forms which new modes of child-friendly governance might take are likely to differ from place to place and across cultures. However, an acknowledgement of the universality of children's rights, and the obligation countries have to meeting them, suggests a number of imperatives guiding the principles for policy and practice in bringing about children's participation:

- ensure that children are included directly in research and needs assessment;
- promote their direct participation in the design, development, management, running and evaluation of programmes;
- invest in training and capacity-building among development workers, service providers and researchers so that they are able to involve, listen to, communicate with and interpret children's views, as well as facilitate their direct representation;
- provide opportunities for key local authority officials to reflect on their own values and realize the value and importance of involving children in local affairs;
- where appropriate, appoint staff with special responsibilities for consulting children, for example local ombudspeople, children's rights' commissioners or youth and LA21 officers;
- develop methods and approaches which enable and support children to express their own views and interests, especially in judicial or administrative procedures;
- produce an annual policy review and budgetary statement of financial support for the development of participatory structures for children;
- where appropriate, ensure that children have a right of access to information held about them, and that support is provided in accessing such information and understanding its implications;
- develop mechanisms to include children's views in decisions which affect them, as well as to provide them with opportunities to exercise their rights as citizens in public debate; and
- build on and adapt existing structures and departments so as to provide the necessary conditions and support for extending local authority activities to include children's participation.

The creation of a children's agenda for participation at the local authority level calls in turn for the support of central government. Since much of the legislation that affects children's participation is enacted at national level, and in the absence of a clear and concerted manifesto commitment to children, the role of a minister for children or children's ombudsperson is imperative (see Hodgkin and Newell 1996, Rosenbaum and Newell, 1991).

Box 6.9: Toppling the ivory tower; children, participatory research and academia

The ivory tower

Academia performs an important role in society. It is regarded by many as the fount of all knowledge, a world inhabited by the most intelligent, the birthplace of theories, policies and inventions. It is considered a foreign environment to the majority of people, including many of those who study within it. Perhaps it suffers from an 'ivory tower' syndrome. This reputation is not without foundation, for there are those who assume their position in the tower, live by its rules and happily assert without question their knowledge (equating to power) over those outside. For children, the ivory tower is indeed a distant world, one that does not allow for their involvement in research agendas, syllabuses or theses and a world that is unfamiliar, intimidating or uninteresting. For those in the tower, children are the antithesis of all the academic world represents. Their thoughts are irrational and unfounded and their modes of operating immature. They offer little and have much to learn. Imagine, then, the shock as movements to involve children begin to knock at the tower's door. The notion of children as research subjects is rare enough but as partners – what a ludicrous idea! What and how could children possibly contribute? What on earth could they teach those who teach them?

Challenging academia

This scenario is exaggerated and simplified, of course, but it does introduce some of the real problems facing those in academia with an interest in researching with children. Traditional academic concern for the child has been limited to the fields of education and development psychology but within the last decade this scope has broadened to disciplines such as sociology, anthropology and geography. Accompanying this, there has been a phenomenal growth in the use of participatory research methods, not just in academia, but in the NGO and international agency sectors too. These changes are demanding fundamental shifts of thought and action and they represent a serious challenge to academia. The greater involvement of children in this world will demand not only new ways of thinking but sometimes significant changes in modes of operating.

Barriers to children's participation

The nature of the challenge is highly variable, dependent on the structural constraints of the institution and the culture of individual disciplines. The demand for accurate pre-engagement methodological detail, for example, is at odds with the flexible and locally constructed nature of participatory research. Similarly, the idea of children researching and evaluating their own existence through drawing and performance does not sit comfortably alongside academic demands for rigour and integrity. The isolated individualistic agenda of academia is in stark contrast to the more holistic community-orientated efforts of NGOs and local-action groups. The emphasis on academic recognition through internal channels rather than open dissemination represents a low return to the community in terms of investment in any collaborative efforts. By far the greatest barrier is a concern for the academic legitimacy of information generated through participatory research and particularly by children. Closely associated is compartmentalization into subject groups, a barrier because disciplines only consider part of the whole, with possible misinterpretations of realities.

Hope for the future

Interdisciplinary and learner-centred approaches are already having an impact on the operation of the university and its definitions of success. Initiatives for children can already be identified and are worthy of brief. For example, many universities and colleges encourage students to link with local schools and youth groups as mentors, helpers or simply to talk about their experiences. At Sussex University in the UK, students who do such work are awarded certificates, deservedly acknowledging such non-academic activity. Similarly, colleges are frequently involved in events that promote or defend the interests of the child at local, national and international level. Tertiary institutes are beginning to acknowledge the ability of their own students (normally aged 18–25) to identify and solve issues pertinent to their condition. This is leading to a growing respect for participation and critical reflection on the relationship between youth and academia. The principles being established are encouraging for the future involvement of younger people.

A culture of negotiation and participation is unusual within tertiary institutes and, by extension, between them and the wider society. The ivory tower is still in place but its shutters are slowly opening to community and, specifically, child involvement. As a result, teaching and learning may become more accessible and policy impact increasingly realistic and effective.

Rob Bowden

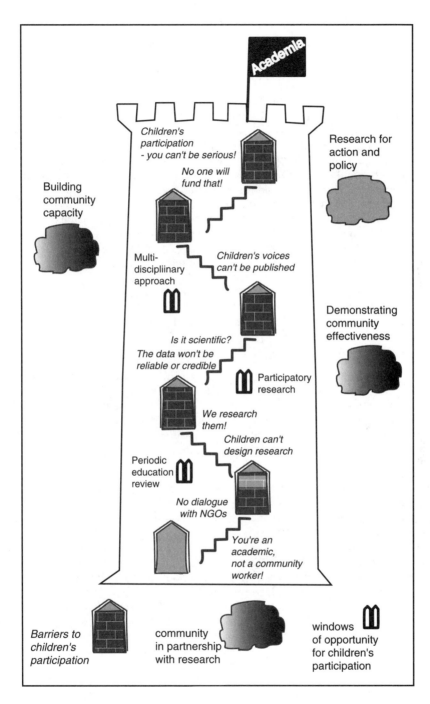

Figure 6.8: *The ivory tower*

6.15   Child-sensitive local government structures in synergy with children's representative bodies

JOHN PARRY-WILLIAMS

Until recently a major way to affect attitudes towards children at the local level was to make the local structures that affected their lives more aware of and sensitive to their needs. One example of this is in Uganda, where it has been made a general duty of councils from the village or ward, through parish, sub-county and county to the district level, to safeguard and promote the welfare of children. In addition, a children's ombudsperson has been incorporated into each elected council. This person's role is referred to in the Local Government Act 1993, and the Children's Statute 1996 as the Secretary for Children and was taken on by the vice-chairperson of these councils. Their role is to mediate in any situation where a child's rights are infringed. However, what this system does not encourage is children organizing themselves to express their views on matters that concern them.

In South Asia there are examples of children coming together to influence the environment in which they live. In Ladakh, in the state of Jammu and Kashmir in north-west India, children are being assisted to form Children's Committees for Village Development (CCVD) by an NGO, the Leh Nutrition Project, supported by SCF(UK). The objectives are:

- to promote recognition of children as a group, while building an atmosphere of collaboration between them and adults;
- to help adults and village communities to make the best use of children's contributions by way of ideas, views and initiatives; and
- to give children the opportunity to increase their understanding of developmental issues and to learn the life skills necessary in their developing roles as citizens.

The CCVD is formed with the consent of the villagers and is intended to be the representative body of all children in the village. They elect the committee depending on the composition of the children in the village; there are representatives for the 5–10 and 11–17 age groups from both sexes and also from children who are out of school and disabled. It is recommended that there are two adult facilitators, one a teacher and the other from the village education or development committee. The schools and pre-schools are central in the development of CCVD activities. Linkages with village adult bodies are seen as vital. The committee itself is run on democratic lines. Committee members have portfolios, there are regular meetings, procedures are laid down and records and plans of action are made.

The children of Igoo village have done their own PLA research on the problems they and adults in the community face and their ranking in importance, from which they drew up a year's action plan. For Igoo, this included improvements to the school, e.g. furniture, drinking water, electricity, walling, sports equipment and a playground. In the community, it was to organize health awareness in collaboration with medical aid centres, the village education committee and schoolchildren, and also to raise money for the medical treatment of a family with eye problems. They are also campaigning to have a child on the village education committee.

They have presented some popular theatre drama on anti-smoking and appear to have influenced some adults, as one member testified to us in a discussion after the performance. They have also used drama and songs to show their parents the importance of education and care for the environment. They have assisted the community in practical ways, such as washing the clothes of the very elderly and whitewashing *stupas* (Buddhist shrines). They feel that their working together has improved their interaction with adults.

There is a long-term plan in Ladakh to have the committees elect members to a block and then to district committees. A body that has gone some way in doing this exists in Tilonia in Rajasthan, where children elect representatives to seven field-centre assemblies in a block covering 110 villages, which are seen as states in the 'republic' of Tilonia, and also to the 'parliament' in Tilonia. These bodies are organized on the lines of India's state assemblies and central parliament. Their interaction is primarily with the Social Work Research Centre (SWRC), a leading NGO in non-formal education, which runs over 60 night schools and a few day schools around Tilonia, whose 2500 students form the electorate. The staff of SWRC have acted as the civil servants to the elected child representatives. This development, called *Bal Sansad* (Children's Parliament), has involved them in reviewing their education and in developing various life skills, such as co-operation and decision-making. It has also emphasized that democracy should be above gender, caste and creed. Children representatives are now being encouraged to participate in village issues other than education.

These children's representative bodies are working towards a situation where the views of children interact and overlap with local government structures and maybe eventually have a national impact. Where local structures are already sensitized to respond to children's needs and interests, as in Uganda, children's representative bodies will be well placed to influence them and to ensure it is those rights and needs most important to children, especially the most disadvantaged, that are addressed and realized first. Also that the role of children as citizens is more widely accepted and respected.

6.16   Children as partners with adults: a view from the North[2]

BERRY MAYALL

Protection, provision and participation

The 3Ps in the UN Convention on the Rights of the Child – protection, provision and participation – are useful tools to help us look at issues in child–adult partnerships. It is crucial to see the 3Ps as interlinked and interactive when we are considering any aspect of children's rights, and when we think about children's participation in shaping and constructing social worlds.

If we aim for children to participate with adults, then we must think about protecting children and providing for them at the same time because children live in social worlds where adults hold the cards and have power over children. You cannot have true participation until you have gone some way to keep children safe from danger, including that posed by adults, and until you have provided them with a minimally adequate standard of living so that they are free to participate.

By protecting children and providing for them, we can enable them to participate. I use the word 'enabled' rather than 'empowered'. In my view, children cannot be truly empowered, since structurally they constitute a minority group in relation to adults. It is relevant therefore, to proceed with the 3Ps simultaneously because all three are interlinked in terms of their effects on each other and on the lives of children and on concepts of childhood – and share common characteristics – all of them are about the distribution of material and social resources. I want to stress, therefore, that when thinking about participation we have to be careful to remember that true *participation* depends on *provision* for children and childhood, and *protection* of children and of childhood.

Children and childhood

When thinking about children's participation, we must take account of what we mean by children and childhood. 'Child' is a relational concept, that is, children are those who adults define as not adults, as lacking the characteristics of adults; what children can do depends very much on what adults say they may do. 'Childhood' is the life lived by children. Its quality and character is, again, determined very largely by what adults allow and prohibit. Though children can try to influence the quality of their lives, they have to accept the broad structures that adults dictate.

According to adult definitions (at least in the North) a defining feature of children is that they are inferior to adults. In northern Europe and America, a huge child-development industry documents this inferiority and the stages children go through before becoming properly human, that is adult. These ideas about children and about how they should live their childhoods are serious barriers to genuine participation. One worrying feature of globalization is that we export our ideas, describing them as facts, to other countries.

Social rights and protection

I suggest that (in the North) children are, by comparison with adults, a minority group. In several respects, adults find it easy to say so. Children are biologically inferior – small in size, experience and knowledge. They are constructed as vulnerable, as incompetent. Child–adult relationships are organized, characterized and implemented by adults.

Therefore, since children occupy minority status, children and their childhoods must be protected. They have to be protected physically until they are strong enough to participate. They also have to be socially protected against adults, against their behaviour, norms, commands and instructions. They have to be protected by being provided with physical and social places which pay attention to their smallness and give them space to grow and learn.

Civil rights and provision

The socio-economic position of children all over the world has worsened in the last few years (except in the Nordic welfare states) and, as we know, child poverty matters crucially, even more than that of adults. It leads to ill-health and poor education, with life-long effects and consequences for the next generation. So how can children acquire or be given a voice in political processes, to demand a better deal, a better distribution of resources? The provision of material and social resources is crucial, so that children are healthy and well-educated enough to participate. Also essential for participation are arenas, channels, and lobbies.

Political rights and participation

It is a long road up here in the North for children to be regarded as citizens. There is a tendency to subsume children under family, to say parents speak for children, to direct social policies towards families rather than directly towards children. Children tend to be excluded from adult social and political arenas, so work needs to be done on including them – to recognize their right to be heard, to be taken account of; to work locally on the implications for social policy and for their daily lives of the UN convention. We need to look at how to enable, provide for participation and protect participation.

We must provide *arenas* for participation – in schools, villages, homes, streets. We must consult with children about what best suits them, and about what social arenas suit them: what groupings of children, and what enabling circumstances. Issues of protecting children continue here – giving them freedom to speak.

It is important to think about *channels* – means, lobbies and avenues. Perhaps this requires setting up new structures for children, not just adding them on to existing adult structures where their participation may end up as symbolic rather than effective. Again, it is clear that we must consider how to provide these channels/lobbies and how to protect children's use of them against powerful adult forces.

Careful thought by children, with adults, is needed on *stages of participation* – defining issues, planning activities, carrying out activities, including research, dealing with findings, getting the points across, all at a range of levels. And of course we must look for appropriate *methods of participation*. What do children and adults consider the best ways of working together? What methods suit what topics? Experience suggests there are no simple blueprints; part of the activity of participation consists of together devising productive methods.

Why should we work for children's participation

Why is it important to work for children's participation? There is the justice argument: adequate resource allocation to this important social group probably demands that we hear what they want; the human knowledge argument: understanding the experiences of children, how they understand their childhoods, what resistances they engage in, their take on social structures and social policies; and the social policy argument: that children's interests are attended to (and the future secured), and that interventions will be appropriate.

Final points

Finally, I should like to add some discussion points on participatory research in the North, as compared to the South. In both regions there are interesting dilemmas if we want to encourage children's participation in working towards the future.

- In the North: we have separated out the lives of children from those of adults, and defined children as very different from adults. Children's lives are locked into huge, complex institutional arrangements that define them as learners, and adults as workers and carers. There are clear conflicts between the interests of children and those of adults. So children's agendas may be very different indeed from adults'. These points can mean that it is hard for adults to talk freely, on equal terms with children. On the other hand, children in some Northern countries are accustomed to voicing their views, to living in fairly egalitarian families, to participating in learning (rather than being passive vessels for information). This can mean children are willing to discuss research and social agendas.
- In the South: the lives of many children are less separated from those of adults. Many children engage in work and caring that is useful to the household and the local economy. Schooling has more obvious relevance to future life as a citizen and is more obviously a good (though not available for all). However, in some countries, adults and elders have high cultural status and children are required to be obedient, silent and respectful of them. So, in some respects, adult–child tensions may be less pronounced and adults and children may have in some cases more common ground on which to talk with each other. On the other hand, adult ideas about how children should behave and what weight should be given to their voices may be an inhibiting factor in participatory work.

6.17   Children's conferences and councils

DAVID WOOLLCOMBE

There are many examples of youth participation afforded by the United Nations' departments and agencies that have championed the cause of youth partnership in decision-making in their documents. However, most of these efforts have met with mixed results because the UN is not ready to obey the first principle of youth participation: an acceptance of youth culture in the partnership. Young people can be persuaded to behave like diplomats but the result is like watching a performance. They lose the very qualities that would have made working with them worthwhile. The clash of cultures has led to some distortions of the partnership process that are worth looking at, if only to learn what not to do. We shall then look at some examples of youth participation in governance at a local level where the results have been far more successful.

The World Summit for Children closed with the words: 'I address myself particularly to the children here: it is up to them to ensure that we keep the promises we've made here today...'. The speaker was the chair of the very committee that, six months previously, had taken a decision not to allow any children to present their views at the summit. Many young people's organizations fought that decision fiercely.

The World Summit for Children was a perfect opportunity for trying out different forms of young people's participation. After much negotiation, UNICEF organized a Children's Open Day to be held two days before the summit on an open-air stage outside the UN. Children sang, children danced, children made passionate appeals but nobody listened. The children were literally singing for the birds. When the heads of state arrived, two children were selected to meet two leaders. The kids were told to 'make it quick' as they were ushered in to see the two politicians, who were both exhausted after a long day of meetings. Nervous and flustered, the children gabbled their presentation, pushed the papers over the table and left feeling angry and betrayed.

At the summit itself, children dressed up in national costumes and ushered their leaders to the stage where they signed the summit documents. Six of them read the summit declaration in the six UN languages. I noted the experience in my diary thus:

> Children in national costumes usher their leaders to the dais where they sign the Declaration and Plan of Action. Back in their places, six children step up to microphones and read the preamble in the different UN languages – reading words that they had no hand in writing, watched by two-dimensional portraits of the kinds of impoverished children which these words are designed to assist and by three-dimensional politicians who are entirely responsible for providing that assistance. Nothing could symbolize the powerlessness of children more accurately than this – and yet these children cry out the words with a passion! The Chinese girl speaks with fire in her belly and a blaze in her eyes that all can relate to. Brilliant! If only such a person were given the levers of power to implement the fine words, we know she would not rest until it were done. Instead the levers of power rest in the hands of people in the serried rows around her, many times her age. Yet they excuse their lack of enthusiasm for child participation by repeating the old phrase I have heard twice today, once from a UNICEF/PR person, and once from a Brazilian diplomat: 'When you go to a children's hospital, you do not expect to have brain surgery done by a child!

In the UNESCO children's environmental conference held in Paris in May 1995, there was absolutely no participation by children in the set-up, planning or execution of the event. The decision to hold the conference was taken by UNESCO, together with the Disney corporation, which funded the event. Eight hundred children had come in classroom groups from 25 countries as a result of winning an environmental competition in the Disney Mickey Mouse magazine. Like a roller coaster in slow motion, the children were moved in regimental discipline from the minute they arrived: to buses, to theme-park rides, to Wild West Shows, to meals, to bathroom breaks.

They were supposed to meet, share ideas and prepare a comprehensive statement on the environment, which they would illustrate with their own paintings. The children did not meet or confer at all, they travelled in separate buses, worked in separate language groups and sat separately at the plenaries, waving their national flags at each other. What was unforgivable was that the Children's Environment Charter was drafted by staff and approved for printing weeks before the children arrived. At the presentation to the UNESCO director, it was read not by children but by actors. Professional artists even repainted the children's paintings, for fear that the kids' own paintings would not be up to scratch. During the 52-minute presentation, children spoke for a total of four minutes; in the closing ceremony, no child spoke at all.

Local and national government experience

Among other European governments, Germany and Austria have made commitments to explore improvement of child participation in decision-making as a priority. Austria's current practice promotes 'self-determination for the child' in relation to its rights under the law, and in numerous lesser areas like a child's responsibility in 'pocket-money transactions' where commitments made by the child can be legally enforced:

> Irrespective of their citizenship, children have the statutory right to vote in the election of their class speaker from 5th grade onward and their school speaker from 9th grade onward. The school speakers, equal in number and rights to parents and teachers, have an important say in all school matters, above all as regards school autonomy. In addition, there is a statutory youth body representing the interests of pupils at the *Lander* (state) and federal levels, whose members are elected by all Austrian school speakers.

In this way, Austria declares its commitment to young people's involvement in decision-making. The German system is almost identical. In practice, though, participation is not easy. Henry, a 19-year-old student from Germany, observes:

> The class speakers are almost always the most nerdy, most unpopular pupils in the class – elected as their role is seen to be a punishment rather than a privilege. The meetings are of the most stifling boredom with long discussions of things that have no interest to students, like the nature of teachers' expense claims, teacher re-training in the holidays, school inspection and relationship to national and regional authorities. On the rare occasions where something of interest to students does come up, the teachers and parents listen sympathetically to what the students have to say, then go on to do exactly what they want. It's like there is a conspiracy between the

parents and teachers against the students and, of course, they are always the majority. So the students have no real power. And they know it – so they feel defeated before they even get into the room.

It is no surprise to me that smart kids do not want to get involved. It is no fun. Why not spend the time doing sports, going to parties, shopping or at the movies? I myself think that and yet, when I became a part of the new German system, I was more idealistically motivated than any of my peers. I genuinely wanted to make it work. I tried extremely hard for many months, but I couldn't. We need to go back to the drawing-board and start thinking it through all over again.

That process of thinking it through has not begun. In most of the rest of the world, the Austro-German system for involving young people in governance is deemed to be technically the most efficient and progressive in the world. Jones and Wallace (1992) cite it as the 'most advanced and well-developed in Europe'. Several schools in the UK, Switzerland and other places follow it and make it work. However, Henry's experience is clearly real and demands that we find out why a theoretically perfect system does not work in practice.

In July 1996, in Racine, Wisconsin, USA, a meeting, 'Promoting Young People in Governance', was held. The report of the conference included some revealing comments by young people, which give a lucid glimpse of how youth participation can affect them:

> The justification for expanding youth governance is both moral and practical. From the principles of diversity to democracy, to the benefits of better-informed reliable young people, more creative decision-making, and the production of a new generation of skilled community and business leaders – all derive from effective, well-planned young people's participation. (Tim Burke)

> It's a two-way street. In my year with the California Association of Student Councils, my skills and my knowledge have grown exponentially – I've been like a human sponge. And the council with students in charge keeps the school boards on the ball. Technology is moving at such a rate, if you don't have kids on board, you're going to be left behind. The kids who are going to inherit the earth were playing computers at age five and setting up websites at age twelve. (Steve Arnowitz)

> Boards must nurture young people's talent, not kill it. Young people are willing to take greater risks, so it can be scary to give them power. But why worry about taking risks when we're already failing?! Why be so nervous, as when we don't take risks, nothing happens!' (Paul Schmitz)

The Community Education Council (CEC) of South Derbyshire made a serious effort to involve young people in the governance of their youth service. In its report of June 1991, it explains how it initially set up a youth sub-committee that met 'the County Council's criteria regarding the substantial involvement of young people...'. It proved to be problematic because:

(1) The Young People felt out of place. Despite very positive training which had been undertaken, the traditional committee approach remained off-putting. The young people who came were all well-motivated and

239

academically able, which in itself was a problem as they were not truly representative of their peers. Even they felt uncomfortable when faced with the formal committee structure with its long agendas and adult environment. Their initial enthusiasm evaporated quickly.

(2) Because of academic and other commitments, on-going commitment to the committee was hard to sustain.

(3) Because the committee representatives were all young people, the part-time adult working staff felt no ownership of the committee process and may have been alienated by it. Facing up to the failure of the committee, youth workers and young people themselves met and discussed how to do it better, and consulted with other NGOs, like the uniformed young people's movements – scouts, guides etc. The result was a group which the young people themselves called the Power Pack.

The Power Pack is a young people's sub-committee composed entirely of young people. Each statutory youth club in South Derbyshire has the right to send four representatives to attend (preferably two male, two female), and each club has one vote. Any four can come to any meeting so there is no need for an on-going commitment by individual kids. Notes from each meeting are posted on the youth-club noticeboard so all know what is happening at the pack all the time. Each club also nominates one of its part-time youth workers to take responsibility for participation in the Power Pack, organizing transport to meetings, etc. Uniformed young people's groups are also allowed to send representatives, as are adult youth workers, but no adults are allowed to speak at meetings unless specifically called upon by the young people to do so. They created a constitution which outlined their duties, responsibilities and purposes, with membership criteria and the exact manner in which the meetings are to be run – circulating chairmanship by a young people's representative, etc. A resource pack was created with structure diagrams, a voting card, an introduction to the Power Pack and an explanation of budgets available, which amount to £60,000 a year.

There are some deep cultural gulfs lying between children and officials, and bridging them is fraught with many complex practical difficulties. Recognizing the capacity of children and young people to set agendas and run things is part of how those bridges are built, because it means respect for kids and results in interest from kids. Children and young people can run their own organizations and conventions. This gives them the power and interest to negotiate and work with adults in ways that are not otherwise possible.

6.18   Promoting children's participation in an international conference: what can we learn from the Save the Children Alliance experience in Oslo?

RACHEL MARCUS

Despite sustained pressure from Redd Barna, working children's organizations and other NGOs, the Norwegian government refused to make provision for the significant participation of working children in the International Conference on Child Labour held in Oslo in October 1997[3]. Eventually three children, one each from Africa, Asia and Latin America were invited but requests to increase the representation of working children were turned down. To increase the opportunities for children to make their voices heard in the conference, on behalf of the Save the Children Alliance, Redd Barna, Rädda Barnen and SCF (UK) organized a working-children's forum. Twenty-one children aged between 13 and 18 from Latin America, Africa, south and south-east Asia, elected by their organizations, met for ten days in Oslo before, during and after the international conference.

Twelve of the children had previously participated in international working-children's meetings, the other nine had not, though all but two had been involved in national or regional meetings. The Alliance deliberately invited children from a range of movements, both those closely linked to supporting NGOs and also working-children's groups[4], in order to increase the range of experiences, types of organizations and approaches to children's participation represented.

The children's forum was clearly a valuable experience for all those who participated and one from which the Alliance agencies have learnt a great deal. Some of the main issues arising from our attempts to increase the opportunities for children's voices to be heard in the Oslo conference are discussed below.

Lessons from the children's forum

Participation in the official conference

- *Children's participation at events of this kind can change attitudes*, to both child participation and child-labour policies and practice. The fact that the children expressed different views clearly challenged claims that they are all manipulated by adults to say the same thing. There is, however, a need for more rigorous assessment of the cumulative value of their presence at such events. Our positive sense of changing attitudes is based on anecdotal evidence.
- *Formal participation of children in conferences on equal terms with adults appears to have a greater impact than fringe meetings*, though these were the most that could be achieved in Oslo. Unsurprisingly, what the three child delegates said was quoted, and often incorporated into other delegates' speeches to a greater extent than the views they and the

241

other children had expressed in meetings with key individuals or the mass media.

- Contrary to prevailing assumptions, *children as young as 13, who are experienced in discussing issues, are able to contribute meaningfully* as participants in conferences of this kind. Adults should not assume that conferences are unfriendly spaces for children and exclude them 'for their own good'.

Linking the children's forum and the official conference

- *The goals of such meetings should be limited, defined clearly, and preferably negotiated with participants in advance.* Given the short time-frame available, prior negotiation was not possible at the Oslo meeting. A lack of shared commitment to the goals of the forum contributed to conflict between participants. The goals of increasing opportunities for children to feed into the main conference, exchange experiences and discuss future co-operation, all in ten days, were probably too ambitious.

- *There are trade-offs* between: (i) facilitating opportunities for children to put their views to key players (e.g. UNICEF or the ILO) and to the mass media, and making time for them to discuss and exchange experiences among themselves; (ii) allocating sufficient time to prevent meetings becoming too pressured, and ensuring that children are not forced to be away from school, work or families for too long. The amount of time children, like adults, need to get to know one another and to work comfortably together, particularly when they come from such a wide range of cultural backgrounds and such divergent work and organizational experiences, should not be underestimated.

- *Greater discussion and clarity on the role of adults is critical.* Despite clarification at the beginning of the meeting that adults should support the children, giving explanations where necessary, but not attempting to influence their views, many of the accompanying adults strayed across that boundary, which is, of course, difficult to define. The fear of missing opportunities presented by an international conference to promote both children's participation and particular views on child labour may well have pushed several adults into the strong influencing role observed in Oslo. The timing and content of interventions from alliance organizers and observers aiming to clarify an issue or move beyond an apparent deadlock were also not always judged well.

- *The degree of adult facilitation needed is likely to vary* with the children's experience of organizing themselves and running meetings and with their cultural background. It would be helpful in future meetings to have on hand a facilitator experienced in conflict resolution, though the children manage to handle incompatibilities and differences of opinion mostly by themselves.

242

6.19 International agencies, government and NGOs working together in Yemen

SHEENA CRAWFORD

In 1997, the Yemen Ministry of Insurance and Social Affairs, UNICEF, the World Bank and Rädda Barnen (Swedish Save the Children Fund) joined together to produce the first report in Yemen on the status of children and women living in especially difficult circumstances. All the organizations contributed to financing and carrying out the surveys necessary for the report, and funds were also provided by the Royal Netherlands Embassy.

The co-operation of these different bodies was quite special. The ministry had voiced a fear that donors often conduct research without other agencies knowing. Research topics are sometimes duplicated and the results not properly disseminated. What is found out is not put to good use. By involving all the relevant agencies in the background research, lack of co-ordination was avoided. With a financial stake in the report, all agencies had an interest in ensuring that its findings be effectively utilized.

Until we started working on the report, children and women living in especially difficult circumstances in Yemen had hardly had a voice and had not been seen as active participants in the development process. We decided, then, to call the report 'To be seen and heard' (Crawford, 1997) which took, in all, four months to produce, including time for setting up the working committee, holding inter-agency meetings, deciding on the format and a broad framework for the contents for the report, finding the necessary secondary sources of information (in Yemen and abroad), designing the appraisals, training the research teams and putting together the final document.

Some people were initially wary of using participatory methods. They felt that more statistical information was needed if the research was to lead to effective strategies for action. Others of us felt it was necessary to get qualitative information from the research: to build knowledge and understanding with the children and women, to find out with them what makes their circumstance particularly difficult and to learn what their hopes, fears and life expectations are. This new understanding would be used to enhance existing statistical data (principally from the results of the Yemen Census, 1994) and to help us design new strategies for intervention and change. Box 6.10 shows how officials came to be convinced of the worth of participatory appraisal.

Some of the survey results didn't come as too much of a surprise. We saw that boys and girls have different access to existing basic services such as shelter, health and education, and that whether you live in the town or the country has a marked effect on ease of access to services. We also found out that, for some children, wherever they live, access to *any* services is going to be difficult, if not impossible. These children, mostly from the traditional cleaner's class and from among particular groups of returnees after the Gulf crisis, don't even make it into the houses of correction or the state orphanage. Only boys can go to the orphanage anyway, there are no facilities for girls.

Box 6.10: What people thought of using participatory research methods

When the participatory appraisals were carried out for the status report, it was the first time in Yemen that research had been designed especially with children in mind and with them as the main participants. We were unable to involve children directly in planning the appraisals but we made sure that they were able to contribute issues that they considered important.

We formed and trained three appraisal teams. In 'Abyan, on the south coast, men and women from the Ministry of Agriculture's Training Centre did research in two farming villages and two villages where the people are very poor and depend largely on fishing for their livelihoods. On the central upland plain, in the city of Dhamar, workers from the municipal office carried out research with disadvantaged people who had returned to Yemen during the Gulf Crisis in 1991 and with people from the 'traditional cleaners' class. In Sana'a, appraisals were undertaken with people living in the squatter settlements and with boys in the House of Correction and the state orphanage. We were also able to draw on experience from the Community Rehabilitation Programme for disabled children, which the ministry implements with Rädda Barnen support, and on community education projects supported by UNICEF. The 24 people involved in the field research each said that the new methods were very useful and that they had enjoyed the process and learned far more than expected. The children who participated did so with great enthusiasm!

At first, officials from some offices of government were concerned when we pointed out that the appraisals would not be done with a 'representative sample' of children in especially difficult circumstances, would not use questionnaires and would not provide statistical results. When they came to share in the results of the appraisals, they immediately became enthusiastic about the new methods. They accepted quickly that we could not have chosen a representative sample anyway because we weren't even sure at the beginning of the research, who 'children living in especially difficult circumstances' were or where we would find them. Part of our purpose was to decide on working definitions of these circumstances, together with the children and their families.

Most importantly, the officials were pleased to share what they considered real knowledge and understanding about the lives of some of the worst-off children in the country. The decision-makers in government may wait a long time for the results of social research and then feel that what has been discovered simply hints at things they already know and is often, therefore, a waste of time and money. The Yemeni officials felt that using participatory methods increased their involvement in the research process and enhanced their understanding of the lives of the group of children under study.

Figure 6.9: *The Mountain of Opportunity*

One of the most important things that we learned from the children is that, until they reach about 12 years of age, all of them have similar kinds of aspirations. This means that boys, whether they come from secure, middle-income (and above) families or from highly disadvantaged circumstances, all say that they want to get a good education and to become doctors, engineers or pilots when they grow up. Girls, too, want to learn, and they want to grow up to be beautiful brides and to have a secure home. These desires are constant, even though the most disadvantaged children are at the same time fully aware that the highest immediate priorities for them are shelter and food, being loved and living in secure conditions. Boys sometimes want to work to contribute to the family income and, maybe, to pay for their education. After 12 years of age, most of the children living in especially difficult circumstances abandon their dreams. They learn, simply, to cope with their difficulties, to lower their sights and strive just to survive as best they can.

When we shared these, and other, findings with government agency officials, everyone agreed that we must work together to find integrated strategies to tackle the problems of children in especially difficult circumstances. Government is convinced that this can be best achieved not only by donor and technical organizations co-ordinating their efforts but also by involving these bodies in civil society. New laws governing national non-governmental organizations (NGOs) have recently been passed. This has led to an upsurge in the number of NGOs, and there are now over 1200 registered. A coalition of some 30 NGOs has been formed, with support from Rädda Barnen, to work to ensure the implementation of the UN Convention for the Rights of the Child (UNCRC). NGOs in Yemen now cover a range of types, including religious foundations, unions and charity groups. The government is aware of the need for everyone who is working to secure the UNCRC to co-operate. It is fully committed to this task. This example in Yemen shows that international organizations, such as the World Bank and UNICEF, are committed to increasing their work with civil-sector bodies. The next phase is the development of co-ordinated strategies and action plans from all the agencies working in support of the CRC. Only in this way will it be possible for all those living in especially difficult circumstances 'to be seen and heard' and for them to participate fully in the effort to bring about positive social change.

6.20   Government and international agencies

WORKING GROUP REPORT

Ways forward for local and central government

When central government asks local authorities to establish a plan specifically for children, a range of very productive local-level initiatives can result, for example the UK's Children's Services Plan, South Africa's Development Facilitation Act and Uganda's Children's Statute have all been foundations for innovative local projects. The leader of the local council in Kirklees in the UK has become personally committed to children's rights and associated projects which the council is pursuing in partnership with Save the Children, while the Mayor of Johannesburg has become associated with projects attempting to increase children's involvement. In both these cases, high-level support laid the ground for prioritizing children's participation and involving independent allies who combined inside knowledge with outside stimulation.

Experience shows that there has not always been an emphasis on sustainability, although lasting (but flexible) structures for children are so vital to their involvement. They need to have regular opportunities for participation and support systems that allow a continuous flow of different children to join in as others pass through and move on. In order to do this, these structures need to ensure that the majority have a voice in the design of the system, but need also to guarantee that the voices of those children who are less articulate and usually get left out are also heard. Local government agencies (including schools) should ensure that opportunities for participation are built in from the very early years. If young children are involved from their earliest youth, they will be confident and skilled in participation by the time they reach adolescence (e.g. Kirklees/Save the Children joint initiative targeted on children under 8).

Capacity-building
Local government officers do not always understand children's needs and concerns or understand the barriers that impede their involvement. Children can play a significant role in providing them with training (e.g. the Frontier Foundation with street youth in Toronto). Children and young people act as advocates for participation by demonstrating the extra insights and added value which come when their involvement is actively appreciated.

Barriers

- National and local plans of action for children are of limited use without funding
- The workers who are easiest to convince about children's rights to participate (social workers, workers with street children, etc.) may have been won over, but the next levels are highly resistant. Those who work in institutions where they have authority over children (e.g. teachers, residential-care staff) will not easily give up any power because they fear it will be at their expense.
- Specialist children's rights officers can become a barrier if they don't learn to collaborate with others, if they remain ignorant of other people's working constraints or if they fail to understand power structure, and how decisions are made.
- If parents are ignorant of the UN Convention on the Rights of the Child (CRC), or lack support for its approach, children will have no early experiences of having their rights respected.
- Social and political attitudes are the major stumbling-block. Unless these are changed, changing structures will achieve nothing. New structures involving the same people (with unchanged attitudes) will not constitute progress. Current structures, but involving people with changed perceptions of children, can be made to work.

The Convention on the Rights of the Child

The CRC provides an excellent starting-point for development of regionally or locally specific conventions and has proved its worth in a great many countries. It is one of the most widely ratified conventions, and in 1997 only two countries had not signed up to it. The CRC is, however, an institution that is weakened by its global nature and its need to provide a single convention to fit all cultures. In certain cultures local people have claimed that the rights laid down are not relevant to their own moral codes and have had difficulty in implementing its provisions, so have laid it aside. In other cases, new or unstable governments have been unwilling to agree to put international agreements into place.

Strategies for change

There are a few key strategies for change that could make a significant impact on the lives of children around the globe:

- CRC should be acknowledged at all levels in local and national government. Central government has the responsibility to inform others of its work in implementing the convention. Central government should require local government to audit the progress it makes in its implementation. There is a need for a wide range of agencies to be involved and to own collective responsibility for that implementation.
- Children may be integrated into improved structures of local governance. There is no need to re-structure completely!
- Other stakeholders can be identified (they may not recognize themselves as stakeholders) and involved.
- The media should be involved in progress on children's participation so that they have a more positive and active image of young people and they should reflect this in their reporting.
- Children's organizations can act collectively to establish and pursue joint strategies. This collective can also include NGOs. Such a coalition of children's groups should be as independent and self-sustaining as possible.

Changing government's vision of children

How are children perceived and valued for their contribution and involvement? How can we change this for the better? We need an attitudinal change at national, local and neighbourhood levels. Much as we would like to devise a totally new way by which children could come together to express and make their views felt, it is more realistic to accept that we would need to operate through and change existing structures. One of the most important of these structures is the UN Convention.

At central-government level, having ratified the CRC, an independent National Children's Commission (NCC) or equivalent could be a dynamic force to keep central government to its obligations. The commission would be a powerful lobbying force, informing and supporting local government, in all its forms, of their CRC commitments. It would involve children and young people in its research studies and advocacy. It would also work collaboratively with NGOs and the mass media to bring positive change in attitudes and perceptions towards children, particularly by involving children in these campaigns.

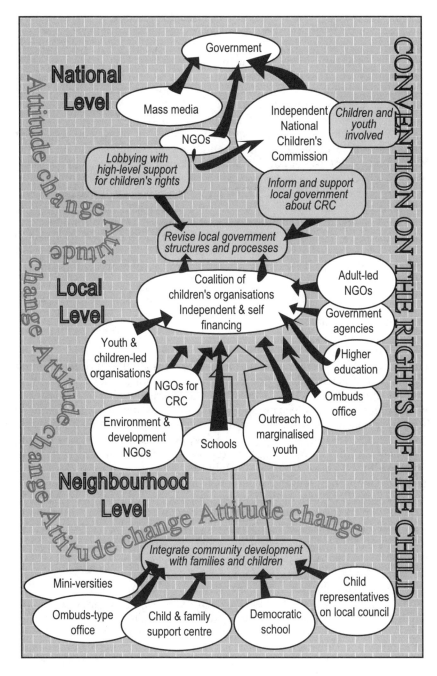

Figure 6.10: *Changing Government's Vision of Children*

With the NCC, the most potentially effective force to raise the influence and involvement of children is a Coalition of Children's Organizations, which needs to be self-sustaining and independent of government. (This would seem the appropriate body to write the supplementary report on the CRC to the CRC committee in Geneva). It is the task of this body to interact and facilitate the development of a variety of organizations in their efforts to make a reality of the convention. Its linkages should include the range of agencies and groups run by and working for children.

At the neighbourhood level there is a need for an integrated community-development approach with families and children, which would include representation of children on local decision-making committees, and democratic schools. This is vital for the proposed processes to become dynamic and self-sustaining in the community; everything that is relevant for the community should also have its expression and voice shared here.

With this degree of awareness, there is a real possibility of children at the grassroots level starting to have some influence on its own environment and on how it is perceived by local government. All this could mean that government at all levels will develop a greater sensitivity in its attitudes towards children.

International agencies

Global structures: local inertia
There are structural difficulties in the organizational culture of large bureaucracies that affect which programmes are adopted or abandoned. Promotion systems may reflect less the interests of children than those of the institution and its higher echelons, because the interests of children are so varied and difficult to represent. It is also not uncommon that innovative ideas are dismissed by old hands, who point out that participation is naïve and wastes time and that strong leadership is a practical reality for an international body. While large institutions have impressive global leverage through their capacity to mobilize public opinion and substantial funds, they may also be limited by political considerations in their campaigns and programmes. Equally, it is not possible to respond to a large and varied membership, so international organizations are restricted to a network of contacts that may not be fully representative.

Marketing and representing children
In marketing themselves and their campaigns, international organizations often genuinely seek participation by children, but logistical and structural constraints can distort these efforts towards insulting tokenism. Young people often find children's summits and councils boring and patronizing. The opportunity presented, however, is significant, and children's gatherings, parliaments and presentations have had much positive influence on policy and practice. International agency policies are becoming more supportive of children's rights, providing a fundamental underpinning of institutional commitment and an influence on global practice. The United Nations has also adopted children's committees as a means of providing accountability and power

sharing for the big children's events; these are generally well meaning, but are not always vested with full powers equal to those of other stakeholders.

Some key problems that need to be accounted for in making strategies:

- young people are not necessarily interested in participation with the international scene;
- adults claim to talk on behalf of children; and
- children often see that the process is fake, that it is tokenism and not real participation.

Some positive aspects and possibilities of the big organization and the multinational gathering are as follows:

- stakeholder involvement is increasing, with children often defining the agenda;

The *status quo* is a castle that is defended by the old guard who consider themselves as gatekeepers and who imprison young people if they catch them. Inside, there are some true believers, who try to help. Outside, the castle is under attack from various groups. One is an International Youth Association that is trying to rally youth behind it, without real participation by them. The youth themselves are challenging the *status quo* with demonstrations (illustrated by a catapult) as did the schoolchildren during the fall of the Berlin Wall. Some youth and older people are networking on the tactics and strategy, talking together by radio. Another young person is using a megaphone to let the youth voice be heard. There is a Trojan Horse that will be let into the castle by the true believers, which represents the international children's summits.

Figure 6.11: *The Trojan Horse*

251

- International meetings are a chance to share positive experiences;
- children's voices can challenge the prevailing culture and provide a catalyst for change;
- the fringe can have a powerful voice;
- using today's computer technology, children can voice their realities without reprisal;
- adult culture needs to look inwards and examine its own procedures; and
- children can provide inspirational ideas

The strategies suggested are as follows:

- Youth-led strategies can get around lack of interest and motivate young people. To reduce their fears of being able to do it 'right' or getting into problems, they can network together and with adults who can support them. They form independent youth groups that sustain themselves through continued responsiveness and their ability to deal with difficulties. The outcomes are unknown but they are generally likely to be beneficial and responsible, which also helps towards sustainability.
- Institution-led strategies can be beneficial in allowing the voices of young people to be heard and incorporated into global and national policies. Properly inclusive international conferences can be highly effective.
- Adults need access to workshops that allow them to experience children's participation and learn how to hand over responsibility to children
- Positive images and examples should be encouraged in the media.

Figure 6.12: *'We stand in a circle and take one step in. We close our eyes, hold hands across the circle and tie ourselves up in a human knot. We work together to untie it This exercise illustrates how the people who can best work out solutions to problems are the ones who have the problems themselves.'*

6.21   Conclusions

VICTORIA JOHNSON and PATTA SCOTT

The image at the beginning of this analysis of institutionalizing children's participation was of layers of influence; different institutions surround the child, from the family in all its different forms to community and local-level institutions, to national and international policy structures. By the end of the analysis, the image formed is of a web, with lines of influence and power relations going between the different levels, the different institutions and the different children. As we look at this web of influence, we should always be asking the question, who benefits? Amy Kaspar (6.1) suggests that there should be assurances that children's participatory rights are advanced and should benefit the child. There are numerous examples in Part 6 that show the value of children's participation in policy, research and community programmes, yet the positive and negative impacts for children and young people need investigation. Degrees of participation should be evaluated from a perspective of whether children themselves feel they have benefited from the process and whether they have enjoyed it. Do they have enough time to participate in different types of decisions in different institutions, to what extent and for how long? Do they want to participate in adult-initiated fora and projects? What are the risks of participation for the different children involved? Young individuals should always be given the choice of opting out of adult-initiated schemes that seek to increase their involvement in areas in

Figure 6.13: *The web of stakeholder relations*

253

which they may not want to participate. This brings us back to some of the ethical issues raised in Part 2 that should be at the forefront of our minds when entering any analysis of the successes of participation.

The lines of communication and power relationships within and between institutions need to be understood. People who work on children's issues have varying levels of awareness of questions of difference between young people or their skills in dealing with contrast and conflict. It is often found acceptable to give a voice only to those who are articulate, rather than to include those voices which are more difficult to hear. Issues of gender, class, ethnicity and disability can be some of the divides that exclude children and young people from involvement in different groups and processes.

Children's participation poses a fundamental threat to adult–child power relationships which makes institutionalizing children's participation an even greater challenge than institutionalizing other types of stakeholder participation. Changing adult attitudes towards children's participation may be a gradual process through the life-cycle of a project – examples in Part 6 have shown that adults, including parents and decision-makers, do become convinced of benefits and propose that the process must allow time for this. Children and young people also gain confidence and self-esteem as a project invites them gradually to increase their participation and control. It is in this way that power-sharing becomes possible and adults gain the confidence to give up some of their power and control. Robert Chambers (in Blackburn and Holland, 1998: xvi) suggests that it is a priority that we learn:

> How to enable powerful people to recognise that power is not a commodity to be amassed, but a resource to be shared; and how to enable them to gain satisfaction, fulfilment and even fun from disempowering themselves and empowering others.

Children can be good advocates of their own participation – both children and adults need proof that a project is going to work, which they gain through the project process. It is only in this way that adults will relinquish power.

Training for staff within organizations, and adults involved in children's lives and projects may often hold the key to greater understanding and acceptance. It is important to recognize the family, in its many forms, as one of the most immediate and direct institutions which influences the engagement a child may have with broader society. Initial work with parents and guardians to gain informed consent can be transformed into a process of deeper parental involvement, capacity-building and participatory monitoring and evaluation. As a result, the attitudes of parents, children and workers begin to change, and a more trusting and productive relationship can develop.

Understanding children and young people's own informal networks and groupings, and also their own motivations, is vital to understanding the best routes to more effective participation. It may be in more informal groupings that children are most comfortable discussing issues and developing their own capacities to share in aspects of the broader society. Supporting and funding youth organizations and groups, set up and directed by young people, is productive and important. Funding agencies need to be aware of the time that it can take to achieve more meaningful and effective participation by children and young people. Funding cycles and reporting structures need to be made more flexible in order to allow for long-term benefits from participatory processes involving young people.

It is ironic that the UN Convention on the Rights of the Child (CRC) is used to give validity for children's participation alongside protection and provision, as some of the legal structures deemed necessary in different countries to protect children may also in some ways limit their involvement. In institutionalizing children's participation, cultural and legal boundaries and frameworks need to be fully understood. Legal measures are important to ensure that children are not exposed to risks that may harm their mental and physical development. Within different cultural and institutional contexts, projects can work with young people to develop appropriate strategies and working methods that embrace their views, opinions and needs more fully, while maintaining protection and provision.

Young people are in a special position to contribute to social change. Often they do not have such a vested interest and such a weight of responsibility, as do many adults. In their formal and informal groupings, children and young people around the world already play important roles as social actors and agents of change and the future of children's participation can build on this foundation, developing partnerships and celebrating diversity and innovation. It is a challenge to institutions to become more open to the talent, enthusiasm and courage of the young.

Notes

1. These are based on the seven responsibilities for local decision-makers identified by Save the Children (1995).
2. This paper was given as a welcoming address to the worshop participants.
3. The new government which took office a week before the conference is more positive towards children's participation than was its predecessor; it invited an extra delegate from the children's forum to present conclusions to the ministerial part of the conference. Four children out of 320 delegates cannot, however, be seen as other than tokenistic.
4. These tend to have a more automomous identity, though all continue to receive support from NGOs, trade unions or churches.

PART 7

Children as Active Participants

Editor and co-author: EDDA IVAN-SMITH

Co-authors: ROB BOWDEN,
VERA VAN DER GRIFT-WANYOTO, ADAM HAINES,
DONALD KAMINSKY, GRACE MUKASA, IMANI TAFARI-AMA,
ANDREW WEST

Summary

Part 7 focuses on the qualities of a programme or research project that are needed in order to facilitate children's participation. The difficulties of applying a uniform definition of participation are also discussed. With contributions from Jamaica, UK, Uganda and Honduras, Part 7 provides us with a wide range of 'snapshots' of different geographical and cultural locations and the attendant strategies that work, and also some of the pitfalls of working in a participatory way with children, young people and adult communities.

Key issues raised in Part 7:

- Participation cannot be imposed on children and young people.
- Adult researchers need to recognize and validate children's knowledge and perspectives.
- Children and young people can be highly effective catalysts of change.
- Children and adults may have different participation agendas which may cause conflict.
- Children and young people may identify appropriate methodologies for participation; researchers need to be flexible in order to adapt to these.
- When embarking on a project or programme involving children's participation, it is important to include the wider community in the process.
- Adults need to be clear about who benefits from children's participation.
- The research process can be flexible and act as a stepping stone towards children's empowerment.

7.0 Introduction

EDDA IVAN-SMITH

Children acting on their own behalf and challenging adult views are two of the more emotive aspects of children's participation. The issue of children as active participants in the development process raises a host of legal and moral dilemmas that will be discussed in this part. In concept and practice, children's participation is fraught with the problems of definition, and there is a growing body of literature on this subject that demonstrates these divergent views. Andy West (1996a: 3) poses some interesting questions regarding children' s participation:

> The term participation is essentially contested – the exact meaning is elusive because common agreement as to precise definition and use is difficult or impossible to achieve. At one level, participation means being a member of a group or even talking to someone; on another level, participation

259

concerns power-sharing and decision-making... For children and young people there is a question of what's in it for me?

The lack of definition about children's participation means that practitioners are often unsure where to start. In their training manual on participatory research with children, Jo Boyden and Judith Ennew (1997: 39) provide some basic approaches.

> Throughout the 1990s there has been considerable discussion about child participation, often without any very clear ideas about what it entails. It should mean children are at the least informed about and consulted in actions taken for their welfare, and may be involved in planning, implementing and evaluating these actions. Too often it means that children are displayed at public events to sing songs or give testimony, in order to justify adult projects for children. To participate meaningfully, children need information about the reasons and the consequences of what they are doing, and the social skills for decision-making, debate and action. This need not be confined to teenagers; even pre-school children can participate if adults are willing to share power.

Even when there is clarity about the definition of children's participation, the application of it can be difficult:

> Behind many of the problems around 'operationalizing children's participation' is the shift of thinking that is needed to take it forward.

Figure 7.1: *'What's in it for me?'*

ology. The research was designed to provide data for the establishment of a Social Investment Fund, a joint project between the Jamaican government (through the Centre for Development, Population and Social Change at the University of the West Indies, Mona), and the World Bank which would simultaneously provide the international financial body with the opportunity to extend its resources to the community level.

Peter Espeut notes that the emergence of the concept of a garrison community can be traced to the creation of the politically monolithic community, Tivoli Gardens, by then sociologist Edward Seaga (for many years now, leader of the Jamaica Labour Party), as an enclave to secure votes. He elaborates further that:

> We need to remind ourselves how these garrisons got formed in the first place: it's all about the distribution of scarce benefits and spoils by the Ministry of Housing. Under the JLP (Jamaica Labour Party) government of the 1960s Back-O-Wall was bulldozed to make way for the buildings which are now Tivoli Gardens. So far no garrison; but distribute homes and apartments along party lines to JLP supporters alone, and have a master sociologist create an enclave spirit, and now you have the garrison *par excellence*. Tivoli Gardens has symbolic value as the first garrison, and the most complete, with social infrastructure and services to create almost a separate island.
>
> Taking a leaf out of Mr Seaga's book, the PNP (People's National Party) Government of the 1970s beefed up its Ministry of Housing and created poor copies of Tivoli Gardens all around Kingston, without its cultural and economic foundations...The politicians who consciously and deliberately conceived them and then played midwife had a specific purpose in mind: to construct a bedrock of votes which would guarantee them electoral victory or the hands to bogus any election.

(The Gleaner, 14 May, 1997).

The 1990s have so far seen a change in the nature of violence in these communities; internal power conflicts in PNP and JLP strongholds have given rise to the creation of gangs, particularly among the youth who gained increasing access to guns as a result of the drug/gun trade with outside agents. The reason for the violent conflicts within and among garrison communities has therefore shifted from partisan politics (although these are still pervasive) to the arbitrary enforcement of power through gun law.

Children as active participants in development

Youth are culture bearers and therefore active agents in the process of social change. The research uses an intergenerational map[1] to analyse the process of gender-identity construction among young people growing up within the structural and social frameworks of poverty and violence in Southside, one of the garrison communities.

A criminal career is, for some boys, thought to result from the status and therefore self-esteem which it brings as well as from the income it provides in the face of chronic unemployment. The young adolescents' inability to secure employment is due in a large measure to the stigma that the scourge of violence confers on community. Lack of access to adequate training and skills reinforces this vicious cycle of poverty and hopelessness.

On the other hand, according to the study, some young girls in the same age cohort start having sexual relationships sometimes as a strategy for escaping from the same poverty cycle. Dependence on a man is common. A girl in her early teens might even be encouraged by her mother, invariably the sole parent and herself a juvenile, to have a relationship with a 'Namebrand' man or a don. It is this powerful man who can protect her from exposure to harassment and provide her with the material goods her family may be unable to afford. It is inevitable, however, that the girls' dependency on male support and the violent contradictions with which these relationships are sometimes fraught will compound their social difficulties. Early childbearing also serves to reinforce female dependency; girls drop out of school early, thereby destroying their chances to carve out a viable career.

The cycle of early childbearing, which generally starts at the age of 12, contributes significantly to parents being unable to command the respect required to influence positively their own children's behaviour. At the same time, the meagreness of the material means available to parents results in hopelessness and frustration on the part of both generations. In other instances, migration of parents as a recourse to eke out a better economic existence often results in children being neglected by relatives or friends who feel no real obligation to add to their own responsibilities.

These worst-case scenarios need not inevitably typify the identities of young adolescents. On the contrary, a combination of psycho-social endowments and the intervention of institutions can contribute to the choice continuum and make it possible for the youth to construct alternative survival identities. Although the international media might depict the Jamaican subculture of poverty and violence as the propensity of all inhabitants of the country, it is, on the contrary, a small proportion of the population of two and a half million which could be said to fit this stereotype.

Following the completion of the above-mentioned study, I returned to Southside to discuss with a group of children and other community participants their experience and perceptions of living in a poor, urban community haunted by the spectre of violence. The multi-method engagement included popular education techniques in the languages used locally. From this exercise, I produced a twenty-minute video documentary, 'Living, loving and losing in Southside', which captured some of the contradictions of this social situation.

I am particularly concerned to focus on the age cohort of 10–15 years; youth in this age set are most at risk from the impact of poverty and violence (Moser and Holland, 1996; Levy et al, 1996). Although we present a dialectic movement from subordination through consciousness, struggle and resistance to the realization of agency and active voice as ideals, there are undoubtedly significant proportions of poor populations who are silenced and immobilized, seemingly in perpetuity.

The process of critiquing continuously all assumptions about the immutability of knowledge obliges the researcher to consider all expressions of social texts as significant. I have chosen poetry, therefore, as one medium representative of the voices of the researched in a language that they find intelligible, as well as to problematize the role of the researcher as ethno-grapher and social analyst. In other words, in as much as I am critically analysing the identity of children in a garrison community in Jamaica, my own combined identities are infused with values that affect my representation of the research participants and their community.

Conflicts in a Garrison

Sitting on a side
walk in Southside
with young girls
talking about boys and periods of bloody encounters
of sex
of pregnancy
of just feeling bodies
changing
and wondering
how to manage these transitions
i too talked of my encounters with the pain and confusion
and confidence
to assert being female
and loving it
time was so short
i will return i said, maybe even live
here
for a while...

The way forward

The multi-method approach initiated during the introductory phase of the research process will be maintained in future investigations. Data-gathering techniques will include participatory rapid appraisal, audio-visual documenta-tion, in-depth and semi-structured interviews, group discussions and work-shops, and participant observation.[2] These explorations will facilitate a discussion of identities embodied in the interlocking mosaic of the self that cannot be disaggregated discretely in the lived experience; we are embark-ing on a complex task both conceptually and in practice. The meanings which it is hoped will be gleaned from the research project will elaborate the norms and boundaries of gender/sex identities and suggest what are con-sidered accepted behaviours, roles or transgressions, or rebel identities and actions.

We also have to identify the resources, including personal endowments, social networks and other formal and informal institutional facilities, which provide the space and means for social actors to resist the structural forces of domination and develop and deploy strategies to ensure their survival. Some of these resources which we will unpack later include the family/household, school, church, social clubs, corporate and development agencies, peer-support networks and other social relationships, the (political and drug) don and the geographical location on the Kingston waterfront in the heart of the capital city's commercial area.

We recognize that power is not a one-way street or a unidimensional concept. We can explain power through the discourses of children who embody the contradictions inherent in concepts of the family or in whatever primary institutional arrangement they are first socialized into, in peer and other social relations in the community, and as they passively and actively interact with the wider society.

Children are one of the most mute categories among the poor. We are proposing to interrupt that silence at two levels: by recognizing the ways in which children's finding voice and realizing agency is facilitated by their own cultural networks and practices as well as institutions and values; and through the process of engagement, encouraging self-reflexivity that can contribute to the process of consciousness of one's humanity and capacity for exercising agency, which Freire defines as conscientization. As Freire suggests, without critical reflection on ourselves we cannot hope for emancipation.

Our engagement with the community will therefore be a conscious attempt to contribute to this process of self-reflexivity. I expect that through the process the research participants may become more confident about their agency, in spite of the social circumstances working against their autonomy. This reflexive consciousness of self and agency through the process of listening and talking (Hooks, 1990; Freire, 1985) aims to fulfil the Freirean recommendation that participants should be engaged in a process of consciousness-raising through research. This approach is a particularly appropriate statement of the scope of change hoped for by this project.

7.2 Voyce: environmental care and young people's participation

ADAM HAINES

Voyce (Views of Young Concerned Environmentalists) was formed in 1995 by Kim Jackson, an environmental education officer at Brighton and Hove Council. She noted a gap in the younger end of environmental-awareness groups in Brighton. Many schools and young people became enthusiastic about her project, and Voyce was born.

Voyce likes to get hands-on sleeves rolled up and stuck in. This is one of the great benefits of involving young people. One of the first projects was the refurbishment of Brighton sea-front beach deck. It was to be rebuilt and smartened up with a line of recycled glass bricks. Many kind people had recycled their old wine bottles but none of them had washed them or removed any labels, so the Voyce task force set to work with vigour for their first assignment. Rubber gloves were donned, scrubbing brushes brought out and several hours later a healthy pile of furnace-ready bottles was shining in the corner. Voyce had successfully completed its first mission. During this time, Voyce was becoming involved in advocacy work. We sent a representative to the international children's conference in Eastbourne, Sussex, where our spokesperson presented Voyce's work and approach to local environmental issues.

Several Voyce members attended the Children's Rights festival in 1995, which was set up by Brighton council to give local youth a say in what went on, and give children an opportunity to work closer with adults in the local community. Voyce held a stall at this festival and also built a recycled can sculpture in the shape of *V.O.Y.C.E*, the letter *Y* being a person with outstretched arms.

An event called 'Low Tide' was held several months later, where Voyce had a stall with Brighton council, and a few of our members conducted environment-week surveys to discover public views and opinions on the sea, beach, local environment and other related subjects. Around this time the group really started to take off and lots of events were organized. It wasn't long until Voyce T-shirts were donned, together with gloves, litter pickers were handed black bin-liners and a whole load of members took to the eastern end of Brighton beach to clear up any objects that weren't pebbles! Around eight sacks of junk were collected, ranging from drinks' cans to fishermen's net rope, and a very rusty large saw blade. The beach looked much better!

Brighton has an old, and original wooden tram shelter sited on a main road. For years it has been plain and almost faded in the background until Voyce got together a plan to sponsor this shelter and brighten it up. Contacts from the Magpie recycling centre helped to draw the sketches and assist with the plans, then one October weekend in 1996 the tram shelter was transformed from grey to brightly coloured; pictures adorned all the walls, lovingly handpainted by Magpie and Voyce, and a poem on an environmental theme was written on the inside ceiling. A glass display was erected, telling bus-stop users about Voyce and the painting. From local residents' responses, it has certainly brightened up many people's days and physical environment.

Soon after this, Voyce was asked by the Walden Schools environmental panel, a group of young people concerned with environmental issues, to meet and exchange ideas. They suggested a fun day out, with a serious side to the day of bonding closer local young peoples' groups in Sussex for the good of all. The morning began with a discussion and group working games whereby people mixed with others they didn't know to gain knowledge and meet each other.

The momentum of Voyce activities continued rapidly with the advent of the Garb and Garbage fashion show held at Brighton College of Technology. This coincided with the launch of youth-work week in November 1996, on an environmental theme. Hardworking Voyce members made outfits of their own designs, all from recycled materials such as packets, bin-bags, old rags. You name it, clothes were made from it!

Voyce then became involved in a mural painting project, on the theme of the four seasons: how they should be, and thought-provoking pictures of how the seasons will change if left to a careless and ignoring society. Our friends at Magpie asked us to team up with them on this project, and lots of painting sessions were held at their recycling centre to complete the murals. During the final varnishing, two Voyce members appeared for ten minutes on a morning radio programme talking about the mural project and other Voyce

Figure 7.2: *Garb and Garbage fashion show*

activities. The murals are now hung just off Western Road in Brighton and without a doubt 'Brighten up' our local town!

Next came the national campaign Get a Grip on Litter week in April. Voyce donned the gloves once again, picked up the litter pickers and black bin-liners, put on a special Get a Grip on Litter badge each and set to work. Despite the wind and rain, several sacks of rubbish were collected from the seafront in central Brighton.

Soon after this event Voyce was asked to make some banners and flags to decorate the city's Madeira Drive on several different environmental themes as part of the annual dance parade: ecology and environment; Brighton sea-side in summer; and music, art and dance. The banners were displayed in the parade and have since gone on to star in other Voyce events.

For Voyce, the highlight of 1997 was our involvement in the lions street carnival, and through lots of luck and friends, we were given the use of a lorry plus a 40-foot long trailer for the day. The theme of the float was to be 'Ali Baba and the 40 recycling themes' which meant everyone had to dress up in either environmentally-sound costumes or traditional Arab dress. Voyce members then let fly with their materials (recycled items, scissors, glue, Sellotape, water-based paint, cane sticks and polythene) to create the float.

A cave was created for the front of the float, to shelter the band and its equipment should it rain, wheelie bins were attached to the lorry to house

VOYCE ~ VIEWS OF YOUNG CONCERNED ENVIRONMENTALISTS

Figure 7.3: *Environmental posters*

environmentally-aware costume wearers dressed in many materials: plastic, cans, paper, newspaper, organic materials, cardboard, textiles, glass, oil and foil. The moment the lorry arrived, the heavens opened and rain set in for the day – great!! Just what we needed! The band hastily loaded all the musical equipment into the waterproof cave and set up while the others loaded everything they could, barring the kitchen sink! It was a real team effort (everyone wet together). By the time the lorry set off, the water-based paint on the cave had half washed away, producing the world's first transparent rock, and everyone involved was soaked through!

The carnival proceeded slowly to Preston Park attracting many people (who seemed pleased) alongside, and was great fun to be part of. On arrival at the park, we were told that Voyce had won first prize in the youth category. A video camcorder was used to film this event, plus other Brighton-based activities on the beach and inland, for a video-maker competition, but unfortunately it got stolen before Voyce could get their teeth into yet another project.

Box 7.1: Environment and regeneration in cities

A participatory group was formed as part of the Brighton (and, since 1998, Hove) Community Environment Partnership (BriHCEP)[3], of which Voyce is a part. It planned to go out into the community and get the views of different people on their environment to feed into the Local Agenda 21 process. The group painted a milk float and set off for events on the seafront and in the Brighton Festival to gather ideas. One event they attended was the 1995 Children's Rights Festival. Children and adults took part and members of Voyce helped the participatory group to gather ideas on the local environment. Apart from the more obvious techniques – marking places that children and adults liked and disliked on the map and then asking the reasons for their choices – the participation group tried to think of ways to draw people into the process and decided to paint a 'problem wall' and an 'ideas tree'. 'Bricks' and 'leaves' were cut from cardboard and filled in by passing members of the public to stick on the wall and tree. Environmental problems were put on to the wall and positive ideas and action to improve environmental conditions were hung on the tree. The results were then fed into the local council and the Agenda 21 process. Despite the group facing problems in following through the full process of how the results have been used in the council, some of the methods have been useful elsewhere in the UK.

In Roundshaw Estate, Sutton, UK, a team of local authority workers and residents have used participatory methodologies to involve children in a well-being needs' assessment. The team spent time at the local play centre, the youth club, two local primary schools and also talked to children in informal settings. They used a range of participatory techniques to identify issues of importance to the children and to explore the kinds of changes they might want to see. A popular activity was mapping the estate, together with the 'problem wall' and the 'ideas tree'. The problems and ideas identified by the children became part of a community-planning exercise set up as a response to the needs' assessment (Cornwall, 1998).

These methods have since come back to Brighton in a training where the Roundshaw team reported on their successful work to a participatory training of community workers (organized by PACT Community Project as part of the Urban Community Support Programme). Many of the training participants remarked at the end of the week how exciting the process had been and that the time they had spent with children had been very informative. They had gone into Whitehawk, a poor area of Brighton, and had found that a whole range of techniques had been successful, including the problem wall and ideas tree, mapping, ranking and prioritiziation of ideas by scoring. Many said they would use some of these participatory techniques to continue their ongoing assessments of needs and appropriate action in Whitehawk.

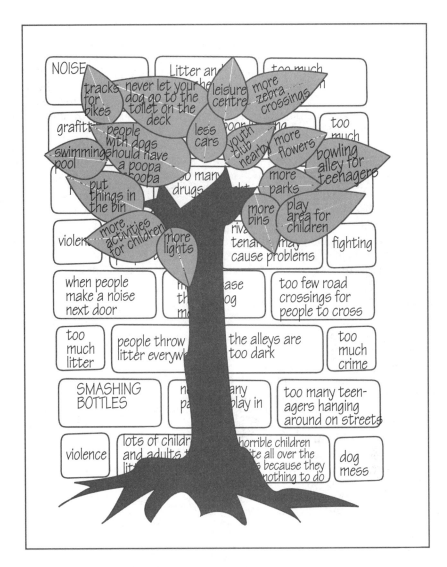

Figure 7.4: *Problem wall and ideas tree*

7.3 Different questions, different ideas: child-led research and other participation

ANDREW WEST

Children's participation is increasingly advocated and implemented around the world. By participation is meant a varied range of activities, and a

271

typology of forms has been described and illustrated (eg, Hart, 1992, Treseder, 1997). The focus in this paper will be on child-led participation and issues arising from adults' rationale for developing that involvement.

The range of children's potential participation can be illustrated briefly through practical activities, for example in participatory research and in children's organizations. Participatory research is generally taken to mean involving people in the research process, seeing them not as subjects or objects but as participants, valued primarily for their existing knowledge and expertise. Participatory research with children can take several forms. It can mean simply devising better ways of seeing their perspective on life or on particular issues, but there are many other variations, for example:

- using children in focus groups to develop research questions;
- children being given an adult-prepared questionnaire to interview other children;
- peer research developed and done by children (peer research is really a misnomer, for it is initiated and resourced by adults); and
- children-led research, as a process of joint inquiry with adults but where decision-making lies with children.

There is clearly a continuum of approaches and methods, with different tensions and balances between adults and children. The point is that language (the word `participation') can cover up and obscure realities, so there is a need to find ways of being clear about activities when the term 'participation' is being applied.

A further practical example of children's participation in the UK are children's councils, which aim to involve children in local government decision-making. These vary from structures which replicate adult decision-making bodies to those run, in reality, by adults, those facilitated by adults, and to those led by children and serviced and resourced by adults, again demonstrating how language obscures reality (West, 1996a).

This paper will outline the problem of adult rationale for promoting children's participation; why should adults initiate and promote children's participation; who defines what is successful? Two background issues, quantity and quality, must first be considered.

Quantity

A personal awareness of the range of children's participation, of practice and writing, and of the interest shown by many individuals and agencies may suggest to many that participation seems to be increasing around the world. It probably is, but it is increasing from a comparatively small practice base, and children's involvement in decision-making is still contested and limited in scope. Children's participation still needs to be promoted. The bases and forms of promotion include: taking a moral stance – it is a right for children; espousing methods – it can be done; and describing the benefits. This last is usually seen as the best way of communicating the participation message, for example, that there are benefits for children (skills, confidence, personal development), and for adults and the community (children's ownership of neighbourhood issues, better services, fewer social problems).

272

Two questions emerge from a focus on benefits: (i) who is defining these benefits and whom do they benefit? and (ii) will the emphasis on the practical (benefits) obscure other issues? Is such a focus limiting, by suggesting that participation is only to be valued if it is beneficial so that it will be discounted when or if it is seen not to be beneficial, again begging the question of who is defining those benefit criteria.

Quality

There is a need to look at the quality of work undertaken in the name of children's participation, not in terms of privileging one form of activity over another, nor just to define the limits and extent of participation, but in order to check aims and to think about children's and adults' reasons for involvement.

Issues arising here include the need to be pragmatic about existing power relationships, recognizing that adults have power, that time is needed for sustainable participation to develop, and the need not to romanticize children's participation as the panacea for social or organizational ills, remembering especially that children's reasons for taking part may be very different to those of adults.

Practice

These issues can be explored briefly through practical examples. For now it is useful to distinguish arbitrarily two contexts of children's participation. This is important because ultimately such distinction concerns adults' visualizations of children and of issues affecting them, and in large part reflects adults' rationale for children's participation, from a Northern perspective at least:

(1) children's participation in the context of vulnerability and the problems they face; work with socially excluded children; work with particular groups; and

(2) children's participation in the broader context of inclusion, involving children in advancing their views and perspectives.

Both contexts are about inclusion, but the first is generally with specific groups while the second, although posited for all children, in practice generally involves those whose lives are sufficiently stable, that is majority groups. (There is a third context, not explored here, concerning children as users of particular services. This might be subsumed under the previous two, with both minority groupings and majority organizations having children as users or members.)

These distinctions may not reflect the reality of children's lives nor their own categorizations and explanations. One important element, often forgotten by adults, is the rapid change in the lives of the young, which has major consequences for their participation and implications for developing practice.

Child-led research

Participatory research projects involving children are usually initiated by adults. Why would adults want to do this? Varied reasons are advanced, including elders' personal perspectives on children's rights, but also the practicalities of, for example, getting access to specific groups of children, acquiring better data or particular kinds of information.

Other reasons can be illustrated through research examples, such as the Save the Children's (UK) work on children leaving care in England in 1995 (children looked after by local government for reasons of sexual or violent abuse, neglect, being orphaned, etc.). Why might adults initiate such research? Moral reasons include the experience and circumstances of those children. Their lives are, as they say, 'not good' and, for example, they are over-represented in the homeless population. Adults' practical reasons for research include the development of new, and improvement of existing, services along with participation being the best way of reaching some children, hearing their voices and exploring new methods of work.

This piece of work, and a subsequent project with street children in Dhaka, Bangladesh in 1997, adopted a similar approach and methodology. In both there was a focus on children-led participatory research. The young people decided the aims, issues, methods, developed questions, conducted interviews, undertook qualitative analysis, made recommendations and participated in the launch. Two particular points might be noted. In SCF's research, the young people (older children) rejected the idea of developing some participatory rural appraisal (PRA)-type techniques (drawings, etc), because of credibility. In their view young people's research would be challenged and needed a robust method, and from their experience research meant questionnaires, so we settled on semi-structured interview schedules. Another lesson from the leaving-care research was the need to incorporate fun into workshops.

One central feature of these and similar projects is that adults are, in reality, looking to the future, to the next generation. They realise that there is a problem, looking at children's circumstances today, with a view to improving services tomorrow, effectively for the next age-group of care leavers. Children agree that provision for their successors is vitally important and, for example, promote the needs of future street children. Children are keen on implementing changes for others but they also ask about themselves: What about us, now? What will happen to us over the next year, or month? Adults' ideas of children's requirements, for example the independence for young care leavers, may be different to the young people's need for support. Adults' perceptions of children's concerns, such as the prospects for young women from the street in Bangladesh, may be expressed differently from those of children. Through such participatory research children are throwing down a challenge to adults. What about our lives now? This is in addition to the question that must be posed of what happens to the particular participant children at the end of the project.

Adult explanations of problems must also be considered and recognized as contestable explanations, not facts. In exploring problems, adults often want to examine why children went into care or came on to the street in the first instance, where they are from, how they came to be where they are, etc. For adults, these are important causal factors. In their own research, children did not pick up on these questions. Their families and identity were important but what mattered was their present circumstances and the future. The recognized forms of knowledge are different, almost different epistemologies.

Children and local government

A current phenomenon in the UK, especially in England, is the development of children's participation in local government consultation, usually in the form of youth councils aimed at older children. These initiatives stem from particular local governments' responses to policy directives to improve social-service provision, and numerous adult concerns about young people, especially fear of them if they are excluded and therefore seen to be unmanageable. There are, in addition, moral concerns about their plight and their rights.

But there are issues around this participation, not only as to whether it is tokenistic but how it is done. What some adults want is a set of children's structures that reflect their own in order to feed into existing forms of local government. This means that children and young people must take on formal adult structures of communication, such as committees and debate. These methods and processes are controlling forms because they exclude those children who are unable to participate in these ways because of social status, skills, confidence, self-esteem and personal circumstances.

There is a tendency to see children as a homogeneous group bounded by age, which means that adults often assume that to consult one implies consulting all; the participation of a few stands for that of many. Little attention is paid to problems of representation or to the plethora of children's identities and experiences.

Where attention is paid to the heterogeneity of children, and to the development of different methods and structures, other issues can arise. One ideal has been to develop children's own organizations and child-led groups. These are usually initiated or supported and resourced by adults in order to gain any recognition and authority, but within them the children can decide on activities or alternative action to those of adults. An example of this is a group developed, facilitated and resourced by adults, with the aim of working on issues important to children and to communicate their views especially to local government. The group, composed primarily of 12–15-year-olds, met regularly and developed skills which included organizing events, running workshops, speaking in public, identifying issues and exploring new ways of communicating with adults that were accessible to their peers (including the use of drama). They took control of the management of the group, jointly with adults but felt that they were not heard by politicians, saw no change occurring, little response, and found the panel format preferred by adults difficult to speak to. In this context, the children began to work on issues in other ways, setting up a peer-support group and undertaking practical work on environmental issues. This produced some conflict with the adults. The adults wanted children's participation and their involvement in decision-making but the children were deciding on a way forward which did not include participating even in the open-ended format already devised. This was not the reason that adults had resourced the group.

An important point here is change — in the lives of individual children, in the group, and in the social and physical environment. Children entered the group at different times and at different ages and points in their lives. The children involved and the environment shaped the group as a whole, which changed over the months, while individual children developed personally in different ways. Older children with longer involvement, who had developed a number of skills, began to move on. The dynamics of the group altered as participatory processes moved spirally, learning from the past but moving through particular stages reflecting the development of individual children and their entry into the group. The children moving on maintained their own support group.

Change and cultural reproduction

Children's lives are changing more rapidly than the structures formed by adults, while adults' aims and reasons for establishing a particular project cannot properly be fulfilled without flexibility and strong commitment. Participation of children aims to achieve change, at the very least in social processes if not also in outcomes. Societies and cultures are dynamic and change over time, but must also reproduce themselves. The idea of change is in tension with the maintenance of broad social structures and the detail of cultural forms that also contribute to personal identity. The participation of a powerless and oppressed group challenges the strong and subtle processes of social and cultural reproduction.

The tension between change and social reproduction indicates the importance of how children's involvement is conceived and expressed. A focus on the practical benefits will only too often rely on an underlying adult agenda, the criteria defining those benefits being located in an adult conception and version of community life. Children's real perspectives are lost in the pace of change.

The tensions between adults' and children's versions of the community, and of change, can be seen all around us in England and across the world. A consistent theme emerging from consultation with children and their participation in local issues, is the problem of the car and other vehicles. Children have said: 'I want the road to be a park and no cars to come'. Ultimately this is a conflict over the use of public space, with different children and adults espousing different views but generally divided along the lines of age and personal lifestyle. Although no extensive poll has been undertaken to give a large-scale breakdown of views, it is clear that the adults with cars dominate with few, if any, concessions to children, however much they participate. Change will take time and commitment, and participation must be emphasized as much as possible and integrated with the other two Ps of the Convention on the Rights of the Child – protection and provision – if it is to happen.

Box 7.2: Children's research and perceptions of exclusion in Bangladesh and Britain[4]

In 1997–8 Save the Children undertook four child-led participatory research projects in Bangladesh, drawing on a model of work used in young people's research on leaving care in Britain (West, 1995, 1996b, 1998). The projects were led by street children in Dhaka (Khan, 1997), children from charland areas in Kurigram and Shariatpur, and girls working in the informal sector in Dhaka. In each project a group of children chose the research aims and method, devised questions and interviews, conducted the research, and were involved in analysis, write-up and recommenda-tions. At the completion of the research they took part in and led aspects of dissemination, advocacy, press conferences, etc. The children were aged between 9 and 15 years. Each project focused on issues selected by them, and threw up challenges to adult perceptions of children's lives and ideas. Some interesting international comparisons of children's own per-spectives can begin to be drawn (see West, 1998), and will be developed further as more such material is gathered.

One particular international theme is children's exclusion. A common element in children's perceptions was that poverty, low incomes, poor housing, lack of food, fuel, etc. was only one characteristic of their exclu-sion: 'Why can't we live a decent life', as the street children put it. Their material and environmental exclusion was exacerbated by another factor of equal importance: the attitude and actions of adults toward them. A few aspects of this are noted here. For older children (16–17 years) leaving care in England, the attitude of the general public was found to be gen-erally antagonistic. They experienced being treated as dangerous, as a criminal or prostitute. Parents refused to let their children associate with those in care, on leaving care, young people found themselves refused employment. The police were also found to be a problem and 'not under-standing'. These factors made worse the already difficult circumstances of many who were unemployed, on low incomes, in poor housing and lacking emotional and practical support. In Dhaka, the street-children's research found that adults' attitudes were a major problem in their lives, with elders of all types who 'frequently misbehaved with them, which ranged from verbal abuse to physical torture' (Khan, 1997: 16). In partic-ular, the police harassed and abused the children, especially the girls. In addition they found it difficult, if not impossible, to find good jobs, and raised the issue of gender, because 'all adult people hated girls who stayed on the street', and asked what of the future for all street children but especially the girls. In the other children's research in Bangladesh, relationships with adults were again an aspect in children's exclusion. The charland children, for example, identified the 'good behaviour' of adults towards children (and vice versa) as an important issue. Social exclusion is now seen as an important policy issue in Britain. Children have indicated that it will not be enough to focus on the material ele-ments in their lives. Adults must look at their own attitudes and actions if children's exclusion is to be addressed.

Andy West

7.4   Giving children a voice

GRACE MUKASA AND VERA VAN DER GRIFT-WANYOTO

Child's voice:

When our parents get money from people and they don't pay their debts, we feel we should tell them but we fear.

Adult's voice:

In this house I am the president and my wife is the vice.

In Uganda, children have extensive responsibilities in the community as they participate significantly in daily work. Many families are dependent on their labour to survive. Children's customary obligations and duties do not, however, give them a corresponding right to participate in decision-making or to voice their opinion. By giving them a voice and listening to their ideas, knowledge and wants can be integrated into the communal process of brainstorming, planning and decision-making in a participatory rural appraisal (PRA) project. This is a way to empower our children who are 'seen but not heard' in our communities.

Redd Barna, Uganda targets children at national, district and community levels. Nationally it is in partnership with the National Council for Children (NCC) which supports child advocacy and the development of district plans of action for children. These mainly target local leadership in order to understand, give expression to, and integrate children's issues in all district planning processes.

At the community level, we use participatory approaches such as PRA and mediated learning experiences (MLE) to advocate for and with children and involve them in all development activities. It has not been easy, hence the development of a PRA model which gives voice to children.

Giving voice to children

In the model we aim at giving children the possibility of conceptualizing their world and so heightening their awareness. The knowledge generated jointly will touch on children's capacities, insights, resilience, self-confidence and responsibilities.

As facilitators, we try to understand their everyday life, cultural values, gender differences and natural/social environments. Their lives and thoughts tell much about the society, in that they live and engender a more purposeful dialogue with them. The children are involved in an interactive process that expands their perception of the world.

In this approach we use the following methods:

- mapping;
- transect walk;
- drawings and role plays, focusing on everyday life, natural and social resources;

278

- riddles and proverbs;
- events in the village;
- social networks (qualities of relations); and
- personal images which can show expression of feelings and emotions such as sadness, fear, joy, shame, anxiety, cultural values and philosophy about life.

Children's voices

They weigh the left and right arm, if the left arm is heavier than the right, you go to Hell. The road to Satan is wide and beautiful, but the road to God is very poor. (Formula for going to Heaven)

The children gain confidence by analysing their situation, identifying problems and solutions, prioritizing them and taking action. Thereafter, they become more assertive in advocating for their rights and articulating their issues to the rest of the community:

For us children, it is not a big problem when our fathers marry second or even third wives if they can afford it. What is of importance to us is that we are not discriminated against, especially in matters of education where children of the youngest wife are favoured. (Baliraine Charles, P5, Namagonjo Primary School).

Children start by working in small projects aimed at improving their welfare. They buy basic necessities for themselves. If the initial project is successful and the benefits are not hijacked by the adults, the children begin engaging willingly in wider communal activities and membership of the village management committees.

Diversity

The analysis of intra-communal difference is based on the division of the community into five interest groups (based on gender and age): younger women, younger men, older women, older men and children. The children's group has diverse needs and interests, providing a challenge to its facilitators. Children vary in age, gender and social class based on parents' education and social status. There are school-going and non-school-going children, those with (differing) disabilities, some traumatized children and those from different cultural, religious and language contexts. The challenge to Redd Barna is to develop its capacity to work with and empower all these different children.

The socio-cultural context

Uganda boasts 39 different ethnic groups and this is well reflected in the children themselves. These dictate the roles and attitudes of children and parental acceptance of their offspring in PRA processes. Whenever we meet for the first time, the girls group themselves together, as do the boys. There is always the underlying fear that Redd Barna Uganda wants to penetrate the community through its children. Parents worry about our influence and their loss of control. Children, meantime, live in fear of a backlash and abrupt censure from the involvement of their parents. Redd Barna Uganda tries to build community confidence through sensitization on children's rights and responsibilities by involving local facilitators with particular qualities:

- someone who loves children;
- who is fluent in their language;
- has knowledge and appreciates their cultural attitudes;
- has skills in communication and ability to mediate interest and active listening; and
- with the capability to mediate genuine warmth, joy and playfulness.

The worse-off children

Redd Barna's mandate is to reach children in especially difficult circumstances: children who lack the minimum basic needs, do not go to school and whose status and self-esteem are, consequently, very low, and who are extremely busy from dawn to dusk. Even with deliberate effort to seek them out, the choice of who should join us is made by the well-off local leadership which ends up sending its own children in the expectation of some handouts.

Strengths of children's participation

Children, if properly handled and facilitated at their own pace can open up to new ideas and contribute to the fulfilment of their rights and responsibilities as embedded in the UNCRC, Organization of African Unity (OAU) Charter and Uganda Children Statute 1996.

Our experience is that the process becomes a sounding-board for them openly to air their problems. They are adventurous and responsive to new ways of doing things. In Bulende Bugosere, one of the villages in which

Figure 7.5: *What is child abuse? . . . breaking the 'self-confidence of the child.'*

280

Redd Barna is working, the children's groups have turned into a pressure group for awareness-creation and have demystified the parental fear of child participation.

Due to their openness and frankness, children of this community are able to monitor the processes they go through. They have initiated their own projects, can assertively participate in community meetings and community decision-making processes and can document/elaborate the benefits that have accrued to them directly and the changes that have occurred in their community over a period of time.

Conclusion

The PRA process eventually empowers children to participate on their own without necessarily depending on outsiders. The major benefits achieved with the PRA process are the parental recognition of the heavy workload they have been enforcing on their children, the dramatic increases in school enrolment and children's ability to assert themselves in community meetings.

7.5   Children, power and participatory research in Uganda

ROB BOWDEN

As awareness and action in child-focused research continues to grow rapidly, the dilemma is now not so much whether we should consider children but how to address and include them? To date, children have been located in an assuming altruistic discourse, particularly within the area of gender studies, but this has neglected the heterogeneity of childhood, and ignored the perspective of the child, rendering children passive recipients of development. In short, current development discourse perpetuates the power relations of adult over child, maintaining a social hierarchy taken for granted because we have failed to address the assumptions behind it.

Researchers and practitioners have only recently begun to listen to children and develop methods that involve them as active participants. Those who have accepted this role face challenges, arguably greater than at any other level of development research. Questions regarding priorities, power structures and empowerment, common to many forms of social research, are exacerbated in working with children. Methodologies require adaptation and innovation to meet their capacities, and analysis must develop techniques that lend both academic legitimacy and practical application to the data collected.

Informal non-academic networks are slowly developing, such as the newsletter *Pikkin Palaver* (Children's Debate), designed to bring together youth leaders, academics, practitioners and children to share ideas, methodologies and resources. Within a year it has attracted substantial attention and interest but getting contributions from people has been a struggle. It would seem there is always a report that is more important or a journal that is more credible for their contribution. This is understood, but if we are serious about the rhetoric of promoting interdisciplinary and multi-layered open research then we must be committed to using such networks to develop the critical mass needed to gain legitimacy for our work.

Partnerships between academia and NGOs are also beginning to emerge, and my current PhD research will work in close co-operation with Redd Barna (Uganda) in the pursuit of more effective participatory methods for working with children. The research is currently being designed in collaboration with Redd Barna to overcome issues such as varied agendas, operating parameters, time-scales and ownership of results, as well as more practical local considerations. It is expected that the experiences of collaborative research between the academic institute (University of Brighton, UK) and the NGO (Redd Barna Uganda) will itself be as instructive as any subject matter retrieved.

Whilst collaboration of this nature is still perhaps unusual, individual researchers often have close ties with specific practitioners and have achieved great progress in working towards child-related policy and practice through the sharing of knowledge and experience.

In teaching, also, children's participation is starting to appear and through my own teaching opportunities I have managed to convince senior academics to include a consideration of children in broader development-studies curricula, even to exam level. This has stimulated significant interest, with many students now choosing to research further with children in their special options and dissertations, a move that has forced the library to improve its stock of appropriate literature. Advocating this simple awareness of children and their capacities can thus be seen to play a significant role in lowering academic barriers.

Choosing to study children in development is in itself a major challenge to the researcher, for it is often not considered a worthy subject. It is rather a category taken for granted – seen but not heard, acted upon but not with. As a geographer I have found myself justifying the subject matter of my research to colleagues even before entering the field. In considering the changing political economy of children in rural Uganda it is intended, however, to expose the complex and highly dynamic realities of their childhood to a sceptical audience and demonstrate their value in the development process. The research will consider how and when children should be consulted, and through careful consultation with existing social structures and agencies, evaluate how their needs and priorities might be incorporated in future programmes and initiatives.

The research[5] will contribute to an emerging concern for the perspective of the child, through using participatory methodologies to address current development issues. Rigorous experimentation and replication will develop a portfolio of techniques to demonstrate the validity of children's contributions in real contexts. Working across various locations it is intended to identify techniques that lend themselves to the type of rapid appraisal associated with the time and budget constraints of much development planning. Finally, through close association with Redd Barna (Uganda) the problem of institutionalizing children in the development process, through training, extension and improvements in practice, will be addressed.

It is hoped that the research will identify opportunities for allowing children into the development process through exploring and reporting on their capacity to research. In this instance, that is the extent of the project for it has its own agenda, namely that of a PhD thesis, an agenda that in itself must be acknowledged and accepted by all participants from the outset to avoid misguided expectations. In terms of development planning and action the collaboration with Redd Barna may, however, contribute towards involving children in more open negotiation with existing power structures, a process that, if institutionalized and sustained beyond the research period, may help establish children as active participants in the development process.

7.6 Approaches to peer education and youth advisory councils – experiences in Honduras

DONALD KAMINSKY

Two major avenues for children's participation are: (i) through involvement in child-to-child activities and peer education; and (ii) in leadership roles which can be provided through youth advisory councils. In Honduras, both of these mechanisms have been instituted.

Project Alternatives and Opportunities, (hereafter referred to as 'the project') is a non-governmental organization which works with working children and their families in the informal sector. The Foundation for Development, Friendship and Answers (FUNDAR) operates at the middle/secondary school level with a programme whose activities are based at the largest formal education institute in the country. Both have developed peer-education activities and the project has a youth advisory council. The peer-education programme was developed first at the informal level and the experience was then extended to the secondary-school level.

Selection criteria for participants in the programme have been similar at both the formal and informal levels. They include:

- desire by the youth to participate and be involved in peer education and community development activities after the training;
- average and above grades in school (the project youth go to school one half of the day and work the other half day in the informal sector);
- time available to participate actively, and interest and permission of their guardian; and
- leadership potential.

Leadership potential was much stronger at the formal level as there is the interest in creating a leadership core for the educational institute, which has 10 000 students, who then could carry the responsibility for sustaining the programme and actively working as leaders in their communities. Training for both groups is performed with a series of basic modules that are reinforced with periodic sessions and the addition of new material.

The modules include content areas (e.g. substance abuse, HIV/AIDS, environmental concerns), training methodologies (e.g. use of role play puppets/theatre), communications principles, planning and evaluating techniques, social-skills building and leadership skills. This area is stressed more with the group at the formal level. Monitoring is performed by staff on a regular basis. This is important for assessing the quality of transmission of information and for the youth to feel that there is always an adult there for them when they need advice and assistance. After training, the youth carry out peer-education sessions in their schools, churches, community institutions and non-governmental institutions. They seek ways to be involved in the development of their community through such activities as organizing youth or sports clubs. Those youth who work in the informal sector, in the markets, have planned and implemented clean-up campaigns.

The direct results of introducing peer-education activities are that the participants are developing knowledge and life skills, their self-esteem is improving, their communications skills with their peers and their parents are better, they are sharing their knowledge in their home, at school and in their community. They are looking for mechanisms to improve their community. They are converted into known and recognized leaders in their schools and communities. Indirect results include an adequate use of their free time, learning how to schedule their time better, and in some cases an improvement in school qualifications. In other cases school notes have worsened so that we have learned that it is important for the staff to monitor the school notes. The promotion of children's participation has become a basic objective for all activities of the project, and not only for the child-to-child programme. The success of the FUNDAR effort has provided the incentive to extend the work to other formal educational institutions and to plan a mid- to long-term commitment of expansion.

The youth advisory council of Project Alternatives and Opportunities serves as a mechanism for the youth to interact with the project's young participants and its staff. The 17-member council was selected from those participating in the peer-education activity according to the criteria used above. They are organized, with a board of directors elected by their membership. They meet as a council once a month; commissions working on special schemes meet more frequently on an *ad hoc* basis. The council is accompanied in the meetings by two professional members of the project's staff who serve to direct the youth. Once again, it is important that adults are present for consultation when the young people feel this is necessary. They also need a regular feedback mechanism to the project. The council states as its lines of action: to seek the active participation of youth in the decision-making process, to integrate the various zones where the project operates; to discover the potential of youth to serve as leaders in their community; and to establish co-ordination between them and the project's personnel.

An adolescent of just 17 years, who works and goes to secondary school one half day and who is president of the council expresses his opinion about children/youth as active participants in the development process as follows:

- *Who should participate?*
  Everyone should participate but principally youth since they are the persons who are passing through a state of change, that is to say seeking

their personal identity, and this will help them in the process so as to have a better development of the life of the youth.

- *When should they participate?*
  They should participate all the time since there is always something new to learn and this helps them to have better relations with others, learning and developing better every day.

- *Why should they participate?*
  Because this helps both our personal as well as social development, learning and teaching others so that every day things will go better.

- *Where should they participate?*
  They should participate at any time and place, since we learn in all forms, whether positively for our betterment or in taking care of future development.

- *How should they participate?*
  Youth should participate in a positive and active manner demonstrating all of their abilities and capacities, providing their opinions and points of view for the betterment of the learning and development process.

Our experience indicates that to optimize children's participation opportunities one needs to think about involving everyone, both adults and children. It is important to have the full support of the guardians for their children to act as development protagonists. Regular communication should, therefore, be established with them. Although selecting those with leadership potential for training and participation in an effort to involve youth more widely is not a fully democratic process, it is done with a vision of creating youth leaders. These leaders will then take the responsibility for facilitating the participation of all children and youth within a democratic process, whether they have the potential for leadership or not.

7.7   Conclusions

EDDA IVAN-SMITH

The different benefits and pitfalls of initiating children's active participation have been highlighted in these five chapters. One of the issues that has emerged from this part is that participation, by its very nature, cannot be imposed. Traditionally, research has been an extractive process, even with adults, where subjects of the research have had little control over the process and analysis. Research with children, presents a different set of problems as children can be reluctant to refuse involvement; additionally, adult agendas are often not clearly explained. Thus researchers working with children need to learn particular participatory methods that will be appropriate to children and young people of different ages and genders and cultures.

Simply including children in a research process does not merit the accolade

285

of a participatory approach, as was pointed out by Andy West in his paper. In order to recognize and validate children's knowledge, experiences and perspectives, we need to be prepared validate and legitimize the opposing views of children. Validating this experience and perspective means being open to change the research process and content and to develop methodologies that will assist the true participation and partnership of children in a piece of research work. Children themselves may identify methodologies or approaches that are more appropriate, and researchers need to be flexible enough to incorporate these changes.

We have seen that the consequences of working with children can be very positive. In Imani Tafari-Ama's paper the effective change that children made to their environment were central to the lessons learnt in that piece of research. Very often research is viewed as a static process that is simply written up and left. The Jamaican example details how a piece of research can be used as a stepping stone in the road to empowerment for young people and their community. This illustrates the difference between simply involving children in a process and fostering their active participation. This active participation can lead to changes in the objectives of pieces of research or programme. This is probably one of the more complex areas of children's participation, as it can raise political issues that are sensitive. It also means that sometimes, as Andy West pointed out, the adults have to relinquish some power and allow the process to evolve in a way that was perhaps not expected.

Adult researchers need to be equipped with the tools to respond to young people's request to take research further or to embark on some sort of community action. Clearly, the inclusion of children in a piece of research may be their first opportunity to be heard and taken seriously. The research process and outcome may be the beginning of something quite important not just for the children and young people but also for the community in which they live.

Involving communities in children's participation is essential, as we have seen in Grace Mukasa's paper. Some communities may be hostile or suspicious about children's participation. Therefore, it is important to include them in the process and to explain clearly the objectives of participation. Children do not live in isolation and their experiences and perspectives are informed by the dynamics of their community. Working with children and adults often provides a different view of a particular community. Attitudes to gender, class and disability will affect the particular experience of children, and therefore it is important to work with the wider community as well to gain a comprehensive view of the situation of children.

In many societies it is not possible to begin work with children without negotiating the consent of parents or guardian. This consent has to be negotiated and reviewed throughout the process and not just at the beginning of a piece of work. Informed consent will need to be negotiated differently depending on the complexity of work and the age of the child or young person. Adults and children need to know the consequences, outputs and purpose of a piece of research and need to feel that they have some ownership of the activity.

Locating children's participation within their cultural context is an important starting point. When embarking on a project that includes children we need to start where the community and society is and not impose precon-

Figure 7.6: *Young researcher sets forth*

ceived ideas about what level we should be starting at. There is a tendency to work within a hierarchy of participation without a given context. This can lead to unrealistic expectations.

There is also a need to recognize that different societies will have different definitions of participation and this needs to be accounted for when working with children and young people. Although the ethos of participatory approaches to work is based on the importance of inclusion, the approach and explanation of participation can often exclude certain children and young people. It is also important not to lose sight of the objectives of children's participation in our quest for more participatory approaches to our work with children. Adults need to be clear about the purpose of the participation of children and young people. Are we embarking on participatory projects with children simply to make our programmes 'look better' or actually to develop the capacities of children and their communities?

Children's participation should not be seen as just one isolated component of a programme or project but as an approach and process that is applied at different levels and times to all aspects of programming and research. It is only by being honest about our objectives and examining them that children and young people will feel secure and enabled to participate on their own terms as well. There are also dangers and risks in embracing participation blindly; we need to be aware of these dilemmas and ethical issues and learn from our mistakes. Lastly, our approach must be underpinned by a framework of principles and ethical approaches. This framework needs to be informed by the experiences of children and adults in all areas of work.

Notes:

1. Although the concentration of the research will be on youth in the 10–15 age group, elders from various age sets in the community will also be interviewed in order to gain an understanding of the historical development of local youth.
2. I shall also be able to evaluate gendered hierarchies which exist within the community and which may be altered by access which one may have to institutional support at family and community levels and which community actors may have to resources outside of the community.
3. Details of BriHCEP from Brighton and Hove Council, co-convenors of the group at the time were Jane Knight and Vicky Johnson (and Peter Brissenden at start of project) with much help from other voluteers.
4. Material drawn from a paper presented at the Children and Social Exclusion conference, University of Hull.
5. This research is funded by the University of Brighton (1996–2000) in partnership with Redd Barna (Uganda) and Makerere University. I would like to thank the Dudley Stamp Memorial Trust for their financial support.

Figure 7.7: *'Imagine the room is full of mosquitoes and we must squash them. Look! They're in front of us! Now behind! To the left! To the right! Above our heads!'*

PART 8

The Way Forward

Co-authors: EDDA IVAN-SMITH and VICTORIA JOHNSON

The Way Forward

EDDA IVAN-SMITH AND VICTORIA JOHNSON

Part 8 examines the conclusions from the book and puts forward the key elements needed to enable the true active participation of children and young people in the development process. Devising strategies to take forward children' s participation encompasses many of the issues that have been discussed in previous chapters, such as ethics and approaches, working with different institutions and cultural issues, so this chapter is really a synthesis of the different components of children' s participation that draws together some of the principles and guidelines needed to achieve this.

Lines of communication and power

The practice and theory of children's participation is still a relatively new area. Although there are people working in this field and there is a wealth of experience from which to draw, work has been discrete and people often work in isolation on the issues within their own institutional context. The development of networks involving local stakeholders would help gain support and benefit from shared experiences. In setting up networks we must think about expanding the accessibility of information to a broad range of interested parties, including academics, students, development practitioners, youth workers, children and young people, and the media. The media can be valuable partners in disseminating information and can be an effective means of getting information to people who are not part of formal networks or organizations.

Documentation of experiences and accessibility of materials is another key issue. Because of the nascent nature of this field, there is no university department or library index devoted to materials concerned with children' s active participation in either research or programming. The study of children using participatory approaches has not been legitimized in its own right and has been subsumed under more general disciplines such as psychology, sociology or general development studies. Centralized documentation centres or systems in different countries or regions to hold material on children's participation and to highlight progressive practices could be useful in taking the arguments forward. This would help to give this area credibility and give people an overview of current debates and recent case-studies.

There is a dilemma facing those advocating more meaningful attempts to engender children's participation. On the one hand, gradual progress has been made in the field of gender that has come about through increasing evidence and documentation on the importance of gender analysis in development, accompanied by systematic pressure from donors on organizations to incorporate such an analysis into projects. There is an argument for pressure to be put on organizations or parts of organizations to prove how they are improving the lives of children. On the other hand, there is a fear that project staff and managers may be forced into a check-list approach where they do not necessarily believe in children's participation or yet have the capabilities really to address this area of work without putting children at risk or coming up with tokenistic solutions. A preferred option may therefore be to continue to document successes and build up more analysis on the importance of children's involvement. It is also important to make sure people are aware of children's rights, including the participation rights expressed in the UNCRC.

The workshop process went some way towards developing a dialogue between different constituencies in the field of children's participation, including that of young people. The experience was unique for most participants, as it was a week devoted entirely to issues of children's participation in research and programming with a core of people working on these issues in very different contexts. This started the building of a multi-layered and rich learning matrix. There is, however, still much to learn and room for improvement. Networking is not only a vertical process but one where as adults we have to be open to networking with young people and children in a way that may be uncomfortable and unfamiliar for us because it means relinquishing power. Endorsing participation in both thought and deed can be a difficult process, for adults, of relearning social skills we had as children. The workshop process, which was very participatory, served as a microcosm of society's dilemmas when involvement is approached in an egalitarian way. Some participants did not want to take the responsibility of participating or make consensual decisions; they were, at times, more comfortable to be told what to do and when, while others felt better by telling others how to proceed.

The road to participation is neither smooth nor easy. It is fraught with ethical issues, particularly around power. A delicate balance is needed between giving up too much control and thus abdicating responsibility as an adult, and maintaining too much power and therefore running the risk of being tokenistic and dictatorial. Adults must be open to participate in new and different ways. For too long the participatory process with children has been one that elders have devised and set up and then invited children and young people to join. It is often presupposed that it is the children and young people that have to come forward to be involved in this process.

Adults need to step back and observe the ways in which children and youth interact with each other and perhaps be willing to take part in that process. A recent example of this can be found in an HIV/AIDS workshop run by an NGO that was primarily an adults' workshop, with children observing and monitoring the inclusion of children's issues and adults' willingness to let young people participate. After the first few days one adult was heard to say: 'I was not quite sure about having children invited in this at first, as some of them were shy and reluctant to join in and seemed rather awkward; but after some time they seem more confident and better able to participate with us'. The young people at this conference had the same reaction to the adults' participation, but neither of these groups ever actually discussed or explained their fears and difficulties with each other.

This example highlights the importance of clarity and transparency when adults, children and young people are working together, as very different agendas may be in place without their being discussed or negotiated. Thus, before we embark on the process of working in a participatory way with children and young people, we need to be aware and sensitive to the host of ethical issues that underline and inform the quality of work we do and its outcome.

Ethics

Starting a process with clarity and transparency is one of the key lessons learnt from the experiences of contributors to this book. Very often this clarity is taken at face value in the guise of research and programming procedures. For example, with the issue of informed consent, programmers or researchers may feel that it is too difficult to explain a process to children so will simply tell them the bare facts and not discuss the ongoing process with them. This leaves children in a powerless position that can be easily manipulated by the adult, even if that is not the intention. We need to bear in mind that children also have the right *not to* participate in a given process, as do adults. We also have to be prepared for our programmes and research plans possibly to go awry as 'logical frameworks' and other similar procedures may not be applicable. Children and young people may want to participate in a particular way or only at a specific time during a project or piece of research. The long-term implications of a participatory project with children and young people must be discussed and, if possible, prepared for. Being transparent about the intent and lifespan of a particular project with children and young people will enable them to make a truly informed decision and will enable all, both children and adults, to discuss the implications on a continual basis. Developing trust and sustainability is the real test of a positive building block in the participatory process.

Ethical issues must be revisited throughout the lifetime of a project or research process, and some, such as informed consent, may need to be renegotiated at different stages of the project process. The way in which information, gathered in a participatory way, is interpreted and then disseminated again rings ethical alarm bells. It is sometimes assumed that if information is gathered in an innovative and participatory way then that is the end of the story. However, much of the data can be abused and the messages interpreted wrongly if care is not taken to carry participation of children and young people throughout the whole life-cycle of the project.

There are protocols and ethical codes of conduct that are applied to research carried out with adults, so this is not a new idea. The rigour of taking into account ethical conduct in research and in carrying out practical projects should be highlighted and insisted upon even more in the case of working with children. Too often it is presumed that they will say yes, compounded by the fact that children may think that they should do as an adult asks. The solutions to ethical questions raised in Part 2 of this book may vary depending on legal, institutional and cultural contexts; however, there may be value in further developing some basic code to include fundamentals such as informed consent of both children and their parents or guardians without which one should not even start research with children. The kinds of ethical issues and questions raised in this book can at least serve as a starting point.

Figure 8.1: *Start from where you are and take care!*

How to: the process

The ethical dilemmas and practical approaches to participatory work with children are inextricably linked, as one informs the other. A pillar of any ethical process is communication. If there is no clear communication and clarity of intent children will at best be confused, at worst they could be adversely affected or damaged by such a situation. If communication is important, adults need to know the best way to develop that skill and what its pitfalls are when dealing with children and young people, in particular, very young children. Practical issues of developing a participatory process with children, such as where one talks to them, how and what level of involvement, must be underpinned by sensitivity to the local political and social context or culture within which they are living. Some methods may be inappropriate in a particular setting. Adjustments and the need for flexibility are paramount when working with children and the larger community.

The types of research processes and approaches that are successful with adults may not be the same for children. Research should be fun and children should have the chance to opt out if they are not enjoying the process. Many hours can be spent at the drawing board, devising innovative and systematic research methods; however, when you go out in the field they may not be the type of activity that the children or young people you are working with want to get involved in. Some of the more classic participatory methods have been successful with some groups of children, for example mapping and ranking, but many practitioners and researchers have found that children enjoy the use

294

of different media, such as video, photo appraisal, theatre and movement, to express issues of importance to them. Making popular television and radio can also be a successful way to more meaningful children's participation and to adults taking the issues seriously, as shown in the case of Ghana in Part 3. It is the flexibility of the approach and the openness to trying new ways of interacting with young people that seems to be the key to finding a more participatory approach.

Culture

Considering culture should be a prime objective for the way forward. Much of the thinking and literature that is available on children's participation has emanated from Western developed countries. The majority of this literature is rooted in the psychological tradition that looks at the individual behaviour of children in isolation. This material rarely explores the dynamics between different groups of children or within communities. There is a dearth of shared experiences of how their involvement has been adapted in different contexts and cultures. More documentation on this would lead to a better understanding of how children's participation can be effective in different situations throughout the world, as well as within different groups of children, such as girls, and children with disabilities or those in conflict situations.

The documentation and experience of micro-level research in diverse cultural contexts can be used to tap the knowledge and experience of children and adults in different social and cultural locations. As research has, up until recently, had a tendency to be Eurocentric, drawing on different experiences would help to curb this trend. The development and process of research protocols to help highlight children's perspectives can and should be adapted to local circumstances; this would help give children ownership of the research that is conducted with them, rather than imposing irrelevant models on them. The contextualization of children's participation in research and programming means being sensitive not only to national cultures but the sub-cultures of children's lives; this means bringing different disciplines and approaches to working with children, including those types of communication used by and between children themselves.

Finally, discussion about culture does not make sense without the perspective of children and young people. Children's language, social mores and means of interaction with each other constitute a sub-culture of the wider, more visible adult culture. These sub-cultures are neither homogeneous nor static. Children and young people move in and out of different groups and gangs that provide them with a self-identity appropriate to their stage of development and circumstances. We must also be aware that some cultural traditions are particularly harmful for individual or particular groups of children. Damaging practices or behaviour towards children established in cultural tradition should be subject to the same scrutiny as less traditional practices. Cultures are not static; they are changing and adapting constantly and being challenged. It is important that we do not allow tradition to dull our vision of the best interests of the child. This is especially important in crisis situations, where the material well-being of children is, understandably, a priority. However, this often overlooks children's own capacity to cope in difficult situations, which could improve approaches to working with them in emergencies and conflict situations.

Crisis

Crisis situations can be seen as yet another sub-culture of the prevailing culture. In countries where conflict has been longstanding, ways of working with children need to have a developmental and not just a short-term crisis-management approach. Where agencies have seen a crisis situation as an opportunity to effect positive change in children's lives during and beyond the crisis, children have been able to make a valuable contribution to programme and research development. In particular, participatory approaches have proved useful in emergency situations, such as conflict resolution, and in refugee contexts. Departing from less traditional methods of recording data in politically unstable situations may be one way forward. For example, developing visual or oral-history methods may be more appropriate and carry less risk. Building on children's strengths and resilience requires researchers and programmers to develop means that will enable children to discuss their feelings and ways of coping.

Including children's perspectives will enhance understanding not just for children but for their parents, as all community members react differently and have different coping strategies. If these are pooled and used as resources the impact on children could be a positive one with long-term effects. If qualitative methods are used alongside quantitative ones a more comprehensive picture of the true effects of difficult situations, as well as the capacity of children to manage them, can emerge. For this type of approach to be taken up effectively, agencies must have clear-cut polices and guidelines that are monitored with children throughout the process. This is sometimes difficult as large international donors, especially those that fund emergency work, are often less concerned with qualitative methods, prioritizing outputs and quantitative results. This can be damaging both to children and adults, as issues of age, gender and ethnicity are often not taken into account, further dislocating an already disrupted community. Development agencies and other institutions need to devise methods and approaches to work with all community members and perhaps change their own institutional cultures to foster this type of change.

Institutions and power

In order for development agencies and donors to change, they must examine the power relationships that hinder the participation of adults and children. Too often participation has been seen by governments and development agencies as an issue of equality rather than equity. An equality approach to how children and young people are included means that there is an expectation that they will fit into existing structures which may be inherently exclusive. Taking an equity approach involves analysis and identification of the different levels of exclusion, acknowledges issues of difference and formulates ways in which existing structures can accommodate those who are naturally excluded from the process. It is not enough simply to invite children and young people to participate in institutions. Institutions have to work to enable children and adults to feel comfortable and safe in taking risks in the face of new dynamics which will emerge in a participatory process. Recognizing and validating children's own networks and structures can be part of this learning and analytical process. It may be in these informal networks that children feel most at ease and able to analyse and discuss issues of importance to them. As was discussed in the Part 6, seeing children as partners and agents of change can illuminate and strengthen the participatory process between them and adults and institutions. Structurally changing an institution, and particularly the family, can often be threatening to the *status quo* and be met, therefore, with resistance. Those with power, be they in families, governments or NGOs, have much to gain by maintaining the *status quo*. Equally, if open to a new approach to power, adults as well as children can gain much by more participation. Statutory institutions will better reflect the people they seek to serve, and non-governmental organizations (NGOs) and other voluntary bodies will be more accountable to a larger constituency as children's needs and concerns are reflected in policies at all levels. It is also possible that families of all types would be in a better position to resolve or avoid damaging conflict.

The issue of different 'theoretical' cultures or frameworks not being integrated into the children's participation and development debate is a complicated one. 'Theoretical cultures' can be interpreted as meaning different models or approaches to work and analysis. For example, a cultural anthropologist will have a different mode of examination of children than an environmentalist. Equally, within the children's participation debate, departures from the hierarchical models of participation should be incorporated into our analysis. Abrioux's spherical model of participation (see Part 2) provides a useful alternative to the hierarchical one by looking at degrees of participation which can be achieved, given different contexts. This allows us to develop children's involvement at the most appropriate point and to look at degrees of participation that can better measure that involvement. If we concentrate too much on attaining abstract goals of participation not rooted in the reality of children's lives there is a danger of trying to attain the impossible while affecting children and young people adversely. Bringing in perspectives from the fields of cultural anthropology and economics, as well as people who have different experiences and attitudes to child-rearing, would enable a more sophisticated debate around cultural change and children' s capacities within those different cultures. From this we can learn the different definitions of children's participation in a given context. Working with children as partners in research rather than as passive objects would enhance the investigative process and promote children's self-confidence and general development. Thinking of children as partners requires adults to develop specific skills appropriate to many different contexts.

Where do we go from here?

An obstacle to developing children and young people's participation is the behaviour of adults. If adults are genuinely to involve young people we have to learn to listen to them and create an environment where that is possible.

Researchers and practitioners have to prepare themselves for hearing things from children that they do not like. Children have a wealth of knowledge and experiences that can enlighten the communities within which we live, but they can be easily marginalized, especially if their views run counter to those of the adult majority. At the same time adults must take their responsibilities seriously and not necessarily place the whole weight of participation on children and young people. Much of this will come from training and active involvement in projects.

Relating to children and young people as active participants in the development process means a shift in adults' attitudes. It also means that part of the participation process is about learning from children and young people and being willing to unlearn many of the assumptions and prejudices that cloud adults' perceptions of the young. Once participatory processes are in place in a particular project it is important not to view them as just an optional extra. Children and young people's participation should not be seen as an isolated component of a wider process but as an integral part of a project, where participation can gradually and with sensitivity be applied during all stages of a particular piece of work.

We must realize that participation is not always a priority for children and young people, neither is it the panacea for all their ills. Children have a right

Figure 8.2: *A closing circle to share what we learned and bring us close to each other.*

298

not to participate and that must be respected as well. There is a temptation to become evangelical about children's participation and overlook some of the dangers or risks for them or their communities. There are also different levels of involvement. Participation is a dynamic process in which both children and adults have to adapt and change on a regular basis. The way forward demands a shift in thinking in adult attitudes to children and young people. Developing better methods of working with children and enabling their participation is beneficial not only to children. By including some previously invisible groups we are making our research, our programmes and our communities more inclusive, more functional and effective. Omitting a large sector of society means that everyone loses and fails to see the big picture. If we are unaware of the problems and issues that concern children and young people we cannot hope to devise strategies or solutions that will address their concerns, and will constantly be struggling to make sense of the world without some of the vital information we need.

Appendix 1: the workshop process

PATTA SCOTT

Idea, announcement and invitations

Personally, for me the most valuable aspect of it was the workshop process itself, that demonstrated the value of the participatory approach *in vivo*. (Vesna, Yugoslavia)

In 1996 and 1997 a number of international gatherings on various aspects of participation were held, yet few were able to achieve participation in the way they were organized or facilitated. The five organizers of the workshop on children's participation attempted to find a way around the communication and bureaucratic obstacles to holding a participatory event.

The event was advertised in *PLA Notes*, which has a global circulation of just under 3500. The organizers sent out announcements to our contacts and networks, to everyone on our databases who had expressed an interest in children's participation and to all the regional offices of Save the Children (SCF). Each respondent was asked for 200 words on what they would like to share at the workshop. We provided several options: a paper, a workshop idea, a poster or a way of helping out. We wanted the process to be as participatory as possible, but how were we going to reject or accept people in a participatory way? Who was going to have access to the announcement or feel able to respond to it? Around 45 people replied with wonderful ideas and experiences. This was the number we could accommodate, so we did not need to deal with the difficult question of rejecting applicants. Only those who submitted ideas well past the deadline had to be asked to participate next time.

I think the number we had was definitely the maximum to make it work. For a future workshop I would prefer even fewer people, even though the number probably was small already for an international workshop on a subject that so many people are working on. (Esther, Tanzania)

Participants

It was a great mix of people from different countries. (Claire, UK)

It was an enriching experience, given that participants were from different backgrounds, although a more diversified organizational background would have generated even more ideas. (Grace, Uganda)

The group which attended included practitioners of children's participation from all over the globe, from NGOs, government institutions, academic institutions, local community organizations and youth groups. The bias, however, was towards NGO workers and researchers, two-thirds of the participants were female and the common language was English. It was a well-balanced group, but it was not one that was representative of all the stakeholders in children's participation. In particular, we found we did not get many responses from children and young people interested and able to come. The people who saw the announcement did not necessarily link the idea of attending a workshop in the UK with the idea of inviting children. This is partly because the announcement was formal and so expectation was for a formal event, which might not have seemed particularly comfortable or interesting to younger people. As it is, the participants will now have much more confidence in promoting the involvement of children and young people in a follow-up workshop.

> On reflection, I do not think that the young people who attended were actually representative of children, i.e. the under-18s. They seemed to me to be 18 and over. Also they seemed to be exceptionally articulate and not really representative of most young people. The process had been carefully worked out and did foster interaction. I would also have liked it if there had been more young people and that the programme was more their agenda and they were the resource people rather than an addition. However, I realize this is hard and needs a lot of prior involvement. This is where we who are working with children in the field have a distinct advantage, as their participation comes as part of their on-going interaction with adults. Although with the interesting things going on in places like Kirklees, children could have been involved if it had been part of a long-term planning process. (John, Nepal)

> Young people should be represented on the planning team. Invite participants to bring case-studies written or produced by children to the workshop. (Julia, Palestine)

> Most people who were present seemed to be from programme level. It would be worthwhile, I think, also to have people present who have regular, direct contact with children such as street-workers. Of course there could be difficulties, with language etc., but then again, isn't that what the whole subject is about? If someone, or some group has a contribution that is worthwhile and would help the whole process forward, it is worth investing time and effort to ensure they take part. Another point is to include children's own perspectives and views on participation. How do children themselves see child participation, do they feel it is important, and on what levels do they see their participation as most useful/necessary? What in their view are the barriers and what kind of problems do they encounter? (Esther, Tanzania)

In the overall process of understanding and promoting children's participation, it seems we need a multiplicity of events to offset the conflicting demands of communication and diversity. A range of workshops in different languages and formats needs careful design and cross-referencing to allow groups of people to understand one another to cross-pollinate ideas.

Themes

The workshop agenda was divided into six themes, based on the submissions of the participants: ethical issues; cultural issues; methods of participation; participation in emergencies; institutional issues; and children as active participants in society. Everyone attending the workshop was to be a member of one theme team. Some ideas seemed to span more than one theme so we juggled a little. Then we sent to everyone the proposed agenda and asked if they agreed with the theme area they had been allocated and explained the idea of team facilitation for each workshop day. When we received their responses, we adjusted accordingly. The length of workshop time allocated for each theme was based on the number of people in that team. For each team we appointed a facilitator and a minute-taker. In the end, however, the teams made their own decisions about facilitation, minutes and organization.

Participation tends to throw up a wide range of issues, all of which are valuable in the debate between the participants, but which may also be too much to cover in a single event. The means by which people then reduce the issues to workable portions has a significant effect on the outcome. In the workshop, we decided to leave the planning of this aspect to the participants themselves. It is at this point that they used their skills and experience to achieve a meaningful session.

> The programme was designed to cover very big issues in very short spaces of time (workshop participant).

It was inevitable that many areas remained uncovered. The interesting point is that the workshop format laid the basis for strong links between the participants, links that were used subsequently to follow up on significant issues.

> In terms of topics it would be good to have more focus on working with children with different abilities, sustainable mechanisms for on-going participation by children and evaluating children's participation. There was such an amazing sense of solidarity and moving forwards with the group. Such links and friendships are on-going sources of inspiration, support and information with untold beneficial consequences. (Claire, UK)

> It is useful to be in contact and share and exchange the experience and knowledge, which is one of the primary aims of such gatherings. (Vesna, Yugoslavia)

The workshop

On the first day of the workshop, after the introductions, each theme team planned their day of the workshop. They were given responsibility for planning how presentations would be made, issues analysed, workshop sessions run and facilitation organized. The organizing group from IDS, IOE and SCF provided logistical support. At first the participants were a little surprised. No organized sessions, no formal paper giving, only a little facilitation and leadership by the organizing committee? We're not prepared! The effect was wonderful, energizing, exhausting.

On day one, the ethics team provided us with a heady mix of presentations and difficult questions that we tried to answer in small groups, sorting cards and sharing examples. On the second day, the methods team presented us with a multi-media selection of a range of methods from around the world, interspersed with energising and learning games from Ernesto Cloma of the Philippines Educational Theatre Association. On day three, the culture and emergency teams got us discussing in depth the issues raised from case-study presentations mixed with diagramming in small groups. The fourth day saw the institutions team facilitating myriad small-group exercises, diagramming, modelling and games. On this day, the group decided not to make presentations of their papers and posters to the plenary but to contribute them in the different working groups that ran in parallel throughout the day. The final day included presentations, card sorting and role-plays and helped to wrap up our thinking and excitement about the workshop, its themes and the way forward. On each day, a new group found a different way of organizing the rest of the participants and putting across their points, while finding space for discussion and interaction.

I found the approach quite innovative and allowed everyone to share a significant part of planning and managing the workload involved in staging each day's activities. Each successive group seemed compelled to find more innovative ways than previous groups to make their subject area stimulating. (workshop participant)

People shared their work in a manner not normally captured and indeed in writing this I am struggling to convey the spirit of sharing and camaraderie ... It allowed activists, NGO staff, students and youth representatives to have equal impetus in an environment too often dominated by academics and institutionalists. (Rob, UK)

Each team's day of facilitation responded to the lessons of the last; each format was appropriate not only in exploring the subject matter but in complementing or contrasting with those used in previous sessions. In this way, the 45 participants together guided the process, and the varied mix of practitioners, young people and researchers all found opportunities to share their ideas in comfortable and innovative ways.

One of the best aspects of the workshop was that it limited monologues from individual speakers and instead encouraged interaction and group discussions. It also forced all participants to be actively involved in planning different parts of the workshop rather than being passively 'entertained' by the organizers. (Julian F., UK)

The process of the workshop was innovative and challenging. I think it was an experiment that came off really well. Everybody had a responsibility that went beyond her or his own presentation and participants were actively involved throughout the week. The fact that each group was responsible for one day brought out some competitiveness, but in a positive way. The different groups felt an obligation to present something new, in a way to do better than the previous groups. This led to creative presentations, and a wish to make things work. (Esther, Tanzania)

The process had some flaws that should be elucidated. For one thing it was exhausting, there should have been more time to rest and reflect on each subject, but we had felt unable to reject people's submissions in order to limit the programme to fit the time available:

> The pace of the whole week was pretty fast and pretty intense – as there were so many issues to cover, so many people and so many ideas! This fast pace seemed to work OK – as people seemed keen to address as many issues as possible. However, I found there were so many ideas that after two days I didn't know where any more would fit in my brain! Excess ideas wove their way in to my dreams each night... (Claire, UK)

The dual responsibility of facilitating and listening was sometimes distracting:

> Although brilliant in many respects and truly participative, workshop participants' concentration (at the very least mine) was divided between planning their respective session and staying fully involved in the entire workshop (workshop participant).

Just like a participatory activity in a community, the process had the effect of bonding the participants together, of underlining their common ideals and exposing their differences. By the end we were good friends, we had learned much from one another and we knew where each other stood in terms of the participatory work to which we are all committed. Now we feel we are a loose network, we share information and ideas and contribute to expand the links with other children, young people and adults who are involved in promoting and understanding children's participation.

> I was impressed by the on-going commitment to participation throughout the planning and running of the workshop. It was very evident that a lot of planning and effort had been put in to run the workshop in a way that maximized space for people's participation. I thought the week was a huge success – the level of enthusiasm, participation, exchange of ideas, laughter and general friendliness (I feel) are all indicators of a successful planning process. (Claire, UK)

Reflections on the impact

The workshop included a daily evaluation of the process arranged by each facilitation team and the last day included a brief questionnaire. Both these generated excellent suggestions, many of which were incorporated as the days went by. Rob Bowden, editor of *Pikkin Palaver*, contacted a number of the participants in the succeeding months and they sent him contributions to the newsletter on children's participation that has now become an important means of sharing ideas for many of the group. We sent out an e-mail in February 1998 and received some great replies about the impact of the workshop on subsequent work and thinking:

> I think the workshop has mainly served to affirm the course SCF's Caribbean programme is taking of making child participation a fundamental approach to child-focused work with partner agencies. We have

become much more sensitive to questions of culture when applying child participatory measures. (Denise, Jamaica)

Although I had ideas on participation before the September event, I was also conscious of the impact that the workshop made on my thinking. The collective approach to documentation is a current practice of much of my work with adults following field trips and training activities. (Julia, Palestine)

I think the workshop opened my eyes to some of the possibilities, especially the fact that work in this area is going on in the UK as well as overseas. In a way, that is very important, as the participation of children should not just be seen in the overseas development context. The fact that it is successfully happening in a few places in the UK and involving senior council members, etc. is a confidence boost to the legitimacy of the idea and stops the feeling that it is a marginal activity for overseas consumption only. (John, Nepal)

◄◄·►►

Through the workshop there are some issues related to child participation that I'm more aware of and try to deal with. Something I am struggling with, for example, is that most child participation is on adults' terms, initiated by adults, with the goals and ways of reaching them set by elders. If it goes well, children take over and make the project their own. But how often does that happen? Then again, how to avoid adult-initiated projects, especially in 'advocacy' organizations that usually don't work directly with children. I just can't imagine a group of children walking into my office one day and saying 'let's produce a booklet'. Then again, maybe it's my job to make that happen. A lot of what we call participation is still very much just listening to children and taking them seriously, trying to reflect what they say.

◄◄·►►

Also there is a danger of seeing participation as an end in itself, the magic solution. Once children can participate fully in all activities, then everything is fine. Of course this is an exaggeration, but if you talk about participation for a week and talk about all the problems and obstacles on the way, it seems that when you get there, that's it. But it isn't. Child participation should be a prerequisite for any programme working with, or usually for, children, not a goal in itself. (Esther, Tanzania)

The whole event was a huge learning curve. It made me far more aware of the cultural context in which we live and work and the implications of different contexts. It enhanced my enthusiasm and commitment to using a range of creative methodologies when working with children and young people. It has enabled me to share good ideas with children and young people that I work with about what other young people are doing in other parts of the world. The networking and exchange of ideas and materials has continued since September. Just today, I have received some stunning materials from Grace in Uganda. (Claire, UK)

◄◄·►►

Some of the specific techniques that were applied were new for me and are now a part of my repertoire of techniques. This resulted in my using the child-to-child approach more intensively (in the child rights field). The other thing, or rather the essence of it, is that I have had a definite confirmation of my belief that whatever you do, and however dedicated you are to your work, you have to be aware of cultural specifities in your country or region in order to avoid the import of trends which are not of priority. (Vesna, Yugoslavia)

Activities underway

My leaving for Tajikistan is to do an evaluation with groups of children on a female-headed household income-generating project with a pay-back feature into the local village schools. The children, we hope, are going to be the evaluators; they are 13–16 years old and some may have benefited from the project. They may be illiterate, so we are using the 'Ah-Hah' method of drawings. SCF (UK) and a group of children will be researching awareness about HIV/AIDS amongst children and young people in eastern Nepal, both in refugee camps there and in the adjacent communities. They will be planning their own awareness-raising programme, which will take place in a regional workshop and they will together be the main resource people. The children will also bring edited films of their work and the process they used; they will be trained to use a camcorder to record what goes on but the rushes will be professionally edited. (John, SCF UK, Nepal)

-<-->-

I've just finished my proposal for the restarting of the [*Mambo Leo*] magazine. The proposal has been very much influenced by what I've heard and learned at the workshop. Most importantly, I've learned to be less ambitious and more realistic, at least where scale and pace of the project are concerned.(Esther, Kuleana, Tanzania)

-<-->-

In Lebanon, I was co-ordinating a collective approach to preparing a poster and a case-study of SCF's programme for Palestinian children in the refugee camps of south and north Lebanon. The purpose of the activities was to identify the achievements and impact of the programme from the different points of view, to acknowledge the challenges that have been faced since 1984 (Lebanon war, the camps war, regular aggressive military action by the Israelis in the south, the uncertain future of these people due to the 'peace' process from which they are excluded).

The activities included:
(1) Discussions and drawings with kindergarten children
(2) A focus-group activity with 12 children aged 12–17 years, who have been orphaned or have lost their fathers. They have been integrated into local homes, instead of being put into institutions such as orphanages.

(3) A workshop with 15 children aged 12–14 years who demonstrated their evaluation of their programme through drama, artwork, discussion and handicrafts. They then completed an activity on children's rights, identifying their top nine articles in a diamond ranking.

(4) An adult workshop with five children participating, several facilitating the flip-chart feedback after mixed group work.

(5) A group of children prepared ideas for a poster, which will be used for education and advocacy work this year (it is the 50th anniversary since they fled from Palestine). They chose photos that they had taken in last year's photography training at summer camp, and prepared some written material, organizing their presentation. (Julia, Palestine)

◄◄·►►

The experience from the workshop has greatly facilitated our work in Uganda. I wrote a report about the workshop for Redd Barna management, which was highly appreciated, and I was encouraged to follow-up in our programme work. We organized a workshop on child participation for all our field staff who work directly with children in which I gave a feedback from the seminar. Ideas from the workshop have already been tried out in the 12 districts, especially those on good practice when following up children's groups. Child participation was a major issue for discussion during our annual review in December and those discussions led to child participation becoming a major component of our 1998 annual plans and budgets. We have come up with a training model, which we have already tried out on our local partners. Using the experience I derived from the workshop and the local experiences from our staff, we intend to produce a booklet which we will share with our local partners, other Redd Barna countries and children themselves, especially the Child Rights' Clubs. (Grace, Redd Barna, Uganda)

◄◄·►►

Working in collaboration with Claire O'Kane (University of Wales Swansea/International Centre for Childhood Studies) later in 1997 was an action-replay of the Sussex participatory approaches in a happening event. We workshopped with a group of children brought together for two separate days from different parts of Wales to make recordings for the ICCS Children & Decision-Making Project. The project had initially included 40 children, who were in care, in an extensive series of interviews. Eight of the original 40 had subsequently volunteered to take part in making recordings for the production of an audio-cassette. The initial workshop sessions were about selecting text from the original interviews, deciding what to include and who would say what. With radio, illiteracy is not a problem; it is easier to set up grassroots participation in this media; involvement in radio-making improves literacy skills by confidence-building and motivating people to learn. (Sarah, Unlimited Productions, UK)

Appendix 2 : ladders of participation

PAT PRIDMORE

A number of useful typologies have been developed to help us recognize the way in which participation is a process rather than a product. An early example was presented by Sherry Arnstein (1969) (see Figure 1). At the time of publication the ladder of participation was considered to be a deliberately provocative typology of citizen involvement. It has, however, since been taken up and adapted widely by others (Hubley, 1993). More recently the dialogue has moved into frameworks of empowerment (Cornwall, 1996; Hart, 1992). Hart's ladder of children's participation has proved a valuable tool for project evaluation (see Figure 2). As Hart (1997: 41) explains:

> Whilst the upper levels of the ladder express increasing degrees of initiation by children, they are not meant to imply that a child should always be attempting to operate at the highest level of their competence. The figure is rather meant for adult facilitators to establish the conditions that enable

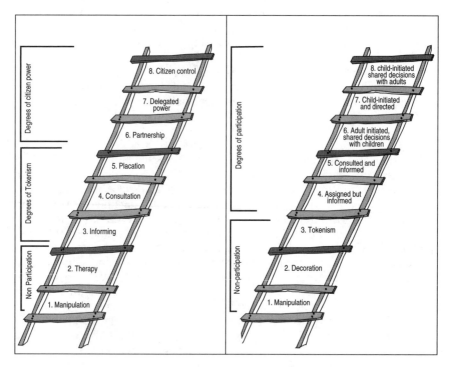

Figure 1: *Ladder of citizen participation*
(Origin: Arnstein, 1969: 70)

Figure 2: *Ladder of children's participation*
(Source: Hart, 1997: 41)

groups of children to work at whatever levels on different projects or different phases of the same project. Also, some children may not be initiators but are excellent collaborators. The important principle is to avoid working at the three lowest levels, the rungs of non-participation.

Appendix 3: The United Nations Convention on the Rights of the Child – history and background

EDDA IVAN-SMITH

The United Nations Convention on the Rights of the Child (UNCRC) is the most widely ratified international legal document in the history of human rights. As of December 1997, 191 of the United Nations' 193 member states had signed and ratified it. The two countries not to have ratified are Somalia and the United States of America.

The Convention was adopted by the United Nations General Assembly in 1989. The 1990 World Summit for Children declared that: 'The Convention on the Rights of the Child provides a new opportunity to make respect for children's rights and welfare truly universal'. The Convention was new and innovative at this time, for two main reasons: it was the first international document specifically to acknowledge participation as a child's right; and although there had been previous declarations in 1924 and 1959, this was the first convention on children's rights which was legally binding. Unlike declarations, or agendas for action, conventions are legal instruments. Member states first declare their intention to abide by a convention when they sign it; they then ratify it when they have brought their own laws into line. Once a country has ratified the Convention, other member states can intervene to ensure that the rights of the Convention have been ensured. This is done through the United Nations Committee on the Rights of the Child which requires ratifying countries to report on their progress every five years. The committee also welcomes and encourages alternative reports from non-governmental organizations.

Main principles of the Convention

The CRC comprises 54 articles. The first defines a child as every human being below the age of 18, unless majority is attained earlier according to the law of the country. Although when drafting the Convention it was not considered possible to attain common agreement on the age of majority, age 18 remains as a general benchmark definition.

There is a common misconception that the CRC is anti-family/parents as it focuses solely on children. A cursory glance may give this impression, but the convention in fact is supportive of families. In many of its articles it highlights the importance of the child being able to grow up in a secure and loving family environment, and it states that the family should be given all necessary support and assistance by the state.

Although there are a number of articles in the Convention addressing specific issues of children's rights, four main principles or guidelines run through the CRC. When governments, parents or professionals working with children try to make sense of the Convention in practical terms, these four principles are referred to frequently:

1. *Non-discrimination:* This could be called the 'issues of difference' principle as it is identified as the principle which ensures that all children enjoy their human rights. All governments have an obligation to provide equality of opportunity among children as expressed in *Article 2*, which states that:

   States parties shall respect and ensure the rights set forth in the present Convention to each child within their jurisdiction without discrimination of any kind, irrespective of the child's or his or her parents' or legal guardian's race, colour, sex, language, religion, political or other opinion, national, ethnic or social origin, property, disability, birth or other status.

2. *Best interests of the child:* This recognizes that children, particularly when very young, are especially vulnerable and need special support to enable them to enjoy their rights fully. Whenever official decisions are taken which affect children, their interests should be seen as paramount; this is one of the more significant messages of the CRC set out in *Article 3*:

   In all actions concerning children, whether undertaken by public or private social-welfare institutions, courts of law, administrative authorities or legislative bodies, the best interests of the child shall be a primary consideration.

3. *The right to survival and development:* This is perhaps the principle most readily associated with the Convention and it relates directly to children's economic and social rights. Both the words 'survival' and 'development' are rare for a human rights treaty and give this article a more qualitative tone. The Convention makes it quite clear that development and survival are about governments and parents not just meeting the basic health needs of children but also developing their intellectual and personal growth and happiness. *Article 6* states:

   'States parties shall ensure to the maximum extent possible the survival and development of the child'.

4. *The views of the child:* Perhaps the most provocative and crucial principle of the CRC is that concerned with respecting and acting upon children's views and opinions. Despite its controversial nature, sound logic is at work here. In order to gauge what is in the best interests of the child it follows that we should listen to her/him, as *Article 12* states:

   States parties shall assure to the child who is capable of forming his or her own views the right to express those views freely in all matters affecting the child, the views of the child being given due weight in accordance with the age and maturity of the child.

Other participation-related articles are as follows:

Article 13: the child's right to obtain and make known information, and to express his or her views, unless this would violate the rights of others;

Article 15: the right of children to meet with others and to join or set up associations, unless the fact of doing so violates the rights of others;

Article 17: the state shall ensure the accessibility to children of information and materials from a diversity of sources, and it shall encourage the mass media to disseminate information which is of social and cultural benefit to the child, and to take steps to protect him or her from harmful materials; and

Article 18: parents have joint primary responsibility for the upbringing and development of the child, and the state shall support them in this. The best interests of the child will be their basic concern.

Since the adoption of the Convention, there has been a shift of thinking about attitudes to children in all spheres of life. Though the CRC is not a practical tool, and for some that is its major flaw, it has proved to be a useful frame of reference for practitioners and advocates of children. As it is so widely ratified, it has also proved to be a useful advocacy tool for many groups, which call governments to account over their treatment of children.

Appendix 4: the lead organizations in the preparation of this book

Development FOCUS
Development FOCUS is a research and consultancy partnership based in Brighton, Sussex, working on issues of environment and development. Victoria Johnson was contracted to the Institute of Development Studies to carry out work on children's participation, one of the key areas of specialization of Development FOCUS.

Institute of Development Studies
The Institute of Development Studies is one of the world's leading centres for research on development issues, and has a reputation for combining rigorous investigation with a practical focus on real-world problems. IDS also has a strong tradition of teaching and training, and an active programme of information dissemination and knowledge sharing. The participation group at IDS is a team working to deepen understanding of participatory approaches through partnerships that link practitioners and researchers worldwide.

Save the Children (UK)
Save the Children is the UK's largest voluntary agency concerned with international child health and welfare. It works in the UK and 50 of the world's least-developed countries. Save the Children works to achieve lasting benefits for children within the communities in which they live by influencing policy and practice, based on its experience and study in different parts of the world. In all of its work, Save the Children endeavours to make a reality of children's rights.

Institute of Education, University of London
The Institute of Education is a graduate college of the federal University of London enrolling students from more than 80 countries. It is the largest institution in the United Kingdom devoted to the study of education and related areas. The Education and International Development Group undertakes teaching, research and consultancy on educational issues in developing countries. It offers courses, supervises research students, conducts research projects and has an extensive network of contacts with multi- and bi-lateral development organizations and international institutes of education.

Appendix 5: Children's participation in research and programming workshop: participants' contact list

Abrioux, Emmanuelle: c/o Action Centre la Faim, 9 Rue Dareau, 75014 Paris, France

Adams, Eileen: 75 Gaskarth Road, London SW12 9NN, tel/fax: 0181 675 6194

Allen, Denise: Save the Children (UK), PO Box 8907, Central Sorting Office, Kingston, Jamaica, tel: 876 922 7799, fax: 876 922 5997, email: 106174.714@compuserve.com

Bowden, Rob: Geography Subject Group, Department of Construction, Geography and Surveying, University of Brighton, Mithras House, Lewes Road, Brighton BN2 4AT, Tel: 01273 642425/671057, fax: 01273 642392, email: rcb6@bton.ac.uk

Carnegie, Rachel: 337 Petersham Road, Richmond, Surrey, TW10 7DB, UK, tel/fax: 9181 940 7436

Cloma, Ernesto: Philippine Educational Theater Association, #61 Lantana Street, Quezon City, Philippines, tel: 632 4100822/709637, fax: 632 4100820

Coomaraswamy, Priya: Save the Children (UK), 35 Bagatale Road, Colombo 3, Sri Lanka, tel: 941 593595, fax: 941 593353, email: scfsl@sri.lanka.net

Damen Halaseh, Safa: Questscope for Social Development in the Middle East, PO Box 910729, Amman, Jordan, tel: 926 661 8951, fax: 962 661 8952, email:questscope@nets.com.jo

Dejanovic, Vesna: Save The Children (UK), Generala Hanrisa 1, PO Box 855,11000 Belgrade, FR Yugoslavia, tel/fax: 381113971421, email: 106007.2462@compuserve.com

Faulkner, Julian: Flat 1, 19 Lennox Gardens, London SW1X ODB e-mail: julian@synergies.u-net.com, home page: www.synergies.u-net.com

Farhana Faruqui: House no.50, Street 155, G-11/1 Islamabad, Pakistan, e-mail: farhana@raf.sdnpk.undp.org

Feeney, Mark: Kirkless Council, Oldgate House, Huddersfield HD1 6QF, West Yorkshire, tel: 01484 225113, fax: 01484 225360

Gilkes, Julia: Save the Children (UK), PO Box 2899, Larnaka, Cyprus, tel/fax: 04 627108, email: scfcyp@spidernet.com.cy

Gordon, Gill: Institute of Education, University of London, 20 Bedford Way, London WC1H 0AL and 33 Leicester Road, Lewes, East Sussex, BN7 1SU, tel/fax: 01273 479 293, email: gmgordon@netcomuk.com.uk

Haines, Adam: VOYCE, c/o Kim Jackson, The Community Health and Environment Team, Hove Town Hall, Norton Road, BN3 3BQ, UK, tel: 01273 292254

Haque, Mahfuza: Save the Children (UK), PO Box 55, House 28 Road 16 (new), Dhanmondi RA, Dhaka, Bangladesh, tel: 880 2817561, fax: 880 2817278, email: scfukbd@bangla.net

Halasah, Safa: Questscope, P.O. Box 910729, Amman, 11191, Jordan, fax: 9266 461 8952, email: questscope@nets.com.jo

Harrison, Kate: AHRTAG, Farringdon Point, 29-35 Farringdon Road, London EC1M 3JB, tel: 0171 242 0606, fax: 0171 242 0041, email: ahrtag@gn.apc.org

Hart, Roger: Children's Environment Research Group, University of New York, New York, email: rhart@email.cuny.edu

Hill, Joanna: ActionAid Nepal, PO Box 6257, Kathmandu, Nepal, email:joanna@aanepal.mos.com.np

Hinton, Rachel: Department of Social Anthropology, University of Edinburgh, Adam Ferguson Building, George Square, Edinburgh, EH16 5AY, UK, tel: 0131 650 3936, email: r.hinton@ed.ac.uk

Inglis, Andy: Scottish Participatory Initiatives, 3 Queen Charlotte Lane, Leith, Edinburgh EH6 6AY, tel: 0131 555 0950, fax: 031 555 0340, email: 101234.2170@compuserve.com

Ivan-Smith, Edda: Save the Children (UK),17 Grove Lane, London SE5 8RD, tel: 0171 703 5400, fax: 0171 793 7630, email: e.ivan-smith@scfuk.org.uk

Johnson, Vicky: Development Focus, 23 York Avenue, Brighton BN3 1PJ, East Sussex, tel/fax: 01273 722336, email: vjohnson@devfocus.u-net.com

Kaminsky, Donald: Project Alternatives and Opportunities, PO Box 1587, Tegucigalpa, Honduras, tel: 504 226179, fax: 504 22 0543, email: fundar%alter@sdhon.org.hn

Kaspar, Amy: The Treasury, Somerville College, Oxford University, OX2 6HD, UK, tel: 01865 270 623, email: amy.kaspar@some.ox.ac.uk

Lamptey, Alice: Save the Children (UK), PO Box C. 976, Cantonments, Accra, Ghana, tel: 23321 772600/772601, fax: 23321 772146, email: 100633.2504@compuserve.com

Manyau, Charity: Save the Children (UK), PO Box 4689, 10 Natal Road, Corner of 2nd Street, Belgravia, Zimbabwe, tel: 2634 7931 198/9, fax: 2634 727508, email: 100075.2761@compuserve.com

Mayall, Berry: Institute of Education, University of London, 20 Bedford Way, London WC1H OAL, tel: 0171 580 1122

McNeill, Sarah, Unlimited Productions, PO Box 2041, Hove, Brighton, Sussex BN3 2EW, tel/fax: 01273 724 948, email: sarahmcneil@dial.pipex.com

Mukasa, Grace: Redd Barna – Uganda, PO Box 12018, Kampala, Uganda, tel: 341714/341693, fax: 341700, email: rbu@imul.com

Ngcozela, Thabang: Ilitha Lamso Children's Organisation, Cape Town, South Africa, tel: 272 14618338, fax: 2721 461 236

Obeng, Christiana, PO Box 514, Accra, Ghana

Obdam, Esther: Kuleana Centre for Children's Rights, PO Box 27, Mwanza, Tanzania, tel: 25568,500911/500912, fax: 25568 42402, email: kuleana@tan2.healthnet.org

Olivier, Amanda: PO Box 81, Buhrmannsdrift 2867, South Africa, tel: 27140 681 044, email: hawa@ilink.co.za

Osuga, Ben: Sikiliza International, PO Box 31618, Kampala, Uganda, tel/fax: 256 42 211 86, email: djohnson@imul.com

O'Kane, Clare: Butterflies Programme of Street and Working Children, U-4 Green Park Extension, New Delhi, 110016, India, tel: 91 11 6855910, fax: 91 11 6858117, email: *bflies%bflies@sdalt.ernet* or Children and Decision-Making Study, International Centre for Childhood Studies, University of Wales, Singleton Park, Swansea, SA2 8PP, tel/fax: 01792 295767

Otaala, Barnabas, Dean of Education, University of Namibia, Private Bag 13301, Windhoek, Nambia, fax: 26461 206 3980

Parry-Williams, John: Save the Children Fund (UK), South Asia Regional Office, Pulchowk, Lalitpur, GPO Box 5850, Kathmandu, Nepal, tel: 977 1527 152, fax: 977 1527 266, email: John@scfscaro.mos.com.np

Percy-Smith, Barry: Nene Centre for Research, Nene College of Higher Education, Park Campus, Northampton NN2 7AH, tel: 01604 735500, fax: 01604 791114

Pridmore, Pat: Institute of Education, University of London, 20 Bedford Way, London WC1H OAL, tel: 0171 612 6601, fax: 0171 612 6632, email: p.pridmore@ioe.ac.uk

Scott, Patta: Institute of Development Studies, University of Sussex, Brighton BN1 9RE, tel: 01273 606 261, fax: 01273 621 202/691 647, email:p.scott-villiers@ids.ac.uk

Stephens, David: University of Sussex, Centre for International Education, Education Development Building, University of Sussex, Falmer, Brighton BN1 9RG, tel: (01273)606755, fax: (01273)678568, email: cie@sussex.ac.uk

Swift, Melinda: TRAC PO Box 62535, Marshalltown, 2017,South Africa, tel: 2711831060/3/4/, fax: 2711834 8385, email: trac@wn.apc.org

Tafari-Ama, Imani: Seinpostdain 32586 EA, Den Haag, Holland, tel:0703515745

Theis, Joachim: Save the Children (UK), c/o La Thanh Hotel, 218 Doi Can, Ba Dinh District, Hanoi, Vietnam, tel: 844 8325319/8325344, fax: 844 8325073, email: scfukhan@netnam.org.vn

West, Andy: Save the Children (UK),1 Eastgate, LEEDS, LS2 7LY, tel:0113 242 4844, fax: 0113 242 5032

Woollcombe, David: Peace Child, The White House, Buntingford, Herts, SG9 9AH, tel: 0176 327 4459, fax: 0176 327 4460, email: 100640.3551@compuserve,com

Zelleke, Abebaw: Save the Children (UK), PO Box 7165, Addis Ababa, Ethiopia, tel: 251 1611177/611178/610876, fax: 251 1611055, email: 100440.1465@compuserve.com

Additional Contributors[1]

Baker, Rachel: Department of Social Anthropology, University of Edinburgh, Adam Ferguson Building, George Square, Edinburgh, EH8 9LL, tel: 0131 650 1000, fax: 0131 650 3945

Blagborough, Jonathan: Anti-Slavery International, The Stableyard, Broomgrove Road, London, SW9 9TL tel: 0171 924 9555, fax:0171 738 4110, e-mail:antislavery@gn.apc.org

Crawford, Sheena: Department of Social Anthropology, University of Edinburgh, Adam Ferguson Building, George Square, Edinburgh, EH8 9LL, tel: 0131 650 1000, fax: 0131 650 3945, email: s.crawford@ed.ac.uk

Harris, Lucy: 62 Queens Park Terrace, Brighton BN2 2YB, East Sussex, tel: 01273 382855

Lewes, Mary Ellen: Children's Environments Research Group, City University of New York/ New York City High School, tel: 212 337 6800/ 212 683 3526

Marcus, Rachel: Save the Children Fund, 17 Grove Lane, London SE5 8RD, tel: 0171 703 5400, fax: 0171 793 7630, email: r.marcus@scfuk.org.uk

Saurin, Amanda: Environmental education and arts in schools, Willowcote, Wellgreen Lane, Kingston, Lewes BN7 3NR, East Sussex, tel: 01273 479383

Woodhead, Martin: Centre for Human Development and Learning, School of Education, The Open University, Walton Hall, Milton Keynes MK7 6AA, tel: 01908 652894, fax: 01908 654111

[1] These are people who have made contributions to this book but did not attend the workshop.

Bibliography and References

Part 1

Bhavnani, Kum-Kum (1991) *Talking Politics: A psychological framing for views from youth in Britain*, Cambridge University Press, Cambridge

Boyte, H.C., (1995) 'Beyond deliberation, citizenship as public work', PEGS Conference, Feb 10–11, 1995

Chambers, R. (1997) *Whose Reality Counts? Putting the last first*, Intermediate Technology (IT) Publications, London

Ennew, J. (1994) *Street and Working Children: a guide to planning*, Development Manual 4, Save the Children (UK), London

Gaventa, J. (1998) 'Poverty, Participation and Social Exclusion in North and South', *IDS Bulletin*, Vol. 29, No. 1, 50–57

Guijt, I., Fuglesang, A. and Kisadha, T. (ed.) (1994), *It is the Young Trees that make a Forest Thick: a report on Redd Barna's learning experiences with participatory rural appraisal, Kyakatebe, Masaka District, Uganda*, IIED, London, and Redd Barna, Kampala, Uganda

Hart, R.A. (1997) *Children's Participation, the theory and practice of involving young citizens in community development and environmental care*, UNICEF, New York and Earthscan, London

James, A., Jenks, C. and Prout, A. (1998) *Theorizing Childhood*, Polity Press, Cambridge

Johnson, V., Hill, J., Ivan-Smith, E. (1995) *Listening to Smaller Voices: children in an environment of change*, ACTIONAID, London

Johnson, V. (1996) 'Starting a dialogue on children's participation', *PLA Notes* No. 25, Special Issue on Children's Participation, IIED, London

Jones, G. and Wallace, C. (1992) *Youth, Family and Citizenship*, Open University Press, Buckingham

Merrifield, J. (1997) 'Finding our loadstone again: democracy, the civil society and adult education', in 'Crossing borders breaking boundaries', Proceedings of the 27th annual SCUTREA conference, Birkbeck College, London

Putnam, R.D. (1993) 'The prosperous community, social capital and public life', *American Prospect*, Vol. 13

Theis, J. and Thi Huyen, H. (1997) *From Housework to Goldmining: child labour in rural Vietnam*, Save the Children (UK), Hanoi, Vietnam

Welbourn, A. (1992) 'Rapid rural appraisal, gender and health: alternative ways of listening to needs', in de Koning, K. and Martin, M. (1996), *Participatory Research in Health: Issues and Experience*, Zed Books, London and New Jersey and NPPHCN, Johannesburg

West, A. (1995) *You're on your Own; Young people's research on leaving care*, Save the Children, London

Wilkinson, R.G. (1996) *Unhealthy Societies*, Routledge, London and New York

Willis, P. Bekenn, A. Ellis, T. and Whitt, D. (1988) *The Youth Review: social conditions of young people in Wolverhampton*, Avebury, Aldershot

Part 2

Adams, E. with Kean, J. (1991) *Education for Participation: Schools and the Environmental and Design Professions*, Newcastle Architecture Workshop

Adams, E. and Ward, C. (1982) *Art and the Built Environment*, Longman, Harlow, Essex

317

Adams, E. (1990a) 'Teachers, architects and planners: collaboration in education' in *Issues in Design Education,* ed. David Thistlewood, Longman, Harlow, Essex

Adams, E. (1990b) *Learning through Landscapes: a report on the use, design, management and development of school grounds,* Learning through Landscapes Trust, Winchester

Alderson, P. (1995) *Listening to Children – Children, ethics and social research,* Barnardos, Essex, UK

Bassey, M. (1983) 'Pedagogic research into singularities: case-studies, probes and curriculum innovations', *Oxford Review of Education,* 9, (2)

Bassey, M. (1991) 'On the nature of research in education (part 2)', *Research Intelligence,* British Education Research Association Newsletter 37

Bell, G. (1994) 'Art education as action enquiry' in *Aspects of Education,* No. 42, University of Hull

Black, M. with additional material by Blagbrough, J. (1997) *Child Domestic Workers. A Handbook for Research and Action,* Anti-Slavery International, London

British Psychological Society (1995) *Code of Conduct, Ethical Principles and Guidelines,* The British Psychological Society, Leicester

Butler, I. and Williamson, H. (1994) *Children Speak: children, trauma and social work,* Longman, Harlow, Essex

Chawla, L. (1997) *Growing Up In Cities Project Report,* Children and Environment Programme of the Norwegian Centre for Child Research, Trondheim, Norway

Dadds, M. (1993) 'Thinking and being in teacher education' in Elliot, J. (ed.) *Reconstructing Teacher Education,* Falmer Press

Damon, W. (1977) *The Social World of the Child,* Josey-Bass, San Francisco

Elliott, J. (1991) *Action Research for Educational Change,* Open University Press, Milton Keynes

Ennew, J. (1994) 'Street and Working Children: A Guide to Planning', *SCF Development Manual 4,* SCF, London

Fine, G. and Sandstrom, K. (1988) *Knowing Children: participant observation with minors,* Sage, New Delhi

Garratt, D. with Chell, E. Tock, L. Westerby, M. and Sellers, T. (1997) 'A participatory appraisal of domestic violence: community perceptions and a review of the Beechdale Project', Report for the Walsall Domestic Violence Forum, University of Hull

Harahan, J. (1976) *Design in general education: eight projects,* Design Council

Hart, R. (1979) *Children's Experience of Place,* Irvington, New York

Hart, R. (1992) 'Children's participation: from tokenism to citizenship', *Innocenti Essay,* No. 4, UNICEF, Rome

Hart, R. (1997) *Children's Participation: the Theory and Practice of Involving Young Citizens in Community Development and Environmental Care,* Earthscan, London

James, A. (1995) 'Methodologies of Competence for a Competent Methodology', Paper at Children and Social Competence Conference

Johnson, V. (1996) 'Starting a dialogue on children's participation' in *PLA Notes No. 25,* Special Issue on Children's Participation, IIED, London

Kemmis, S. (1990) 'Action research in retrospect and prospect' in Kemmis, S. and McTaggart, R. (ed.), *The Action Research Reader,* Deakin University Press, Geelong

Kohlberg, L, (1984) *Essays of Moral Development,* Harper Collins, New York

Lomax, P. (1994) 'Action research for professional practice: a position paper on educational action research', Paper presented at the Practitioner Research Workshop, annual conference of the British Research Association, September, Oxford

Lynch, K. (ed.), (1977) *Growing Up in Cities,* MIT Press, Cambridge, MA., USA

Morrow, V. and Richards, M. (1996) 'The Ethics of Social Research with Children: an overview'. *Children and Society,* Vol.10, No.2, 90–105

Piaget, J. (1954) *The Construction of Reality in the Child,* Basic Books, New York

Qvortrup, J. and others (ed.) (1994) 'Childhood Matters: social theory, practice and politics', European Centre, Vienna

Sellers, T. and Westerby, M. (1996) 'Teenage facilitators: barriers to improving adolescent sexual health' in *PLA Notes* No. 25, IIED, London, and in *The SHIP: Sexual Health Information Pack,* (Holden, S. and Welbourn, A. ed.), IDS, Sussex, UK

Singh, K. (1993) 'Participatory Rural Appraisal (PRA): learning from and with rural communities', *Drought Monitor*, Nov/Dec.

Socio-Legal Studies Association (1995) Statement of Ethical Practice' in *SLSA Directory of Members*, Butterworths

Thoburn, J., Lewis, A. and Shemmings, D. (1995) 'Paternalism or Partnership? Family involvement in the child protection process', *Studies in Child Protection*, HMSO, London

Treseder, P. (1997) *Empowering Children and Young People: training manual*, Children's Rights Office / Save the Children, London

Uzzell, D. (1979) 'Four roles of the community researcher' *Journal of Voluntary Action Research*, 8: 1–2

Van Bueren, (1996) 'The 'Quiet' Revolution: children's rights in international law' in M. John (ed.) *The Child's Right to a Fair Hearing*, Jessica Kingsley Publishers, London

Woodhead, M. (1997) 'Is there a place for work in development?', report for Rädda Barnen Children and Work Project

Part 3

ActionAid Nepal (1997) DA2 and DA3 MTR Reports (translated sections on children)

Baker, R. (1996) 'PRA with street children in Nepal' in *PLA Notes*, No. 25, IIED, London

Baker, R. and Hinton, R.C. (forthcoming) 'Do focus groups facilitate meaningful participation in social research?' in Baker, R. and Kitzinger, J. (ed.), *Focus Group Research: politics, theory and practice*, Sage, London

Bedford, Laura, J. (1995) 'Ondleleni: Children on their way. Street children in Durban, pasts, presents and futures – constraints and possibilities', report, October 1995, South Africa

Boal, A. (1974) *Theatre of the Oppressed*, trans. Charles A. and Mania-Odilia Leal McBride, Pluto Press, London

Boal, A. (1992) *Games for Actors and non-Actors*, trans., A. Jackson Routledge, London

Bonati, G. and Hawes, H. (1992) *Child-to-Child: a Resource Book*, The Child-to-Child Trust, London

Braden, Su (1996) 'Video work with communities' *Anthropology in Action*, Vol. 3, No.1, Oxfam 'Video as a participatory process: a one-programme approach', *Cross-programme learning report*

Chambers, R. (1997) *Whose Reality Counts: putting the first last*, IT Publications, London

Duchscherer, D., Duchscherer, C., Namgyal, R. and Iqbal, M. 1996 *Child Participation in Practice: SCF NWI's experiences in programming*, in 'PRA with Children', IDS PRA Topic Pack, December

Edwards, M. (1996) 'Institutionalizing children's participation in development' in *PLA Notes*, No. 26, IIED, London

Gordon, G. (1997) 'Participatory approaches to the use of drama in sexual and reproductive health programmes' in *Performance and Participation, PLA Notes* No. 29, IIED, London

Hart, R. (1997) *Children's Participation*, UNICEF/Earthscan

Hill, J. and Sapkota, P. (1997) 'Children: the actual managers', in SCF UK *South and Central Asia's Children* (1997), No. 8, Spring

Hinton, R.C. (1995) 'Trades in different worlds: listening to refugee voices' in *PLA Notes*, No. 24, IIED, London

Hinton, R.C. (1996) 'Using participatory methods for gender and health research', *Journal for Applied Anthropology in Policy and Practice: Anthropology and Refugees*, Vol. 3, No. 1, 24–34

Hubbard, J. (1991) *Shooting Back: a photographic view of life by homeless children*, Chronicle Books, San Francisco, CA

IPPF (1997) *Sexual and Reproductive Health: a new approach with communities*, IPPF Publications

Johansson, L. and De Waal, D. (1996) 'Giving people a voice rather than a message', in *Engaging Participation: the use of video as a tool in rural development*, Farmesa/FAO

Johnson, V. Hill, J. and Ivan-Smith, E. (1995) *Listening to Smaller Voices,* ActionAid, London

Johnson, V. (1996) 'Starting a dialogue on children's participation', in *PLA Notes No. 25,* February, Special Issue on Children's Participation, IIED, London

Kane, E. (1996) 'Groundwork: participatory research for girls' education', Manual and Video. EDIHR/ASTHR The World Bank, Washington DC

Kumkum, Ghosh (1997) 'Learning from children', in *South and Central Asia's Children, No. 8, Spring 1997. Working for children's rights and participation.* UNICEF and SCF

Mbowa, R. (1997) 'Rehearsing for reality', in *Performance and Participation, PLA Notes* No. 29, IIED, London

Ogolla, L. (1997) *Towards Behaviour Change: participatory theatre in education and development,* PETAD Publication, Wood Avenue, PO Box 476339, Nairobi

PLA Notes No. 29 (1997) *Performance and Participation,* IIED, London

Pridmore, P. (1996) 'Children as Health Educators: the child-to-child approach', PhD Thesis, Institute of Education, University of London

Pridmore, P. and Landsdown, R. (1997) 'Exploring perceptions of health: does draw and write really break down barriers?' in *Health Education Journal,* Vol. 56, 219–30

Sapkota, P. (1997) 'Economic Contribution of School-going Children in the Majhi Community of Ghata Tole': a report compiled for child-centred participatory research (Draft), AAN

Sey, H. and VanBelle-Prouty (ed) 'Classroom Observations and Participatory Learning for Action Activities: a view of the experiences of girls, prepared for USAID Africa Bureau, Office of Sustainable Development and the Institute for International Research

Sharma, U. (1997) *ACCESS Program Process Report,* DA3, AAN

Singh, N. and Trivedy, R. (1996) *Approaches to Child Participation,* SCF, UK

SNV – Kenya Street Children Programme 1996 'Participatory Action Research with Children', Report of a training workshop on participatory action research with children for social workers and street educators

The Child-to-Child Trust in association with UNICEF (1993) *Children for Health,* TALC and UNICEF

Theis, J. and Hoang Thi Huyen (1997) *From Housework to Gold Mining – Child Labour in Rural Vietnam,* SCF/UK, Hanoi

van Beers, H. (1996) 'Participatory Action Research with Children', Report of a training workshop on participatory action research with children for social workers and street educators, Naro Moru, Kenya

Waiba, K. (1997) 'Impact Study Report of Programme on Children' (Draft), AAN

Welbourn, A. (1995) 'Stepping Stones: a training package on HIV/AIDS, communication and relationship skills', *Strategies for Hope,* Training Series, No. 1

Part 4

Alderson, P. and Mayall, B. (ed.) (1994) *Children's Decisions in Health Care and Research,* London, Social Science Research Unit, Institute of Education, University of London

Armstrong, A. (1995) 'A Child Belongs to Everyone: law, family and the construction of the "best interest of the child" in Zimbabwe', *Spedale degli,* Innocenti, Florence, Italy

Bailey, D., Hawes, H. *et al.* (ed.) (1992) *Child-to-Child: a resource book,* The Child-to-Child Trust, London

Bernard van Leer Foundation, (1991) *Child Development in Africa: building on people's strengths,* Bernard Van Leer Foundation, The Hague

Boyden, J. (1990) 'Childhood and the policy-makers: a comparative perspective on the globalization of childhood', in James, A. and Prout, A. (ed.) *Constructing and Reconstructing Childhood,* Falmer Press, London

Burman, E. (1996) 'Local, global or globalized? Child development and international child rights legislation', *Childhood:* 3, 1: 45–67

Cole M. (1992) 'Culture in development', in Bornstein, M.H. and Lamb, M.E. (ed.) *Human Development, an Advanced Textbook,* Erlbaum, Hillside, New Jersey

Dalin, P. (1993) *Changing the School Culture*, Cassell, London

Ennew, J. and Milne, B. (1989) *The Next Generation*, Zed Books, London

Feuerstein, M.T. (1981) *Report of the Evaluation of the Child-to-Child Programme*, Child-to-Child Trust, London

Francis, V. (1993) 'Health Education – a key to community eye health: but where are the locksmiths?' *Community Eye Health*, Vol. 6, No. 12: 17–19

Government of Uganda (1992) *Education for National Integration and Development – the White Paper*, Government of Uganda, Kampala

Gyekye, K. (1996) *African Cultural Values (an introduction)*, Sankofa Publishing Company, Accra, Ghana

Harrison, K. (1997) 'Child-to-Child and PRA: holistic and participatory approaches to school health promotion', Unpublished MA dissertation, Institute of Education, University of London

Hawes, H. (1988) *Child-to-Child: another path to learning*, UNESCO Institute of Education, London

Hawes H. and Scotchmer, C. (1993) *Children for Health*, Child-to-Child Trust, London

Hess B. B. *et al.* (1988) *Ethnocentrism and Cultural Relativism*, Macmillan, New York

Hodgkinson, C. (1983) *The Philosophy of Leadership*, Blackwells, Oxford

International Labour Organization (1996) *Child Labour: targetting the intolerable*, Geneva, International Labour Office

James, A and Prout, A. (ed.) (1997) *Constructing and Reconstructing Childhood*, 2nd ed. Falmer Press, London

Klitgaard, R. (1994) 'Taking Culture into Account: from "Let's" to "How?"', in Serageldin, I. and Taboroff, I., *Culture and Development in Africa*, World Bank, Washington

Lansdown, R. (1995) *Child-to-Child: a review of the literature*, Child-to-Child Trust, London

McKechnie J., Lindsay S. and Hobbs S. (1996) 'Child employment: a neglected topic?' *The Psychologist* 9, 5: 219–22

Ministry of Basic Education and Culture (MBEC) (1989) *Universal Children's Rights, Zimbabwe*, Ministry of Basic Education and Culture, Harare

Ministry of Education (1996) Ministry of Education Primary Education Programme (PREP): report on the adminstration of primary 6 criterion – referenced tests, Ministry of Education, Accra

Mostert, M. L. and Zimba, R. F. (1990) *Child-to-Child in Namibia*, University of Namibia Printery, Windhoek

Myers, R. (1992) *The Twelve Who Survive*, Routledge, New York

Otaala, B. (1994a) *Child-to-Child in Northern Namibia: new initiatives*, Frewer's Printers, Windhoek

Otaala, B. (1994b) *Child-to-Child in Southern Namibia*, Frewer's Printers, Windhoek

Otaala, B. (1995a) *The Contribution of Educational Psychology in Africa: the Namibian case*, University of Namibia Printery, Windhoek

Otaala, B. (1995b) 'Health through the school' Proposal presented to the Research and Publications Committee, University of Namibia, Windhoek

Otaala, B. (1995c) 'Resilience in Namibian children: a preliminary study' in Grotberg, E. (1995) *The International Resilience Project: promoting resilience in children*, University of Alabama at Birmingham, Civitan International Research Centre, Birmingham

Otaala, B., Myers, R. and Landers, C. (1988) *Children Caring for Children*, UNICEF, New York

Pridmore, P. (1996) 'Children as Health Educators: the child-to-child approach', Unpublished PhD thesis, Institute of Education, London

Pridmore, P. and Bendelow, G. (1995) 'Images of Health: exploring beliefs of children using the "draw and write" technique', *Health Education Journal* 54: 473–88

Reynolds, P. (1991) *Dance Civet Cat: child labour in the Zambezi Valley*, Zed Books, London

Smith, P. and Bond, M. (1993) *Social Psychology Across Cultures: analysis and perspectives*, Harvester/Wheatsheaf, Hemel Hampstead

Statistical Service Department (1995) *Ghana Living Standard Survey* (GLSS), Government of Ghana, Accra

Stephens, D. (1994) 'Using culture to improve the quality of educational research in developing countries', in Takala, T. (ed.) *Quality of Education in the Context of Culture in Developing Countries*, Tampere, Finland

Thorne, B. (1993) *Gender Play: girls and boys in school*, Rutgers University Press, New Brunswick, New Jersey

Tolfree, D. (forthcoming, 1998) – Report to Rädda Barnen, Stockholm

UNESCO (1991) *Education for All: purpose and context. Roundtable Themes 1*, World Conference on Education for All, UNESCO, Paris

UNESCO (1996) *What makes a good teacher? Children speak their minds*, UNESCO Associated Schools Project, Paris

UNICEF (1990) *Cross Currents: a review of NGO/UN action for children 1979–1989 commissioned by the NGO Committee of UNICEF*, UNICEF, New York

UNICEF (1991) *A Situation Analysis of Children and Women in Namibia*, NISER for UNICEF, Windhoek, Namibia

UNICEF (1997) *The State of the World's Children*, Oxford University Press, New York

Vanistendael S. (1989) 'Traditional educative models to a transcultural approach', in Tay, A. K. B. *Child-to-Child in Africa: towards an open learning strategy*, UNESCO, Paris – UNICEF Cooperative Programme, Digest No. 29

Verhelst,T. (1987) *No Life Without Roots: culture and development*, Zed Press, London

WCEFA (1990) (World Conference on Education for All): *World Declaration on Education for All: our framework for action to meet basic needs*, 5–9 March, Jomtien, Thailand

Welbourn, A. (1995*) Stepping Stones: a training package on HIV/AIDS, communication and relationship skills*, Strategies for Hope, ACTIONAID, Chard/London

Wellington, K.E. (1988) 'The Dipo Custom of the Krobos', Unpublished dissertation presented to the Ghana Institute of Journalism

White, B. (1996) 'Globalization and the child labour problem', *Journal of International Development* 8, 6: 829–39.

Woodhead M. (1990) 'Psychology and the cultural construction of children's needs' in Prout, A. and James, A. (ed.) *Construction and Reconstruction of Childhood*, Falmer, London

Woodhead M. (1996) *In Search of the Rainbow: pathways to quality in large-scale programmes for young disadvantaged Children*, Bernard van Leer Foundation, The Hague

Woodhead, M. (1998a) *Young Working Lives: a study of children's perspectives*, Rädda Barnen, Stockholm

Woodhead, M. (1998b) 'Combating child labour – listen to what the children say', manuscript

Woodhead, M. (1998c) 'Quality in early childhood: a contextually-appropriate approach', *International Journal of Early Years' Education*

Woodhead, M. (1998d) 'Standardizing childhood – the role of psychology', manuscript

Woodhead, M. (1998e) *A Place for Work in Child Development*, Rädda Barnen, Stockholm

Woodhead, M., Faulkner, D. and Littleton, K.S. (ed.) (1998) *Cultural Worlds of Early Childhood*, Routledge, London

Zimba, R. F. and Otaala, B. (1991) *Child Care and Development in Uukwaluudhi*, Northern Namibia, UNICEF, Windhoek

Zimba, R. F. and Otaala, B. (1995) *The Family in Transition: a study of childrearing practices and beliefs among the Nama of the Karas and Hardap Regions of Namibia*, University of Namibia Printery, Windhoek

Part 5

Attwood, H. (ed.) (1996) *PRA Disasters, Refugees and Emergencies Pack*, Institute of Development Studies, University of Sussex, Falmer

Baden, S. (1997) 'Post-conflict Mozambique: women's special situation, population issues and gender perspectives to be integrated into skills training and employment promotion', ILO Training Policies and Systems Branch, ILO Action Programmes on skills and entrepreneurship training for countries emerging from armed conflict, Geneva

Baric, L. (1996) *Health Education and Health Promotion: handbook for students and practitioners,* Barns Publications, Altrincham

Cohler, B. (1991) 'The life story and the study of resilience and response to adversity', *Journal of Narrative and Life History,* Vol. 1: 169–200

Cuny, D. (1994) *Disasters and Development,* INTERTECT Press, Dallas

Ferron, S. and Pridmore, P. (1988) 'Education in Hope – the need for new approaches to health education in emergencies', *Journal of Practice in Education for Development,* Vol. 3, No. 3

Frankl, V. (1993) *Man's Search for Meaning: an introduction to logotherapy,* Washington Square Press, New York

Garbarino J. and Bedard C. (1996) 'Spiritual challenges to children facing violent trauma', *Childhood,* Vol.3, No. 4: 467–78

Grotberg, E. (1995) *International Resilience Project: promoting resilience in children,* University of Alabama at Birmingham: Civitan International Research Centre, Birmingham

Hanbury, C. (ed.) (1993) *Child-to Child and Children Living in Camps,* Child-to Child Trust, London

James, A. and Prout, A. (1990) *Contemporary Issues in the Sociological Study of Childhood,* Falmer Press, London

Jensen, J. P. (1996) 'War-affected societies and war-affected children: what are the long-term consequences?' *Childhood,* Vol.3, No. 3: 415–421

Muecke, M. (1992) 'New paradigms for refugee health problems', *Social Science and Medicine,* Vol. 35, No. 4: 515–213

Naidoo, S. and Wills, J. (1994) *Health Promotion, Foundations for Practice,* Bailliere Tindall, London

Rodin, J. and Langer, E. J. (1977) 'Long-term effects of a control-relevant intervention with the institutionalised aged', *Journal of Personality and Social Psychology,* Vol. 35: 897–902

Rädda Barnen (1996) *Throwing Children Into Battle,*World Watch, New York

Van Damme, W. (1995) 'Do refugees belong in camps? Experiences from Goma and Guinea', *The Lancet,* Vol. 346, 5 August: 360–62

Walker, P. (1996) 'Assuring quality for disaster victims', *The Health Exchange,* June: 8–17

Part 6

Blackburn, J. with Holland, J. (1998) *Who Changes? Institutionalizing participation in Development,* IT Publications, London

Chambers, R. (1997) *Whose Reality Counts? Putting the first last,* IT Publications, London

Chawla, Louise (1997) 'Growing up in cities: the results of a seven-country study', Urban Childhood Conference presentation, Trondheim, Norway

Crawford, S. (1997) 'To be seen and heard', Report for UNICEF, Rädda Barnen, World Bank and Yemen Government, Sana'a

Edwards, M. (1996a) 'New approaches to children and development: Introduction and overview to policy arena: children in developing countries' (Edwards, M. ed.) in *Journal of International Development,* Vol. 8, No. 6 pp. 813–827

Edwards, M. (1996b) 'Institutionalising children's participation in development', in *PLA Notes* No. 25, special issue on children's participation, IIED, London

Franklin, A. and Franklin, B. (1996) 'Growing Pains: the developing children's rights movement in the UK', in Pilcher, J. and Wagg, S. (ed.) *Thatcher's Children,* Falmer, London

Gibson, T. (1994) 'Showing what you mean (not just talking about it)', *RRA Notes,* No. 21. IIED, London

Guijt, I. (1996) 'Part I – Moving slowly and reaching far: institutionalising participatory planning for child-centred community development', interim analysis for Redd Barna, East Africa, carried out in collaboration with IIED

Hart, R. A. (1997) *Children's Participation: the theory and practice of involving young citizens in community development and environmental care*, Earthscan Publications London with UNICEF

Hodgkin, R. and Newell, P. (1996) *Effective Government Structures for Children*, Calouste Guibenkian Foundation, London

Holland, J. with Blackburn, J. (1998) *Whose Voice? Participatory Research and policy Change*, IT Publications, London

James, A. and Prout, A. (ed.) (1990) *Constructing and Reconstructing Childhood*, Falmer, London

Johnson, V., Hill, J. and Ivan-Smith, E. (1995) *Listening to Smaller Voices: children in an environment of change*, ActionAid, Chard, London

Jones, G. and Wallace, C. (1992) *Youth Citizenship and Social Change*, Open University Press, Buckingham

Kaspar, Amy (1997) 'Looking out: lessons and visions for young people's participation in the urban built environment', MA thesis, Oxford Brookes University, England

Kumar, S. (ed.) (1996) *ABC of PRA: Attitudes, Behaviour and Change*, a report on a South-South workshop on PRA: attitudes and behaviour, ActionAid India and SPEECH, Bangalore

Lansdown, G. (1995) *Taking Part: children's participation in decision-making*, IPPR, London

Local Government Management Board (1996) *Local Agenda 21 Roundtable Guidance: Local Agenda 21 and Young People*, Local Government Management Board, London

Matthews, H. and Limb, M. (1998) *The Right to Say: the development of youth councils/ forums within the UK*, AREA, Vol. 30, No. 1

Nieuwenhuys, O. (1996) 'Action research with children: a role for street educators', in *PLA Notes* No. 25, special edition on children's participation, IIED, London

Percy-Smith, B. (1997) 'Neglected spaces: exploring the geography of adolescents', Paper presented at the Urban Childhood Conference, Trondheim, Norway

Qvortrup, J. (1990) 'A voice for children in statistical accounting: a plea for children's rights to be heard' in James, A. and Prout, A. (ed.) *Constructing and Reconstructing Childhood*, Falmer, London

Rich, P., Swart-Kruger, J. and Swift, M. (1997) 'Growing up in cities: Canaansland: children's views of life in an informal settlement', South Africa Project Team, Urban Childhood Conference presentation, Trondheim, Norway.

Rosenbaum, M. and Newell, P. (1991) 'Taking children seriously: a proposal for a children's rights commissioner', Calouste Guibenkian Foundation, London

Save the Children (1995) *Towards a Children's Agenda: new challenges for social development*, Save the Children, London

Save the Children (1997a) *All Together Now: community participation for children and young people*, Save the Children, London

Save the Children (1997b) *A Matter of Opinion: research into children's and young people's participation rights in the North East*, Youth Issues North, Save the Children, Newcastle

Sharma, U. (1997) 'ACCESS programme progress report', ActionAid, Chard, London

United Nations (1995) *Concluding Observations of the Committee on The Rights of the Child: United Kingdom of Great Britain and Northern Ireland*, CRC/C/15/Add.34

Woollcombe, David (1996) 'The process of empowerment: lessons from the work of Peace Child International', *PLA Notes* No. 25, special edition on children's participation, IIED, London

Part 7

Boyden, J. and Ennew, J. (1997) *Children in Focus – a manual for participatory research with children,* Rädda Barnen, Stockholm

Cornwall, A. (1998) 'It's our estate too: voices in participatory well-being needs, assessment on the Roundshaw Estate, Sutton', available from IDS, Sussex

Ennew, J. (1994) *Street and Working Children: a guide to planning,* Save the Children (UK), London

Freire, P. (1985) *The Politics of Education: culture, power and liberation*, Macmillan, London

Hart, R. (1992) *Children's Participation: from tokenism to citizenship*, UNICEF, Florence

Hooks, B. (1984) *Feminist Theory: from margin to center*, South End Press, Boston, MA

Hooks, B. (1989) *Talking Back: thinking feminist, thinking black*, Sheba Feminist Publishers, Boston, MA and London

Hooks, B. (1990) *Yearning: race, gender, and cultural politics*, South End Press, Boston, MA

Hooks, B. (1993) *Sisters of the Yam: black women and self-recovery*, South End Press, Boston, MA

Ivan-Smith, E. (1997) 'Seven Things You Always Wanted To Know About Child Focus But Were Too Confused To Ask', Save the Children (unpublished), London

Kakama, P.T. (1993) *Children and Their Rights: village perceptions*, Department of Probation and Social Welfare, Ministry of Labour and Social Affairs, Kampala

Khan, S. (1997) *A Street Children's Research*, Save the Children, Dhaka

Kisadha, T. and Bitekerezo, M. (1995) 'Wild flowers growing instead of food' Unpublished report, Kampala, Redd Barna

Kisadha, T. and Chandler, D. (1996) 'Breaking the gourd', Unpublished report, Kampala, Redd Barna

Levy *et al.* (1996) 'They cry respect: urban violence and poverty in Jamaica', *Community and Social Change*, University of West Indies, Jamaica

Levy, H. (1996): *They Cry 'Respect': urban violence and poverty in Jamaica*, Centre for Population, Community and Social Change, University of the West Indies, Mona, Kingston

Levy, H. and Blumen, J, (1994) 'The existential bases of power relationships: the gender-role case', in *Power/Gender Social Relations in Theory and Practice*, H. L. Radtke and H. J. Stam (ed.) 67–88, Sage Publications, London, Thousand Oaks and New Delhi

Moser, C. and Holland, J. (1996) *Research Report on Urban Poverty and Violence in Jamaica*, World Bank, Washington DC

Mukasa, G. and van der Grift-Wanyoto, V. (ed.) (1997) 'A stick far away cannot kill a snake', unpublished report, Kampala, Redd Barna

Sandborg, K. (1996) 'Giving voice to children', Unpublished report, Kampala, Redd Barna

Sandborg, K. (1996) 'The Ugandan girl child – notes on poverty and tradition as obstacles to her rights', Unpublished report, Kampala

Save the Children (UK) (1997), *Global Programme Strategy*, London

Sewaggude, J. and Mugisha, G. (1997) 'The PRA process in Bulende-Bugosere village', Iganga District, Unpublished report Redd Barna, Kampala

Treseder, P. (1997) *Empowering Children and Young People Training Manual*, Children's Rights Office and Save the Children, London

Van Beers, H. (1995) *Participation of Children in Programming,* Rädda Barnen, Stockholm

West, A. (1995) *You're On Your Own: young people's research on leaving care*, Save the Children (UK), London

West, A. (1996a) *But What Is It . . . ? A critique of undefined participation*, Save the Children (UK), Leeds

West, A. (1996b) 'Young people, participatory research and experiences of leaving Care, *PLA Notes* No. 25, IIED, London

West, A. (1998) 'Family, identity, children's rights: notes on children and young people outside the family, *Journal of Social Sciences*

Appendix 2

Arnstein, S. (1969) 'Eight rungs on the ladder of citizen participation', reprinted in Cahn, E. and Passett, B. (ed.) (1971) *Citizen Participation: effecting community change*, Praeger Publishers, New York

Cornwall, A. (1996) 'Participatory research methods: first steps in a participatory process', in de Konig, K. (ed.) *Participatory Research in Health: issues and experiences*, Zed Books, London

Hart, R. (1992) 'Children's participation: from tokenism to citizenship', *Innocenti Essay*, No. 4, UNICEF, New York

Hart, R. (1997) *Children's Participation: the theory and practice of involving young citizens in community development and environmental care*, Earthscan, London

Hubley, J. (1993) *Communicating Health*, Macmillan, London

Index

3Ps 8, 233
see also participation; protection; provision
abuse 40–1, 95, 120, 139, 159, 276, 280
disclosure of 40–1, 54
academia 229–31, 282
accommodation 70, 73, 75
action research 46, 48
ActionAid 9
Nepal 92–5, 201
active participants 259, 261, 263–5, 281, 284, 285–6
adolescents 29, 31, 205, 263–4, 275
adult-child relationships 37, 49, 94, 102, 105, 175, 178, 234, 254
adults 56–7, 89, 91, 94–5, 132, 178, 181, 242, 273–4, 297–8
facilitators 30–1, 212–13, 242
Afghanistan 25–7, 61
Africa 137, 148, 198
American proverbs 149
Ammam, Jordan 144
analysis 69, 103, 105, 115
arenas 235
Ashiana Day Centre 25–6
Asia 148, 232
Association of Household Workers 35
attitudes 132–3, 159–60, 175, 178, 215, 218–19, 227, 241, 254, 298
Austria 238

Bahay Tuluyan 106
Bal Sansad 233
Bangladesh 34, 76–8, 274, 276
barriers 41, 217–19, 220–1, 222, 227–8, 230, 247
see also resistance
behaviour 72, 133, 145–6, 175, 178, 237, 263–4, 297
Belvedere, Grenada 185
'best interests of the child' 140, 295
Bhutan/Bhutanese 96, 97, 98
biases 69, 97, 99, 103–4, 115
boys 68–9, 186, 210, 243–4, 263
see also girls
Brazil 88–91
Brighton Centre 205–7
Brighton, UK 205, 266–70
Britain *see* UK
Building blocks 51
'bush boarders' 69–70, 72, 73, 75

Camfed 70
camps *see* summer camps; refugees
Canaansland/Kanana, South Africa 42–5
care system 36, 168, 273, 274, 277
carnival 268–9
CBOs 217
CCPR 92
CCVD 232
CDWs 92
CEC 239
Centre for Social Welfare 168
challenges 44–5, 94, 176, 186, 204
change 5–6, 46–7, 178, 192–4, 216, 223, 248–50, 255, 276
in personnel 200–1, 275
positive change 157, 170, 171, 210, 248, 286
channels 235
charlands, Bangladesh 76
Child Care and Development in Uukwaluudhi 138
child development 27–31, 125–6, 176, 234
child labour 3, 13, 81–4, 124–8, 241, 262
see also domestic workers
Child Participation Programme 169
child-adult relationships 37, 49, 94, 102, 105, 175, 178, 234, 254
child-directed/led approaches 211, 271, 273–4, 275, 276
child-focused approaches 81, 162, 163–4, 171
child-rearing 132–3, 138, 139–40
child-to-child approach 13, 69, 120–1, 129–31, 133, 136–7, 153, 164
childhood 6, 12, 13, 119, 125–6, 149, 176, 234
Children's Activity Day 36
children's councils 236–40, 272
Children's Environment Charter 238
children's forum 241–2
children's groups 92–4, 178, 218, 254, 262
Children's Open Day 237
Children's Parliament 233
children's participation 8, 133–4, 136, 141–2, 161–2, 186–8, 218, 225–9, 235, 260–62, 272–3, 291
Children's Perspectives Protocol 127–8
children's rights 86, 95, 136, 138–41, 228
see also CRC
Children's Rights Festival 267, 270

Children's Statute [1996] 232
Children Act [1992] 95
Children and Decision-Making Study 36
children/young people 3, 7–8, 29, 77, 85, 89, 106–8, 133, 134, 194
  see also adolescents; boys; girls; pupils; rural children; street children; urban children
citizenship 5–6, 224
City-as-School High School 203–5
clans 143
CLC 202
Coalition of Children's Organizations 250
communalism 133
communication 30, 41, 49, 54, 55, 89–90, 114, 134, 291, 294
community 102, 133, 138, 197, 200, 204–5, 214, 250, 286
concentration 71
conferences 236–42
confidence 29, 34, 115, 134, 185, 210, 213, 223–4, 280
  less-confident people 36, 67, 76, 95, 102–3, 113, 116, 163, 212
confidentiality/privacy 40–1, 52, 54, 59
conflict/confrontation 72, 75, 89, 104–5, 157–9, 162, 275, 296
  violence 144–5, 263–4
  wars/war trauma 106, 143, 159–60
  see also crisis situations
consent/permission 48–9, 163, 286
  informed 38–9, 53–4, 163, 167, 293, 286
consultation 107, 167, 200
contact-cards 167
context 23, 25–6, 27, 120, 125–6, 151, 181–2, 273
  see also culture; cultural context
contributions 194, 196–7
control 57–8, 89, 222
  see also power
Convention on the Rights of the Child see CRC
coping/survival strategies 3, 75, 84, 158, 159, 264, 265, 296
corporal punishment 139
CRC 8, 31, 86, 135–6, 187, 247–8
  articles of 127, 137, 225, 262, 310–12
  see also children's rights
crisis situations/emergencies 14, 157–61, 171–2, 296
  see also conflicts; difficult circumstances; survival strategies; transitional situations
CTC 106–7
cultural context 104–5, 109, 119–20, 151, 172, 279, 286, 294
culture 27, 68, 120, 122–4, 132–5, 147–51, 170, 276, 295
  cultural resistance 184, 212–13
  reproduction 276

  see also cultural context; organizational culture; school culture

dance 237
  see also drama
data/information 54–6, 101, 293
  gathering 34–6, 82–4, 89, 99, 185–6, 187, 243
DCWC 95
decision-making 36, 139–40, 188–9, 197, 209, 225, 238–40
degrees of participation 25–6, 61, 297
democracy 224
designers 47
development 122, 292–3
Development FOCUS 313
developmental psychology see psychology
Dhaka, Bangladesh 34, 274, 276
differences/diversity 5–7, 23, 52–3, 60, 186, 195, 216–17, 243–4, 275, 279
difficult circumstances 25–6, 61, 157, 243, 246, 280, 296
  see also conflict; crisis situation; survival strategies
disability & disabled children 53, 113, 168–9, 194
discrimination 25–6
disease/illness 96, 98, 100
Disney corporation 238
displaced persons camp 158
  see also refugees
distortion/'interpretation' 67, 89, 101, 103–4, 115
documentation 31, 50, 99, 103, 291–2, 295
domestic & household workers 34–6, 82, 84
drama & role-play 35, 69, 71, 105–6, 188, 233
  see also dance; songs; theatre
drawing 26, 35, 68, 71, 93, 113
dump site 106–7
durbar 134

ECPAT newsletter 33
editors 211, 212–13
education 46, 93, 122–4, 135, 137, 169, 186–7, 201–3
  see also schools; teachers
emergencies see crisis situations; conflict
empathy 80
empowerment 114
enablement 234
enabling factors 88, 94
ENDA 36
England see UK
entretiens participatifs 36
environment 200, 204–5, 266–70
Environmental Protectors' Club 210–11

328

ethics/ethical issues 11–12, 21–4, 31–7, 45–6, 52–9, 101, 163, 293–4
Ethiopia 214–17
Eurocentric ideas *see* North; Western ideas
European proverbs 149
evaluation 50, 58, 80–1, 88, 92, 216
'examples' 149–50
exclusion 5–7, 25–7, 237, 261–2, 276
expectations 52, 79, 97, 102
'experts' 233

facilitators/facilitation 36, 76, 80, 81, 92, 103, 113, 181, 280
  see also adult facilitators
family 190, 194–8, 235, 254
feedback 50, 90, 105, 115, 172, 208–9
FFW 216
findings/outcomes 70, 73, 75, 93–4, 103, 105, 115
flooding/riverbank erosion 76
fostering 168
Foyers Maurice Sixto 34
FRY [former Republic of Yugoslavia] 166–71
fun/fun activities 67, 172
FUNDAR 283

Gambia 69
games/energizers 71
Garb and Garbage fashion show 267–8
garrison communities 262–6
gate-keepers 38, 110, 251
Germany 238–9
Get a Grip on Litter week 268
Ghana 86–7, 132–5
Ghana National Commission on Children 86
girls 25–7, 67, 68–9, 78, 186, 210, 243–4, 264
  see also boys
  see also local government
Grand Anse RC School 186
governments 16, 246, 248
Grenada 185–8
GrenSave 185
groups 67, 71, 99, 111, 113, 114
  see also children's groups
Growing Up In Cities [GUIC] 42–5

Haiti 34
healing & therapy 106, 159, 171
health 73, 78, 97, 158
  education 25–7, 129, 134, 136, 137, 164
  see also disease; well-being
health visitors 197
hierarchy/authority 97
Ho Chi Mhin City, Vietnam 84, 85
Honduras 283–5
hope 183

ideas tree 271
identity 159, 265, 276
IDS 9, 313
Igoo, India 232–3
IIED 9
Ilitha Lomso Children and Youth Organization 79–81
illiteracy *see* literacy
illness/disease 96, 98, 100
inclusion 5, 273
income-generation project 163, 164
India 178, 232
Indonesia 35
information *see* data
informed consent 38–9, 53–4, 163, 167, 286, 293
initiation ceremony 132
Institute of Education 9, 313
Institutions 14, 108, 175–7, 180, 193, 253–4, 296–7
  see also organizations
international agencies 16, 250–2
International Conference on Child Labour 241–2
intervention 126
interviews 11, 33, 34–5, 167, 168, 186, 274
invisibility *see* visibility
involving children 134, 135, 216
'ivory tower' 229, 231

Jamaica 208, 262–6
James' four-fold typology 38
Jijiga, Ethiopia 214–17
Johannesburg, South Africa 42–5
Jordan 143–7
journalists/reporters/broadcasters 32, 33

Kabul, Afghanistan 25–7
Kanana/Canaansland, South Africa 42–5
Kenya 66
Keschey 187
key issues 5, 12, 21–2, 65–6, 110–11, 119, 157, 175, 259
Kirklees, United Kingdom 220–4
Kuleana Centre for Children's Rights 53, 211, 213

labour 81–2, 84, 94, 124–8,
  see also child labour, domestic workers
Ladakh 67, 232, 233
ladders of participation 7, 26, 50, 61, 210, 308
landscape projects 199–201, 204–5
language 30, 45, 67, 77, 87, 113, 134, 137, 264, 272
latrines 164
laws/legal structure 25–6, 106, 140, 232, 255

leadership 209–10, 283–5
learning 94–5, 205–7, 221, 222
Leh Nutrition Project 232
lessons learnt 70–2, 78, 110–11, 222–3,
    241–2
literacy/illiteracy/non-literacy 26, 68, 88,
    186, 202–3
Local Government Act [1993] 232
local government/authority 36, 220–9,
    238–40, 246–7, 272, 274–5
love/compassion 159–60
'Low Tide' 267
'lowers' 102, 103, 104, 116

magazine/newsletter 53, 211–14, 281
mainstreaming/integrating 94, 95, 116,
    218
Mambo Leo 53, 211–14
Manila, Philippines 35
marginalized children/people 52, 180, 208,
    210
matrix diagrams/rating 96, 98, 99
MBEC 140
media 11, 31–4, 86–7, 197, 291, 295
    see also news; radio; television
methods 65–73, 77, 82, 113, 116, 278–9,
    294–5, 303
    activities 67, 127–8, 134, 172
    see also matrix; seasonal calendars;
        visual
Metro Theatre League 107
Mola Secondary School 70
Mola, Zimbabwe 72, 73, 75
motivations/incentives 45, 49, 56–7, 72,
    101, 135, 182–3, 273–4
Mountain of Opportunity 243
Mozambique 158
MTR 92
murals 267–8

Nama 139–40
Namibia 136–8, 161
NCC 248, 278
needs assessment 79, 215
neighbourhoods 42, 143–7
Nepal 67, 92–5, 96, 97, 98, 201–3
Netherlands 243
networks 291, 292, 297
New York, USA 203–5
news 32
newsletter/magazine 53, 211–14, 281
NGOs 15, 217–19, 246, 282
North 27, 233–6
    see also Western ideas
Norway 241
Norwegian Centre for Child Research 42
note-taking, avoiding 103, 115, 157, 172

'Oath to Freedom' tour 105

objectives 69, 72, 109, 232, 286, 287
objectivity 90
Oliver 184–5
opinions *see* views
organizations 178, 217–19, 222
    culture of 178, 250
    see also institutions; NGOs
Oslo conference 241–2
outreach strategy 104–5
ownership/control 50, 54, 85

Palestine 190
Paradise Project 185–8
parents/guardians & foster-carers 72, 168,
    203, 210, 264, 279–80, 286
Parklands Partnership 204
participants 283, 300–1, 314–16
    see also active participants
participation 29, 152, 169, 179, 182–3, 233,
    237, 272, 284–5, 299
    see also children's participation; degrees
        of participation; ladders of
        participation; PLA; PRA; spherical
        model
Participatory Educational Theatre [PET] 66
participatory video *see* video
Partners/partnership 47, 50, 136, 146, 152,
    194, 204, 209, 218, 282
patience 78
payments 57
Peace Child 53, 188–9
peers 28, 36, 181, 283
perceptions 36–7; 58
perspectives/views 29, 45, 86, 94, 124, 127,
    132–3, 140–1, 215, 220
Philippine Educational Theatre Association
    [PETA] 105, 106–7
Philippines 35, 105–9, 192
photo appraisal & photography 85, 113,
    115, 206
Pikkin Palaver 281, 304
PLA 74, 119, 232
PLA Notes 67
PLAN International 134
play 11, 28, 77
playground 144–5
poetry 264
politics/political change 25–6, 158, 171,
    183, 191–4, 227, 235
pollution 108
portrayal of children 32–3
poverty 75, 235
power 57–8, 97, 188–9, 192, 223, 266, 292,
    296–7
    imbalance 11, 37, 101, 142, 237
    powerlessness 237
relationships 22, 37, 99, 175–6, 178, 181,
    209–10, 254, 264
    see also control

Power Pack 240
PRA [participatory rural appraisal] 69,
    72–3, 144, 162, 176, 214
PRA with Children 67
problem wall 271
problems/priorities not considered by adults
    77–8, 144–5
Project Alternatives and Opportunities
    283–4
Project Grow 203–5
projects/programmes 163–6, 168, 180, 206,
    208, 214, 217
Promoting Young People in Governance
    239
protection 31, 75, 125, 126, 144, 180–1,
    233, 234–5
proverbs 147–9
provision 233, 235
psychology 27–9, 176, 295
puberty rites 132
pupils/schoolchildren 47, 69, 101

Questscope 144
quotations 124, 128, 141, 300–7

Rädda Barnen 125, 127, 128, 160, 241, 243,
    246
radio 32, 87, 267, 295
rap 90
Rap TV 91
reality gap 130–1
rebelling 194
recreation 77
recycling 266, 268–9
Redd Barna 241
    Uganda 278–83
refugees/displaced people 96–7, 158, 167,
    214
relationships 47, 49, 143, 178, 264
    see also adult-child relationships
religious beliefs 132
Report of Situation of Children and Women
    138
representation 233, 238
Rescue Missions 53, 188–9, 192
research 81–5, 135, 141–2, 144–6, 169, 185,
    243–4, 271, 285–6
    see also action research
resilience 157, 158–61, 172
resistance 184, 209, 247, 297
    see also barriers
respect 48, 80
responsibilities 188–9, 194
restrictive contexts 25–6
Reunite, Operation 167
rights 25–6, 86, 95, 121, 127, 135–6, 235
    see also children's rights; CRC
Rio de Janeiro, Brazil 91
role-play 66, 69

see also drama
RPE 88, 89, 91
rural children 81–4, 87, 134

safety/security 25–7, 30, 34, 73, 104, 145,
    205, 234
sanitation project 163–5
Saturday School 43
SCF 76, 165, 167–8, 185, 208, 214–17, 222,
    261, 276
    SCF Alliance 241
    SCF Ghana 86
    SCF Sri Lanka 163, 166
    SCF UK 9, 70, 161, 222, 273, 313
    SCF Vietnam 81, 84, 85
    Swedish SCF 125, 243
    see also Rädda Barnen; Redd Barna
schools 15, 104, 119, 129–31, 188–9,
    199–203, 213, 238–9
    culture 123–4, 131, 212
    curriculum 46, 202
    environment/grounds 46, 199–200
seasonal calendars 96, 98, 101
seating 79–80
security/safety 25–7, 30, 34, 73, 104, 145,
    205, 234
self-esteem see confidence
self-reflexivity 266
Senegal 36
Separated Children in Exile 167
settings 79, 104–5, 113
sexuality/sexual issues 66, 134, 264
SFI 106
Shoishab 34
Shona 140
shy/less-confident people 36, 67, 76, 95,
    102–3, 113, 116, 163, 212
situational analysis 69
six-step approach 129
Smokey Mountain 106
social actors, children as 157, 158
social capital 5–6
social centre, Ammam 144–5
social exclusion (see exclusion)
Social Investment Fund 263
society see context; culture
Somali refugees 214–17
songs/singing 67, 71, 233, 237
    see also drama
South 236
South Africa 42–5, 188–9, 191–2
spherical model of participation 11, 61, 297
squatters 42, 69
    see also bush boarders
Sri Lanka 161–6
staff 26, 171, 200–1, 218–19, 222
status 97, 142, 144
Stepping Stones 66
street children 23, 24, 68, 99, 100, 106, 119,
    144, 274

Sucharitha Women's Society 163
summer camps 144–5, 209
survival/coping strategies 3, 75, 84, 158,
    159, 264, 265, 296
SWRC 233

Tanzania 211–14
Target the Intolerable 125
teachers 47, 73, 130, 141, 199–201, 202–3,
    204–5, 216
television 32, 86–7
    making programmes/films 12, 33, 86–7,
        91, 115, 295
    see also video
theatre 66, 105–9, 116, 192, 233
    see also dance; drama; songs
Theatre for Development 66
Tilonia, India 233
time/time-frames 60–1, 163, 180, 183, 202,
    215–17, 221–2, 242
Tivoli Gardens 263
To be Seen and Heard 243
tokenism 250–1
top-down approach 158
tourism 185, 186–8
traditional knowledge 97, 99
transitional situations 166, 170
transparency 59, 101, 103, 292–3
Trincomalee District Development
    Association 163
Trojan horse 251
trust 159, 172

Uganda 5, 129–31, 190, 232, 278–81,
    281–3
UK 46, 192, 199, 220–4, 226, 239–40,
    266–70, 272–7
UN 236–7, 250
    see also CRC; UNESCO; UNICEF
UNCRC see CRC
UNESCO 42, 237–8
UNICEF 138, 237, 243
'uppers' 102
urban children 84, 134, 143–7
urbanization 143
USA 203–5, 239

vehicles 276
video/video-making 12, 66–7, 87–91, 113,
    114, 115, 168, 269
Vietnam 81–6
views/perspectives 29, 45, 86, 94, 127,
    132–3, 140–1, 215, 220
Visayan Forum 35
visibility/invisibility 6, 52–3, 95
visual arts 107–8
    see also drama; theatre; TV; video
visualization/visual tools 69, 97, 103, 105,
    115
voice, giving/hearing [porte parole] 3–4,
    32–3, 37, 88, 90, 146, 266
Voyce 266–70

Walden Schools 267
web of influence 253
well-being 97, 158, 261, 295
    see also health
Western/Eurocentric ideas 27, 119, 125,
    135, 176, 295
    see also North
wildlife project 199–201
Women-Headed Households Income-
    Generating Project 163
work see labour
workshops 9, 43, 76–8, 106–12, 137,
    147–51, 214, 292, 300–7
World Bank 243, 263
World Decade of Cultural Development
    122
World Declaration on Education for All
    121
World Summit for Children 237

Yemen 243–6
young people see adolescents; children
youth councils 226, 275, 283–4
Yugoslav Child Rights Centre 169
Yugoslavia, former see FRY

Zimbabwe 69–75, 140

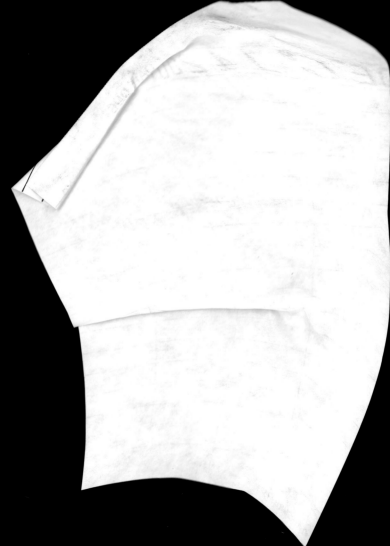

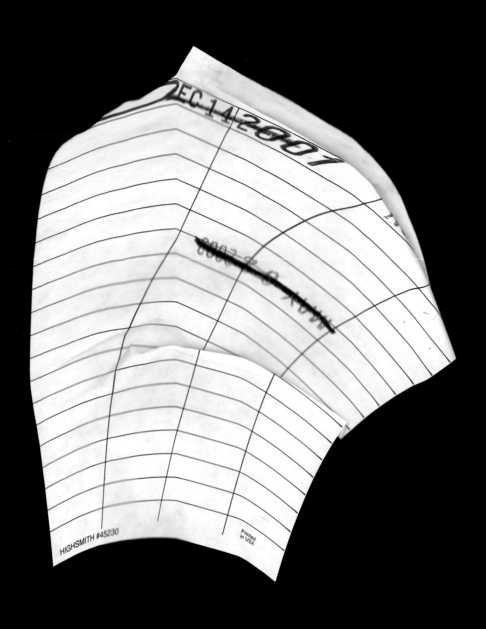

DEC 14 2001

MAY 04 2008

HIGHSMITH #45230

Printed
in USA